Yale
Publications
in the
History of Art
38

George L.
Hersey
Editor

# Loudon
# and the Landscape

## From Country Seat
## to Metropolis

## 1783–1843

## Melanie Louise Simo

Yale University Press
New Haven and London

Designed by
Esther Pullman
and set in Bodoni Book
by The Composing Room
of Michigan.
Printed in the United
States of America by
Halliday Lithograph,
West Hanover, Mass.

The paper in this book
meets the guidelines for
permanence and
durability of the
Committee on Production
Guidelines for Book
Longevity of the Council
on Library Resources.

10 9 8 7 6 5 4 3 2 1

Library of Congress Cataloging-in-Publication Data
Simo, Melanie Louise, 1949–
    Loudon and the landscape.
    (Yale publications in the history of art ; 38)
    Bibliography: p.
    Includes index.
    1. Loudon, J. C. (John Claudius), 1783–1843.
2. Landscape architects—Great Britain—Biography.
1. Title.   II. Series.
SB470.L69S56 1988      712'.092'4      87-15974
ISBN 0–300–03745–7 (alk. paper)

For my parents
and my
husband, Paul

Art is not tame, and Nature is not wild,
in the ordinary sense. A perfect work of man's art
would also be wild or natural in a good sense.
Man tames Nature only that he may at last make
her more free even than he found her, though he
may never yet have succeeded.

Henry David Thoreau
*A Week on the Concord and Merrimack Rivers*

# Contents

# Plates

# Figures

Frontispiece: John Claudius Loudon (1783–1843), portrait by unknown artist, ca. 1812, frontispiece in *Self-Instruction for Young Gardeners* (London, 1845). Courtesy, Westminster City Libraries, Archives Department.
1

Thomas Stothard, R.A., *A Distant View of Edinburgh*, 1809. Courtesy, Yale Center for British Art, Paul Mellon Collection.
2

G. Arnald, A.R.A., *London Bridge &c.*, 1811, engraved by Hay for *The Beauties of England and Wales*. Author's collection.
3

J.C.Loudon, "Working Plan for Forming a New Approach" (to Gunnersbury Park, West London), from the *Gardener's Magazine* 12 (February 1836): 54–55. Author's collection.
4

Tomb of J.C.Loudon, in Kensal Green Cemetery, London. Photo by author.
5

John Constable, R.A., *Stour Valley and Dedham Church*, 1814. Warren Collection; courtesy, Museum of Fine Arts, Boston.
6

Scene on the grounds of Hope End, Herefordshire, formerly the seat of Edward Moulton-Barrett and childhood home of his daughter, Elizabeth Barrett Browning. Photo by author.
7

George Morland, *Carters with a Load of Slate*. Gift of Miss Amelia Peabody; courtesy, Museum of Fine Arts, Boston.
8

J.C.Loudon, "Naked and Decorated Scotch cottages," from *Treatise on Country Residences* (London, 1806), vol. 1, pl. 5, figs. 2 and 4. Courtesy of the Frances Loeb Library, Graduate School of Design, Harvard University.
9

J.C.Loudon, "A residence formed . . . in Mr. Brown's style — generally prevalent at the present day, 1806," from *Treatise on Country Residences* (London, 1806), vol. 2, pl. 26, fig. 3. Courtesy of the Frances Loeb Library, Graduate School of Design, Harvard University.
10

J.C.Loudon, "A residence . . . in the style of the author, J. Loudon," from *Treatise on Country Residences* (London, 1806), vol. 2, pl. 26, fig. 4. Courtesy of the Frances Loeb Library, Graduate School of Design, Harvard University.

36

J.C.Loudon, Plan of a house with a large conservatory and vinery, from *Treatise on Country Residences* (London, 1806), vol. 1, pl. 12. Courtesy of the Frances Loeb Library, Graduate School of Design, Harvard University.

37

Benjamin Thompson, Count Rumford, Fireplace: ground plan, elevation, and section, from Rumford, *Essays, Political, Economical, and Philosophical* (London, 1800), vol. 1, p. 385. Courtesy, Harvard College Library.

38

J.C.Loudon, Diagram of an improved cottage fireplace, from *Treatise on Country Residences* (London, 1806), vol. 1, pl. 6. Courtesy of the Frances Loeb Library, Graduate School of Design, Harvard University.

39

J.C.Loudon, Elevation of a house to be covered with ivy and creepers, from *Treatise on Country Residences* (London, 1806), vol. 1, pl. 4. Courtesy of the Frances Loeb Library, Graduate School of Design, Harvard University.

40

W.H.Bartlett, "Colzean Castle, Ayrshire," from William Beattie, *Scotland Illustrated* (London, 1847), vol. 1., opposite p. 188. Courtesy, Harvard College Library.

41

J.C.Loudon, Perspective view of a house covered with ivy and creepers, adapted to its particular site, from *Treatise on Country Residences* (London, 1806), vol. 1, pl. 8. Courtesy of the Frances Loeb Library, Graduate School of Design, Harvard University.

42

"Deepdene," the residence of Thomas Hope, Esq., in Surrey, from the *Gardener's Magazine* 5 (October 1829):591. Author's collection.

43

J.C.Loudon, Design for a Botanic Garden, from *Hints on the Formation of Gardens and Pleasure Grounds* (London, 1812), pl. 17. Courtesy, The British Library.

44

J.C.Loudon, Design for a conservatory, sited in the center of a flower garden: sections, elevations, and plan, from *Hints on the Formation of Gardens and Pleasure Grounds* (London, 1812), pl. 20. Courtesy of the Frances Loeb Library, Graduate School of Design, Harvard University.

45

A.K.Johnston, "Map of Part of Russia, to illustrate the Campaigns of 1812," printed for William Blackwood & Sons, Edinburgh and London. Author's collection.

46

Conservatory of the Taurida palace, St. Petersburg, formerly the residence of Potemkin, from Loudon, *Encyclopaedia of Gardening* (London, 1830), fig. 22. Author's collection.

47

Sir George Stuart Mackenzie, Proposal for an Improved Forcing House: elevation, plan, and section, 1815, from *Transactions of the Horticultural Society* (London), vol. 2 (1817). Courtesy, Gray Herbarium Library, Harvard University.

48

J.C.Loudon, Sketches of curvilinear hothouses, from *Encyclopaedia of Gardening* (London, 1830): 315–17. Author's collection.

49

Vignettes of gardens in London, including the Palm House at Kew Gardens by Richard Turner, from Charles Knight, *Cyclopaedia of London* (London, 1851), p. 25. Author's collection.

50

J.C.Loudon, Elevation and plan of colleges for working men, from *Mechanics' Magazine*, no. 443 (February 4, 1832): 321. Courtesy, the Literary and Philosophical Society, Newcastle-upon-Tyne, Northumberland.

51

J.C.Loudon, "Eighty dwellings for the labouring classes," plan, from *Encyclopaedia of Cottage, Farm, and Villa Architecture* (London, 1853), fig. 440. Courtesy, Harvard College Library.

52

Robert Gauen, Apparatus for forcing fruit trees by concentrating solar energy on a hollow cast-iron ball, from *Gardener's Magazine* 3 (September 1827): 101. Author's collection.

53

J.C.Loudon, Proposed apparatus for warming the earth by solar concentration, from *Gardener's Magazine* 3 (January 1828): 367. Author's collection.

54

Charles Barry, Revision of the northwest façade of the *"Beau Idéal* Villa" by Selim, from Loudon, *Encyclopaedia of Cottage, Farm, and Villa Architecture* (London, 1836), p. 818. Courtesy, Berkshire County Library, Reading.

55

T. Webster, "Perspective view of the Kitchen of Baron de Lerchenfeld at Munich," designed by Benjamin Thompson, Count Rumford, from Rumford, *Essays, Political, Economical, and Philosophical* (London, 1800), vol. 3, pl. 1. Courtesy, Harvard College Library.

56

William Manning, Prefabricated portable cottage for the Australian colonies, from Loudon, *Encyclopaedia of Cottage, Farm and Villa Architecture* (London, 1853), fig. 456. Courtesy, Harvard College Library.

57

J.C.Loudon, "Model cottage for a Country Labourer," plan, section, and perspective, from *Gardener's Magazine* 6 (April 1830): 155, 160. Author's collection.

58

A. Pugin, Jr., "Fontainebleau: view toward the gardens," from L. T. Ventouillac, *Paris and its Environs* (London, 1831), vol. 1, opposite p. 78. Courtesy, Harvard College Library.

59

"Pantheon Bazaar," interior, from Charles Knight, *London* (London, 1842–1844), vol. 5, p. 400. Author's collection.

60

"Bellaggio, Lago di Como," woodcut from John Ruskin's original drawing, from the *Architectural Magazine* 5 (June 1838): 246. Courtesy, Harvard College Library.

61

John Robertson, "Cottage in the Old English Manner," from Loudon, *Encyclopaedia of Cottage, Farm, and Villa Architecture* (London, n.d., a new edition by Mrs. Loudon), design 28. Courtesy of the Frances Loeb Library, Graduate School of Design, Harvard University.

62

Andrew Jackson Downing, "Symmetrical Cottage," from Downing, *The Architecture of Country Houses* (New York, 1850), design 7. Courtesy of the Frances Loeb Library, Graduate School of Design, Harvard University.

63

Covent Garden Market, London, by Charles Fowler: bird's-eye view, from *Gardener's Magazine* 7 (June 1831): 266. Author's collection.

64

Covent Garden Market, London, by Charles Fowler: perspective view, from *Gardener's Magazine* 7 (June 1831): 273. Author's collection.

65

The London Horticultural Society's gardens at Chiswick during an exhibition, from Charles Knight, *London* (London, 1842–44), vol. 5, p. 305. Author's collection.

66

West bank of the Seine at Ris-Orangis, France, formerly the site of the Horticultural Institute of Fromont, directed by the chevalier Etienne Soulange-Bodin. Photo by author.

67

The *Gardener's Magazine* 5 (1829), title page. Author's collection.

68

T.A., Plan (*1*.) and elevation (*2*.) of a gardener's house designed to serve as a watchtower, from the *Gardener's Magazine* 8 (December 1832): 661–62. Author's collection.

69

"*Serre Ornée*," or ornamented conservatory, in the commercial botanic garden of M. Boursault, in the rue Blanche, Paris, from P. Boitard, *Traité de la composition et de l'ornement des jardins* (Paris, 1825), frontispiece. Courtesy, the Lindley Library of the Royal Horticultural Society, London.

70

*Populus monilifera*, or Canadian (Black Italian) Poplar, portrait of a full-grown specimen at Syon House, Brentford, seat of the duke of Northumberland, from *Arboretum Britannicum* (London, 1844), vol. 7, p. 274. Courtesy of the Frances Loeb Library, Graduate School of Design, Harvard University.

71

Baltard, "View of the great jet at St. Cloud," ca. 1815. Author's collection.

72

J. Nash, "The Gardens of the Tuileries: View from the grand entrance," from L.T. Ventouillac, *Paris and its Environs* (London, 1831), vol. 2, opposite p. 188. Courtesy, Harvard College Library.

73

"Kenwood, View on Entering the Gates," near Hampstead Heath, London, woodcut from Loudon, *The Villa Gardener* (London, 1850), p. 453. Courtesy, Ushaw College Library, Durham.

74

J.C. Loudon, Design for the Birmingham Botanical Garden (1831), from the *Gardener's Magazine* 8 (August 1832): 414–15. Author's collection.

75

John Nash, "Plan of an Estate belonging to the Crown called Marylebone Park Farm [now known as Regent's Park]" (1812) from Parliamentary Papers: *First Report of the Commissioners of His Majesty's Woods, Forests, and Land Revenues*, June 4, 1812. Courtesy, The British Library.

76

Gabriel Thouin, "Jardin fantastique anglais," from Thouin, *Plans raisonnés de toutes les espèces de jardins* (Paris, 1820), pl. 19. Courtesy, the Lindley Library of the Royal Horticultural Society, London.

77

F.L. von Sckell, Plan of the Nymphenburg Gardens, near Munich, from the *Gardener's Magazine* 9 (August 1833): 388–89. Author's collection.

78

J.C. Loudon, Circular range of hothouses proposed for the Birmingham Botanical Garden (1831), from the *Gardener's Magazine* 8 (August 1832): 420. Author's collection.

79

J.C. Loudon, Conical, or beehive-shaped, hothouses for the Birmingham Botanical Garden (1831), from the *Gardener's Magazine* 8 (August 1832): 422. Author's collection.

80

J. Storer, engraving of Coleshill House, Berkshire, formerly a residence of the earl of Radnor, from John Britton, *The Beauties of England and Wales* (London, 1801). Courtesy, Berkshire County Library, Reading.

81

J.C. Loudon, "Design for Re-arranging the Pleasure Grounds at Coleshill," 1843. Courtesy, the National Trust, England.

*Pure Water the Cities of London and Westminster* (London, 1828). Courtesy, The British Library.
95
View of Kensington Gardens, looking east to the Serpentine River. Photo by author.
96
Jonas Dennis, "View of the West Front of Buckingham Palace," from Dennis, *The Landscape Gardener* (London, 1835), frontispiece. Courtesy of the Frances Loeb Library, Graduate School of Design, Harvard University.
97
"Seven Dials," St. Giles's Parish, London, from Charles Knight, *London* (London, 1842–44), vol. 3, p. 257. Author's collection.
98
"Cruchley's new Plan of London and environs," 1835, detail, Holland Park and Kensington Gardens. Courtesy, Local History Library, London Borough of Camden's Libraries and Arts Department.
99
J.C.Loudon, Concentric greenbelt scheme, entitled "Hints for Breathing Places for the Metropolis," from the *Gardener's Magazine* 5 (December 1829): 687. Author's collection.
100
"Cary's new Plan of London & its Vicinity," 1845, detail, Regent's Park and Hampstead. Courtesy, Local History Library, London Borough of Camden's Libraries and Arts Department.
101
John Constable, R.A., *A View on Hampstead Heath with Figures in the Foreground*, 1821. Courtesy, Yale Center for British Art, Paul Mellon Collection.
102
View from Hampstead Heath to the London Metropolis, ca. 1840. Courtesy, Local History Library, London Borough of Camden's Libraries and Arts Department.
103
"Mogg's [map, showing] 45 Miles of the Country Round London," 1831, detail, from central London and Westminster to Gravesend, on the east. Courtesy, Local History Library, London Borough of Camden's Libraries and Arts Department.
104
J.H.Forshaw and Patrick Abercrombie, Open Space Plan, from their *County of London Plan* (London: Macmillan, 1943), opposite p. 46. By permission of Macmillan, London and Basingstoke.
105
Jeremy Bentham, Panopticon, section and plan, as reproduced in Leonardo Benevolo, *The Origins of Modern Town Planning* (Cambridge: MIT Press, 1967). By permission of Gius. Laterza & Figli, Bari, Italy.
106
Gabriel Thouin, "Project for an experimental farm," from Thouin, *Plans raisonnés de toutes les espèces de jardins* (Paris, 1819), pl. 51.

Courtesy of the Frances Loeb Library, Graduate School of Design, Harvard University.

107

Sir John Soane, "Design for a Royal Palace [made in] Rome, 1779," proposed for Hyde Park, from Soane, *Designs for Public and Private Buildings* (London, 1828), pl. 34. Courtesy of the Frances Loeb Library, Graduate School of Design, Harvard University.

108

Ebenezer Howard, diagrams 2 and 3 of his Garden City, from Howard, *Garden Cities of To-morrow* (London, 1902). Courtesy of the Frances Loeb Library, Graduate School of Design, Harvard University.

109

J. M. W. Turner, "Boulevards," from Turner, *The Rivers of France* (London, 1853), opposite p. 308. Courtesy, Harvard College Library.

110

View in the grounds of Birkenhead Park, near Liverpool, laid out by Joseph Paxton in 1844. Photo by author.

111

Thomas Shepherd, "The Coliseum, Regent's Park," from James Elmes, *Metropolitan Improvements; or, London in the Nineteenth Century* (London, 1829), opposite p. 24. Courtesy, Harvard College Library.

112

Two views of the Thames Tunnel, interior (*a*), and longitudinal section (*b*), from Charles Knight, *London* (London, 1842–1844), vol. 3, pp. 48, 55. Author's collection.

113

W. A. Nesfield, Two views of his residence, Fortis Green, in Muswell Hill, North London, from Loudon, *The Villa Gardener* (London, 1850), pp. 284, 280. Courtesy, Ushaw College Library, Durham.

114

E. B. Lamb, View of Loudon's house, Porchester Terrace, ca. 1838, from Loudon, *The Villa Gardener* (London, 1850), p. 136. Courtesy, Ushaw College Library, Durham.

115

View of Nos. 3 and 5, Porchester Terrace, Bayswater. Photo by author.

116

No. 3, Porchester Terrace, Bayswater, detail of veranda. Photo by author.

117

J. C. Loudon, Plan of his own residence, Porchester Terrace, from *The Villa Gardener* (London, 1850), p. 135. Courtesy, Ushaw College Library, Durham.

118

J. C. Loudon, Polygonal conservatory, from *The Green-House Companion* (London, 1825), p. 17. Courtesy, Gray Herbarium Library, Harvard University.

119

John Britton, Map of St. Pancras and Marylebone, 1834, detail of Bayswater. Courtesy, Local History Library, London Borough of Camden's Libraries and Arts Department.

120

Jane W. Loudon, Portrait. By kind courtesy of Bea Howe.

121

John Linnell, Portrait of J.C.Loudon (1840–41). Reproduced by permission of the Council of the Linnean Society of London.

122

*Loudonia aurea*, from John Lindley, "A Sketch of the Vegetation of the Swan River Colony," South Australia, in *Edwards' Botanical Register, Appendix to the First 23 volumes* (London, 1839), p. xliii. Courtesy, Arnold Arboretum Library, Harvard University.

123

Reconstruction of a plan for the Southampton Cemetery, drawn by the author, from Loudon's written description in his official report, dated August 31, 1843.

124

Remnants of "imaginary squares" designed by J.C.Loudon for the Southampton Cemetery. Photo by author.

# Preface

John Claudius Loudon, the Scottish landscape gardener (1783–1843), was a meticulous designer, a sound theorist, an eminent horticulturist, and a charitable, sometimes charming man. Imaginative and far-sighted, he was often the first to propose an innovation that would later be developed by others. In 1816 he invented a wrought-iron sash bar, which made possible the construction of curvilinear glasshouses, such as the Palm House at Kew, in London, and the conservatory of the New York Botanical Garden. In 1829 Loudon devised a plan for multiple greenbelts to penetrate the dense, expanding London metropolis. In 1839 he laid out the Derby Arboretum, generally considered to be England's first public park.[1]

Through his writings, Loudon also made contributions to social and political reform, national education, and regional planning. His work and thought excite more than historical interest, however, for his greatest aesthetic and social concerns are among our own today: the expansion of metropolitan regions, the design and siting of buildings, conservation of the landscape, the quality of education and housing, wages and unemployment, the dignity of the individual, and the right to a "fair chance in life."

Unfortunately, the formidable bulk of Loudon's publications has obscured his own distinctive views. As the editor of popular encyclopedias of gardening, architecture, and agriculture, he is best known today for his compilations of the work and thought of others, including designs for cottages, villas, suburban gardens, country houses, and farm buildings. In his greatest encyclopedic work, the eight-volume *Arboretum et Fruticetum Britannicum; or, The Trees and Shrubs of Britain* (1838), the portraits of trees — some serviceable, some poignantly beautiful — were all executed by other hands. Still, whatever images appear in Loudon's works somehow bear his stamp. They are all "Loudonesque"; and they had a pervasive influence, long after his death, on the buildings and landscapes of Victorian Britain and, directly or indirectly, in America, Australia, and other parts of the English-speaking world.

This study is an attempt to look beneath the Loudonesque surface of nineteenth-century buildings and landscapes, to find the essence of Loudon's own aesthetic and social views. If he did not intend to promote all the changes that occurred in his name — if he was actually distressed, for instance, to see that the simplicity of the British rural landscape was threatened by the scarlet geraniums and purple petunias bedded out over expansive lawns or "bosomed up" in the borders of old shrubberies — then what were his views? Henry Noel Humphreys, a warm personal friend of Loudon's, offers a clue: "To read [Loudon's] works in chronological order is like reading the history of the man, whose character we see continuously broadened, softened, and improved by his intense love of the never-cloying beauties of Nature."[2]

Here, Loudon's views, like his character, will be understood as they developed over time, and in the context of the work of his contemporaries, such as Humphry Repton, John Nash, Charles Barry, William Wordsworth, Jeremy Bentham, John Ruskin, and Thomas Carlyle. As a young man, Loudon was bright, earnest, quick to learn, quick to criticize, and impatient with rules, formulas and preconceptions. The mature Loudon, secure in his reputation for horticultural knowledge and refined taste, sincerely acknowledged the talents of others — including his well-known predecessors, Lancelot "Capability" Brown and Repton; and his promising young rival, Joseph Paxton. In his early career, Loudon had designed romantically wild, picturesque landscapes and utilitarian glasshouses, providing controlled environments for plants. In later life, he spent more of his waking hours writing than designing. Yet, even in his waning years, bearing up against rheumatism, chronic bronchitis, and the loss of his right arm, he prepared plans for laying out parks, gardens, and cemeteries.

As Loudon matured, his political and social views became more liberal and his editorial tone more tolerant. His optimism and idealism were confirmed, rather than shaken, by the experience of political and social revolutions. A man who embraced the ideals of democracy, he considered George Washington and Thomas Jefferson "the greatest men that ever lived, or, speaking relatively to age and country, probably ever can or will live."[3] And Loudon longed for seeds from any common tree or plant on their estates. Only the persistence of slavery — which he abhorred — dampened his enthusiasm for a visit to America (which never materialized). A child of the Romantic era, Loudon remained fascinated by great natural or man-made phenomena that could elevate the human spirit. A crumbling ruin could stir his mind to nostalgic or philosophical reflection. The debacle, or breaking up, of the ice-covered river Neva in St. Petersburg could remind him of another sublime upheaval which he believed would occur just as quietly and predictably: the spread of "high, equal and universal education" to all human beings.

The Introduction of this book offers a biographical sketch of Loudon. The following chapters are arranged in part chronologically, in part by subject. The first five consider Loudon's early career, while he lived mainly in the British countryside, laying out gardens and farms, managing estates, and writing. Chapters 6 through 8 are concerned with Loudon's travels in Russia, his experiments in hothouse design, his project for multifamily housing, and his architectural writings. Chapters 9 through 11 focus on a few of Loudon's later designs for public and private gardens, his horticultural writings, and his special concern for the living and working conditions of the hired gardener. Chapters 12 and 13 consider Loudon's later Continental travels, and his views on planning and design at the large scale — metropolitan, regional, and national. Chapter 14 focuses on Loudon's mature social and political views. The final chapter reveals Loudon at home in Bayswater, which, within his lifetime, changed from a rural hamlet to a suburb of the London metropolis. There, among descriptions of his own house and garden, and recollections of friends and colleagues, appears Loudon's young wife, Jane, who shared the last thir-

xxv

teen years of his life, bore him a child, helped him to write some of his best works, and became a horticultural author in her own right.

Loudon diffused his energies in many directions, assuming the roles of writer, teacher, activist, publicist, man of ideas, inventor, designer. He was more a craftsman than an artist. He had a keen, critical eye; an analytical mind; and a love of order. He could perceive beauty in different modes, or styles, of gardening, architecture, and urban design; and, as a designer, he could bring together all the elements of a program into a pleasing whole. At times, his fascination for the science of gardening interfered with the creation of a thing of beauty. But ultimately, he reconciled the art and science of gardening in a way that could be visually satisfying, even if it lacked that ineffable quality, artistic genius.

Loudon was a genius of another order, a man whose mind was a treasure-house of useful information and idealistic schemes. He patiently articulated sound principles of architecture, landscape design, and planning, and he was passionately committed to reaching as wide an audience as possible. His vision of progress was at once Utopian and pragmatic. And, unable to wait for inevitable social change, he took great pains to bring some happiness into other people's lives while he lived. This is the man who should emerge in the following pages.

My interest in Loudon was sparked by a graduate seminar on British architecture offered by George Hersey at Yale some fifteen years ago. Since then, three fellowships have made possible a few years of travel and research in Britain: a Fulbright-Hays fellowship for doctoral dissertation research at University College London, a private fellowship jointly administered by Yale University and the Royal Institute of British Architects, and a Leverhulme Visiting Fellowship for research in residence at the University of Newcastle-upon-Tyne.

The librarians, archivists, curators, and staff of many institutions in Britain, France, and the United States have been generous with research materials and personal assistance. Unusually helpful were Barbara Callahan and Jon Perry at the Gray Herbarium Library, Harvard University; Bernadette Callery at the Hunt Institute for Botanical Documentation, Carnegie-Mellon University; Dr. Brent Elliott at the Lindley Library of the Royal Horticultural Society, London; Christopher Hail at the Frances Loeb Library, Harvard Graduate School of Design; and Margaret (Alec) Wills at the School of Architecture Library, University of Newcastle-upon-Tyne.

Among the many individuals who have offered advice, assistance, and encouragement, I would like especially to thank Charles Beveridge, Susan Casteras, Judith Colton, Tom Faulkner, John Gloag, Janet Godden, Patrick Goode, John Harris, Noel Hill, Mrs. Peggy Jay, Beatrice (Howe) Lubbock, Michael Nagy, Nicholas Penny, Vincent Scully, John Stilgoe, James Weirick, Peter and Jenny Willis, and Rachel Wilson. Garrett Eckbo, in particular, has encouraged me through his writings and our far-ranging conversations; more than any other practitioner of landscape architecture today, Garrett has reinforced my belief that the democratic ideals, environmental goals, and artistic freedom that Loudon espoused are still worth writing about and striving for.

Among those who have read parts of this book, in one version or another, I am particularly indebted to Mavis Batey, James Broderick, J. Quentin Hughes, Will Lee, and G. B. H. Wightman. Reyner Banham, my adviser at University College London, and Laurence Fricker read an earlier version of the present book and offered considerable stimulation and guidance. Later drafts were read by Ann Leighton (Isadore L. L. Smith) and John Murray. For their insights and continual, genial support, I am deeply grateful. George Hersey followed the progress of this work for more than a decade, guiding it through early stages and assisting its completion in many ways. Given the meticulous editing of Cynthia Wells and Judy Metro at Yale University Press, I feel unusually fortunate. For whatever imperfections remain, the responsibility is my own. (Because this is a historical study, the botanical names of plants have not been modernized.)

Inevitably there are persons to whom most authors are indebted, not so much for any particular insight into their subject, as for their friendship, love, sympathy, or shared experiences and values. For many years, until her death in December 1985, Ann Leighton was my constant inspiration, a fellow writer on gardening and landscape who combined a keen intellect with compassion and grace. My parents and my husband, Paul, have given more than I can acknowledge here — except to note that their cheerful encouragement and genuine interest in Loudon, the man, were invaluable.

# Abbreviations

The following works written or edited by Loudon are cited frequently:

| | |
|---|---|
| *Arboretum et Fruticetum Britannicum; or, The Trees and Shrubs of Britain. . . . 1838.* | *Arb. Brit.* or *Arboretum* |
| *The Architectural Magazine. . . . 1834–39.* | *Arch. Mag.* |
| *A Treatise on Forming, Improving, and Managing Country Residences. . . . 1806.* | *Country Res.* or *Country Residences* |
| *Designs for Laying out Farms and Farm Buildings, in the Scotch Style; adapted to England. . . . 1811.* | *Designs for Farms* |
| *An Encyclopaedia of Agriculture. . . . 1825.* | *Encyc. Ag.* |
| *An Encyclopaedia of Cottage, Farm, and Villa Architecture and Furniture. . . . 1832–33.* | *Encyc. Arch.* or *Encyclopaedia of Architecture* |
| *An Encyclopaedia of Gardening. . . . 1822.* | *Encyc. Gard.* |
| *The Gardener's Magazine, and Register of Rural and Domestic Improvement. 1826–44.* | *Gard. Mag.* |
| *Hints on the Formation of Gardens and Pleasure Grounds. . . . 1812.* | *Hints on Gard.* |
| *An Immediate and Effectual Mode of Raising the Rental of the Landed Property of England. . . . 1808.* | *Landed Prop.* |
| *The Magazine of Natural History. . . . 1828–36.* | *Mag. Nat. Hist.* |
| *Observations on . . . Useful and Ornamental Plantations; on the Theory and Practice of Landscape Gardening. . . . 1804.* | *Obs. on Gard.* or *Observations on Landscape Gardening* |
| *Remarks on the Construction of Hot-houses. . . . 1817.* | *Remarks on Hot-houses* |
| *Sketches of Curvilinear Hot-houses. . . . 1818.* | *Sketches of Hot-houses* |
| *The Suburban Gardener and Villa Companion. . . . 1836–38.* | *Sub. Gard.* |

| | |
|---|---|
| *Treat. Hot-houses* | *A Short Treatise on several improvements recently made in Hot-houses. . . .* 1805. |
| "Treatise on Scone" | "A Treatise on the Improvements proposed for Scone. . . ." 1803. |

Other works frequently cited include the following:

| | |
|---|---|
| *Annales Soc. Hort.* | *Annales de la Société (Royale) d'Horticulture de Paris, et Journal Spécial de l'Etat et des Progrès du Jardinage.* Vols. 1–34. (Paris). 1827–44. |
| *Bon. Jard.* | *L'Almanach du Bon Jardinier* (Paris). 1825–44. These volumes were edited by Alexandre Poiteau. |
| *DNB* | Sidney Lee et al., eds. *Dictionary of National Biography.* Oxford: Oxford University Press, from ca. 1909. |
| *Gard. Gaz.* | *The Gardener's Gazette: A Weekly Journal of Science, Literature and General News* (London). (January 7, 1837 [vol. 1, no. 1] through November 13, 1941). |
| "Life of Loudon" | Jane Loudon. "A Short Account of the Life and Writings of John Claudius Loudon." First published in J. C. Loudon, *Self-Instruction for Young Gardeners.* References are to this essay, as reprinted in John Gloag, *Mr Loudon's England* (Newcastle-upon-Tyne: Oriel Press, 1970) 182–219. |
| "Recollections" | Henry Noel Humphreys. "Recollections of John Claudius Loudon," a series of six articles published in the *Garden* (volume 1 [June 29, 1872] through volume 3 [January 18, 1873]). |
| *Trans. Hort. Soc.* | *Transactions of the Horticultural Society.* Vols. 1–3. London: Bulmer, 1812–20. |
| *Wellesley Index* | Walter E. Houghton, ed. *The Wellesley Index to Victorian Periodicals, 1824–1900.* 3 vols. Toronto: University of Toronto Press; London: Routledge & Kegan Paul, 1979. |

# Introduction

This biographical sketch introduces the people, places, and events that influenced Loudon's intellectual development. He, in turn, influenced several generations through his popular encyclopedias and magazines. One impressive work, however, nearly ruined him financially.

Before Loudon was thirty years old, he had amassed a personal fortune of some fifteen thousand pounds ($75,000). This financial independence — remarkable for a small farmer's son — came to him after nearly two decades of diligent apprenticeship and professional practice. He had been apprenticed to some nurserymen and landscape gardeners while he studied botany, chemistry, and agriculture at the University of Edinburgh. He had laid out country seats in Scotland, England, Wales, and Ireland and had consulted on projects to reclaim land from the sea. He had worked as a tenant farmer and land agent (profiting from favorable rates of inflation during wartime), and had designed his own house, gardens, and farm buildings. He had briefly conducted an agricultural school and had published treatises on landscape gardening, hothouse construction, farming, and political economy. Now, in 1813, he was eager to leave Britain for a while and cast off the "confining coil of insular thought."[1]

Some extraordinary men in Britain had already impressed Loudon with their breadth of knowledge and their more cosmopolitan views. He had met Sir Joseph Banks, president of the Royal Society, who in turn introduced him to the scientific world of London. He had met Jeremy Bentham, whose concern for the "greatest happiness of the greatest number" became Loudon's own standard for assessing change. With a command of French, German, Italian, and Latin, Loudon had read the best-known works on gardening, agriculture, and landscape design, including Philip Miller and Jean de la Quintinie on practical gardening; John Evelyn and William Marshall on planting trees; and Thomas Whately, Uvedale Price, Richard Payne Knight, and René de Girardin on laying out picturesque landscapes. Adam Smith, Sir Joshua Reynolds, and Jean-Jacques Rousseau had nurtured his mind, his eye, his imagination. Now Loudon was eager to experience what the French call *dépaysment*. He had to extricate himself from Britain, physically and mentally, in order to arrive at a sympathetic understanding of other landscapes, customs, people, and ideas.

In March 1813 Loudon sailed for Europe — not for Calais and the south, however, like cultured young men on the Grand Tour, attracted to the lands of the classical poets. Instead, he went via Gothenburg, straight to the capitals and battlefields of northern Europe, which were at last open to travelers as Napoleon's army was retreating. This first Continental journey lasted eighteen months; Loudon would return four times, most often to Paris.[2]

These travels offered Loudon adventures, professional contacts, and a wealth of material for his written works. More important, they stimulated some profound changes in his thinking. In matters of landscape design and town planning, Loudon saw that the Germans and the French had sometimes surpassed the British; and he recommended some of their practices, particularly for public parks and the systematic management of streets and roads. On political and social issues, Loudon grew increasingly more liberal. Having seen how a sound education, decent housing, and access to parks and museums had benefited the working people of southern Germany, he became more concerned about the immediate needs of working people in Britain. In time, his proposals began to rely less on private wealth eventually to diffuse prosperity to the poor.

"Diffusion" was still, in Loudon's mind, a workable means for improvement. But, from the 1820s onward, it was education — or intellectual capital — not merely monetary wealth, that Loudon wanted to see diffused. He continually urged the creation of a National Education Establishment in Britain, under which children of all social classes would be educated together until age sixteen. Loudon never believed that intellect or wealth would thereby become equalized, but he did hold the radical belief that the children of both rich and poor should be given a "fair chance in life," from the beginning. And instead of appealing to self-interest, Loudon began to emphasize self-cultivation and cooperation. In 1808 he had written that "all the great improvements, whether inventions or economical modes of practice, that have been made since the beginning of the world, have been made by individuals." By 1829 he was convinced that "no man can steal a march on his age. All improvement is more the result of the general mind of society than of the mind of the individual who is the immediate instrument."[3]

These changes in outlook all occurred before 1830, the year in which Loudon met and married his remarkable wife, Jane Wells Webb. The author of a three-volume science fiction novel at nineteen, Jane Wells Loudon became her husband's amanuensis at twenty-three; and the two began to work daily, sometimes half the night, writing and editing works on gardening and architecture for a wide audience. In these works, Loudon revealed a special affection and sympathy for young working gardeners, often speaking to them directly about what he had learned through a lifetime of travel, study, experimentation, and design. Friends who knew of his severe chronic illnesses and reviewers confronted with his enormous encyclopedias alike referred to Loudon as "indefatigable," a "tiger," a "demon for work." A few must have recognized the motivation for Loudon's labors: his firm conviction that "Knowledge is pleasure as well as power; and that of any two individuals in society, whether rich or poor, the more highly cultivated, other circumstances being the same, will possess the greater share of happiness, and will be the more valuable member of society."[4] Ultimately, environmental education — on housing, gardening, landscape design, and planning — was Loudon's most permanent contribution to "the greatest happiness."

In his lifetime, Loudon was recognized by some as an amiable and

benevolent man who occasionally revealed a sense of humor. John Linnell's portrait of Loudon at fifty-seven suggests some of these qualities (see
fig. 121). But an unknown artist's sketch of the young Loudon, perhaps in
his late twenties, is his more familiar image today: the self-confident,
mildly complacent, apparently successful self-made man, the ungrateful
successor to Brown and Repton, the fastidious critic of gardens great and
small (see Frontispiece). To reconcile these two contradictory images of
Loudon, one must go back to the beginning, before the young man left his
father's farm.

John Claudius Loudon was born on April 8, 1783, in Cambuslang,
Lanarkshire, southwest of Edinburgh. The eldest of several children, he
might have remained at his father's farm, Kerse Hall, near Gogar, and
continued to work the land like other efficient Scots in the Midlothian
countryside. But Loudon had other ambitions. When his father gave him a
small garden, Loudon laid it out with miniature walks and beds. Collecting new seeds for the garden, reading, and sketching landscapes were his
childhood pleasures. Later, when he lived with an uncle in Edinburgh and
went to a local school, he particularly enjoyed botany and chemistry.
Before long he recognized his all-encompassing vocation: landscape
gardening.

With his father's reluctant permission, at age eleven or twelve,
Loudon became a part-time draftsman and general assistant to John
Mawer, a nurseryman, landscape gardener, and hothouse expert at Easter
Dalry, near Edinburgh. And what an opportunity for a schoolboy that was!
Mawer was just then, in 1794, experimenting with new methods of heating
glasshouses, erecting boilers to produce steam for his pineries, peach
houses, and vineries. "We tried all sorts of things," Loudon later recalled.[5] Having learned from Mawer's experiences, as well as from the
writings of Count Rumford and Walter Nicol, he went on to experiment
with his own utilitarian glass structures, focusing on the essentials: light,
heat, soil, water, and air. Whatever might detract from the end in view —
any ornaments or thick wooden or stone members — he soon discarded.

While he held a job and studied part-time, Loudon found the study
of languages tedious and would gladly have dispensed with French and
Latin. One day, however, his uncle, a collector of fine prints, was showing

*While Loudon was growing up on his father's farm, lay-
ing out miniature walks and beds in his own patch of garden, the Scottish capital lay some five miles to the northeast, roughly in the direction of Stothard's view.*

Fig. 1
Thomas Stothard, R.A., *A Dis-
tant View of Edinburgh*, 1809.
Courtesy, Yale Center for Brit-
ish Art, Paul Mellon
Collection.

an engraving to a friend and asked Loudon to translate the French title. Unable to read it, the mortified boy quietly resolved to learn the language. He eventually paid his teacher with what he earned by translating a life of Abelard for *Shrarton's Encyclopedia*. From age thirteen he kept a journal (for many years written mainly in French); he also studied Italian. In his twenties, he taught himself German, Hebrew, and Greek.

When Mawer died in 1798, Loudon became apprenticed to the firm of Messrs. Dicksons and Shade, nurserymen and landscape planners in Leith Walk.[6] While he boarded with the Dicksons, Loudon alarmed the family by sitting up two nights a week to study, staying awake with strong green tea. During vacations, he worked so hard on his father's farm that the laborers confessed they "were all shamed by the young master."[7] Years later Noel Humphreys wrote of Loudon's diligence, determination, and considerable store of information on a great range of subjects acquired during those years. And Jane Loudon deduced from old family papers that her husband had been a modest young man, quiet, not fond of displaying his knowledge but able to astonish his listeners with what he did know about certain subjects.

Though Loudon's quest for knowledge was self-motivated, his studies at the University of Edinburgh — an *intellectual* hothouse — must have further stimulated his inner drive. There he would have met fellow Scottish students — sons of farmers and artisans — with funds as modest and aspirations as keen and high-minded as his own. In time Loudon became the favorite of Professor Andrew Coventry, who lectured on husbandry, planting, gardening, and "ornamental agriculture," with some reference to the writings of Whately, William Gilpin, Marshall, Price, Knight, and Repton. In rural improvements, "durable economy" should always take precedence over "shifting Taste," Dr. Coventry insisted. Utility should be the decisive factor. And husbandmen would usually find that whatever was "most extensively beneficial" was "most exquisitely ornamental" — in other words, Beauty is Use; Use, Beauty.[8]

Loudon gradually adopted these views in theory and in practice. In his early experiments with hothouse designs, however, he was most concerned with utility — not beauty. At twenty, he clearly distinguished his orderly, utilitarian hothouses from more elegant conservatories, to which he would add columns, entablatures, and balustrades. Years later, in 1831, he would eliminate the classical trappings when he proposed either a hemispherical or a beehive-shaped glasshouse as the centerpiece of the Birmingham Botanical Garden.[9] By then, utility and beauty had become inseparable.

Had he been a true disciple of Dr. Coventry, Loudon might have consistently associated beauty with utility. But he was also drawn to the more elegant writings of Sir Uvedale Price, a man of acute aesthetic sensibilities, for whom land was primarily *landscape*. Price examined the subtle distinctions between beautiful, sublime, and picturesque landscapes, as found in nature and as they might be improved, taking hints from the unified compositions of the great landscape painters — Claude Lorrain, Salvator Rosa, Nicolas Poussin, Peter Paul Rubens, Thomas Gainsborough, and others. For improving *real* landscapes, too, Price emphasized the unity of a composition, undisturbed by distinct, isolated objects and enhanced by whatever could obscure the edges of things —

dappled lights and shadows, weeds and wild undergrowth, mosses and evidences of decay.

In the case of inhabited landscapes, Price did not ignore convenience and utility. He recognized that, near the house, picturesque effects would have to be sacrificed to neatness. But such a sacrifice should not "wantonly" be made. [10] This association of the lax or immoral with the prim and neat is amusing — and typical of the way Price overturned commonsense notions of beauty and ugliness when he explored the visual appeal of the picturesque. Even machinery and evidence of industry could be picturesque. Old mills nestled in narrow river valleys could offer delightful images of decay, in the lights and shadows falling on wheels and weather-stained woodwork, with plants cropping up in the joints between stones.

Loudon, the young mechanical designer of hothouses, did not see machinery as picturesque. Still, Price offered him a comprehensive approach for viewing the natural and man-made world and for making any entire scene visually coherent. [11] Loudon accepted this picturesque vision and thereafter adopted the principles of landscape painting as guides for designing real landscapes, including buildings as well as their sites and prospects.

Price also offered a painless way of looking at poverty, by softening its harsh edges in the landscape. For instance, the cottages of poor laborers could be viewed as delightfully picturesque, especially when, shrouded in vines, they enhanced the rustic character of the landscape. Accordingly, in 1806 Loudon recommended that luxuriant vines and creepers should enhance the rustic, picturesque character of cottages — and even of large country houses. Two decades later, he would propose more *useful* changes when he insisted that the humblest cottage share with the mansion the essential comforts of flush toilets, large windows, and elevated ground floors. After examining the interiors of cottages in many parts of Britain and on the Continent, he knew that the homes of laboring people needed improvements which connoisseurs of the Picturesque might never detect — or appreciate.

At the age of twenty, in 1803, after experimenting with hothouses and embankments and improving country residences in Scotland, Loudon went to London for the first time, carrying Dr. Coventry's letters of introduction to influential scientists and landed gentlemen in the metropolis (fig. 2). In this way, Sir Joseph Banks and James Sowerby, both distinguished naturalists, became kind friends and supporters. It was Jeremy Bentham, however, who had perhaps the greatest influence on Loudon's life and work.

Bentham was approaching sixty when Loudon met him — an eccentric man, somewhat reclusive, with views that were considered revolutionary and dangerous. But Loudon, already persuaded by Coventry's arguments for utility, was intrigued to find Bentham applying the same principle to a broad range of social and political concerns, from constitutional codes and parliamentary reform to the design of workhouses and the quantification of human happiness. Loudon tended to qualify, not quantify, degrees of happiness. He would temper his own concern for utility with a desire for beauty. Still, Loudon admired the elder man's essential humanity. Years later he referred to Bentham as "the greatest benefactor

to mankind, in our opinion, since the commencement of the Christian
era."[12] Not surprisingly in Loudon's writings and designs are some unmis-
takable "Benthamite" qualities: a comparable search for grand, comprehensive theories; a similar insistence on system, order, and coherence
among the parts of a whole; in architectural design, the same geometrical
clarity and centralization; in social commentary, the same primary concern for the great mass of society.[13]

Loudon had not been in London a year when the *Literary Journal*
published his first proposal for metropolitan improvements: a plan to lay
out and plant the public squares of London with hardy trees and flowering
shrubs, so as to form picturesque compositions viewed from within and
without the squares. This article appeared in December 1803, two months
after Loudon completed his "Treatise on Scone," an elaborate bound
manuscript similar to Repton's "Red Books," containing Loudon's proposed improvements for the earl of Mansfield's ancient Scottish seat, near
Perth. For the next few years, Loudon continued to practice landscape
gardening in the British Isles. He became a fellow of the Linnaean Society
in February 1806 and later a fellow of the London (now Royal) Horticultural Society. He attracted clients as well as critics with his early
writings; and his first, *Observations on Landscape Gardening* (1804),
caught the eye of one of his most memorable clients — William A.
Madocks, a Radical member of Parliament and devotee of the Picturesque.

In 1806–07, Loudon offered Madocks professional advice on an
embankment project at Tremadoc, North Wales; in turn, Madocks offered
Loudon an exposure to another world: one of sublime mountains, fine
wines, boisterous wit, and delicate airs sung by the illustrious Elizabeth
Billington of Covent Garden. Leaving Tremadoc with vivid recollections
of the enterprising, public-spirited Madocks and his engaging friends,
Loudon returned to London on the night mail coach — unfortunately,

LONDON BRIDGE &c.

riding outside in the rain. He caught cold, then developed rheumatic fever. His knee become ankylosed, and he was left with a permanent limp; also his right arm was permanently contracted. Suffering severe pain, Loudon retired from practice for a while and took a room in a farmhouse in Pinner, Middlesex.

There, while convalescing, Loudon continued his agricultural studies and landscape painting and began to translate from French and German works. The relative inactivity was frustrating. "How much have I neglected the important task of improving myself!" he had written in his journal of 1806. "What new ideas have developed themselves before me, and what different views of life have I acquired since I came to London three years ago! Yet now I am twenty-three years of age — perhaps one whole third of my life having passed away, and what have I done to benefit my fellow man?"[14] This attitude towards life and work never left him. The means which Loudon recommended for improvement would vary, from self-reliance and rugged individualism to experiments in cooperation. The end — the benefit of his fellow man — remained constant.

In 1807 Loudon persuaded his father to join him as a tenant of Wood Hall Farm, in Pinner, where the two introduced "Scotch" farming to the south of England. The elder Loudon took up another lease, for Kenton Farm, near Harrow, Middlesex. And young Loudon, still in his mid-twenties, published a pamphlet on landed property (1808), in which he urged proprietors to raise land rentals, offer longer leases, and rationalize agriculture — for their own greater profit and for the diffusion of prosperity to all classes of society.

This pamphlet caught the attention of General George Frederick Stratton of Great Tew, Oxfordshire, who asked Loudon to revalue his estate in the spring of 1808. Loudon proposed to double the rentals, and that autumn he became a tenant there himself, assuming responsibility for nearly one thousand acres. In 1809 he bought a farm in Ramsbury, Wiltshire, and planned a central farmstead with an efficient radial pattern of hedgerows. There he intended to erect several new cottages, a chapel, and a "Lancasterian" school, to be founded on the innovative educational principles of Joseph Lancaster. These enterprises may have been curtailed, however, by the elder Mr. Loudon's death in December 1809. In the spring of 1811, young Loudon sold his lease on Tew Lodge Farm, closed his agricultural college, and returned to London, where he continued to write on agriculture and landscape design. Meanwhile, he supported his mother and younger siblings.[15]

These responsibilities could not keep Loudon from going to the Continent as soon as the retreat of Napoleon's army cleared the way. He sailed from Harwich to Gothenburg, and traveled through Scandinavia and Poland, then on to Russia, passing by the traces of war: "horses and men lying dead by the road-side, and bands of wild-looking Cossacks scouring the country."[16] Once his carriage was attacked by Cossacks, who would have stolen the horses but for the lashing whips of the driver and servants. Between Riga and St. Petersburg, he paused to sketch a picturesque old fort. Presumed to be a spy, he was arrested, detained for questioning, and finally released.

On this first Continental journey, Loudon observed the roads, the forests, and the educational systems of Sweden; tree-lined avenues, bad drainage, and filthy narrow streets in Berlin; the palace and gardens of Schönbrunn in Vienna; a picturesque cemetery overlooking the Polish city of Wilno; and a panopticon prison erected by Jeremy Bentham's brother, General Samuel Bentham, in St. Petersburg. After eight months in Russia, Loudon came away with impressions of extremes. The boors, slaves, and freemen of Russia had no gardens worth mentioning; the noblemen had some of the most magnificent palaces and horticultural establishments in Europe. More pineapples were grown in the hothouses round St. Petersburg than in the rest of Continental Europe combined, but few Russians had as yet developed a taste for certain domestic comforts and simple picturesque landscapes.

Loudon returned to London in September 1814 as a member of the Imperial Society of Moscow, the Natural History Society of Berlin, the Royal Economical Society of Potsdam, and several other institutions. His newly acquired information and fresh perceptions would inform his encyclopedias, treatises, and magazines for the next several decades. In his absence, however, his hard-earned fortune had been dissipated through his banker's speculations; apparently he had lost nearly everything. Under this financial strain, Loudon's health suffered. In 1816, unable to resume the vigorous practice of landscape gardening, he rented a small house with a large garden in Bayswater, where his mother and sisters came to live with him — at a place he called "the Hermitage."

Loudon was now thirty-three. For the rest of his life, he would suffer from chronic rheumatism. His right arm would be broken twice, then, in 1825, amputated. For a man who had once shown great promise as a calligrapher and had occasionally exhibited paintings at the Royal Academy, the loss of the arm must have been particularly hard to bear. Still, by all accounts, Loudon always showed a stoical acceptance of physical pain and misfortune.

Within a year of his moving to Bayswater, Loudon had begun to experiment with hothouse construction. In 1816 he invented a wrought-iron sash bar which would allow him to construct curved, dome-shaped glasshouses for plants. He then began to combine curvilinear forms with ridge-and-furrow glazing — all in response to calculations of the angles of the sun's rays at different times of the day. By 1818 Loudon had constructed a variety of curvilinear hothouses in his own garden in Bayswater, had published the results of his experiments, and had sold the rights to his sash bar to the firm of W. and D. Bailey, Ironmongers, in London — who were to reap the financial benefits.[17]

At that time, profit from the commercial development of the sash bar did not interest Loudon; assuming the public would benefit from his invention, he became preoccupied with some of its wider applications. In 1818 he could already see the potential of using curved-iron and glass construction for a new transparency, durability, and beauty in any structure where maximum light was important: in warehouses, depots, churches, homes, shop fronts, and office buildings. His sketch of a "cathedral conservatory" now looks prophetic of Victorian railway stations and of Joseph Paxton's Crystal Palace of 1851, where Loudon's ridge-and-furrow glazing would have its most famous application.[18] Evidently he was searching for new ways to reconcile utility and beauty when he envisioned hothouses as spherical bodies of "almost perfect transparence." He asked, "Can that edifice then be in correct taste, whose architecture is at variance with its use? which as it is rendered more beautiful, becomes less useful?"[19]

The same fundamental questions of use and beauty were beginning to challenge Loudon's views of landscape design. Although his designs for the grounds of private residences were still picturesque and clearly Reptonian — as at Bullmarsh Court (1818), in Berkshire (see plates 6 and 8) — his views on public gardens and parks were expanding. On the Continent in 1815 and 1819, Loudon found that most public gardens were laid out with straight, tree-lined avenues, broad and sunny or narrow and shady, for people's enjoyment at various times of the year. Now, for a century, eminent British writers had ridiculed straight lines and symmetry in the garden, yet ever since the time of the ancient Greeks, men had used straight lines and symmetry to design public open spaces that satisfied human needs. Was there not a kind of beauty in these apparently useful spaces? Loudon would try to resolve these questions in his *Encyclopaedia of Gardening*, where he discussed the influence of climate, culture, politics, and the state of civilization on the design of public and private landscapes.

In 1822 the first edition of that massive work appeared, marking a turning point in British garden literature. Though the individual sections were compiled from hundreds of other works, the totality was original: an assimilation of technical information, horticultural and botanical science, history, aesthetic theory, and professional practice, including several sketches and plans interspersed with text. This new format and content also established the new direction which had begun to emerge in Loudon's writing from about 1811, when he settled permanently in the London metropolis. Many of his earlier works had been expensively produced, set in large type, with fine engravings and sometimes hand-colored lithographs. Only one large quarto publication, his *Hints on Gardens and Pleasure Grounds* (1812) had been aimed at a wide audience, offering designs for a great range of gardens, from tiny front yards in the city to rural properties of a hundred acres or more. From 1822 onward, most of Loudon's works would be smaller octavo publications, set in small type and illustrated by plain woodcuts. The earlier works had been dedicated to royalty, the nobility, and the gentry. The later works, though still purchased by the upper classes, would tend to speak directly to self-educated, self-improving young gardeners, craftsmen, and middle-class householders. (An exception was Loudon's eight-volume *Arboretum et Fruticetum Britannicum; or, The Trees and Shrubs of Britain* [1838], dedicated to the duke of Northumberland and addressed to great landed proprietors, as well as to practical and amateur gardeners, nurserymen, and foresters.)

What accounts for these gradual changes in Loudon's writings? The British reading public was, of course, expanding along with industry, urbanism, and the significance of the middle classes. Later in the 1820s, publications such as the *Mechanics' Magazine* and the *Library of Useful Knowledge* would speak to many of the people whom Loudon had in mind. Certainly the efforts of philosophers and social reformers — Bentham, Robert Owen, Lord Brougham, Francis Place — could have stimulated Loudon's interests in diffusing useful knowledge. But events in Loudon's personal life, too, must have prompted changes in his outlook: the broadening experiences of travel, the loss of a substantial fortune, and the chronic illnesses which curtailed the possibility of his working directly as a landscape gardener for noblemen and gentlemen. All these events would tend to redirect his sympathies towards a wider audience of gardeners — both at home and abroad.

In France, the only professional landscape gardener who had already begun to publish designs for "everyman" was Gabriel Thouin, author of *Plans Raisonnés de Toutes les Espèces de Jardins* (1819), a series of model plans for the grounds of suburban and rural dwellings, ranging from the small garden to the regional experimental farm. Loudon may have noticed this unusual new book on his second visit to Paris in 1819. Three years later, he used several of Thouin's picturesque plans in his *Encyclopaedia of Gardening* to illustrate the practice of landscape gardening, along with his own plans and some woodcuts after Repton. At the time, Loudon considered Thouin one of the two best designers in France. (The other was Thomas Blaikie, a Scot.)[20] Loudon could also appreciate Thouin's balance between utilitarian concerns — pure air, shade and sunlight, space for exercise and repose in public and private landscapes — and the appreciation of beauty in *both* picturesque and symmetrical gardens. This kind of broad vision was essential for Loudon if he was ever to develop a comprehensive theory of landscape design throughout the ages and if he hoped to communicate with an international public.

From the 1820s onwards, Loudon assumed an international audience for his works. Some of his encyclopedias were translated into German, extracts were translated into French and Danish, and some of his articles were reprinted in other European and American magazines. For the *Arboretum Britannicum*, he sent out three thousand questionnaires to colleagues and friends on several continents, requesting information on all the hardy trees and shrubs native to, or naturalized in, Britain. And while traveling in Germany in 1828, he conceived the idea of an international horticultural society.

Loudon's *Gardener's Magazine* (1826–44) became an international forum for information and ideas, with correspondents such as Thomas Blaikie and the Chevalier Soulange-Bodin in France; Giuseppe Manetti in Italy; Charles Sckell in Germany; Andrew Jackson Downing and John Torrey in America; and others from Denmark, Russia, South Africa, and Australia. More than a miscellany of "Rural and Domestic Improvements," the *Gardener's Magazine* was broadly environmental in scope, including articles on architectural design, town planning, and metropolitan improvements. There, in the tiny print reserved for the conductor's (editor's) comments, one could read also the periodical unfolding of Loudon's personal development. Gradually his blunt, tactless criticism of men and gardens gave way to a more tempered appraisal of intentions, principles, and possibilities. Still he antagonized some readers by boldly criticizing the design and management of gardens and calling for better wages, hours, and lodgings for the hired gardener. Though he lost a few subscribers in the process, he used his magazine to promote, as well as to record, social and environmental improvements.

Loudon's most impassioned pleas for reform appeared during and immediately after his fourth Continental journey in 1828–29. While trav-

eling in France and southern Germany to record new developments in
gardening and agriculture, he began to report on the actual conditions of
working people — not as he had once described them, as picturesque
"flocks" of humble humanity, subservient to amelioration — but as individuals. In the fig gardens of Argenteuil, north of Paris, for instance,
Loudon talked with an aged couple employed as *gardes champêtres*, and
with an unusual tenderness he afterwards described their wretched condition and their painstaking methods of tending and pruning the figs. This
vivid portrait carried an implicit plea for reform. Loudon, somewhat
shaken by the experience, took comfort in the belief that an improving
society would not allow such misery to persist.[21]

In southern Germany, Loudon found society actively improving by
means of education. En route from Stuttgart to Heilbron, he talked with a
young housemaid, daughter of a stonecutter, who could read and write and
was able to tell him about the local ancient monuments, the way to make
wine, the orbits of the moon and the earth, and the weekly newspaper. In
Munich, he discussed what he had seen of cottages and schools with
Charles Sckell, director general of the Court Gardens of Bavaria, and with
the directors of schools in Karlsruhe and Stuttgart. Loudon concluded that
southern Germany had experienced a revolution as great, in effect, as the
French Revolution of 1789. Education, the great revolutionary force, had
created in Württemberg, Baden, and Bavaria some of the most civilized
communities in Europe. Practical lessons in gardening and agriculture
were offered at most schools, and children were required to attend between the ages of six and fourteen. Loudon found no beggars, few people
on "poor rates" (or public relief), and very little crime. He left convinced
that a high and equal education for all classes was essentially the birth-
right of each individual in a civilized state and that education was one of
the safeguards of a stable society.[22]

In 1828 these were radical views. Society in Britain was still hailed
by some as a great pyramid whose stability depended on the broad base of
the working classes.[23] People feared that, given a liberal and scientific
education, workers would become insubordinate, the base of the social
pyramid would erode, and the whole structure would crumble. Loudon, a
product of Scottish education, never believed this. But he did not become
an ardent educational reformer until he had actually seen the "benefits" of
German school systems in the refinement and happiness of the people.
Before he returned to England, in mid-January 1829, he published a
pamphlet in Paris on the educational systems of southern Germany and
joined the Parisian Society for Elementary Education.[24]

In London, Loudon circulated among his friends an "Outline of a
Plan for a National Education Establishment" based on German precedents. One copy fell into the hands of Rowland Detrosier, Secretary of the
National Political Union, who passed it on to Francis Place, the outspoken
advocate for education, Radical member of Parliament, and, later, co-
author of the People's Charter. For the more conservative subscribers to
the *Gardener's Magazine* (many of them clergymen), Loudon published an
expurgated version of his plan, entitled "Parochial Institutions," in which
all references to the disestablishment of the Churches of England and
Scotland were omitted.[25]

In the daily newspapers, Loudon was most candid. "The strength of every country lies in the mass of the population," he wrote in a letter to the *Morning Advertiser*, reprinted as a pamphlet, "The Great Objects to be Attained by Reform," on December 1, 1830. (He sent Bentham an inscribed copy.) In it were Loudon's urgent pleas for free trade, election by ballot, fair representation of the people, a national education establishment, and more. A year passed. On April 12, 1832, after the Reform Bill had been once rejected by the House of Lords and tension was mounting in the streets, the *Times* ran Loudon's letter urging that, if the second reading of the bill were rejected, reformers should unite to stop buying all articles subject to taxation except one — the newspaper.[26] A few weeks later, the Reform Bill was passed; it was signed into law on June 7, 1832.

During these years, Loudon never publicly espoused political movements such as Radicalism or Chartism. His later books and his design for the Derby Arboretum received long, favorable commentaries in the *Westminster Review*, originally begun by Bentham, James Mill, and others. Still, though Loudon moved in Benthamite circles, he was not officially "one" of them. Outspoken about political ideals, he remained aloof from party politics. While traveling in Britain or abroad, he tried to remain objective, jotting down memoranda "as a botanist would describe a plant."[27] On one journey, he exulted in the boldness and freedom of the English constitution. Loudon also cherished Thomas Jefferson's ideals of self-government and expected great things from democracies. At the same time, he could admire what monarchies and centralized governments had achieved in Europe, including well-planned cities with public parks and boulevards that served as much-needed "breathing places."

As a planner without political power, Loudon was usually an opposition party of one, a self-appointed guardian of the interests of metropolitan inhabitants at large. In one case he urged that certain land, threatened by speculative development, be preserved as park land — and failed; in another, he succeeded, when he advocated the construction of gate lodges to shelter the park keepers in bad weather.[28] His most radical plan for the London metropolis, a comprehensive scheme for concentric greenbelts, published in December 1829, was conceived as an alternative to random speculative building in the outskirts of London, particularly on Hampstead Heath, a favorite rural retreat of Londoners. Loudon assumed, rightly, that the metropolis would inevitably expand, enveloping more rural villages like Hampstead and Bayswater. To preserve precious open space, then, Loudon continually urged the sound long-term planning of both town and country, coordinated by a strong, representative metropolitan government.[29] Loudon did not live to see such a government formed, but toward the end of his life, he did serve on the committee of the new Metropolitan Improvements Society, established in 1842 to urge a comprehensive program of environmental reforms.

It is at the scale of the metropolis that Loudon's theories of planning and design can best be appreciated. Endowed with an enormous capacity to absorb, analyze, and synthesize, Loudon wanted to seize the wholeness of anything — a city, a garden, a body of knowledge — before considering its parts. Craving order, he had to construct a grand, unified theory to classify and subdivide the various purposes, qualities, and characters of all the arts. In about 1830, he was stimulated by the writings of a member of the French Academy of Fine Arts, A. C. Quatremère de Quincy. From his *Essai sur l'Imitation* (1823) Loudon derived his own general theory of art and his leading principle, the "Recognition of Art."[30]

Repton had, of course, insisted that gardens are works of art. But Quatremère de Quincy had recently constructed a grand, comprehensive theory of all the fine arts — from which the English landscape garden was excluded! The French theorist maintained that all the fine arts, or "arts of imitation," offer the pleasure of comparing the work of art with the work of nature. In his view, the epitome of the English landscape garden was a mere facsimile of nature, however — unlike those gardens, paintings, and sculpture which were clearly recognizable as distinct, man-made creations, imitating, but never merely replicating the accidents of nature. In sum, Art presupposes artifice (see figs. 3 and 6).

The development of Loudon's *gardenesque* garden, or as some would have it, the demise of the English landscape garden, begins here. It is a complex, fascinating and disturbing development, which should have led to a clearer understanding of illusion, the imitation of nature, and the essential purposes of landscape architecture. Some believe it led instead to mere chaos in the garden.

Loudon developed his controversial ideas on the Gardenesque in the early 1830s, before the appearance of his best-known works, including the *Encyclopaedia of Cottage, Farm, and Villa Architecture and Furniture* (1832–33), the *Architectural Magazine* (1834–39), the *Suburban Gardener* (1838), and the *Arboretum et Fruticetum Britannicum* (1838). With

*Here, in Loudon's "gardenesque" manner, is his plan for reshaping the entrance to N.M.Rothschild's house, some 140 yards from the public road. The new drive is clearly man-made in form and direction, and has been lengthened to disguise the slight descent to the house. The trees are not thickly massed, but loosely grouped, both to screen the private grounds from the road and to allow ample light and nourishment for the cedars, oaks, and planes.*

Fig. 3

J.C.Loudon, "Working Plan for Forming a New Approach," (to Gunnersbury Park, West don), ca. 1836.

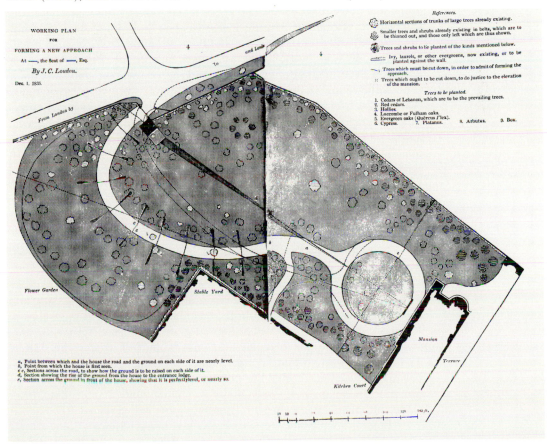

WORKING PLAN
FOR
FORMING A NEW APPROACH
At —, the Seat of —, Esq.
*By J.C. Loudon.*
Dec. 1, 1835.

References.

Horizontal sections of trunks of large trees already existing.

Smaller trees and shrubs already existing in belts, which are to be thinned out, and those only left which are thus shown.

Trees and shrubs to be planted of the kinds mentioned below.

Ivy, laurels, or other evergreens, now existing, or to be planted against the wall.

Trees which must be cut down, in order to admit of forming the approach.

Trees which ought to be cut down, to do justice to the elevation of the mansion.

Trees to be planted.

1. Cedars of Lebanon, which are to be the prevailing trees.
2. Red cedars.
3. Hollies.
4. Luccombe or Fulham oaks.
5. Evergreen oaks (Quércus I'lex).
6. Cypress.    7. Platanus.    8. Arbutus.    9. Box.

From London by

Flower Garden

Stable Yard

Mansion

Terrace

Kitchen Court

*a*, Point between which and the house the road and the ground on each side of it are nearly level.
*b*, Point from which the house is first seen.
*c c*, Sections across the road, to show how the ground is to be raised on each side of it.
*d*, Section showing the rise of the ground from the house to the entrance lodge.
*e*, Section across the ground in front of the house, showing that it is perfectly level, or nearly so.

the constant help of his wife Jane, Loudon produced these works and others in the thirteen years before his death.

The *Encyclopaedia of Architecture*, one of Loudon's most popular works, ran through several editions and revisions, with over a thousand pages of closely printed text and hundreds of wood engravings. Here Loudon revealed once again his noblest intentions: "to increase the comforts of the great mass of society" by diffusing practical information on all that could be considered essential in any dwelling, including sound construction, planning, plumbing, and mechanical services. Charles Barry, John Robertson, E.B.Lamb, and other architects and amateur designers contributed the elevations, plans, and specifications. Loudon, as editor and design critic, gradually introduced architectural principles and criticism. By pointing out the strengths and weaknesses of imperfect designs, he hoped to raise the general level of public knowledge and taste — not only in order to encourage better building, but also in order to improve people's manners and habits of thinking. He still believed that fine architecture, like beautiful landscapes, could help to refine a person's character and sensibilities.

Studies of the animal kingdom, too, he believed, could humanize the heart and elevate character. Loudon began the *Magazine of Natural History* in May 1828 and remained its conductor until the close of 1836. Here he published articles by John James Audubon, the American ornithologist; Charles Waterton, the eccentric British naturalist; the Reverend John Stevens Henslow, professor of botany at Cambridge; and the fifteen-year-old John Ruskin, whose article on the color of the Rhine was his first published work of prose. Loudon also published less analytical, more anecdotal writings, for he was eager to stimulate habits of inquiry among a wide audience, including working people and young people, especially young women. Daughters, he noted, were no longer being educated to become "mere domestic managers or household ornaments," but "rational companions of rational men."[31] Leisure was no longer an aristocratic, but a human concern, and Loudon was surely among the first to emphasize this fact when, in 1828, he wrote, "The humblest and most laborious individual, after fulfilling all his duties to his employer and to his family, has still a portion of leisure, and with him, as with man in every class of society, happiness will be found to depend much more on the manner in which this leisure time is spent, than on the nature of his professional or mechanical occupation."[32]

It is often assumed that Loudon himself had no time for leisure. Apparently his moments of relaxation revolved around the dinner hour, with occasional games of charades and long after-dinner conversations with friends such as Noel Humphreys, author of works on architecture and natural history, and Grant Thorburn, the Scottish emigré and seedsman.[33] Thomas Sopwith, the mining engineer and inventor from Newcastle, was always a welcome guest at the Loudons' table, and it was the flow of friendly conversation that he most enjoyed.[34] One reviewer for the *Gentleman's Magazine* recalled the Loudons' dinner parties, particularly the illustrious company and enjoyable conversation among naturalists, travelers, and men conversant with literature, art, and science.[35]

Loudon's travels were mainly for business, although Jane always accompanied him, eventually with Agnes, their only child. The Loudons would journey through England and Scotland for months at a time, making "garden calls" in order to report on domestic and rural improvements in the *Gardener's Magazine*. Until Loudon's death in 1843, this magazine continued to provide an international medium of communication among professional and amateur gardeners, while covering the wider economic, political, social, and cultural developments that affected the land-scape — such as Parliamentary debates on public walks and parks, new scientific and benevolent societies, economic recession, unemployment and emigration, and the quality of air in industrial towns. Meanwhile, new rival periodicals, such as Joseph Paxton's *Horticultural Register* and *Magazine of Botany*, were increasingly specializing in smaller gardens and floriculture, apparently responding to public demand. Loudon was aware of what the public wanted, but, though he began to offer articles on the design and planting of flower gardens, he still maintained a balance of social and political commentary and continued to promote reform. In 1839 the *Times* considered the *Gardener's Magazine* "the oldest and by far the best of the gardening periodicals."[36]

In the last years of his life, Loudon could not support a family on the income of his publications, particularly after the depression in the book trade of 1841. Thus, in spite of failing health, he resumed his practice of landscape gardening. In 1839 he laid out the Derby Arboretum with a collection of over one thousand different species and varieties of trees and shrubs in the space of eleven acres. His last commissions included three rural cemeteries in Cambridge, Southampton, and Bath; a suburban garden near Shepherd's Bush, West London; and a few country seats, such as Gunnersbury House, in Middlesex, and Coleshill, then in Berkshire. Some of these late designs may never have been completely realized. Certainly none could have been more generally appreciated than the Derby Arboretum, but it was mainly through his writings that Loudon was known during his lifetime and is remembered today.

Two weeks before his death, Loudon sent letters to some noblemen and gentlemen, requesting that they purchase a set of the *Arboretum et Fruticetum Britannicum*, his definitive work on the trees and shrubs of Britain, illustrated with hundreds of fine portraits of living specimens and published at his own expense of over ten thousand pounds. In these letters Loudon briefly alluded to his lifelong infirmities and admitted that he had just suffered an inflammation of the lungs which left him with chronic bronchitis. He was now, at sixty, unable to continue his practice of landscape gardening, and had to depend entirely on the literary labors of his wife — for the income of his thirteen books in print was pledged to his publishers, Longmans, until an outstanding debt of twenty-six hundred pounds for the *Arboretum* could be paid. The letters ended with a quota-tion from the *Quarterly Review*, indicating the great value of the *Arboretum* and congratulating Loudon for finishing his Herculean task, "a task which few men, except himself, would have had the courage to begin, and still fewer the perseverance to complete."[37]

Why did he do it? To send these frank letters must have been painful, though apparently necessary. But why did Loudon begin the *Arboretum* and persevere, even to the point of impoverishing a wife and daughter and ruining his own precarious health?

Loudon wrote the *Arboretum et Fruticetum Britannicum* essentially

*This tomb, said to be of Loudon's own design, has survived as just one of his many self-portraits. The others are his published works.*

Fig. 4 (*see also p. 289*)
Tomb of J.C.Loudon, in Kensal Green Cemetery, London.

for the public good. He believed it an object of national importance to give the public a complete portrait of the most useful and permanent ornaments in the landscape — trees — because he found that people were becoming too much absorbed in acquiring the more delicate and transient novelties, like new varieties of camellias and hybrid calceolarias. Too much effort and expense was being poured into the glasshouse and the flower garden, while the public walks, town parks, and the grounds of country seats were being neglected. The very *art* of landscape gardening was being neglected; for, in Loudon's view, the picturesque scenes that imitated nature's careless ways with the most common trees and plants could never be recognized as fine art. Only hardy foreign trees mingled among the native trees could make the English landscape garden a true work of art. Utterly convinced of this notion and committed to improving the "general face of the country" with useful and permanent beauty, Loudon struggled yet again, throughout the *Arboretum*, to entertain and instruct the public.[38]

"If this work does not repay the author for his immense labour," the *Gentleman's Magazine* warned, "the public deserve to be gibbeted on the trees which they have not had the sense or the taste to value."[39] In this case, kind words and profound admiration were Loudon's only reward, even though many sets of the *Arboretum* were purchased in response to his solicitous letters. On December 14, 1843, he died, leaving to his wife Jane — along with his furniture, his library, his wines, china, and plate — a debt of £2,400.

Many Victorian ladies would have been overcome by this financial burden. But Jane Loudon continued to revise and edit her husband's works and produced original stories and horticultural tomes of her own. With the help of Joseph Paxton, Robert Chambers, Joseph Strutt, Charles Waterton, Sir Walter and Lady Pauline Trevelyan, and other kind friends and subscribers to Loudon's works, Jane managed to pay the remaining debts and provide for her young daughter. Of her husband, in his posthumous book, *Self-Instruction for Young Gardeners*, she wrote, "He was equally estimable as a husband and a father, and as a master and a friend."

Loudon was buried in Kensal Green Cemetery the same year that his work *On the Laying Out, Planting and Managing of Cemeteries* appeared (fig. 4). Inscribed on his tomb — a simple, massive block of stone surmounted by a granite urn — is the single line:

His works are his best monument.

# 1

## Farming in Time of War

Wartime demands for more grain stimulated Loudon's efforts to make English farms more efficient. His improvements involved some disturbing changes, however, in the lives of cottagers and small farmers.

Throughout Loudon's early career, during the Napoleonic wars, Britain was obliged to feed military troops as well as a growing population at home. Under wartime inflation, the price of corn (or wheat) was still considered low — relative to the price of land — but was actually painfully high relative to a laborer's wages.[1] During lean years, prices doubled or tripled. The harvest of 1811 was unusually poor, and that of 1799 was disastrous. In the winter and early spring of 1800, when Loudon was a sixteen-year-old nurseryman's apprentice and part-time student in Edinburgh, public soup kitchens were set up to feed the desperate poor in the city.[2] Grain imports were increasingly expensive, given wartime restrictions and the obstructions to commerce when the exporting of gold bullion was checked.[3] In 1801 the national debt was estimated at £460,000,000.[4] Between 1800 and 1812, Britain spent some £100,000,000 on imported grain, and about half that sum went to France.[5]

In 1812 Loudon warned that every British payment to France for imported corn was a "great tribute to Napoleon." Furthermore, given the inefficiencies which Loudon perceived on many farms in southern England, all payment for imported corn was, in effect, a "tax for slovenly management."[6] The times were right, then, for enterprising and imaginative men to reform the agricultural practices of the nation, not only for their own profit, but also for the sake of rendering Britain independent of other nations for an adequate supply of bread corn. Without this independence, Loudon argued, Britain could not be considered truly powerful (fig. 5).[7]

Whenever Loudon recommended rural improvements to the men who collectively controlled the wealth and power of the nation, he appealed to their self-interest, their patriotism, and their sense of responsibility as trustees, not only for the land, but also for the welfare of present and future generations. There was not only sincerity, but also urgency, in Loudon's appeals. He shared these patriotic and benevolent sentiments. And he hoped to share a small portion of the landowners' profits. In fact, he made a considerable fortune, some £15,000.

The scale of Loudon's early projects was usually large — from about twenty acres to several thousand. His clients were typically drawn from

A few years before Constable painted this scene in East Anglia, Loudon worked as a tenant farmer in Oxfordshire. Here, the plowman and the laborers digging in the dunghill are inextricably part of their timeless environment, which seems affected only by cyclical change, season after season, year after year. But the wars were not yet over, England needed more grain, and Loudon was caught up in more disturbing changes on the land.

Fig. 5
John Constable, R.A., *Stour Valley and Dedham Church*, 1814. Warren Collection; Courtesy, Museum of Fine Arts, Boston.

the landed gentry and aristocracy in Scotland, Wales, and England, such as the earl of Wemyss at Gosford, in Haddingtonshire; Edward Moulton-Barrett, Esq., at Hope End, in Herefordshire (fig. 6); and the earl of Harewood at Harewood House, in Yorkshire.[8] These men must have been willing to listen to a self-confident young Scot who believed in his own bright vision of improvements on the land. Loudon's aesthetic ideals of landscape design were founded in a deep love of Britain's naturally wild, picturesque, and pastoral landscapes. At the same time, his economic arguments for reforms in agricultural land management had to be founded in a thorough understanding of the scientific and technical problems of husbandry. Apparently his arguments were persuasive, for his early books and treatises attracted clients willing to invest their capital under his direction.

From 1807 to 1811, Loudon was also a tenant farmer, with holdings in Middlesex, Oxfordshire, and Wiltshire. At Tew Lodge Farm, in Oxfordshire, he designed and built his own house and farm offices. He improved over a thousand acres of arable and pasture land. He was also an agent, or "valuator," for twenty-four thousand acres of agricultural land in the south of England. Thus he figured as an entrepreneur in what was then Britain's largest industry and source of employment: agriculture.[9]

In 1807 Loudon's father, William, came down from Scotland to join his son and spent the last two years of his life as a tenant of Wood Hall Farm, near Pinner, in Middlesex. For this brief interval, father and son worked together with some success to introduce into the south of England the efficient methods of "Scotch" farming. In February 1810 the *Gentleman's Magazine* notice of the death of the elder Mr. Loudon identified him as one of the first "Scotch Agriculturists" to settle in England.[10] About that time, Sir Joseph Banks, president of the Royal Society, commended Sir John Sinclair, past president of the Board of Agriculture, on his book *The Husbandry of Scotland* and added, "Agriculture has derived, and is deriving, and will derive more benefit from Scots industry and skill

than has been accumulated since the days when Adam first wielded the spade."[11]

Loudon considered the key factor in the success of Scottish agricultural improvements to be the long lease; and he believed he had been the first to emphasize its value for an English audience — in his pamphlet on landed property published in 1808.[12] Acting on that wisdom, he and his father had secured leases of up to twenty-one years on the land they farmed in Oxfordshire and Middlesex. They paid double or triple the old rentals; and, with this long-term security, they were willing to make large capital investments in machinery, roads, and buildings, sometimes sharing the expenses with the landowner.

The two "Scotch" farmers evidently had some difficulty, however, in persuading the native English farmhands to go along with the new northern methods. In *Landed Property*, Loudon alluded to the "silly prejudices of local attachment or national predilection" and deplored the state of lethargy in which farmers seemed to "dream away their existence."[13] In this and several other writings, Loudon offered detailed instructions for draining land, rotating crops, consolidating small pastures, establishing drill husbandry, and introducing new efficiencies by a greater division of labor.[14] England was already profiting from such efficiency in the industrial towns; but "the commercial spirit of this nation has led [men] so totally to overlook the value and management of land," Loudon argued, "that to a person coming from a country where the soil is so highly valued, and so assiduously cultivated, this neglect appears like madness."[15]

Dr. Andrew Coventry, Loudon's former teacher in Edinburgh, was his most frequently cited authority on agricultural affairs. Coventry's *Discourses . . . on Agricultural and Rural Economy* (1808) corroborated Loudon's arguments with a voice of greater experience and a tone of greater tolerance.[16] Loudon often sharply disagreed with the other major agricultural writers of the day, including William Marshall, Arthur Young, and Nathaniel Kent, on topics ranging from the length of leases and size of farms to enclosures and agricultural schools. "Whatever suits

*In this secluded hollow among the Malvern Hills, in about 1810, Moulton-Barrett began to erect his three-story Moorish mansion, soon to be surrounded by shrubberies, walled gardens, orchards, and a park. Loudon's precise contributions, dating from 1811, are not known. The mansion was demolished in 1873; and today the grounds, in their half-wild state, seem to be the work of nature — luxuriantly picturesque, but not "Art," according to Quatremère de Quincy.*

Fig. 6
Scene on the grounds of Hope End, Herefordshire, formerly the seat of Edward Moulton-Barrett and childhood home of his daughter, Elizabeth Barrett Browning.

the market," was Loudon's standard test. In the debate over Commerce versus Agriculture, Loudon sided with James Mill, who defended commerce as a legitimate producer of wealth, and thus dismissed the arguments of William Spence and William Cobbett.[17] Loudon also paraphrased Adam Smith, in the *Wealth of Nations:* "In a nation where private rights of individuals are held sacred, the natural efforts of every man to better his own condition are sufficient to make the State flourish."[18]

At this time, Loudon was such a confirmed individualist that he disparaged most cooperative bodies, even those, like the Board of Agriculture, whose goals of agricultural and social reforms he shared. There were others, too, who questioned the need for such a board. In 1800 one Thomas Stone, representing "A Society of Practical Farmers," had criticized the Board of Agriculture's policy of offering "bounties" or rewards for certain farm practices.[19] Initially, even Sir Joseph Banks had opposed the establishment of the board, since the Royal Society, of which he was president, was already furthering the cause of agricultural improvements.[20] Loudon's skepticism was apparent in his *Landed Property*, of 1808: "Whatever is not worth pursuing for its own sake, can never be rendered so by the bounties of a society; . . . in a free country, such as this, [societies] are of no use whatever. So long as mankind are influenced by motives of self-interest, wherever there is a power to bring these motives into action, there will always be a supply of every kind of skill, ingenuity, improvement, virtue, vice, agricultural produce, and everything else, proportioned to the effectual demand."[21]

Within fifteen years, Loudon's views would change dramatically. He himself would offer rewards to encourage the establishment of subscription libraries for gardeners.[22] His attention would shift from the landowner to the displaced laborers, whose wretched conditions and sheer numbers were demanding even more public sympathy than the distress of the landed gentry. Loudon's deeper compassion for working people, both rural and urban, developed while he lived in the London metropolis, after traveling in Europe, living for a time in some Continental cities, and suffering the loss of his own financial security. His coming of age, however, occurred during the years of the Napoleonic wars, when he lived and worked mainly in the British countryside, prospering from his own exertions. At that time, his views were to some extent conditioned by current preoccupations with national defense and food supplies, by his own self-interest and that of his landowning clients.

As a farmer and agricultural writer, Loudon applied the principles of political economy to the management of landed estates, as did William Marshall, Arthur Young, and Sir John Sinclair, in various ways. Loudon's particularly liberal views on rural affairs were not fundamentally opposed to the views of those who governed the kingdom. Rather, his views simply represented the progressive end of the wide spectrum of political and economic views which dominated both houses of Parliament in the early years of the nineteenth century. These were the last few decades of the "reign of agriculture," which William Marshall recognized in 1804. "The three estates of parliament," he noted, "are composed of agricultural commoners, agricultural peers, and an agricultural king."[23]

Marshall was an agriculturist who applied the principles of political economy to his practice, within certain limits. No friend of Jacobinism or leveling, Marshall thought that the present order of things, in 1804, was "nearly right," with regular gradations from peasant to prince. Consequently, there was a range of small, middling, and great holdings of land, with most holdings in middle-sized farms. This arrangement seemed to encourage the most productive use of the land. Small farmers were encouraged to be industrious and frugal; and, through emulation of their more prosperous neighbors, they might hope to rise a few gradations on the socioeconomic scale. But Marshall stopped short of recommending unlimited capital investments and unlimited sizes of farms. He was strongly opposed to the middleman's taking a share of profits. Loudon, both a middleman and a practical farmer for a few years, had good reason to demur. Still, both he and Marshall advocated better management of agricultural land and a more efficient division of labor to bring about an end to the scarcity of corn.

Arthur Young, secretary of the Board of Agriculture, had been making similar arguments for decades. When he first stressed the importance of agriculture to the national welfare, in his *Farmer's Letters to the People of England* (1767), Young expressed many of Loudon's later arguments for large farms, enclosures, and large capital investments for agricultural improvements.[24] Like Loudon, Young shifted his sympathies to those without capital — the poor — after a critical period of transition in his personal life, around 1799 to 1800.[25] However, even after the personal tragedy and the religious conversion that prompted Young's change of heart, he still insisted that unrestricted private enterprise in agriculture was the key to national prosperity. In 1801 Young warned against the terrors of food scarcity and violent revolutions, and at the same time he exulted in the recent British naval battles, which appeared to bring an end to the French wars:

What a tremendous period! and with what a voice does it call on the government of this country to measure its policy in peace to the future exigencies which may, — which *must* demand all the resources which the multiplied blessings of the Almighty have enabled this country to call into effect. What a requisition to talents, genius, patriotism, and vigour, so to arrange the political economy of the nation, to exert every nerve, and call into life and action all the latent energies of vital strength, by which a people may rise superior to every apparent cause of depression. What a demand upon the legislature to labour with one heart and hand to remove every obstacle that can impede the steps of private exertion in its progress to national greatness![26]

Here was the exuberance of a fellow agricultural reformer with whom Loudon could share national goals, if not always professional opinions. Did the two ever meet? Probably not, judging from the cool, distant tone of Loudon's references to Young. True, Loudon could have been introduced to Young through Sir Joseph Banks, Jeremy Bentham, or General Stratton of Great Tew, Oxfordshire. He might have accompanied Young to the annual sheep shearings at Woburn and Holkham, and dined in the company of dukes, earls, tenant farmers, butchers, the American ambassador, a Hungarian prince, and the distinguished leaders in agriculture and science, including Sinclair and Banks.[27] But Loudon, in his twenties, was stubborn, somewhat inflexible, and highly independent. Not only did he scorn the Board of Agriculture, of which Young was secretary; he may have perceived Young to be another English rival (like Repton) of the older generation whose writings and works he intended one day to surpass. Years later, when Loudon began his *Gardener's Magazine*, in 1826, it was more closely modeled on the Scottish *Farmer's Magazine* than on Young's *Annals of Agriculture* — both in its logical organization of contents (the *Annals* had no apparent organization); and in its emphasis on more progressive political, as well as technical, means for improving the landscape.[28] Still, to some extent, Young's *Annals* were as influential on the progress of agriculture as Loudon's *Magazine* was on the progress of gardening and landscape design. Both periodicals were repositories of practical and technical information, including plates of the latest improved implements (ploughs, threshers, lawn mowers, and so forth). Both contained accounts of tours to inspect farms and country seats, as well as commentaries on the important social and political issues of the day, including the conditions of laborers and battles in Parliament or on foreign soil.

As the Napoleonic wars continued, the commons, wastelands, fields, and meadows of Britain were steadily being enclosed for more productive farming. Both Young's accounts of the pace and effects of enclosures and later, more complex economic analyses explain the transformations on the rural landscape: Small pastures were opened up for larger arable fields. Small farms were consolidated. Tracts of wasteland, low swampy land, and common land were enclosed for cultivation.[29] In 1811, the number of enclosures in Britain reached an all-time high of 133.[30] In 1808, Loudon was generally in favor of these enclosures. Still, he recognized the value of wastelands as healthful open spaces; and he tended to agree with Professor Coventry that before the wastelands and commons were enclosed, the methods of husbandry on the prime agricultural land should be improved. By building on strengths, Loudon argued, the nation's immediate needs for bread corn would best be supplied and the nation's prosperity in the long term would best be ensured.[31]

In the short term, enclosures of commons and wastelands took away the means of subsistence for cottagers who had depended on access to those unimproved lands for grazing a cow or a few sheep, for letting a pig loose among fallen acorns in an oak grove, for gathering wood or peat for fuel, sometimes for fishing or quarrying.[32] Deprived of these resources, poor cottagers had to depend on charity (the "poor rates"), or they deserted their hamlets and villages, drifting to manufacturing towns.

William Cobbett was incensed. In 1802 he launched the *Political Register*, a unique organ of Tory (conservative) radicalism, dominated by his own grating, sometimes ingratiating, voice. Fearless, relentless, and armed with colorful figures of speech, Cobbett supported orthodox Whig or Tory positions only insofar as they approximated his own sympathies for the small farmer and cottager, those less articulate survivors of traditional English rural society. Thus, while Loudon was writing agricultural treatises addressed to the landowners, Cobbett, the robust son of a tavern owner in the town of Farnham, Hampshire, took up the cause of the displaced cottagers. He deplored their loss of livelihood and basic human dignity. In 1804, he was horrified by their migration to the towns.[33]

Loudon, in 1808, showed some sympathy for the sad plight of cottagers and farmers who were suddenly forced to leave the land which their ancestors might have cultivated for centuries. He persistently recommended cottage gardens and cows for all the laborers who remained on the land. But he argued that the future could be bright for all ranks of the rural population. Small farmers who were able and willing to adapt to changing conditions might channel their energies in new directions and become overseers, managers, or bailiffs on the new larger farms. Like Young, Loudon believed that enclosures would increase opportunities for honorable employment, rather than overcrowd the so-called "workhouses." The more energetic and progressive farmers could also become tenants on the newly enclosed, less improved lands of Britain. Although some cottagers would inevitably be obliged to leave the countryside, Loudon was confident that education would soon prepare them for new occupations.

Cobbett, angered by rural depopulation, cared nothing for new occupations; he wanted to see the old occupation — manual labor — restored to its former dignity and self-sufficiency (fig. 7). "I wish to see the poor men of England what the poor men of England were when I was born," he declared in 1807.[34] But however Cobbett might rail against mere "book-learning" and the discontents it engendered among agricultural laborers, Loudon believed that reading, writing, and basic mathematical skills should be taught to all young people. In 1809, when he purchased Mimbury Fort, a farm near Ramsbury, Wiltshire, Loudon planned to establish a school based on the innovative, nondenominational, and highly controversial system of Joseph Lancaster.[35]

If Loudon was reconciled to some degree of rural depopulation, it was because he could envision a new, possibly better life for anyone sufficiently enterprising and educated to move on (as the Scots had done for a century or more). Once the "pernicious" laws of settlement were repealed, he reasoned, the poor would no longer be condemned to remain in their places of unemployment — their native parishes; they could migrate to the sources of new demands for labor, in other parishes or in the manufacturing towns and villages.[36] "And what is this," Loudon asked, "but to collect into flocks the wandering groups of half-starved sheep and

*Two men by a cart of slate have had some unexplained interaction while a third, hunched over his horse, disappears into the shadows. In this brooding, uncertain atmosphere, one is reminded of the contemporary dilemma (ca. 1800) over agriculture and labor: whether to seek a return to conditions of a "happier" past, or to make "progress" in step with a changing, urbanizing world.*
Fig. 7
George Morland, *Carters with a Load of Slate*. Gift of Miss Amelia Peabody; Courtesy, Museum of Fine Arts, Boston.

lambs, and instead of heathy waste and mountains, to place them in sheltered fields of abundant and perpetual pasture; and for the rags and beggary of the country labourer's cottage, to substitute the clean and comfortable apartment of the tradesman and manufacturer: It is evident that this must even *better* the condition of the labourers that remain."[37]

This is hardly the voice of the economist Adam Smith or the philosopher Jeremy Bentham, but, instead, the faint echo of Uvedale Price, whose picturesque vision of humble cottagers was now dimly focused on the bright brick terraces of the incipient industrial town. Price cannot be held responsible for Loudon's dubious simile of sheep and laborers. Price did, nevertheless, provide the broad aesthetic vision, and William Mason, the imagery, for Loudon's scenario of urban "perpetual pastures."

As a young writer, Loudon would quickly snatch images from unlikely sources and apply them in new contexts. At times, his images resembled those of the Reverend William Mason, precentor of York, rector of Aston, and a respectable minor poet, whose principles of garden design Loudon found congenial with his own. Thus, it is not surprising that Mason's imagery should linger in Loudon's mind. In Mason's poem *The English Garden* (1772–81), subservient animals and subservient people gracefully exchanged roles.[38] While sheep figured as "fond foresters" and "harmless epicures," the cottagers' children were "tribes" with vacant gazes, thronging at the cottage door, or they were "troops" basking on sunny hillocks, frolicking with the lambs entrusted to their care. Here, the charming progeny of the poor mingled with the gentle beasts, oblivious in their innocence to the "Penury and Toil" which Mason knew to be lurking behind the cottage door. Unlike the poet George Crabbe (also a clergyman), Mason did not dwell on the painful realities of life in these old English cottages.[39]

The pervading tone of *The English Garden* was generally soothing and optimistic about the current state of the kingdom, yet Mason seems faintly wistful for the primeval loss of an earthly paradise and for the more recent loss, unidentified in time, of social stability:

> there was a golden time,
> When each created being kept its sphere
> Appointed, nor infring'd its neighbour's right.[40]

If such a golden age ever existed, it had receded long before Loudon read this poem (by 1804). As a young landscape gardener and agriculturist, confronting the complex economic and social issues which arose in his practice, he was torn between wistfulness for the legendary stability of an earlier, simpler age and enthusiasm for the great changes and opportunities of his own time. He still retained a few rosy-tinted images of agricultural laborers, even as he saw those laborers drift to the industrial towns. But there the images lost all vitality. Except when applied to a few exceptional towns, the pastoral images were not convincing.[41]

In his twenties, Loudon's ideals of beauty, harmony, and the good society were still firmly based in the late eighteenth-century rural landscape of his childhood, the lowlands of Scotland. There he had watched his father, an energetic, educated, independent small farmer, carrying on the local traditions of constant improvement on the agricultural land.[42] The University of Edinburgh, that renowned Scottish seat of learning where admissions were open and fees relatively low, was only a few miles away. [43] Even closer to home, in the lowland villages, education provided a basis for a "harmony of interests" among people of different backgrounds. Until much later in the nineteenth century, according to James Fergusson, "the sons of laird, farmer, smith and fisherman [sat] side by side on the same school bench."[44] Other reasons for a perceived harmony of interests among people of unlike socioeconomic backgrounds were the strong ties of kinship perpetuated by the clans, the shared simplicity of rural life and manners in lowland Scotland, and a traditional "loyalty to the soil," which bound the laird, tenant, laborer and servant together.

None of these conditions was, in itself, exclusively characteristic of Loudon's Midlothian home. When he was a boy, the old loyalties were already being shaken in the course of progress. Still, the sum of all these conditions did add up to an environment which could implant in a boy's mind the eternal values of social harmony and self-education, and the desire for rational improvements which demanded, in turn, rational acceptance of change.

The fact that poor rates were virtually unknown in lowland Scotland for much of the eighteenth century would also have influenced Loudon's attitudes toward assistance to the poor, while he was working in the south of England. In Midlothian Scotland, as Robert Forsyth explained in 1805, aid to the poor was supplied largely by voluntary contributions made at every church door on Sundays. These contributions, which offered only a meager assistance to the poor, not a legally assured support, tended to promote the spirit of industry, frugality, and decent pride among the lowest class of the community — at least as long as opportunities for employment were not lacking.[45] Thus, when Loudon came to Oxfordshire, he would have come with a particular combination of inherited and personal views of improvement and change, all founded in a social order somewhat different from that of the countryside of southern England. And when he tried to make changes on the land, which would directly affect the livelihoods of the poor, Loudon would assume certain tendencies of human nature that were not necessarily universal — or English — but Scottish.

Loudon was motivated by a particularly Scottish form of idealism: sanguine, high-minded, and serene. He drew encouragement from several of his countrymen, including Henry Home, Lord Kames, the Scottish agriculturist and amateur philosopher, who had left an eighteenth-century model of responsible behavior in *The Gentleman Farmer* (1776).[46] Loudon borrowed from Lord Kames when he tried to characterize the life of the early nineteenth-century gentleman farmer. And he quoted James Thomson, the early eighteenth-century Scottish poet whose best-known work, *The Seasons*, was diffused with philosophical contentment and rural bliss. Loudon did *not* quote Oliver Goldsmith, the Anglo-Irish poet, however. Goldsmith's "The Deserted Village," of 1770, contained a broad indictment of enclosures, commerce, luxuries, and any changes which tended to drive the cottager from his bower of innocence and ease.

Could Loudon have been aware, in the early 1800s, as he surely was by the 1820s, that similar changes had altered the lives of cottagers in his native Scotland? In his *Encyclopaedia of Agriculture*, of 1825, Loudon included Lord Kames's account of early eighteenth-century agriculture.

At that time, the tenantry of Scotland were so "benumbed with oppression or poverty" that the most enlightened instructions in husbandry would not have done much good.[47] In the Highlands, the wastelands and common grazing lands were being enclosed for large sheep farms to be held by a single farmer; and the old independent cottagers, or crofters, were being "cleared" from the land. The infamous clearances brought terrible misery and poverty; and as cottagers rioted and levelled the new fences, the old stalwart virtues of thrift, self-reliance, and pride on the part of the lairds came to be distorted to extremes.[48] It was only after the Rebellion of 1745 that the great momentum for technological improvements in agriculture began in Scotland. From then on, new communications were opened up between the English and the Scots, and a number of Scottish farmers traveled south of the Cheviots and the Tweed, initially to learn from the English, eventually — as in Loudon's day — to teach the English what *they* knew of ploughs, soils, land leases, breeding, drilling and crop rotation.[49]

By the early 1800s, the modern British farmer, newly prosperous from his latest agricultural improvements, was thinking about the modest luxuries of port wine and muslin: a good sign, Loudon thought. Farmers need not exhibit "tasteless profusion and extravagance." The good life in the country could still remain as Thomson had described it:

> An elegant sufficiency, content,
> Retirement, rural quiet, friendship, books,
> Ease, and alternate labour, useful life.[50]

This was the life that Loudon wanted to live — and did live for a few years — at Tew Lodge Farm, Oxfordshire. Thomson implies more ease than Loudon ever knew, perhaps. The poet's words may also imply a few more material comforts than Loudon had known as a small farmer's son in the lowlands of Scotland. But the essential difference between the country lives described by Thomson and Loudon lay in the actual conditions that made those lives possible. The alleged foundations for the "elegant sufficiency" of British rural life during the early eighteenth century had been relative stability and permanence in the ownership, tenancy, or working of landed property. The foundations for Loudon's rural existence in Oxfordshire a century later, however, were progress and change. Before he took possession of Tew Lodge Farm and another Scot took up an adjacent farm at Great Tew, sixteen English tenant farmers had to be persuaded to leave.

A momentum was underway: for rationalizing the use of agricultural land, for applying the systematic methods of business and commerce to farming, for preparing and eventually educating the children of the countryside to assume occupations in towns, and for irrevocably altering the delicate balance of deference and paternalism in the rural life of Britain. Loudon was caught up in this momentum. Though he stimulated, and profited by, the changes, however, he still cherished the poetic and visual images of a lost, somewhat golden age in Scotland, when the kinship of feelings between lowland laird and tenant was strong; and when the status quo was maintained partly through a sense of loyalty to the soil, from which both laird and tenant derived their livings.[51]

# 2

## Gardeners and Poets, Landlords and Laborers

Loudon's ideal, rural society presupposed harmonious relations between landlord and laborer, based on traditions of deference, benevolence, and mutual respect. His aesthetic ideals, inspired by poets and landscape theorists, were both traditional and radical.

For Loudon, landscape gardening was always a moral concern. In his later works on gardening, building, and planning, he would speak plainly about the basic comforts, rights, and responsibilities which all men and women share — or ought to share. In his early writings, however, for example, *Country Residences* (1806), Loudon spoke primarily to the landed gentleman. Though this man might already be cultivating his lands for his own enjoyment and the benefit of society, he could be troubled by domestic problems: His son might be tempted to neglect rural responsibilities in pursuit of amusements and ultimately be seduced by the city's wealth, wickedness, and luxury. His wife and daughters might have dissipated their mental energies because their "education" had merely encouraged them to display a few superficial accomplishments. To these men and women, Loudon recommended the wholesome pursuits and pleasures of a country life.[1]

The attractions of such a life needed no explanation in Britain, where rural values were, and still are, at the very heart of the culture and the civilization. What intrigued Loudon, however, was the psychology of preference for a particular *kind* of countryside.[2] He recognized an analogy between the minds of men and the objects and scenery which surrounded them in childhood. Characteristic, striking scenery seemed to have a powerful attraction for people upon their return from a long absence in cities or in foreign lands. If one's childhood experience of landscape was less memorable, great cities might be the most striking features recalled in later life, and these would become the most powerful magnets for returning native sons.

A person whose childhood was spent in the midst of indifferent surroundings, however — in a place lacking expression or distinctive natural features — might one day decide to retire to the country for his health, amusement, or study. Suddenly he might find himself unable to know whether a particular part of the country was suitable for himself and his family. Having had no lifelong, and at least half-conscious, exercise of judging scenery, a man could find that he was not "conversant with his own character." An active, gregarious man might select an unpretentious, comfortable home in the country with sequestered walks, sublime prospects, and glimpses of distant towns or the ocean. But if it did not give him the opportunity to see people and to be seen, he might never be happy in such a place. Or, overwhelmed by grief, a man might seek a decaying castle among overgrown topiary gardens, orchards, copses, and streams. The choice of scene will intensify the grief, and to counter this effect, a faithful servant is advised to take care to introduce to the environment only sensitive plants and tame animals at first — then cows, sheep, birds, and, later, horses. Becoming accustomed, by degrees, to the sight of cheerful animation, the man might then eventually regain his mental health and return to the active duties of life.

Loudon had little sympathy for the man who wished merely to display wealth or enlarge his circle of amusements in the country. Thinking of the public interest at a time when preservation of the landscape was not yet a popular concern, Loudon pointed out that the whole community could suffer from this man's lack of understanding of landscape character. In fact, in the wilder parts of western Scotland, landowners had already destroyed some of the finest scenery in the land — unknowingly, perhaps, but irrevocably. Thus, Loudon's deepest sympathy lay with the man who would "feel and enjoy all the appearances of nature":

He requires few directions; his habitation, whatever it be of itself, whether an obscure cottage or village garret, will be a situation, if possible, where 'nature, unconfined, displays all her graces.' His property is all nature; and, knowing no bounds to his estate, he may therefore change his residence at pleasure. Content to receive from man only what are called the necessaries of life, he is sure of enjoying the most sublime mental luxuries which heaven and earth afford: — and . . . whether he remarks the 'green blade which twinkles in the sun,' or 'the huge oak which in the forest grows,' his soul is alike exalted in the discovery of divinity.[3]

Today, one thinks of Thoreau. In 1806 Loudon quoted Cowper:

> "He looks abroad into the varied field
> Of nature; and though poor, perhaps, compared
> With those whose mansions glitter in his sight,
> Calls the delightful scenery all his own.
> His are the mountains, and the vallies his,
> And the resplendent rivers. His t'enjoy
> With a propriety that none can feel,
> But who, with filial confidence inspired,
> Can lift to heaven an unpresumptuous eye,
> And smiling say, 'My father made them all'."[4]

To the readers of *Country Residences* Loudon could recommend Cowper's "The Task" (1783–84), just as he would recommend Pope's *Epistle to Burlington* (1731) to readers of *Landed Property* in 1808. Poets could express with studied grace and ease what Loudon wanted to say about art and nature. Though Humphry Repton had already written volumes on the theory and practice of Loudon's art, the young Loudon proclaimed his own originality and distanced himself from Repton.[5] Apparently he would sooner invoke the authority of a great poet than acknowledge the sound precedent of a rival landscape gardener.

As an amateur painter who occasionally exhibited at the Royal Academy, Loudon also advised landscape gardeners to study painting.[6] He knew, of course, that Price, Knight, and Sir Joshua Reynolds had already articulated the principles of painting, derived from their far more intimate acquaintance with masterpieces by Claude Lorrain, Nicolas Poussin, Salvator Rosa, Jacob van Ruysdael, and others. Had Loudon actually examined such paintings, one wonders, while he was laying out the grounds of country houses? By 1806 he had visited Knight's Downton Castle; Chatsworth, seat of the duke of Devonshire; and many other places housing some of the finest art collections in Great Britain. In *Country Residences*, Loudon did allude to Claude's groups of trees (by quoting Uvedale Price). And, in an essay entitled "Of Painting," in the same work, Loudon explained how composition, coloring, expression, and other concerns of the painter were relevant to landscape design. Indeed, among all the arts, painting would contribute most to "improve the ideas" of the landscape gardener, he observed. "But the great use of studying pictures is to direct the improver to proper subjects in nature," to specific trees, plants, soils, and processes of decay, "of which the mere student of painting can form no idea."[7] Ultimately, Loudon's own study of paintings would develop his sensitivity to the essential quality and character of a landscape; and by drawing and painting, himself, he trained his eye to detect subtleties of form, color, light, and shade in a given site. The study of poetry, however, taught him how to see with the inward eye: how to feel.

Cowper's "The Task" was published in 1785, when Loudon was two years old. By the time the boy discovered the poem, it would have described the world he knew best: the hills and groves, spires and villages, the warm, snug exotics in the greenhouse, the general confidence in rural simplicity, and concern for rural continuity, as landscapes were "gaz'd upon a while / Then advertis'd, and auctioneer'd away." Praising the virtuous, balanced life, Cowper warned against the extremes of overcrowding and isolation; happiness could be found in *degrees* of society and solitude.

A faint echo of Thomas Gray's "Elegy" (1750) can be heard when Loudon first urges landed gentlemen to consider the feelings and needs of their cottagers — so often neglected, as they lived in the shadows: "The part acted by the cottager in the great drama of life, though important when viewed collectively, is nevertheless, as to the operations of the individual, scarcely discernible. The first and last time that we see him is in the field or in the highway at hard labour; when he is no longer capable of toil, he retires under the shelter of his cottage, and leaves the world as obscurely as he came into it."[8] One can almost hear the knell of parting day, and see Gray's ploughman:

> The ploughman homeward plods his weary way,
> And leaves the world to darkness and to me.
> (Lines 3–4)

In the early 1800s, Loudon still reflected on the needs of the poor at a certain philosophical distance: "But, notwithstanding these unavoidable circumstances, the importance of the labouring poor to society is too well known to be neglected in an age like the present. This is evident from the exertions of societies and individuals to increase their comforts. Humanity can never be more nobly employed."[9] Loudon did not claim to know intimately the needs of laborers. He did realize that they deserve consid-

*Loudon's early suggestions*
*for cottage improvement*
*focused on two main con-*
*cerns — a warm, dry inte-*
*rior, heated by improved*
*fireplaces, and an endear-*
*ing, picturesque exterior,*
*framed by shrubs and vines.*
Fig. 8
J.C.Loudon, "Naked and Decorated Scotch cottages."

eration, and he was learning, slowly, not to be condescending. When he thought about improving cottagers' dwellings he considered their bodily needs, but also their feelings and their dreams. He advised landlords, for instance, to look in upon their dependents from time to time: "A visit to their dwellings would reanimate their drooping spirits, strengthen their resolution, or prompt them to exertions: it would not occupy much time; would never be remembered with regret; nor would it be forgotten as a vacuum in time, in which no new ideas were acquired, nor any action performed, that could afford pleasure in the remembrance."[10] These references to memory — a backward glance at a person who showed some kindness, a landscape known in childhood — could be clues to Loudon's own past, as well as insights into the minds of laborers. At twenty-three, Loudon did not yet focus on their interests. Still, he recognized that they, too, have memories to stimulate and dreams to gratify. They also must reflect upon the past and the future. The material comforts of their snug, warm cottages, although necessary, were not sufficient for human existence (fig. 8).

In his early career, Loudon attempted to improve the humble cottage by employing a few technical means borrowed from hothouse construction. (See chapters 6 and 7.) Here, our concern is with the larger rural environment, the village in the landscape. For village streets, Loudon generally recommended irregular, picturesque massing of buildings, especially when uneven ground and other natural features would make picturesque design more economical than a regular grid plan. He crit-icized newly constructed villages that were stiff and formal, like the layout

*Naked Scotch Cottage*

*Decorated Scotch Cottage*

Loudon considered typical of Capability Brown: a straight cottage-lined road which bulged in the center to form a double crescent (fig. 9). This example from Loudon's *Country Residences* is pure fantasy, not any particular village of Brown, but it does illustrate what Loudon did not like in village design. In contrast, his own typical village contained cottages which formed three-sided courts, extended wings, and fragments of rows, interspersed with a few free-standing cottages sited along a winding road.[11] These were all elements of the "natural" village, which evolved over time (fig. 10).

In a natural village, Loudon reasoned, a picturesque effect was achieved incidentally and unself-consciously, as cottagers built their own dwellings for comfort and convenience. Here, all cottages were constructed on rising ground, if possible — above the flood plain. They would be sheltered from the prevailing cold winds. In many old villages, the main street seemed to be an afterthought, merely a passageway winding through the aggregation of randomly sited cottages. In the leftover patches of land were trees, bushes, rocks, weeds, and broken ground. Animating the picturesque natural village were the people — old men digging in the garden, women washing clothes by the stream, and children tending cows or running here and there.[12]

This unpretentious picture was not Loudon's ideal village. He did try, however, to maintain something of this unplanned appearance when asked to lay out a new village. The main feature of his village planning was

*This faint caricature of "Capability" Brown's manner of laying out grounds includes, in the upper right, cottages lining a "formal street" with a double crescent.*

Fig. 9
J.C.Loudon, "A residence formed . . . in Mr. Brown's style — generally prevalent at the present day, 1806."

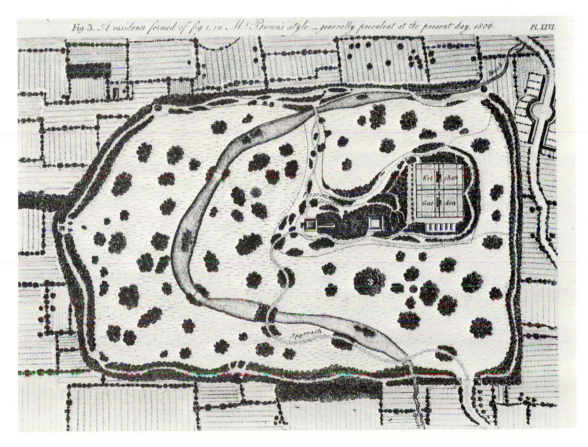

Fig.3. A residence formed of fig.1. in Mr. Brown's style — generally prevalent at the present day, 1806. Pl. XLVI.

*In laying out grounds dur-*
*ing the 1800s, Loudon*
*sought the impression of in-*
*formality and gradual evo-*
*lution — not only in the*
*scattering of open courts*
*and free-standing cottages*
*in the village (*upper
right*) — but in the appar-*
*ently "natural" connection*
*of groups of trees with dense*
*forests.*
Fig. 10
J.C.Loudon, "A residence
. . . in the style of the author,
J.Loudon."

the relative isolation, or staggering, of dwellings, meant to guard against "excessive intimacy" among the poor villagers. The peasant, Loudon reasoned, does not want others to know of his poverty. He conceals his little domestic arrangements from the "prying eye and flippant remarks" of his more independent neighbors. If he lives in a two-family cottage in the village, he may suffer embarrassment or lose some of his native virtue. "It is perhaps in part owing to the greater number of isolated houses, and the smaller number of villages in Britain," Loudon wrote in 1806, "that the peasantry of this country are found more virtuous than that of any other in Europe."[13]

Years later, once Loudon had seen and actually spoken with peasants in Europe, he could no longer cherish this notion. In France, southern Germany, and Switzerland, he met peasants, maids, innkeepers, gardeners, and small farmers who lived in villages and towns and benefited from rural schools and cooperative dairies. He came to realize that isolation might be useful for concealing poverty from the eyes of neighbors and proprietors; but before the poor could be expected to help themselves, they must shake off the "cold, sluggish apathy" which reconciled them to subservience and subsistence.[14] At least the proximity of somewhat more fortunate neighbors could stimulate discontent — which could produce a desire for change and self-improvement.

While Loudon was still addressing the landowners, however, in the early 1800s, he hoped that they would take the initiative for improvement.

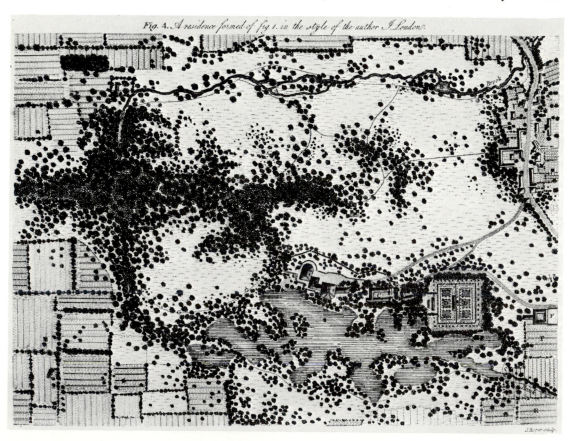

*Fig. 4. A residence formed of fig 1. in the style of the author J.Loudon.*

During these years, despite his earnest considerations, the cottager, the laborer, the "poor," appeared as shadowy, vaguely defined, and picturesquely grouped figures in Loudon's verbal depictions — relegated to what John Barrell has recently termed "The Dark Side of the Landscape."[15] Whether young Loudon consciously and consistently meant to relegate these humbler folk to the shadows is debatable — but not probable. The happiness of the rural poor was the centerpiece of his earliest Utopian vision, and it figured in his overall vision of practical rural improvement. Still, that vision was broad (at times, hazy), and the scope of his stated concerns ranged far beyond gardening, farming, and village planning, into the more ethereal realms of philosophy and theology. In *Country Residences*, he warns readers that "unless true religion and extensive moral reflections enter into all our studies of nature, persons of delicate taste and uncorrupted minds will never enjoy true happiness, even in a country residence. There is an intellectual repose and refined mental pleasure, which arises from the *relative* contemplation of the links of that endless chain by which every thing is connected, and by the perception of that wonderful EXPRESSION OF MIND which pervades the whole universe."[16]

At the height of this rhapsody on contemplating nature — which recalls the famous night described in "Summer," part of James Thomson's poem *The Seasons* — Loudon leaves the endless chain of being and comes down to earth.[17] The study of reflections of Divine Order is not enough — neither in objects of nature nor in works of art. The expression of a marble statue is nothing, Loudon insists, compared with that of a graceful woman. The purely aesthetic or scientific activity of a painter, a sculptor, or a botanist will "contract" the mind if it is not linked with the study of the moral actions of men.

Pope and Thomson had already explored some of these moral and universal relationships. In *The Seasons*, Thomson had even dared to focus on extremes of evil and chaos. "Winter" was Thomson's occasion to reflect on cheerless poverty, secluded distress, and oppression. In the land of liberty, the free-born Briton would not be oppressed by little tyrants forever:

> Ye sons of mercy! yet resume the search;
> Drag forth the legal monsters into light,
> Wrench from their hands Oppression's iron rod,
> And bid the cruel feel the pains they give.
> Much still untouched remains; in this rank age,
> Much is the patriot's weeding hand required.

Though the good who are distressed must still bear the blasts and glooms of Winter, Thomson was reassuring:

> The storms of wintry time will quickly pass,
> And one unbounded Spring encircle all.[18]

In *The Seasons*, a poem that evolved over twenty years, from 1726 to 1746, Thomson presented one comprehensive, optimistic view of Nature, which apparently made a deep impression on Loudon. Here, human suffering and natural catastrophes were ultimately reconciled with joy and the abundance of Nature: it was the unseen Divine Essence which regulated all motions on earth and in the heavens.

Pope had said all of this, and more, with greater eloquence, in his *Essay on Man* (1733). His epistles to aristocratic friends also contained timeless principles of landscape gardening, which Loudon could always recommend:

"Still follow Sense, of ev'ry Art the Soul"
"Consult the Genius of the Place in all"
"In all, let Nature never be forgot."[19]

For vivid descriptions of real scenery and actual country residences, such as Hagley and Stowe, however, Loudon turned not to Pope but to Thomson, whose poem *The Seasons* was still popular at the end of the eighteenth century.[20] Thomson's shaggy banks, secluded ravines, and streams murmuring over twisted roots were still appealing to readers of Rousseau's *Confessions* (1781) and William Gilpin's *Tours*, a series of travel books describing picturesque regions of Britain, published in the 1780s and 1790s. What dated *The Seasons* from a designer's point of view (apart from its nymphs and swains) was the predominance of smooth streams and level green lawns in its landscape gardens; in the eyes of avant-garde critics like Uvedale Price and Payne Knight, these features were too bland, tame, old-fashioned.[21]

Humphry Repton, the pre-eminent landscape gardener of the late eighteenth century, was heir to the tradition of smooth streams and gentle lawns at Hagley, seat of Lord Lyttleton, and Stowe, seat of Lord Cobham, and heir as well to the practice of Charles Bridgeman, William Kent, and Lancelot "Capability" Brown.[22] Beginning in the early 1700s, these professionals and several influential amateurs, including Lord Lyttleton, Henry Hoare, Charles Hamilton, and William Shenstone, laid out some of the finest country residences in Britain; moreover, they had contributed to an evolving aesthetic of picturesque landscape gardening which England could claim as her own unique contribution to the arts.[23] By the end of the century, Repton, with his impressive redbooks for clients and his published works on theory and practice, had established a new, more solid professionalism in landscape gardening (fig. 11). For this reason alone — competent professionalism — Loudon might have chosen to follow Repton, but his artistic and professional ambitions were boundless. Loudon wanted to outperform all rivals and to create gardens, parks, and farms which, in their maturity, would be the very epitomes of their kind, in the most advanced idiom of the day — the rugged, romantically wild picturesque (fig. 12, pl. 2). Thus he followed the lead of the two most articulate amateurs, Price and Knight.[24]

Knight had recently shown that reason could still rule over the luxuriantly wild landscape. Books, solitude, vernal flowers, wavy corn and thoughts of the endless chain of being could co-exist with shaggy shrubs and moss-grown stones in Knight's poem *The Landscape* (1794). Thus Loudon could calmly allude to Knight's poem when he criticized his most distinguished rival, Repton: Loudon claimed that Repton, like Brown before him, designed landscapes that were too tame, bare, and bald for a man of modern sensibility.[25]

The modern art of laying out grounds, in Knight's view, was not simply a departure from shaven lawns, flat insipid plains, and formal

lumps and clumps. The art was an eloquent expression of energy, honesty, and freedom — triumphing over lethargy, officiousness, vanity, tiresome kindness, and even the hallowed serpentine, "blinding beauty in its waving line." In *The Landscape*, Knight criticized the work of Brown and his followers in these well-known lines:

> To improve, adorn and polish, they profess;
> But shave the goddess, whom they come to dress;
> Level each broken bank and shaggy mound,
> And fashion all to one unvaried round;
> One even round, that ever gently flows,
> Nor forms abrupt, nor broken colours knows;
> But, wrapt all o'er in everlasting green,
> Makes one dull, vapid, smooth, unvaried scene.[26]

The less familiar *ending* of Knight's poem reveals the artistic and political freedom which the romantically picturesque landscape could embody. But these lines are much more than a restatement of the familiar associations between landscape gardening and British political liberties. As in Thomson's "Winter," the imagery in Knight's poem is savage; the sentiment is revolutionary. In fact, Knight's lines were written during the first few terrifying years of the French Revolution, in 1793–94. What impact did these lines have on young Loudon, who discovered them sometime before 1804, during the Napoleonic Wars? About that time he was formulating his own vision of a peaceful, productive Britain in the aftermath of such fury as Knight depicts here:[27]

> As the dull, stagnant pool, that's mantled o'er
> With the green weeds of its own muddy shore,
> No bright reflections on its surface shows,
> Nor murmuring surge, nor foaming ripple knows;
> But ever peaceful, motionless, and dead,
> In one smooth sheet its torpid waters spread:
> So by oppression's iron hand confined,
> In calm and peaceful torpor sleep mankind;
> Unfelt the rays of genius, that inflame
> The free-born soul, and bid it pant for fame.
>    But break the mound, and let the waters flow;
> Headlong and fierce their turbid currents go;
> Sweep down the fences, and tear up the soil;
> And roar along, 'midst havock, waste, and spoil;
> Till spent their fury: — then their moisture feeds
> The deepening verdure of the fertile meads;
> Bids vernal flowers the fragrant turf adorn,
> And rising juices swell the wavy corn:
> So when rebellion breaks the despot's chain,
> First wasteful ruin marks the rabble's reign;
> Till tired their fury, and their vengeance spent,
> One common interest bids their hearts relent;
> Then temperate order from confusion springs,
> And, fann'd by freedom, genius spreads its wings.[28]

Implicated in these references to dull pools and torpid waters, Repton bore the spirited criticism of Knight and Price during the picturesque controversy of the 1790s with admirable restraint.[29] In his later writings, he gradually made some concessions to the wilder imagery of nature untamed. By 1806, in his *Enquiry into the Changes of Taste in Landscape Gardening*, Repton admitted that gardening must include not only artificial comforts but "something" of native wilderness, appropriate to the true genius or character of the place.[30] Still, he held his ground against the wild notion that landscape painters, with all their weeds, brambles, and dead branches, and their conventionally fixed foregrounds, middle grounds, and distances, should dominate his professional work. He maintained that landscape gardening was *not* "picture gardening," but a compromise between the two. Extremes must be avoided. Country residences must be, above all, suitable habitations for people.

To Loudon, in his twenties, this voice of experience may have sounded reasonable — but it was too restrained. During these years, he embraced extremes and vacillated between realism and romanticism, between precocious grandfatherly reflection and brash adolescent remarks. "Nothing can be grand or sublime, but as it soars above the common appearance of the like thing," Loudon wrote in 1806. And he went on to suggest that a great park, such as those at Blenheim, Croome, or Dunkeld, could be improved by imitating parts of wild forests (see fig. 12):

The cold inquirer will say, Would not the utility of such parks be injured? So it would, in some degree; but is not beauty or grandeur of character one of the chief objects of such scenes? if not, why change the common character of the country, why make the interesting variety of corn fields, farms, cottages, hedges, coppices, give way to one dull vapid monotonous surface of green, as insipidly varied by trees, — where one might wander an age without seeing any thing else than their naked stems and clump-like heads? . . . Now in a fertile and cultivated country, what can be more truly uncommon with regard to the surface, than making it assume the wild irregularity and excesses of nature, leaving flocks and herds to roam at pleasure, and despising the teeming abundance of cultivation, and the grosser ideas of mere profit or use?[31]

This breezy enthusiasm for nature's excesses, and the accompanying preference for luxuriant scenery over abundant crops, did not survive Loudon's next few years of labor as a tenant farmer in Oxfordshire. What did survive, expressed in more convincing language, was Loudon's high-minded disdain for the merely utilitarian or profitable. He never gave up his yearning to reconcile use and beauty. Gradually, however, he learned to stretch his perceptions of what was truly beautiful.

As a young man formulating his own set of principles for designing landscape gardens that would be both useful and beautiful, Loudon necessarily borrowed much from the eighteenth-century British theorists, particularly from Thomas Whately's *Observations on Modern Gardening* (1770) and Uvedale Price's *Essay on the Picturesque* (1794). He derived his two leading principles from Louis-René de Girardin's *Essay on Landscape* of 1777. There Girardin, marquis d'Ermenonville, emphasized two main principles of landscape design: "l'unité et la liaison des rapports."[32] Loudon, in 1806, insisted on the same two principles: "unity of design and character with regard to the whole; and grouping or connexion in regard to the parts." Of course, Whately and Price had included these principles among others, but it was Girardin who considered these two pre-eminent. Girardin also preferred the simplicity of Shenstone's residence, The Leasowes, to the magnificence of Blenheim and Stowe — a preference which Loudon shared.[33]

Loudon's early career in shaping some of the rural landscapes of Britain depended on his ability to express his ideas in the idioms of both landscape and language. As a young designer, he was already a connoisseur of landscape. As a young author, he was a diligent, fairly competent student of language — but also a spirited lad who squirmed in his seat, longing to leave the stifling classroom of discretion. He was blunt, impatient, petulant, brash with words. Still, he had the eye of a landscape artist and a mind quick to grasp the implications for design in the landscape theories of his first great mentor, Sir Uvedale Price. In the 1790s, Price was also exploring the connections between landscape and language, offering, incidentally, advice on how *not* to write: "Few persons have been so lucky as never to have seen or heard the proser; smiling, and distinctly uttering his flowing, commonplace nothings, with the same placid countenance, the same even-toned voice: he is the very emblem of serpentine walks, belts and rivers, and all of Mr. Brown's works; like his, they are smooth, flowing, even and distinct; and like him, they wear one's soul out."[34] Here, Price was developing an analogy between speech and visual language: "The language . . . by which objects of sight make themselves intelligible, is exactly like that of speech." For a listener unused to a certain language, one had to make clear, labored distinctions and sharp lines, exaggerating the forms or sounds. But then the expressive touches, the grace and the subtleties of landscape and language, would be lost. Price preferred the picturesque: "like a person who speaks with flashes of light; objects the most familiar are placed by him in such singular, yet natural points of view. He strikes out such unthought of agreements and contrasts — such combinations, so little obvious, yet never forced or affected, that the attention cannot flag; but from the delight of what is passed, we eagerly listen for what is to come. This is the true picturesque."[35]

Price, a man of sensibility as well as wit, might have approved of Brown's and Repton's works if he could have seen them today, now that nature has had centuries to complete the landscape gardeners' work. Though charmed by the picturesque, Price could also be moved by the truly beautiful in landscape and language. He continued, "How different is the effect of that soft, insinuating style, of those gentle transitions, which, without dazzling or surprising, keep up an increasing interest, and insensibly wind round the heart."

Loudon was schooled in Price's ideas on the picturesque and the beautiful before he met Sir Joseph Banks and Jeremy Bentham in London in 1803. Afterwards, Price's aesthetic views continued to have a profound influence on Loudon's early practice, which involved some disturbing social and economic issues, as well as the more elegant aspects of shaping the land. Loudon had to learn on his own, however, through trial and error, how to make rural improvements with economy, compassion, and sensibility. He had to find his own voice — with some help from the critics.

In 1811 a charitable writer for the *Monthly Review* observed that

Loudon's *Landed Property* (1808) had "great (some) beauties and great defects," as "philologists have remarked of the English language."[36] The defects lay in his manner: impatience, affectation, arrogance, exaggeration, lack of discretion. The beauties lay in the substance: "a thorough knowledge of the improved husbandry."[37] Today, with hindsight, a few other appealing qualities are evident: Loudon's high enthusiasm and emotional energy; his unflappable confidence in the rational behavior of men, given the right encouragement; his occasional serene reflections; and his delight in articulating a new, partly original aesthetic of garden design.

The critics, however, did not appreciate Loudon's aesthetics, as expressed in *Country Residences*. The *Monthly Review* noted that Loudon recommended roughness in lawns, to give a natural appearance to the country residence, although areas near the house might be mowed and rolled. For most grounds not grazed by sheep, Loudon recommended a variety of grasses, interspersed not only with primroses, violets, daisies, white clover, and camomile, but even with cudweed and hawkweed. William Robinson, active sixty years later, would have been delighted;[38] but in 1807, the *Monthly Review* preferred smoothness and neatness in all areas near the house and did not approve of excessive "wildness" in forests. Clearly, Loudon's new "characteristic style" was opposed to the "modern" system (of Brown and Repton), in which houses and clumps of trees were isolated units, separate from the surrounding countryside. Loudon aimed to harmonize the country residence within its surroundings, and he would take care to unite even the humble offices with the main house, rather than try to conceal them in his picturesque scenes. This last point was commended; but the reviewer warned against the health hazards of excessively picturesque homes, veiled in vines and foliage, as dampness and decay would creep in, and birds and insects would thrive. Then, too, Loudon's partiality for irregular and indented pieces of water — with islands edged by broken ground, rocks, roots, and stones — would merely introduce new mannerisms into the landscape: "A *Loudonian* will be as easily recognised as a *Brownonian* lake."[39]

In the same year as this review appeared, William Wordsworth was likewise criticized for roughness and mannerism. Francis Jeffrey, editor of the *Edinburgh Review*, considered his new work, *Poems in Two Volumes* (1807), as disappointing as Wordsworth's earlier *Lyrical Ballads* (1798). In spite of his strong spirit of originality, pathos, and natural feeling, Wordsworth's diction was inelegant and his versification slovenly. The following lines were merely "affected," no more natural than the ditties of a common song-writer:

> I met Louisa in the shade;
> And, having seen that lovely maid,
> Why should I fear to say
> That she is ruddy, fleet and strong; —
> And down the rocks can leap along,
> Like rivulets in May?
> ("Louisa," lines 1–6.)

In Jeffrey's view, this poet and his circle were alarming innovators; they were mannerists, borrowing from "vulgar ballads and plebian nurseries." However, the critic did appreciate the sonnet which began, "Milton! thou should'st be living at this hour: / England hath need of thee: . . . " In sum: Wordsworth had some talent, which he appeared to be squandering; but let others be forewarned by his extravagancies. Jeffrey's concern was that the "established laws of poetry," that "ancient and venerable code," be restored to their due honor and authority.[40]

Wordsworth was not disheartened by this verdict from Edinburgh. His friends, among them Coleridge and Sir George Beaumont, were strong supporters. In a letter to Lady Beaumont, Wordsworth explained some of his poems and predicted their destiny: "to console the afflicted; to add sunshine to daylight, by making the happy happier; and to teach the young and the gracious of every age to see, to think and feel, and, therefore, to become more actively and securely virtuous."[41] In the prefaces to his works, the poet had already explained his intentions: essentially, to describe incidents and situations from common life, using words and phrases from ordinary language. He would present ordinary things in an unusual way, however — tinged with a certain coloring of the imagination. In the rustic settings of his poems, people acted according to their elemental feelings, their "essential passions of the heart." They spoke plainly, emphatically. Their language was purified by hourly contact with "the best objects from which the best part of the language is originally derived," that is, from objects in the natural world and the humanized, agricultural landscape.[42]

Wordsworth and Loudon were near-contemporaries whose use of the English language and perceptions of the British landscape developed independently. Loudon's emotional response to the natural beauty of glens, mountains, and forests was best expressed in the medium of ground, water, and wood, not in words. His sensibilities as a landscape artist were developed in part, however, by "storing his mind" with the visual imagery of the well-established poets Thomson, Pope, Gray, Cowper, William Mason, and Jacques De Lille.

By 1807, Wordsworth had already looked far beyond these eighteenth-century poets and had developed his own voice — or, rather, several voices — using speech and imagery that initially confounded the critics.[43] Loudon, thirteen years younger than Wordsworth, was then a less experienced innovator, just beginning to develop new approaches to his art. His landscape designs of the early 1800s were as avant-garde as the poems of Wordsworth and the theories of Price and Knight. His boldest innovations, however — his technical and formal experiments with glasshouses — were not yet noticed by the world of art. As a technician, writing about the heating and ventilating of hothouses, Loudon was considered competent, innovative, even ingenious.[44] When he wrote about the art of gardening, however, the critics were unmoved.

In 1806 Loudon was calling for more naturalism and realism in the artifacts of the landscape garden. He was no longer charmed by the emblems and symbols which carried the mind off to distant lands and ancient heroes:

When at Stowe, and told that we are in the Elysian fields or the Grecian valley, the information produces no emotion, but some recollections of Italy or Virgil, which would be pursued with much better effect in the closet over the Eneid, or a work on geography; for still as we pass through these Elysian fields, the attention is caught by new objects, in attending to which properly we either forget the allusion, or, absorbed in reverie, *shut our eyes to the real beauties which surround us*. When the whole is once seen, all the charms of illusion vanish, and the obvious want of utility renders such scenery nauseous and tiresome, and only worth preservation for its singularity and antiquity.[45] (See fig. 13.)

Loudon was not insensitive to the illusions and allusions of Stowe, that classic landscape of another age, which reflected an even more distant past, so dear to all classically educated gentlemen. If he could not be enchanted with that composite creation of Bridgeman, Sir John Vanbrugh, Kent, and Brown, it was because he made different demands on each garden scene, one by one.[46] Loudon had learned from Thomas Whately to look beyond emblems and allegories in the garden, to seek more inherently expressive beauty. And yet, Whately had been charmed by Stowe. He found Lord Cobham's country residence a place of "magnificence and splendour," with a hint of the solemnity of ancient sacred groves, yet pervaded by a spirit of gaiety, "peopled" by busts and enlivened by streams and sprightly verdure. It was a charming "mansion of delight and joy," with perhaps a few too many scenes and buildings — but Whately shrugged off this mild objection with the recollection that "solitude has never been reckoned among the charms of the Elysium."[47]

Solitude and retirement, however, were the very qualities Loudon most valued in the landscape garden. He looked for quieter places in which one could appreciate a lesser number of elegant objects, and he wanted a much more protective, luxuriant screening of one scene from another. At Stowe, where Whately had found a general unity of character within each separate scene, Loudon was more demanding. At the same time as he was looking more intently at objects in the landscape garden, as

*Although the young Loudon objected to the inclusion of so many distracting classical features in this "Grecian Valley" at Stowe, he may have been inspired by what Thomas Whately said about the Grecian Temple (later renamed as the Temple of Concord and Victory), center distance. In 1803 his proposed "Doric" conservatory for Scone (fig. 20) would have had a similar orientation.*

Fig. 13
George Bickham, Jr., engraving after John Baptist Claude Chatelain, "A View from Lord Cobham's Pillar to the Lady's and Grecian Temples" at Stowe, Buckinghamshire, 1753. Courtesy, Yale Center for British Art, Paul Mellon Collection.

*A View from Lord Cobham's Pillar to the Lady's & Grecian Temples.*    *Vue prise depuis la Colomne de Milord Cobham jusqu'au Temple Grec & a celui des Dames.*

a horticulturist and as a designer, he also wanted a more comprehensive unity than his eighteenth-century predecessors had ever asked for: a union of the physical reality of a thing with its immediate, unlearned associations.

Loudon was also seeking a more literal truth than his predecessors had cared to find. "Truth and Nature are the same," he wrote in 1805.[48] Both were founded in utility, yet were not thereby deprived of poetic associations. Loudon was alive to the varied associations which an object — a building, a machine, a tree — might offer. Like Wordsworth, at an early stage, Loudon had been influenced by David Hartley's *Observations on Man* (1749), a methodical, sometimes lyrical study of the association of ideas, and of reveries, dreams, the imagination, pleasures, pains, and other aesthetic and moral concerns.[49] Loudon had also been intrigued by the later eighteenth-century writings of Whately and Archibald Alison, who pursued the flights of the imagination from one idea to another via associations.

From Alison's *Essays on the Nature and Principles of Taste* (1790), Loudon learned to distinguish between *accidental* associations, which depend on erudition, travel, cultivated taste, or some other kind of prior experience, and *natural* associations, which are inherent in the form, color, texture, or fragrance of the object itself. A cypress, for instance, might suggest melancholy, not only because it had been planted in ancient churchyards, but also because it had a uniform, constantly dark green color and a still, solemn appearance. To the rational and romantic young Loudon, these natural associations were fascinating, for they could rivet his attention on the real beauty of the thing itself.

It is for this attention to the reality and integrity of objects — the instinct to focus intently — that Wordsworth and Loudon can best be compared. As noted earlier, Loudon recalled his own wandering from scene to scene at Stowe: frustrated by the overabundance of visual stimulation, he could not focus on one object of art within a secluded or simple natural setting. Then, having lapsed into reveries of ancient Elysian fields, he missed the *real* beauty of the place. In 1807 Wordsworth described how his mind floated "with a kind of dreamy indifference" among the images of his own sonnets. Comparative listlessness or apathy would set in, Wordsworth explained, until all at once an object or an individual came forth, "and my mind," he wrote, "sleepy and unfixed, is awakened and fastened in a moment."[50] Wordsworth was probing more deeply than Loudon into mind, memory, and self-conscious perception. Loudon was usually quite literal, shying away from metaphysics. Yet both had a reverence for the essential, concrete detail of a landscape: a spade, a plough, a leech, a pine, a spire. These were objects on which the poet and the gardener focused their attention.[51]

From childhood, Wordsworth and Loudon had each known intimately some striking landscapes — the former in the English Lake District and the latter in the more romantic parts of lowland Scotland. Mindful of the essential character or mood of a place, they reveled in the particular, typical elements of a scene. Wordsworth was struck by the sight of some ten thousand daffodils — such jolly company as they danced beside a lake, beneath the trees. To Loudon, common forest trees were a source of shelter, beauty, national wealth and naval pride. He also recognized that a single tree could be the noblest ornament of a man's home and that a man could look upon a tree he had planted as his own offspring.

Wordsworth and Loudon had one art form in common: garden design. In the fall of 1806, Wordsworth accepted the invitation of Sir George and Lady Beaumont to design their winter garden at Coleorton Hall, in Leicestershire. In December he sent Lady Beaumont a plan and a lengthy description of a one-acre garden (fig. 14) to be set in an old abandoned quarry.[52] He also coined a new term to supplement the expression "Ge-

*In 1806 Wordsworth sketched this plan of a winter garden for Sir George and Lady Margaret Beaumont, taking a few hints from writers active before the "modern" gardening of Brown and Repton evolved. The poet thought himself a bit old-fashioned in the garden; he even liked jets of water — features which Loudon would try to revive in the 1830s.*

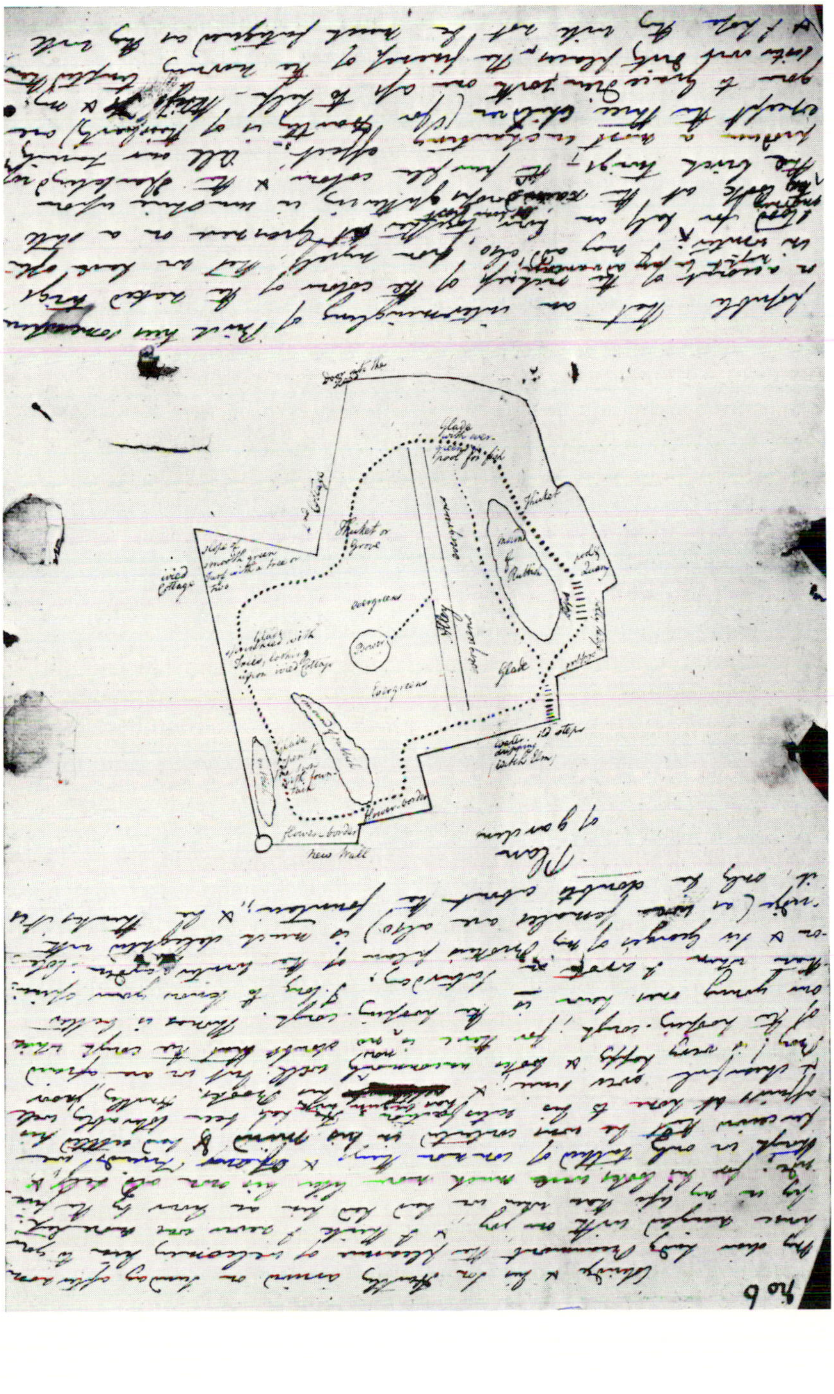

Fig. 14
William Wordsworth, Plan for a winter garden at Coleorton Hall, Leicestershire, seat of Sir George Beaumont. By kind permission of the Trustees of the Pierpont Morgan Library.

nius of the Place." At Coleorton he would try to respect the "sentiment of the place."

The winter garden would first be seen from above, as one stood on a terrace built over a retaining wall. A belt of evergreen shrubs and cypresses, backed by firs, would exclude from sight most of the surrounding scenery, except for a few glimpses of the ivy-clad cottages beyond. Depth, shelter, and seclusion were essential — for this was to be a little paradise "consecrated to winter," with no apparent traces of decay or desolation, not even a fallen leaf from a deciduous tree. There would be several discrete scenes: a showy border, edged in box, backed by a garden wall, and filled with rows of annuals and perennials; an alley bordered by laurel and overshadowed by evergreen trees, leading to an evergreen glade; some artificial mounds (constructed from old rubbish heaps) which would help to screen the different scenes; at the quarry's edge, a pool to reflect the overhanging rocks, the plants, and the towering evergreens; and a secluded lawn containing a single basin for just two gold or silver fish and, here and there, a solitary wild flower.

The appeal of Wordsworth's winter garden lay in its intimacy and its invitation to explore a sheltered, predominantly evergreen world with quiet recesses, cloistral spaces, and places for introspection. However, taking a hint from a scene with a vista described in Thomson's "Hymn on Solitude," Wordsworth left a single opening somewhere in the evergreen enclosure to offer a glimpse of some interesting object in the distance.[53]

Wordsworth knew he was somewhat old-fashioned in the garden, but he liked formal jets of water, for instance, in rural scenery as well as in towns. He enjoyed seeing their diamond drops of light scattering into the atmosphere, producing halos and rainbows on a sunny day. Yet he was also intrigued by Knight's more modern fondness for old quarries as secluded, romantic retreats in a garden.[54] Then, too, Wordsworth was consciously going back to the beginnings of the English landscape garden, before Brown's "system" of modern gardening had set in. The poet turned to earlier poets and painters, and he took up one suggestion from a letter written to the *Spectator* in 1712 (and attributed to Joseph Addison), which described a one-acre winter garden as an evergreen haven for birds and people.[55]

Wordsworth may not have cared to participate in the picturesque controversy of Price, Knight, and Repton. He did, however, offer a veiled criticism of Repton's little milestones and of other devices used to indicate the extent of one man's property. The poet confided to Sir George Beaumont, "Surely it is a substitution of little things for great, when we would put a whole country into a nobleman's livery." Wordsworth would rather have seen a man of wealth and influence making agricultural improvements, adding to the comforts of his tenants, and showing that the "grossest utilities" of the farm are connected, harmoniously, with "the more intellectual arts."[56] This latter point was an objection to Repton's well-publicized opinion that it was ridiculous to attempt to achieve visual harmony between the profitable working farm and the landscape park.[57]

The design and construction of Sir George Beaumont's winter garden occupied Wordsworth during much of the winter of 1806–07, and he apparently enjoyed that diversion from writing. Although Loudon is not known to have visited Coleorton, in 1831 he saw Wordsworth's Lakeland

home, Rhydal Mount, near Grasmere. This "pastoral cottage" he called
one of the few "very perfect" villa residences of the Lake District. Loudon
particularly admired Wordsworth's terrace walk, which displayed the
taste of the painter in its fine coloring and the science of a botanist in the
choice of plants.[58] By that time, Wordsworth and Loudon would be recognized as eminent in their respective pursuits of poetry and gardening. But
in the early 1800s, both men were independently shaping new forms,
having broken away from conventional forms of artistic expression. For
their boldness and roughness, they were criticized.

In the face of adversity, Loudon never had the warm, generous
support of a patron, as Wordsworth had from Sir George and Lady Beaumont. Apart from family; sympathetic employers; and an outstanding
teacher, Professor Coventry in Edinburgh; Loudon stood alone, self-reliant, somewhat arrogant in his youth. He was physically active then,
working constantly, writing at least one book (on hothouses) while traveling by staying up at night in country inns and sending his manuscripts, in
installments, directly to the printers.[59] He also read voraciously, gleaning
from the ancients and the moderns (from Wordsworth, too, one wonders?).
His early works were studded with citations of authors and titles and with
quotations in Latin or English. Tucked in among them, however, standing
out from his generally self-assertive prose, were also fragments of Loudon's life story which revealed an essentially contemporary, romantic
fervor and lack of ease.

Today, Loudon's self-revelations are not shocking; even in his own
time, many literary confessions were more disturbing. Though indiscreet
with words, Loudon was a scrupulously moral member of the Church of
Scotland. He warned against the temptations of dark-eyed tawny gypsies,
who "never fail to corrupt young men wherever they appear."[60] Loudon
preferred traditional virtue and beauty (which he believed were syn-
onymous in a woman). He often compared the charms of a fine landscape
with those of a beautiful woman, insisting — at least when he was twenty-
one — that, in the face of female beauty, all other kinds of beauty
paled.[61]

In an essay written a few years later, Loudon departed from the
general subject of cottage industries among the poor to praise the ladies
who had initiated spinning and knitting in the cottages of Stanmore,
Middlesex. He had a few kind words for the educated English gentlemen
whom he had met south of the Tweed, including men of commerce: they
were, on the whole, liberal and candid. But it was the ladies who drew his
lavish praise. Loudon was then twenty-five, a convalescing landscape
gardener who had a reasonably handsome face beneath dark, wispy curls,
and a stiff, ankylosed left knee that made him limp. After sizing up
English gentlemen, he added this illuminating note:

English ladies too, are no less distinguished for their personal charms than for
their graceful and winning deportment, and their elegant accomplishments. In
their hearts they cherish every stranger; they are Cosmopolites in kindness;
they show their predilection in the most frank yet delicate manner; ever ready
to smooth the rough road of life with a thousand tender offices, which from
them alone can be received, they seem perpetually conscious of their destiny
in life, and in a manner peculiarly their own. Let not the reader suppose that
this picture is drawn from the impulse of merely personal feelings: it is a

general impression resting upon my mind and heart; and if a testimony of this be needed, I may give the melancholy one of my own bodily debility and deformity, which has recently fallen upon me, in consequence of a severe attack of disease. That I lament it, would be superfluous to say; and as I am a man I lament it on the score of my future prospects with the sex: What Cicero says of friendship I would say of love.[62]

Here is the young Loudon, unsure of himself beneath the bravado, yet just confident enough to admit his fears in print. Today, some may not care for his implied sense of women's destiny; this, too, would change in time. In any event, Loudon's spontaneous, sometimes jolting expressions of feeling seem to be characteristic of his own times, the romantic age which included men as different in sensibility as Wordsworth, Shelley, Byron, and Leigh Hunt.

Loudon was never a literary artist, however; and as a young man he did not discuss the political revolutions and the dramatic social transformations that engaged some contemporary writers, painters, poets, and scientists. These were the concerns of Loudon's later life. He was just six years old when the French Revolution first shook the Western world. His early manhood was marked by optimism based in private, self-reliant endeavors, and by a rapid rise to material success in a decade when the management of landed property seemed to him the essential subject for reform. But just as Loudon did not share Wordsworth's enthusiasm for all the humanitarian ideals of the French Revolution, so it appears that he never experienced the poet's profound disillusionment after the ideals of that revolution were betrayed.[63] Loudon's maturity did not arrive with a shattering sense of collective loss, but with a realistic acceptance of a lost fortune, a change of professional goals, and an emerging awareness of sharing his fate with others in society. Thus, Loudon's most moving cries for social reform, and for a change in the "General Mind of Society," came not in the vigor of early manhood, but in the prime of middle age.

For nearly thirty years, half a lifetime, Loudon lived and worked mainly in the countryside. In Midlothian, in Oxfordshire, during intervals in Edinburgh and London, and while traveling throughout the British Isles, he developed an incipient vision of a better world. The vision would change, but for a while it provided a philosophical foundation for all his rural labors. Like Price, his mentor, Loudon believed that altruism should ultimately help to preserve the best in the present social order.[64] Like Repton, his rival, Loudon frequently recommended some benevolent action towards laborers and tenants.[65] But he went far beyond Price and Repton when he published his Utopian image of a better (rural) society. Though his early social ideals approximated those of Price, Loudon was not quite satisfied with the existing conditions and relations among men in the British countryside. He believed that more cheerful relations and deeper bonds could be established between landlord and laborer. Here, then, is his first complete scenario of rural felicity — not as it is, he admits, but as it might be.

The year is 1806. France has had her revolution. Nelson has just won the battle of Trafalgar. At home, in the countryside, some changes are underway. Loudon sketches the domestic scene, perhaps aware that some might find in his picture the figures of Lord Kames, Sir John Sinclair, the marquis of Huntley, and the duke of Gordon (see fig. 15); the lights and shadows of Price, Knight, and Girardin; and Rousseau's tomb on the island of poplars at Ermenonville (fig. 16).[66] No democratic revolutions, no signs of equality among all people are evident here. And no villainy or tyranny can be found in this isolated, imaginary place, somewhere in Britain:

A nobleman returns to his native land after years of serving his country — in the war, perhaps, or in Parliament. Determined to improve his estate — for the sake of patriotism, duty, benevolence, prosperity, and posterity — the nobleman introduces better agricultural methods. His estate managers, "injurious usurpers of authority, who corrupt the poor," have fled; and his tenants, no longer sunken in "misery, sloth and ignorance," take up their duties honorably. The estate prospers. Barren mountains are clothed with plantations, cattle and sheep graze in sheltered glades, and "furrows of golden ridges appear in wavy parallels" over the sloping hillsides.

In a mountain recess thus surrounded, see the ancient castle arise on an abrupt eminence, which shoots forward from the larger and wooded hills. Near it flows a rapid stream, which has its source amid the distant mountains. From them it flows in a romantic glen, beneath canopies of wood and impending rocks, until, washing the adamantine base of the castle, it bursts into liberty, and forms an ample lake, encircled by the park or forest, and beyond that on one side a fertile plain: all which, from the lake, forms a noble foreground to the distant woods and mountains.

The very seclusion of the parish church, sited on an island in the lake, elicits uncommon reverence and piety from the country folk:

*If the urbane visitors boarding the foreground boat were simple country folk, and if the craggy ruin on a promontory were a church on an island, this view would amply illustrate Loudon's first Utopian idyll, which focuses on the humane, noble landlord.*

Fig. 15
Thomas Allom, "Dunolly Castle, Near Oban."

DUNOLLY CASTLE, NEAR OBAN.

In the still clear morning of "the hallowed day," the rural nymphs and swains, in gay simplicity of dress, meeting the eye in variegated clusters, glide over the resplendent waters in little boats and gallies, directing their progress from different shores to the heaven-pointing spire in the island of pines and cypress. Thence, when the hymn of praise, borne on breezes over the waters, and echoed from the cliffs of the neighbouring islands, has ascended into air, and mingled with the songs of birds and angels, they retire to simple fare in cleanly cottages, sheltered by woods, and decorated with gardens and woodbines.

The nobleman delights in visiting these scattered cottages, noting, along the way, the progress of his trees. He listens to the cottagers' accounts of their progress in herding or fence-mending, and they revere him as their "kind father and protector."

Time passes. With the wisdom gained from living long and traveling widely, the aging nobleman advises his son on the care of the estate. He recommends "a country life, and the constant study of the comfort of all his dependents," as the way to find happiness.

Soon after this he quietly expires on a seat in the Saxon alcove at the end of the western terrace, where in an evening of September he had sat down with his family to admire the splendour of the sky, the gloom of the distant mountains, the reflection of the evening sun, and the lengthened shadow of the islands upon the still expanse of the lake. A few days afterwards, about the same hour in the evening, his remains were conveyed over these waters, and interred in the family vault in the burying-ground, in the presence and amid the praises and tears of every individual upon his estate; for all were present, men, women, and children, even infants upon their mothers' breasts wept aloud from the general sympathy: — all were deeply affected, that all might ever remember their father and friend — he that freed them from villany and oppression — and rendered their lives comfortable and happy.[67]

TOMBEAU DE J.J. ROUSSEAU DANS L'ÎLE DES PEUPLIERS, À ERMENONVILLE.

# 3

## Scone Palace, Picturesque and Romantic

For Scone Palace, Loudon produced an elegant bound manuscript similar to the "Red Books" of his rival, Repton. His intention was to render Scone "the first place in the British empire."

One of Loudon's earliest projects of landscape design was to improve the grounds of Scone Palace, Perthshire, seat of the earls of Mansfield. In 1803, at twenty, Loudon was awed by the commission. He knew something of Scone's illustrious past, and in the natural landscape, he could see Scone's magnificent potential.

Scone, the noble country seat two miles north of Perth, was once the capital of Scotland. Over a thousand years ago, the royal city stood in the small area now covered by a wild garden, a Douglas fir, and an ancient market cross. Even earlier, Scone had been a place of contemplation, a retreat for druids. In the sixth century, Scone was a monastery for the religious order of Culdees. In the twelfth century, it was an Augustinian priory, established by King Alexander I. Robert Bruce and Charles II were crowned at Scone. Macbeth was brought home to die there, and Malcolm was to be crowned there. During the Reformation, in 1559, the fifteenth-century Scone Abbey was demolished by a mob from Dundee. By 1580 the ruins of Scone had become the earldom of Gowrie, property of the Perthshire family of Ruthven. After the mysterious violent deaths of the third earl of Gowrie and his brother, King James VI gave the earldom to his faithful cupbearer, Sir David Murray, in 1604. From that time, Scone has been the seat of Murray's descendants and heirs, who have inherited the titles of viscount Stormont and earl of Mansfield. Today the eighth earl and his family live at Scone, now considered the true home of "every feeling man or woman of Scottish descent."[1]

In July 1803, when Loudon arrived at Scone, summoned by David William Murray, third earl of Mansfield, he found William Atkinson's new castellated Gothic palace of reddish sandstone rising near a fragment of the old mansion. Loudon's former professor, Dr. Andrew Coventry, was soon engaged as an evaluator and agent for reletting the farms on the estate. William Marshall, the agriculturist and rural improver, was consulted on leases and methods of husbandry; and one of his pupils served as estate manager.[2] The tasks of the architect and agriculturists were all fairly well defined. But what was there for a landscape gardener to do?

By contemporary accounts, Scone was already a delightful picture of hills, mountains, cultivated fields, plantations, gardens, and gently undulating lawns sloping down to the river Tay. From the remains of the old

*This view, looking north toward Perth along the river Tay, reveals the woods and fields of Scone Palace in the distance, toward the northeast.*

Fig. 17
Thomas Allom, "Perth."

palace, looking southwest, one could watch the play of shifting lights and shadows on a vast theatre of hills two or three miles away, rising beyond the Tay. Some fifteen miles to the northwest were the Grampian mountains, another theatre whose wings and center stage were plantations and cornfields. Within this cheerful scene of industry and skill, nature had been generous with her favors and her protection, sheltering Scone by means of a barrier of northern hills that kept out the mists floating up the Tay from the North Sea (fig. 17).[3]

The parish of Scone, extending over some forty-six hundred Scots acres, was made up of small villages and arable farms. About three thousand acres were cultivated and seven hundred acres planted with forest trees. The rest was common land and muir. In 1803 the village of Scone had 446 inhabitants, known for their sobriety, industry, economy, and decency. Their exemplary character was traced to a wholesome, well-tended environment, ample employment, and the sterling qualities of the earls of Mansfield.[4] Living within sight of the noble residence and grounds, the Scone villagers maintained neat cottages and gardens, and found employment in husbandry, cottage spinning, trade, and odd jobs. Their village had two broad main streets and several byways, a church, a meeting house, a school, and a market with a fine old stone cross. If the villagers shared a particular attachment to the soil and a keen sense of place, these feelings were deepened by the memory of their ancestors, who had proudly witnessed the crowning of Scottish kings. According to tradition, each one would arrive at Scone for the ceremony with so much earth in his boots "that every man might see the king crowned, standing on his own land." Afterwards, the men would cast the earth from their boots upon "Boot Hill," or "Omnis Terra."[5]

Opinions of the new palace were mixed. Some preferred the noble and venerable air of the old early-seventeenth-century palace. It was a decade or two before writers unanimously praised the newer Gothic structure.[6] The picturesque grounds, however, were always admired. Before Loudon arrived, there were gravel walks near the house, a kitchen garden with walks and flowers, a romantic bower, and a secluded shrubbery, where nature seemed "wanton in all the richness, variety and gaiety of foliage." The nursery was surrounded by tall, stately trees, and a small brook ran through a hollow along its southern boundary. There were no rocks or cliffs, however, and few steep banks, except along the brook. People who looked upon Scone from the opposite side of the Tay could see "every object distinctly, round and swelling to the eye."[7]

Loudon admired the picturesque qualities of the given site, but he would do more to enhance and enliven its romantic character. By extensive planting and thinning of forest trees, he would render plantations and clumps less distinct. Viewed from a distance, the woods, groves, and single trees would seem to blend gradually into more picturesque, irregular masses. He would try to achieve richer, more varied plantations as backgrounds for a few grand objects — a single tree, a conservatory, or the palace itself. And in the foregrounds he would plant lawns with nature's own ornaments — wildflowers — usually seen only in a distant meadow (fig. 18, pl. 3).

In October 1803 Loudon submitted for Lord Mansfield's consideration his "Treatise on Scone," a lengthy, elaborate manuscript similar to the redbooks of Repton, but clearly meant to outshine all previous plans for landscape design. In his elegant, flowing script, Loudon wrote that

*Offering this ideal rendering of Scone Palace in 1811, Loudon reported that his recommendations of 1803 had, in part, been followed — including the planting of thousands of oaks, larches, hazels, beeches, and ash. Ultimately the park was meant to appear as the "venerable remains of a forest," partially cleared for the "comfort and conveniency of man."*

Fig. 18
J.C. Loudon, "Scone."

Scone might become "the first place in the British empire." He promised an unprecedented creation, rich in variety of trees and plants, which would display a "propriety and dignity unparalleled in nature or the works of art."[8]

The treatise also contained Loudon's principles of picturesque improvement, including ideas that he had gleaned from wide readings and visits to some of the celebrated country residences of Scotland and England. He had probably seen the oak groves, rhododendrons, and sloping lawns of Kenwood, another seat of Lord Mansfield, five miles north of London, near Hampstead Heath. He may have visited Painshill, south of London, where the Honourable Charles Hamilton had planted specimens of all the rare hardy trees and shrubs available in Britain in the 1740s and 1750s.[9] If he had not yet seen Downton and Foxley, the Herefordshire residences of Richard Payne Knight and Uvedale Price, he had already adopted their main principles of landscape design. He had also taken some hints from the writings of his eminent rival, Repton.[10] Now, while Loudon's first book was in progress, the "Treatise on Scone" was his first opportunity to declare, in writing, his independence from all practitioners before him.

The picturesque controversy of the 1790s had helped to put Loudon's ideas on landscape design into sharp focus. Forewarned by Price and Knight, he would not tame the grounds of Scone, as Brown or Repton would have done. In fact, he was dismayed to find that one Mr. White had already leveled the banks of the river Tay and screened out views of Perth with thick planting along a rivulet.[11] Loudon would begin by opening up views of a handsome bridge with the town of Perth in the distance; and down by the river's edge, he would plant willows, alders, and wild aquatic plants. He would allow no bald, bare river banks, formal clumps, or harsh edges along graveled or sandy paths. Nor would he sacrifice the essential comforts of his employer. Loudon proposed to make Scone the very epitome of refined country life in a naturally romantic setting. Even the woodlands would appear as the "venerable remains of a forest" now managed "for the comfort and conveniency of man."[12] All would be accomplished according to three main principles: Nature, Taste, and Utility.

Two plans demonstrate the essential changes Loudon proposed for Scone.[13] The first shows the existing landscape of undulating ground, drained by a nearly straight, bare rivulet and bordered by a village and arable fields. Dotted about are circular and oval clumps of trees, single trees, and fragments of ancient avenues, all apparently without connection or strong landscape character. The second plan, of Scone improved, emphasizes the romantic character of a nobleman's great park, with dark woods obliterating any views of cultivated fields and village streets, and with irregular clearings, suitable for grazing. The old tight clumps have been thinned, and the rivulet now meanders through open meadows and shady groves. A figure stands fishing from a small boat near the altered, irregular bank of the Tay. And a new approach road from the southeast allows visitors a first glimpse of the palace as they ascend, "bursting from a noble thicket."

Though the Romantic would prevail, other kinds of landscape character would coexist at Scone improved: the intimate Picturesque, the elegant Beautiful, the gentle Pastoral, and views of the awesome Sublime,

each in separate scenes or views, leading insensibly — or at times dramatically — from one to the other. This idea of a carefully controlled
sequence of scenes Loudon could have borrowed from Stowe or Stourhead,
but his description of the walk through his proposed sequence at Scone
closely resembles one long passage which would appear in his book-in-
progress on landscape gardening: a quotation from Rousseau's friend
Louis-René de Girardin on the romantic landscape (fig. 19).

In his essay *De la composition des paysages* (1777), Girardin contrasts naturally picturesque scenery — which occasionally a poet or a
painter can recreate in a landscape garden — and romantic landscape,
which only nature can offer. Girardin's romantic landscape consists of a
sequence of grand and intimate spaces and includes a walk among dark
pines along a mountainside, views of distant snow-capped peaks, and
frequent glimpses of a nearby stream cascading down a rocky ledge to a
trout-filled lake. There below, a little boat gliding through the waters
carries some young girls — a cottager's daughters, who wear straw hats
adorned only with flowers and who sing in natural harmony, taught only by
birds. Beyond the lake, the stream tumbles over twisted roots and multicolored sands to a bath, among herbs, aromatic plants, and balsam pines.
Further, beyond an oak grove and past an orchard, where trees are laden
with fruit and interwoven with the vine, a cottage appears: a sturdy structure of fir planks with a deeply overhanging roof, and only a trellis for
ornament. Inside, the humble cottage is neater than any palace, and the
food is wholesome and pure. Here, the association of landscape beauty
with honesty and simplicity is complete. "We wish to dwell in these
scenes for ever," Loudon quotes Girardin, "for here we feel all the truth
and energy of nature."[14]

From Scone Palace, a similarly romantic, sometimes sublime landscape loomed in the distance among the Grampian mountains. As Loudon
explained,

There, in sailing from Dundee towards Perth [along the River Tay], the general foreground on each side is a level country covered with corn; the middle
distance rising grounds and hills chiefly under pasturage varied by wood,
enlivened by castles, mansions and villages. Behind these arise a chain of
stupendous mountains, the craggy summits of which are covered with snow,
or lost in white clouds, or sometimes obscured by the distant thunder-
storm.[15]

Loudon's proposed walk through the forested dell (now "Friar's Den") at
Scone also recalls Girardin's romantic landscape. Beneath the shelter of
forest trees, Loudon would plant eglantine and honeysuckle in the borders
of a path which crossed and recrossed a murmuring rill. Below, the rill
would splash into a bath, partially concealed by stones and roots, and
sheltered by a weeping willow. There, a single urn or vase might be placed
beneath the drooping branches. Below the bath, the rill would fall to a
lake, which Loudon would stock with carp and perch; and on Prince's
Knoll he would plant an orchard of fruit trees and shrubs. The trellis-
adorned cottage and straw-hatted peasant girls would not appear in the
private grounds of Scone, however; Loudon was thinking of a few secluded
scenes of a more elegant character. On an eminence near the palace, he
would build a Doric conservatory, to be framed by forest trees and oriented

toward the palace, facing west — to catch the light of the setting sun. Here, rising from the ground on which ancient Scottish kings had received their crowns, would be a shelter for delicate plants, a temple-like edifice (fig. 20) which might compete as an object in the landscape with the finest temples of any British landscape garden — even Stowe!

Thomas Whately, one of the writers Loudon most admired, had once described the effects of the setting sun on the Temple of Concord and Victory, "one of the noblest objects that ever adorned a garden" (see fig. 13). Whately's eloquent description of the fleeting quality of light in that particular setting might still inspire a garden designer:

The setting sun shines on the long colonnade which faces the west; all the lower parts of the building are darkened by the neighbouring wood; the pillars rise at different heights out of the obscurity; some of them are nearly overspread with it; some are chequered with a variety of tints; and others are illuminated almost down to the bases. The light is gently softened off by the rotundity of the columns; but it spreads in broad gleams upon the wall within them; and pours full without interruption on all the entablature, distinctly marking every detail; on the statues which adorn the several points of the pediment, a deep shade is contrasted to splendor; the rays of the sun linger on the side of the temple long after the front is overcast with the sober hue of evening; and they tip the upper branches of the trees, or glow in the openings between them, while the shadows lengthen across the Grecian valley. Such an occasional effect, however transient, is so exquisitely beautiful, that it would be unpardonable to neglect it.[16]

Loudon, setting out to make Scone the *first* place in the British empire, could not refuse such a suggestion (though a Greek temple, with its deeply shaded portico, was hardly the best environment for plants). Aside from this conservatory, he would embellish the park with a few other elements of art, sparingly: one solitary Ionic temple and a prospect tower commanding a single straight avenue through the woods. In the dell, the bath would include one mirror-walled room where the liquid sounds of an invisible self-playing musical siphon (an invention of Italian Renaissance origin) would dispel the gloomy silence.

*One of the inspirations for Loudon's vision of Scone was an essay by René de Girardin, benefactor of Rousseau, and eloquent spokesman for simplicity in the landscape garden. In Rousseau's day, Girardin had engaged bands of musicians to wander in the grounds of Ermenonville, giving concerts in the woods or by the lake.*

Fig. 19 (opposite)
View in the grounds of Ermenonville, formerly the seat of René de Girardin, marquis d'Ermenonville.

*Like the Temple of Concord and Victory at Stowe, poignantly described by Thomas Whately, Loudon's "Doric" conservatory on a knoll would have caught the last rays of the setting sun. Below he intended to plant an "unprecedented" collection of hardy trees and shrubs, arranged according to their "natural connection with each other." (Here Loudon meant to incorporate Jussieu's natural system of classification in his own planting design.)*

Fig. 20
J.C. Loudon, Grecian conservatory proposed for the grounds of Scone Palace.

In the flower garden, the traces of art would be limited to the sandy paths and a single jet of water before the Corinthian temple at one end. Loudon knew that the Reverend William Mason had designed a secluded flower garden with a temple at one end at Nuneham Courtenay, Lord Harcourt's seat in Oxfordshire. He was also aware of Mason's original inspiration — a passage from Rousseau's *La nouvelle Héloïse* (1761), in which the heroine, Julie, leads her former lover through her own secluded garden. Planted and arranged with infinite subtlety, that garden seemed truly wild, like an abandoned clearing in the woods. Saint-Preux, the lover, entered from a grove of trees dripping with garlands of honeysuckle and jasmine, to find a lawn rich with thousands of wild-flowers, wild thyme, wild mint, and marjoram, along with a few garden flowers which seemed to grow naturally with their wild neighbors. A dazzling disorder of shaggy rosebushes, strawberries, elderberries, hazelnuts, and gorse, bordered by meandering mossy paths, lay open to the sun. The fruits of such a garden, scattered and uncultivated, would be all the more sweet for the searching and the selecting. Saint-Preux was enchanted, breathless; on penetrating the sylvan boundary, he sensed that he was the first man ever to enter Julie's garden.[17]

All the art of arranging such a wild garden was so carefully concealed that there was no place for even a jet of water. The flower garden at Scone, then, with its jet and temple, would owe something to Mason, something to Rousseau, and perhaps something to Jacques De Lille, who approved of a jet placed in an unpretentious, natural setting. In his poem, *Les Jardins* (1782), De Lille entered nature's own secluded retreats with reverence. He respected the marriage of woodland trees and water in a brook. Yet, because he could be delighted with the "happy contrasts" of art and nature, De Lille never longed for Rousseau's (or Julie's) illusion of pure wilderness in a garden.[18]

Two eighteenth-century botanists had established the scientific classification that Loudon would adopt in the flower garden. In 1789 Antoine Laurent de Jussieu had introduced the natural system of classification, derived from the planting arrangements of his uncle, Bernard de Jussieu, in the garden of the Trianon at Versailles. This new system revolutionized botanical studies by classifying the natural forms of plants, rather than the abstract characteristics that Linnaeus had classified.[19]

The implications of the Jussieuean system for the *design* of gardens were particularly exciting to a landscape gardener with Loudon's love of scientific order and picturesque compositions. He could now lay out plants according to a classification system that was compatible with a basic concern of the planting designer: the need for harmony among the physical forms and characteristics of neighboring masses of plants.[20] This botanically interesting garden need not appear meticulous; no sharp lines of digging need be visible. Rather, Loudon's masses, or drifts, of flowers of a single species would gradually merge with neighboring masses, creating a gentle union of subtly different forms and colors against a background of turf and perhaps a few single trees or shrubs. Since the whole composition of forms and colors would be one integral work of art, however, no other objects — no urns, statues, or busts — would be allowed. Only a beehive might be added — as an appropriate object in a flower garden.

The lawn of the pleasure ground would never need mowing; it would be roughly textured and multicolored, with white and yellow clover, and patches of thyme, daisies, and saxifrage. A few annual flowers, interspersed among picturesque groups of evergreens in the pleasure ground, would be visible from the palace. Not far from the Grecian conservatory would be another unprecedented scene: as in the garden devoted to flowers, the arboretum would contain a collection of every kind of hardy tree and shrub, arranged in picturesque groups according to the natural system of Jussieu. The trees and shrubs would be grouped by their visible similarities, displaying nature's own harmony of forms — which should please both botanists and lovers of the picturesque.

To carry out these plans, Loudon had to make one disturbing suggestion: that the existing village of Scone be moved some two miles to the east. To encourage villagers to leave the cottages they occupied, Loudon advised that a picturesque new village be built without delay. The old church should be rebuilt on some eligible site in the new village, where trees could be planted and ivy trained along the church walls. The cottagers should all have attached gardens, and their cows might be allowed to graze in Lord Mansfield's park in summer. The new village would resemble the old one, with similar curving roads and the same generous, irregular marketplace where the two main roads converged. Such a "settled and agreeable abode" would be so attractive, Loudon predicted, that the cottagers would gladly exchange their old houses to live there. Should they refuse, however, the old village could be retained (and the Grecian conservatory given up).[21] In any event, the proposed new village should be built, Loudon advised — so that both the new and the old would serve as charming, picturesque incidents along one approach road, preparing, by contrast, for the dramatic moment when the visitor first caught a glimpse of the pre-eminent new palace through the ancient gateway.

Loudon completed his "Treatise on Scone" by repeating that, given full scope to realize his picturesque vision, working from the principles of Nature, Taste, and Utility, he could make Scone the first place in the British empire, unparalleled in nature or the works of art. He was confident that "true" taste had changed since the rise of Humphry Repton, and, in effect, he was also defying comparison with the greatest mature works of Capability Brown.

Two years earlier, in the *Annals of Agriculture* of 1801, Arthur Young had described Brown's work at Croome, the seat of the earl of Coventry, in Worcestershire.[22] Nestled in a valley between the Severn and the Avon rivers, and sheltered by the distant Malvern and Cotswold hills, Croome was considered the "first" of noble country seats. After half a century of maturing, Croome's was a gentle landscape which exerted a subtle mastery over all her visible domain. To Young, even the Malvern hills seemed deliberately placed where they might best complete the prospect as seen from the great house.

When Brown first came to Croome, in 1751, much of the land was a swamp. He raised an "excellent" stone edifice in place of the old red-brick mansion and created a serpentine sheet of water which wound through the park for nearly two miles, effectively draining the estate. Two islands rose in this body of water, "one of the most perfect pieces of garden scenery" that Young had ever seen. Bordering the water were many fine trees, including an eighty-foot cedar, a birch, a Turkey oak, and a triple-thorned acacia. Brown was no botanist; but since his time, Croome had become a splendid botanical showplace, "inferior only to Kew." Apart from the shrubberies, greenhouses, and hothouses, Croome had on its grounds a heathhouse, a conservatory, and an orangerie; a menagerie containing gold and silver partridges and pheasants; an American border with every variety of azalea, kalmia, and rhododendron; and an arboretum with twenty-five varieties of *Pinus*, fifteen varieties of *Quercus*, a *Ginkgo biloba*, and other specimens. In Young's view, nothing was too crowded, nothing jumbled in that fourteen-hundred-acre estate. "All is nature . . . not a thistle or a weed can be seen, not a single tree or shrub is out of its proper place."

If this was an accurate description of Brown's finest and now botanically richest work, then Loudon need not worry. The assorted specimens and the manicured lawns that displayed no weeds or thistles were not a threat to his claims for splendor in a wilder, more romantic landscape, naturally picturesque yet scientifically ordered. In time, Loudon would appreciate the neatness and elegance of Croome. In 1840 he would bring out an edition of the complete works of Humphry Repton, Brown's successor. (New editions of works by Whately, Price, and Knight were meant to follow.) By then Loudon looked back on his own early works, such as *Country Residences*, as juvenile efforts. These were products of his ambitious early years of actively transforming large landscapes and concealing the traces of art in deference to a romantic ideal of virgin wilderness. Years later, particularly in his designs for public gardens and parks, he would not attempt to conceal certain traces of art, such as broad, straight main walks. But as a young man, working in naturally romantic settings, he would be almost as discreet as Rousseau's Julie in her wild garden. At Scone, he would even propose to screen certain farm buildings and cultivated fields with thick planting, and to convert some arable lands to pastures, all for the sake of more picturesque views. Loudon was still learning to balance discretion and concealment in landscape design with a frank admission of human needs and a patient search for the real beauties of a place. Meanwhile, he would experience one of Rousseau's ironic longings: to find truth and nature in a garden which was subtly arranged to give the illusion of all the freedom and grace of nature unadorned, unarranged.

Loudon once walked through a passage of wilderness to which Julie might happily have led Saint-Preux. Somewhere near Edinburgh, on the steep wooded banks of a secluded glen between Leith and Colington, a woman once showed Loudon an enchanting place:

No appendage of greatness can ever disturb its quiet. The surrounding rocks forbid the approach of every kind of carriage, and of almost every animal, except sheep, goats and asses. These may sometimes be seen browsing in the wood, or cropping the green meadow in the centre: hares and game indeed are in abundance, and sport themselves secure from the huntsman, as do the trout in the river unalarmed by anglers. The groves, and hanging thickets on the surrounding banks resound with the notes of the thrush and the woodlark, varied at intervals by the note of the cushat dove; and close upon the ear the hum of the wild bee, in its flight from flower to flower, completes a harmony no less in unison with every thing around, than with the emotions ever felt in

such scenes by minds susceptible of feeling the beauties of nature. For-
tunately, this scene is little frequented because known to a few. . . . I will not
assume the merit of discovering this virgin scene; it was shewn me by a
virtuous and amiable mother, who often used to retire thither to mourn the loss
of a much-loved daughter, and who felt herself consoled by its effects.[23]

And in this little sequestered valley, Loudon, too, may have been consoled, when his plans for the romantic landscape of Scone were not
entirely realized.

By 1806 some of Loudon's recommendations for Scone had been
followed — those concerning the roads, plantations, fences, drainage,
and approaches.[24] In the fall and winter of 1804–05, 40,000 oaks,
70,000 larches, 15,400 hazels, 500 chestnuts, 4,400 ashes, 6,400
beeches, and 400 birches were planted at Scone, all from seed: a total of
137,100 trees. The following year, another 137,050 trees were planted.[25]
By 1811 most of the old village of Scone had been removed to the eastern
fringes of the estate, roughly where Loudon had proposed to build a new
village. The new attached cottages had staggered frontages along a curving street, corresponding to Loudon's sketch plan.[26] There were no evic-
tions from the old village, however; most of the cottagers either sold their
property outright or accepted land in exchange. As long as some preferred
to stay, of course, it was impossible to realize Loudon's imagined sequence of gardens from the wooded dell to the Grecian conservatory on
Boot Hill.

By 1837 a five-acre kitchen garden had been planted, and three one-
hundred-foot-long hothouses had been erected along its north wall. A
flower garden with a fine collection of deciduous shrubs and herbaceous
plants had been laid out. It is not clear, however, whether Loudon's
proposed harmony of color and form, his botanical arrangement, and the
character of his natural wilderness were actually achieved.[27]

Today a wild garden and a pinetum, begun in 1848, are thriving
where Loudon had hoped to see his unprecedented Jussieuean arrangement of trees and shrubs. There are some fine Douglas firs, including one
raised from a seed that David Douglas sent back from the Pacific Northwest to Scone. (Douglas, the plant hunter, was born and reared at Scone.)
All the old cottages at Scone have now disappeared. Today visitors catch a
first glimpse of the palace, not from Loudon's proposed approach road
from the southeast, "bursting from a noble thicket," but from higher
ground further east, ascending along a straight avenue. It is the parkland
that best fulfills Loudon's early picturesque vision of Scone. Thinned from
the old tight clumps, the trees stand as tall, fine frames to foreground,
middle ground, and the distant hills.[28]

Of all his early commissions, Scone Palace seems to have been
Loudon's favorite, the one on which he lavished the most effort and
imagination. In 1811, looking back on his early years of practice, he
chose Scone for an "Ideal Sketch" of an improved country seat for a
nobleman (fig. 21).[29] Had the old palace been preserved, he suggests, a
cathedral-like Gothic addition might have been built to command a view
over a man-made cliff above a lake, formed from a branch of the Tay (see
fig. 18). Some old cottages might remain nestled in the woods near the
palace. At some distance, the woods could have been pierced by a web of
avenues that would rival those of Versailles. Some farm offices might have

*Along with the common British trees for the park, Loudon recommended humble wildflowers for the pleasure ground "lawn" — white and yellow clover, thyme, daisies, and saxifrage. Like the trees, these flowers would be planted in masses primarily of one kind, gradually to merge with masses of another kind. The ideal plan of 1811 includes one major addition — the radiating avenues in the forest.*

Fig. 21
J.C. Loudon, "Ideal Sketch of a Design made in 1803–4, for . . . a park on the Earl of Mansfield's Estate at Scone."

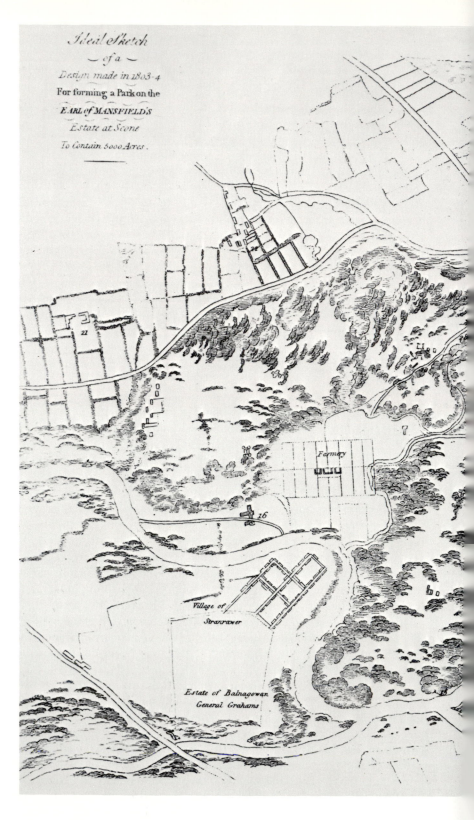

*Ideal Sketch*
*— of a —*
*Design made in 1803-4*
For forming a Park on the
EARL of MANSFIELD'S
*Estate at Scone*
To Contain 5000 Acres.

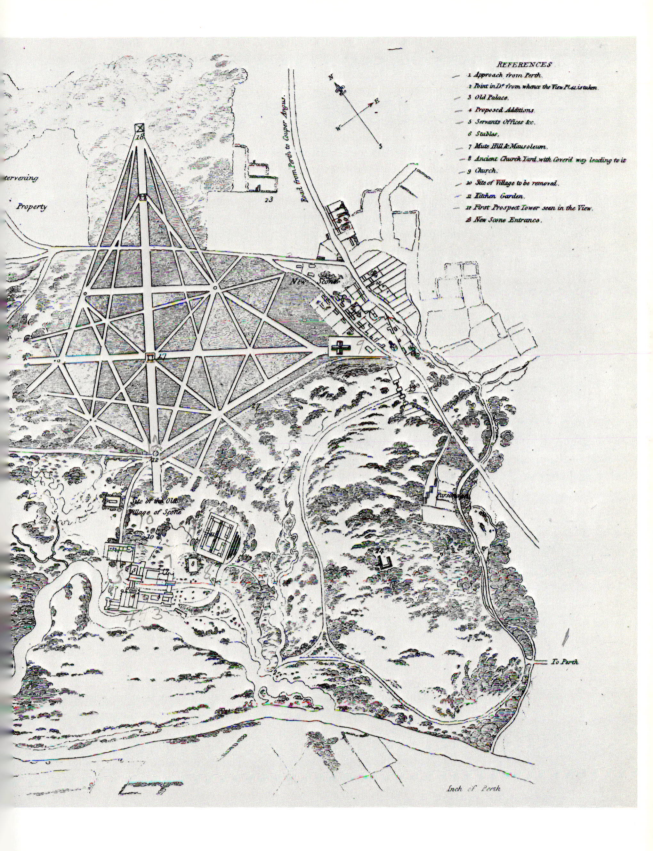

Intervening
Property

New Scone

Site of the Old
Village of Scone

Road from Perth to Couper Angus.

Parsonage

To Perth

Inch of Perth

Fig. 22 (*opposite*)
View from a terrace at Scone Palace, Perth, seat of the earl of Mansfield.

been arranged in a great semicircle, with one diameter of cattle sheds, a central corn thresher, and radiating and concentric sheds, stables, and workshops. (The semicircle was not located on the ideal master plan). In the gardens and park would be scenes which brought to mind melancholy, gaiety, surprise, observation, reflection, and of course — in the agricultural lands — utility. At Scone, Loudon had wanted to compose not simply a great landscape garden, surpassing Stowe, Croome, and other celebrated seats — but a romantic epic, set in a Scottish landscape that resounded with the echoes of a glorious past.

The "Treatise on Scone" reveals some concerns that would remain central to Loudon's vision of rural improvements: the design of landscape scenes in sequence; the emphasis on the natural character, or expression, of a landscape; and the fascination for complete botanical collections, arranged for visual as well as scientific interest. Then, too, for the rest of his life, he would continue to urge that a garden be attached to every cottage. However small, such a portion of the earth's surface would offer every cottager a means of personal expression as well as of subsistence. It seems that, at twenty, Loudon's concern for laborers was not yet truly sympathetic. The Grecian shelter for delicate plants, basking in the glow of a sunset, seems to have taken precedence — at least for one breathless moment while Loudon wrote down his picturesque fantasies. Loudon did make another thoughtful suggestion on the laborer's behalf, however: Lord Mansfield might encourage industry by offering the "dairy couple" a share in the profits of their own labor — a practice described by Columella, Cato, and some British gentlemen.[30]

Taking account of the need of the formidable British navy for wood for ships, Loudon directed the planting of thousands of trees often neglected by gardeners: common oaks, ashes, elms, and beeches. Still, throughout his "Treatise on Scone," he reveals his love for trees as objects of beauty — common forest trees as well as the rare and beautiful specimens in the arboretum. Their aesthetic qualities apparently moved him more than did the quantity of timber they could provide (fig. 22).

At Scone, Loudon would treat the goddess Nature with great respect. He appreciated her useful gifts, but he was more eager to enhance her artless charms. "The whole of my art might be beautifully illustrated by the figure of a Lady," he wrote, "either in full dress or in her natural state." No female nudes appear in his "Treatise on Scone"; instead, Loudon offered the profiles of two women — one with her hair severely pulled back, the other, more beautiful, with soft, abundant curls framing her face. Loudon also offered Lord Mansfield several watercolors of the curly-locked, beautifully contoured landscape of Scone, using the same pale washes and timid deer that Repton had used in his foregrounds. At the same time, Loudon offered persuasive invitations to a new experience of nature subtly enhanced by man. Judging by what he was able to accomplish at Scone, he must have been encouraged. Still, that noble place appears to have been something of a disappointment to him. Like a first love, Scone was an unattainable landscape, which resisted some proposals — and which, to satisfy the lover, was best recollected and recreated in the imagination.

# 4

# Tremadoc
# and the Sublime

Summoned to consult on an
embankment project in a
remote, mountainous region
of North Wales, Loudon
encountered a cultivated,
lively social environment
for which all his studies
and professional contacts
had not prepared him.

*Some people criticized
William Madocks for em-
banking this land from the
sea and thus destroying the
sublimity of tidewater,
cliffs, and mountains. Others, including Loudon,
praised Madocks for introducing agriculture and industry into an economically
depressed land.*

Fig. 23 (*opposite*)
View of Tremadoc, North
Wales, looking toward Mt.
Snowdon.

Night came down on the sea: Rotha's bay received the ship. . . . the moon hid
her red face in the east. A blast came from the mountain . . . "Fly from my
presence, son of night! call thy winds, and fly!"[1]

It was Christmastime in North Wales. The year was 1806. Loudon was a
guest in the fabled land of Ossian and his shadowy warriors of the mist (fig.
23). Gazing northward along the vale of Tremadoc to the peak of Snowdon,
he could study the gaunt Welsh mountain forms in the moonlight. William
Gilpin had been critical; Mount Snowdon, he wrote, was a bleak, dreary
waste, without the rich furniture of forest or rocks that could render
it picturesque.[2] But Gilpin had never seen the Snowdon range from
the sheltered perch of Tan-yr-allt, William Madocks's new villa, which
overlooked the Traeth Mawr sands and the inlet of Cardigan Bay off the
Irish Sea.[3]

Loudon had been invited to Tremadoc in order to advise on
Madocks's latest project to reclaim several thousand acres from the sea. In
return, apart from a fee, Loudon received an introduction to a sublime
landscape and a style of living which he could not have known before, but
only imagined. As his friend Noel Humphreys recounted the story, Loudon was dazzled.[4] From Madocks's villa and the congenial neighboring
homes came the shrieks of heady spirits and the glitter of thousands of
lights — an ironic reflection of the scene once chronicled by the ancient
Gaelic (or Celtic) poet, Ossian:

A thousand lights from the stranger's land rose in the midst of his people. The
feast is spread around: the night passed away in joy.[5]

Now, centuries later, Bacchus grinned from his niche in the hall while
songs were bellowed, trilled, or chanted over bumpers of claret in
Madocks's dining room. Loudon was amazed by the lavish flow of fine
wines and by "the perfect roar of boisterous wit, of the highest class, that
generally accompanied the costly eating and drinking."[6]

For all its wild grandeur, then, for all its poetic associations of a

Fig. 24
The former residence of William A. Madocks, Tan-yr-allt, in Tremadoc.

barbarous age when human passions, in love and war, were fearless and pure, the vale of Tremadoc was no longer a virgin wilderness, invested with supernatural powers, but a land tinged with civilization (fig. 24).

That Christmas season of 1806, one of Madocks's guests especially delighted Loudon. In contrast to the roaring wit of the table, the sweet, clear voice of Elizabeth Billington penetrated the evening mists and consoled a quieted audience for the absence of the nightingale. At the time, some considered Mrs. Billington "the most celebrated vocal performer England ever produced."[7] At Covent Garden in London, starring in an English opera, she had won praise from Haydn.[8] In Naples, Florence, Milan, and Venice, she had sung duets from Italian operas. At Tremadoc she may have sung oratorios of Handel or lighter airs from such comic operas as Isaac Bickerstaff's *Love in a Village*, in which she had played the ingenue, Rosetta, at Covent Garden. Mrs. Billington's lines and lyrics were simple, and the melodies had become favorite old tunes, but her voice Loudon found ravishing.

> Gentle youth, ah, tell me why
> Still you force me thus to fly?
> Cease, oh! cease to persevere;
> Speak not what I must not hear;
> To my heart its ease restore;
> Go, and never see me more.[9]

The white-armed women who kept the fires burning for Ossian's warriors could not have graced the bare Welsh mountains with voices any
more pure.

On this first visit, Loudon was also impressed by his host, William
Madocks, who was then creating a new community in the Welsh wilderness. A young entrepreneur of thirty-three, Madocks was responsible for
the new roads into Tremadoc, for harbors, a canal, cottages with garden
allotments, an improved tannery, a new four-story woolen mill, a vast
reforestation project, and two embankments, which were designed to
reclaim thousands of acres of arable land from the sea. Madocks also
initiated summer horse races, annual fairs, and the weekly markets.
Though not extremely wealthy, he did have some inherited property, as
well as a great deal of imagination and the courage to continue his struggles against both bankruptcy and the unpredictable forces of nature in the
northern wilderness. [10]

In Parliament, Madocks and his friend Sir Francis Burdett were
agitating for reform of the system of representation — against the overwhelming majority, who would rather tolerate a few "rotten boroughs," or
purchased seats in the House of Commons, than invite domestic in-
stability while the nation was at war. (Some members later would be
equally tolerant of the rotten boroughs in peacetime.)[11] Parliamentary
reform was not, however, a major concern of Loudon in 1806. His interests were then focused on agricultural reform, picturesque improvement, and the principles of political economy. Thus, it was not necessarily
Madocks, the radical M.P. for Boston — but Madocks, the philanthropic
improver, the sensitive developer and generous employer — that Loudon
found so impressive. Barely ten years older than Loudon, Madocks became a role model: an energetic, genial man, inspired by a vision of a
productive, dramatic land and inebriated by a variety of the joys of life,
from the sublime and the picturesque to the humane and the absurd.

William Alexander Madocks was the third son of a Welsh barrister
and a merchant's daughter of English and Irish extraction. Born in London
in 1773, he grew up in a Kentish country house that had its own private
theatre. His eldest brother, John, was the squire and his brother Joseph, a
barrister. All three were popular house guests, known for their ready wit,
their singing, and their winsome high spirits. At Wynnstay, the Welsh
seat of Sir Watkin Williams Wynn, near Wrexham, the Madocks brothers
would join the playwright R. B. Sheridan and other guests in amateur
theatricals that lasted for weeks at a time. At home in Tremadoc, Madocks
recreated some of the atmosphere of Wynnstay among his spirited friends,
"the Chaotics," who composed light verse, staged their own private theatricals, and made excursions into the mountains, subjecting themselves,
so they thought, to Death, Rheumatism, and other dangers, all for a
glimpse of the picturesque. [12]

Horace Billington, the landscape painter, a close friend and neighbor of Madocks, used to come to Tan-yr-allt and sketch views of the wild
landscape while the great embankment was still in progress. (Billington's
brother, James, a double bass player, had married the celebrated singer
from Covent Garden.) Another friend, Thomas Love Peacock, came to
Tremadoc in 1811 and immortalized his visit in *Headlong Hall*, a novel in

which no one escaped ridicule, not even such lovers of the picturesque and the sublime as Sir Uvedale Price, Humphry Repton, and writers for the *Edinburgh Review:*

The Dinner

The sun was now terminating his diurnial course, and the lights were glittering on the festal board. . . .

*Mr Mac Laurel*. Really, Squire Headlong, this is the vara nectar itsel. Ye hae saretainly discovered the tarrestrial paradise, but it flows wi' a better leecor than milk an' honey.

*The Reverend Doctor Gaster*. Hem! Mr Mac Laurel! there is a degree of profaneness in that observation, which I should not have looked for in so staunch a supporter of church and state. Milk and honey was the pure food of the antediluvian patriarchs, who knew not the use of the grape, happily for them. — (*Tossing off a bumper of Burgundy*.)[13]

The Chaotics were elitist in one sense: one had to be an "incontestible disciple of Mirth, Taste and irregularity" to enter their circle.[14]

Loudon may have been intimidated. How would these jolly, musical, witty people have regarded him, a twenty-three-year-old Scot from Edinburgh, a Midlothian farmer's son? Would they have recognized him as a promising young author, whose latest treatise, the two-volume *Country Residences,* was dedicated to people like themselves, people whom he had served in his professional capacity as a rural improver? Loudon was not of their world. But he tried to show in print that he could imagine their requirements and their tastes.[15] Although he had occasionally questioned the authority of their reliable guides, Humphry Repton and William Marshall, Loudon took pride in his personal appearance, and he was bright, earnest, willing to listen. Could he fit in?

Loudon was not, by instinct or by breeding, a disciple of Mirth. One wonders whether he had ever stopped to recognize — and admire — such free spirits among the English sons of the gentry and the aristocracy who used to spend a year or two at the University of Edinburgh, between matriculation at public school and Oxford or Cambridge? Madocks, who had gone up to Oxford (Christ Church) during the French Revolution, was now a fellow of All Souls College. He was a good specimen of the typical Englishman who made an appearance at the University of Edinburgh at the end of the eighteenth century, when Loudon was there. Perhaps some of these sons and heirs of landed property sat in on the lectures of Dr. Andrew Coventry, then the only professor of agriculture in the kingdom.[16]

It is difficult to imagine that Loudon would have come to know these high-spirited English students very well. Like most native sons of farmers, Loudon would go directly from the classroom to his lodgings — or to his part-time job at Dickson's nursery. He was engrossed in storing up information from a wide range of arts and sciences, then applying what he had learned in the hothouse or on a client's site. He probably had little time for the clubs and "mutual improvement societies" at the university. (For many years, he would openly disparage societies of all kinds.) At the University of Edinburgh in those days, there were no bachelors' degrees, no exams, no residential colleges, no tutorials. The daily incentives for study had to come from one's own inner resources.[17] On the whole, except for their occasional attendance at lectures, the native Scots found learning a solitary experience.

Edward Topham, an Englishman who had come to Edinburgh in 1774 to "round off" his education, delighted in the company of vivacious Edinburgh gentlemen outside the classrooms. The Scots met one another head on, with quick, penetrating looks. In a severe climate, their fondness for wine and jovial company was eminently tolerable. However they were not, in Topham's opinion, great scholars — in spite of all the time they spent reading, studying, and thinking.[18]

By the time Loudon arrived in Edinburgh, the local reputation for scholarship may have improved. A dry, erudite wit flashed from the pages of the *Edinburgh Review*, that formidable periodical founded in 1802, just as Loudon was about to leave the university town to take up full-time professional practice. Professor Andrew Coventry had moved in the circles of distinguished men of letters such as Lord Cockburn and Francis Jeffrey, the *Review*'s editor, and he may have provided Loudon, a favorite student, with an introduction to the Edinburgh literati.[19]

Whatever opportunities he had had to meet eminent writers and critics, Loudon would have received an education marked by some of the flaws and beauties of the Scottish university system. A Scottish liberal arts education was then criticized for being shallow, "adapted rather for producing a smattering of knowledge on many subjects, than for cultivating habits of careful mental discipline."[20] (Hence some educators' clamor for exams, degrees, and residential colleges). Given the freedoms of the Edinburgh system, however, Loudon was able to indulge his insatiable appetite for knowledge with an enthusiasm not generally cultivated at the English universities. In fact, some Scottish students managed to survive on enthusiasm, independence, lofty dreams — and little else in the way of material comforts. As John Robertson explained, "Seized, perhaps, at the plough, with an enthusiasm for learning, and convinced, that although the attainment is arduous, yet that the consequence is glorious — he redoubles his diligence by day, and his study by night. He disregards the fatigues of his labour, and the poverty of his fare; and looks forward to the evening, when he can unbosom himself to Virgil and Homer."[21]

Something of this personal effort involved in Scottish education — which was then largely self-education — must be understood to appreciate Loudon's awe and admiration for William A. Madocks, an Englishman with a similar, but different, more carefree, kind of enthusiasm for wilderness, industry, and the cultivated good life. The differences between Madocks and Loudon may have been greater than the similarities; for it was not only *what* one had learned, but *how* one had learned, that tended to foster sympathy among strangers. Loudon never knew the Bacchic initiations into the university colleges, where wineglasses had to be surreptitiously emptied beneath the tables if earnest young men wished to stay sober.[22] Loudon did not know the revels, the quiet walks in a courtyard garden, and the long, arduous discussions in students' rooms late into the night, where learning continued and deep friendships were made for life. He was not really prepared, then, to meet the genial human "spirit of the place" at Madocks's sublime mountain retreat. And yet Madocks, in passing and perhaps unconsciously, gave Loudon a few

*To stem tides while work was in progress on an embankment from the sea, Loudon invented this barrier, built of wooden trusses some fifteen to sixteen feet high, covered with boards and oiled canvas or pitched sailcloth. On completion of a segment of the embankment within the barrier, the trussed sections would be moved and realigned to create another enclosure.*

Fig. 25

J.C.Loudon, Embankments, section (marked *fig. 8*) and plan (*fig. 9*) of a recently invented barrier, ca. 1804.

lessons in the high pleasures of life, as the two collaborated briefly in civilizing the landscape.

According to his own account, Loudon had "some share in contributing ideas for these magnificent undertakings" in Tremadoc, including the projected embankment across Traeth Mawr, begun in 1808.[23] Apparently Loudon's first book had initially attracted Madocks's attention.[24] In his *Observations on Landscape Gardening* (1804) Loudon had devoted a long section to land embankments, about which he had learned through trial and error on the estates of Lord Keith and the earl of Selkirk in lowland Scotland. His main premise was that nature's own embankments along rivers and by the sea should be imitated wherever possible, in form, materials, and siting. Since artificial sluices and tunnels were necessary, however, to regulate the ebb and flow of the tides, he had invented an "artificial barrier" to be used during construction, as a temporary shield from the sea (fig. 25).[25]

In the early 1800s the art of embanking land from the sea was not a common practice in Britain. In 1805 the Scottish *Farmer's Magazine*

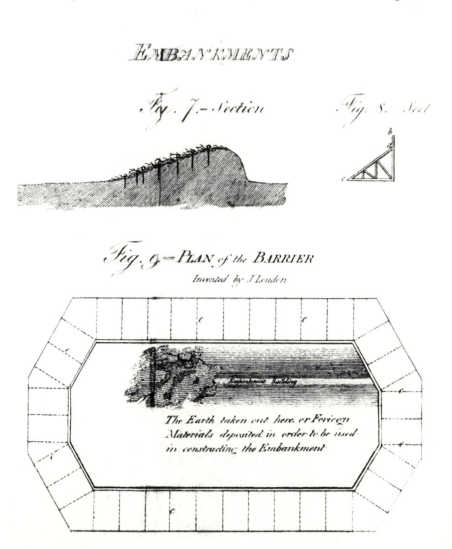

observed that, until recently, the amount of land cultivated in Britain had been considered sufficient for the needs of the country. Wasteland could still be enclosed and cultivated at far less risk and expense than embanked land, if certain legal fetters could be broken. Moreover, the current economic situation — an uncertain wartime economy with inflated paper money and the drain of gold to foreign nations — tended to discourage speculation at great risks.[26] Madocks, in bearing these risks, variously won people's admiration, skepticism, or scorn.

In 1798, after buying some farms along the shore of Traeth Mawr, near Penmorva, Madocks began his enterprise with a dream — to convert the whole estuary, some six thousand acres, to arable fields and pastures. He also wanted to build a town to start up some industries, and to provide a vital link of communication across the Traeth Mawr sands.[27] At that time, the Traeth sands were just barely dry enough for a pedestrian to cross at low tide. At high tide, however, the Traeth was flooded, forming an estuary one mile wide and five miles long, contained on three sides by rocky cliffs and mountains.

By 1800 Madocks and his engineer, James Creassy, had embanked 1,080 acres of the estuary along the northwest shore. Within three years they had planted several different crops in rotation: first oats, then wheat and rape, finally barley and grass.[28] By 1806, when Madocks sent for Loudon, the new town of Tremadoc was already begun. To gain five thousand more acres, Madocks was also building a new embankment, which would carry a road, and perhaps a railway, through Tremadoc, ultimately to connect London and Worcester with Porthdynlleyn (or Porthdinllaen) Harbor on Caernarvon Bay. From there, ships would cross the Irish Sea to Dublin. Tremadoc could then become an important center for transportation and trade, in the midst of flourishing woolen industries, slate quarries, and tanneries. These ventures would bring employment to a generally depressed area, contributing to both local and national prosperity. They would also make Madocks's beloved North Welsh landscape more accessible to travelers, friends, and lovers of the Picturesque and the Sublime.

By the time Loudon arrived, the success of the first embankment at Tremadoc was already a source of local pride, celebrated in the guide books. Roughly parallel to the northwest shore of the Traeth, the embankment was over two miles long and eleven to twenty feet high, facing the sea with a gradually sloping bank of sea sand covered with sods. The second embankment was to run from the northeast to the southwest, spanning the width of the inlet into Cardigan Bay and opposing the full force of the tides. Though only about half as long as the first embankment, the second would be considerably more difficult and expensive to complete.

Madocks persevered after one bill to embank the Traeth had foundered in the House of Commons at the committee stage in 1806. Even the deaths of James Creassy, Madocks's engineer, and of John Madocks, William Madocks's elder brother and financial supporter, did not make the entrepreneur give up hope. With the aid of his steward, John Williams, and his surveyor, Renny Harrison, Madocks finally got his bill passed in August 1807. Henceforth all the Treath Mawr sands and all rentals from the newly embanked land were to be vested in Madocks and his heirs and assignees.

Loudon probably gave Madocks some encouragement before the act of Parliament was passed. A few months later, again at Christmastime, he returned to Tremadoc with his optimistic "Report on the Intended Embankments and Shorelands of Tremadoc," dated 23 December 1807. The expenses of embankment should not exceed twenty-six thousand pounds, Loudon estimated — including an unspecified number of cubic yards of fill, the floodgate with an arch, the railway, the alteration of the course of the brook, and the sowing of five thousand acres of grass seed and oats. The produce of the first year's crop of grass and oats should net within five hundred pounds of the total improvement costs. If the Traeth lands were irrigated or flooded after embankment, the expected return on five thousand acres should be three to four pounds per acre. If the Traeth lands were irrigated or flooded, the lands should still be worth thirty to forty-five shillings per acre annually, for similar profits had been realized at Merse Head, Dumfriesshire, and Cree, Wigtonshire. Loudon knew of no previous embankment that was equally ambitious. However, given the permanent quality of the materials — mostly rock — and the local conditions, the probability of success justified the financial risks.

Not all of Traeth Mawr was originally covered by bare tidal sands. Salt marshes had once covered some of the land recently reclaimed by the first embankment; and some sea grasses remained in the estuary still to be reclaimed. Loudon recalled the rich meadows of Kent and Essex along the banks of the Thames, where art and accident had produced a confluence of about one-third sea water and two-thirds fresh water. At Traeth Mawr, he observed, some of the land might eventually be warped and kept as salt marsh, and the rest irrigated with fresh water for pasture or hay. The seeds of sea grasses from Lincolnshire or Essex, or seeds from a nearby marsh, might be used. Loudon's report contained no mention of wildlife habitats or conservation, per se; his main emphasis was the profitable and productive use of land. The marsh could, of course, provide valuable hay; yet there is a hint of the unworldly gardener in Loudon's suggestion that "nature may be allowed to join her art [to] mature her spontaneous productions" — the sea grasses.[29]

Loudon concluded with some general remarks in praise of the extraordinary scenery, the new roads and industries, and the spirited entrepreneur, Madocks. The town and estate of Tremadoc were, in his view, a "miniature of an agricultural and commercial nation," created for private and public benefit: "It is difficult to conceive any mode of improvement more favorable for public or private advantage for the increase and support of population and the happiness of society."[30]

Attached to Loudon's report was a sketch plan of Tremadoc, now lost, but apparently similar to the "Ideal Plan of Tremadoc" that appeared four years later in his *Designs for Farms* (fig. 26). A conceptual plan, topographically vague, it indicates a regular grid of farm holdings on land reclaimed from the first embankment, meadows in the more vulnerable land sometimes overflown by mountain streams, and the town of Tremadoc, built along a straight road connecting the embankment to the town. Courtyards formed by cottages flank the main road, which terminates at the market place and town hall beneath a precipitous mountain cliff (fig. 27). More cottages, both free-standing and attached, are staggered along a winding road at the base of the cliff.[31]

This ideal plan resembles the actual plan of Tremadoc today, though it presumes a more regular layout and somewhat more growth than Tremadoc ever experienced. The plan also indicates Loudon's proposed diversion of the Glaslyn River (or brook). In 1807 he had strongly recommended that the brook be channeled to a sluice, or floodgate, at the extreme northwest end to take pressure off the more vulnerable central section of the embankment. Had this diversion been effected before the second embankment was begun, Madocks might have saved considerable effort and expense.

After one major disaster — a breach caused by high spring tides in 1812 — the embankment was finally completed, with the aid of some 400 men, 200 horses, and 67 carts.[32] It was never really impermeable to the

*Loudon's idea of "intercepting sewers" for Southampton (later adopted in London) may have originated in his previous experience at Tremadoc. To embank this estuary (to left of inner embankment) from the sea, Loudon pointed out that all inland streams should be intercepted from their normal course across the proposed embankment and diverted to a peripheral canal.*

Fig. 26
J.C.Loudon, Ideal plan of the Tremadoc Estate, Caernarvonshire.

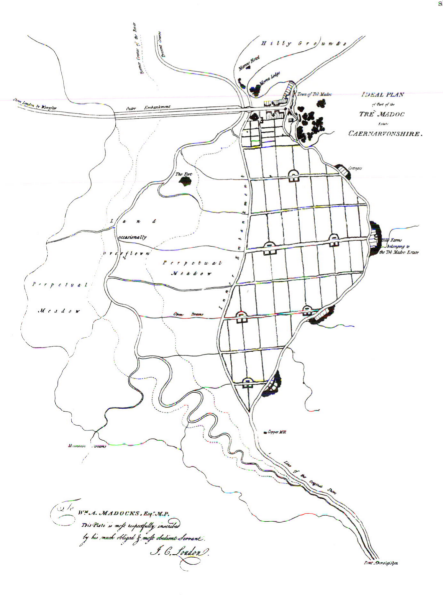

*In Madocks's day, this structure served as Tremadoc's Town Hall. It also contained a dancing room and space for a market or an auditorium. Here Madocks staged amateur theatricals in August 1808. He was also responsible for building comfortable cottages with land attached, a feature Loudon was pleased to report.*

Fig. 27
Market Square, Tremadoc.

force of the sea, however. Madocks's funds steadily dwindled, and some creditors remained unpaid. In the fall of 1812, Madocks rented Tan-yr-allt to a young couple, Percy Bysshe Shelley and his wife Harriet, who remained there less than a year.[33] In 1813, during August, when Tremadoc should have been "in season," the traveler Richard Fenton paused to admire the majestic rocky boundary at the entrance to the Vale of Tremadoc. Arriving at the town, however, he found the inn — which also served as the town hall and theatre — closed. The Gothic stone church was empty; and, at high tide, the sea poured over the embankment, violently dashing against its sides as if impatient to reclaim its former empire.[34]

By 1815 the end of the French wars brought a general economic depression, and Madocks's lands remained a swamp. In 1818 he married a widow of some fortune who took an interest in his projects. By 1824 the harbor of Port Madoc was ready to handle ships. Four years later, Madocks died, leaving his complex enterprise unfinished. The Traeth lands were never completely drained, and today cattle graze there among pools of water.

The town of Tremadoc has changed little since the early nineteenth century. Nearby Portmadoc overtook it in importance and flourished once its harbor and the Festiniog railway were in operation.[35] Today even Portmadoc harbor is quiet, and tourism has replaced the slate trade as the town's major industry. Some local residents regret this new source of wealth and its traces in the landscape: the striped awnings and souvenir shops along Portmadoc's main street, the crowded beaches to the west, and the traffic through the Snowdon mountain range to the north. Even in Madocks's day, some cottagers and landowners resented his intrusions. Two visitors, Shelley and Peacock, recorded differing views.

When he arrived in 1811, Peacock was moved by the grandeur of the wilderness near Tremadoc: "On the top of Cadair Idris I felt how happy a man may be with a little money and a sane intellect, and reflected with astonishment and pity on the madness of the multitude."[36] A few years later, in his novel *Headlong Hall* (1815), Peacock struck a pose of bemused tolerance as he let his characters debate the issue of taming this Welsh wilderness. One cold December day three friends take a walk in search of the Picturesque. They follow a winding road among torrents and cliffs and scale mountains from Bedd Gelert to Aberglaslyn before reaching the great embankment at Traeth Mawr. For one long moment they stand gazing northwards at a scene unique in the British Isles. Their backs to Cardigan Bay and the Irish Sea, they face a range of mountains, which was once reflected in a broad liquid mirror — before Squire Headlong (Madocks) began to drain Traeth Mawr of its tidal waters. The three friends then turn from the muddy plain to the new factories of Tremadoc. Mr. Escot sighs, "I confess, the sight of those manufactories, which have suddenly sprung up, like fungous excrescences, in the bosom of these wild and desolate scenes, impressed me with as much horror and amazement as the sudden appearance of the stocking manufactory struck into the mind of Rousseau, when, in a lonely valley of the Alps, he had just congratulated himself on finding a spot where man had never been."[37]

Mr. Foster looks beyond the Tremadoc woolen factory and tannery to the great triumphs they signify: mechanical power in the service of man, the comforts and conveniences of civilization, and — with employment — the precious gift of life, existence, subsistence. As if to prove Mr. Foster's point, the epitome of snug civilization passes by, in the figure of a rosy-cheeked little girl balancing a basket of heath on her head as she descends along the rocky ravine to their left. Or is she the proof of Mr. Escot's point: that mankind are happy and innocent *before* the taint of men's triumphs over nature? The two philosophers do not stop to inquire into the little girl's means of subsistence, and their companion, Mr. Jenkinson, is silent.

The little girl's father might have been a shepherd, a tanner, a weaver, a stone or slate cutter, or a day laborer. In a mountainous land naturally suited for nothing but grazing or quarrying, jobs were scarce. After the bad harvest of 1799 had left some of the people of North Wales destitute, Madocks's first embankment project created employment and some reason for hope. While critics like Peacock's Mr. Escot might complain, then, the *European Magazine*, among others, would praise Madocks for his spirited service to the community, in spreading industry to such a wild, romantic "desert."[38]

In the winter of 1812–13, when the Shelleys were living at Tan-yr-allt, some neighbors were still skeptical, however, grumbling about Madocks's theatrical friends, who "insulted the spirit of nature's sublime scenery," and about Madocks himself, who had changed a fine prospect into "nothing but a sandy marsh uncultivated and ugly to the view."[39] The poet did not agree. In September 1812 Shelley had praised Madocks in a moving speech before the local gentry of Beaumaris and had helped to raise subscriptions totaling £1,185 for the embankment enterprise. (Shelley's own pledge was £100.)[40] Though Madocks and Shelley had never met, the young poet was then living in Madocks's Welsh home and working on *Queen Mab*, a poem concerned with the end of corruption and ignorance, the restoration of man's natural virtue and happiness, and new kinds of liberty. While Shelley wrote about glorious human potential, there below him, in a splendid panorama, was tangible evidence of the human spirit straining to reach a worthy goal: to hold back some of nature's power for the sake of communication, nourishment, and ultimately the greater happiness of man.[41] Shelley concluded his speech to the Beaumaris gentry with a rallying cry:

How can anyone look on that work and hesitate to join me, when I here publicly pledge myself to spend the last shilling of my fortune, and devote the last breath of my life to this great, this glorious cause.[42]

Four years earlier, at a time when Loudon was no longer involved professionally in Madocks's works, he had paid this calm tribute to the man:

I may surely be allowed, with every feeling and patriotic individual, to express a hope that this amiable and philosophic man, yet in the prime of life, may continue long to enjoy the exalted pleasures which must flow from the consciousness of actions so great and so beneficial.[43]

But what about the factories popping up like fungous excrescences? On the question of conservation, Loudon had no standard response. During his early career, he recognized that "manufactories" posed a threat to fine rural scenery — as he had seen on the river Esk near Roslin, in Midlothian, and along the river Dove, at Matlock, in Derbyshire. Yet he was fascinated by the sight of machinery driven by water or wind in picturesque and romantic landscapes. He recalled that Richard Payne Knight had a fine view of a corn mill at Downton, his castle in Herefordshire. And at Warwick Castle, Loudon had stood before a window in one of the main rooms and gazed upon the driving wheel of a corn mill, enchanted. His only regret was that one could not allow handsome "wind machinery" to be grouped with trees.[44]

Sir Uvedale Price had seen beauty in decayed machinery and delighted in the varied shades of rust and moss. But Loudon liked to see some machinery proudly set in motion. He was dazzled by thousands of lights sparkling against dark mountains. And he was ravished by the sound of a lady's voice, singing in a lonely region too severe for the nightingale to survive. Other minds would immortalize that delicate bird, in poetry and prose. So Shelley wrote, "A poet is a nightingale, who sits in darkness and sings to cheer its own solitude with sweet sounds."[45] Young Loudon was happy just to sit in lamplight, to hear a human voice, and to see a few signs of civilization in an awesome, often monochromatic land.

# 5

# Tew Lodge Farm

As a tenant farmer, Loudon laid out roads, fields, and pastures, introduced new machinery, and built his own home overlooking various prospects: gardens, pleasure grounds, and a productive, somewhat picturesque, agricultural landscape.

For over two and a half years, from 1808 to 1811, Loudon was a tenant farmer at Tew Lodge, Oxfordshire, where he carried out some thirteen thousand pounds' worth of improvements at the proprietor's expense. At the end of his tenure he predicted that, once the trees and hedges had matured, Tew Lodge Farm would become the most magnificent *ferme ornée* in England (fig. 28, pl. 4).[1]

Perhaps Tew Lodge never rose to such magnificence, but this kind of optimism appears throughout Loudon's writings. In 1808 he advised that spirited men should come to England to find the most profitable markets for their skill and capital — in agriculture.[2] In 1825 Loudon was still encouraging young agriculturists:

There is scarcely anything a rational man can desire that he may not obtain, by maintaining on his mind a powerful impression of the necessity of obtaining it; pursuing the means of attainment with unceasing perseverance, and keeping alive that enthusiasm and ardour which always accompany powerful desires. . . . *The grand drawback to every kind of improvement* is, the vulgar and degrading idea that certain things are beyond our reach.[3]

*Ascending the terrace walk, the visitor would pass an avenue of fruit trees and clumps of strawberries before arriving at this more polished scene of flowers and shrubs.*

Fig. 28
J. C. Loudon, "Garden Front of Tew Lodge."

*Garden Front of Tew Lodge.*

Loudon's readers included some English landlords who preferred not to grant long leases to their tenants; they wanted no long-term commitments to a farmer who might turn out to be ignorant, indolent, resentful, or dishonest.[4] Impatient with these preconceived notions, Loudon urged that ignorance and indolence be eradicated, not assumed. All tenant farmers, according to their abilities and ambitions, should have both received substantial formal education and had some practical experience as common laborers by age twenty-five. Even sons of landed gentlemen should work as plowmen or servants, he advised, before assuming their responsibilities as lord of the manor. Loudon had already gone through such an initiation in his youth alongside the laborers on his father's farm. Though determined not to follow in his father's footsteps, he did return to the plow, briefly, as a twenty-five-year-old tenant farmer eager to realize new efficiencies and productivity on some eighteen hundred acres and fortunate to have the financial support of his landlord, General George F. Stratton.

It was Arthur Young, secretary of the Board of Agriculture, who first advised General Stratton to improve the management of his estate at Great Tew. While compiling his survey of Oxfordshire in 1807 or 1808, Young came to Tew and informed Stratton that, under proper management and twenty-one-year leases, his estate might be nearly doubled in value.[5] A short time later, Stratton noticed Loudon's most recent treatise, *An Immediate and Effectual Mode of Raising the Rental of Landed Property* (1808), and he summoned Loudon to appraise Great Tew.

Loudon advised Stratton that, with "Scotch" husbandry and 21-year leases, the total rental of his agricultural lands could be raised from £4,000 to £10,000. Further, Loudon offered to become a tenant himself, at the increased valuation. Stratton could not refuse. He offered to all of his tenant farmers who held leases the chance to sell them back at the increased valuation or for a fixed price. Some refused; four were willing to sell. The few who held their land "at will," without leases, were obliged to quit at a year's notice. Within a few months, then, at Michaelmas (29 September) 1808, Loudon came into possession of 859 acres. As other farmers' leases fell in, Loudon would assume larger holdings. By 1814 he was to have a total of eighteen hundred acres.

Under the terms of Loudon's lease, Stratton would underwrite the cost of a new house, farmyard, water-driven threshing machine, garden, rickyard, and pond — all to be built according to Loudon's plans. Stratton would also repair the old farmhouses, ditches, and fences; plant new fences; build new roads; drain the farmland; and pay for the digging and burning of lime, which Loudon would pay back at 5 percent interest.

Stratton's decision to adopt "Scotch" husbandry made significant changes in the landscape. Within a few years, two Scottish farmers, Loudon and Stenhouse Wood, would take the place of sixteen English farmers on 3700 acres of arable and pasture land. Fewer than 100 large fields would replace 201 smaller ones. Formerly, 87 horses and 10 oxen had been used to draw 24 plows. Now, with two-thirds more land under cultivation, 70 horses would draw 34 plows. The depth of plowing would increase from three inches to between five and nine inches; and a more regular rotation of turnips, grain, and clover would be adopted.

These alterations changed the general appearance of the countryside. Although Wood's holdings remained in arable fields of about the same size, Loudon's lands were transformed from small pastures to larger arable fields. Pleased with the changes, Stratton commented:

All the trees that were in the hedge-rows are left standing, and have a more picturesque effect than they had, which is increased by that of the new roads, which serpentine round the farm on the sides of the hills, (that the level may be kept), and appear like rides through an arable *ferme ornée*. The reservoir for the threshing machine has also a very good effect on the prospect, as water was before much wanted to enliven the scene; and the new farm-house, which stands on the brow of a hill, commanding a beautiful valley, and a view of a great part of the farm, is also a very ornamental object.[6]

Loudon's *ferme ornée*, or ornamented farm, was a modest venture compared with the much larger, more elaborate park farms at Woburn, in Bedfordshire, and Holkham, in Norfolk (fig. 29). He appreciated their integration of practical farming and picturesque landscape design on a grand scale. Woburn, seat of the duke of Bedford, particularly impressed Loudon with its display of "mind and dignity" and its "patriotic exhibitions of agricultural skill and produce."[7] But Philip Southcote's small, early eighteenth-century *ferme ornée* in Wooburn, Surrey, would have been more comparable to Tew Lodge in scale and original aspirations. Southcote had originally wanted simply a garden and a circumferential walk round his farm for convenience and pleasure. Over time, however, he added flowers, temples, and a canal, all of which would recall to Horace Walpole "the habitation of such nymphs and shepherds as are represented in landscapes and novels, but do not exist in real life."[8]

In contrast, Loudon aimed for simplicity, durability, and just enough elegance to distinguish Tew Lodge from an ordinary farm. His new, nearly level roads following the hilly contours might look as if they were winding and picturesque; they were meant to accommodate a loaded cart drawn by a single horse. To create larger arable fields, Loudon had to pull up some of the picturesque old hedgerows, but he planted new ones, laid out as shelters from the prevailing north and east winds. To prepare for plowing, he had to fill in the gutters and ravines that had scarred the old pastures. And in the center of the farm, on a wide valley floor, Loudon had Stratton drain the land to prepare the site for his new farm buildings: the long ranges of stables and offices that would enclose three sides of a quadrangle. On the fourth, open side, Loudon laid out a spring-fed, cement-bottomed oval pond (not a more picturesque stream or lake) for washing horses' legs after a day's work.

The farm buildings, as seen in Loudon's renderings of 1811, are faintly reminiscent of an Italian villa, with low-pitched, hipped and gabled roofs, and plain stuccoed walls occasionally relieved by an arch (see fig. 29). A clock tower rises in the central mass, dominating the one- and two-story wings. The main architectural lines are horizontal, however, accentuated by the long, low roofs. The overall effect, Loudon noted, was one of "lightness and Doric simplicity," made possible, in part, by the use of light, nearly flat, tar-paper roofs. Loudon had not invented these roofs of paper (or cardboard) coated with a mixture of tar, pitch, powdered charcoal, and lime. But he knew that they had held up well in various parts of the kingdom, having covered a church in Dunfermline, Fife, for forty years, and warehouses in Greenock, Deal, Dover, and Canterbury

The panoramic views reveal
many more single trees than
an efficient Scottish farmer
would leave in his cultivated
fields. Remaining from up-
rooted hedgerows, these
oaks and elms were left
standing, however, for their
picturesque appeal. Those in
pastures also sheltered cattle
from summer heat and
winter storms.

Fig. 29
J.C. Loudon, "General Elevation of the Farm Buildings,"
and two panoramic views at
Tew Lodge Farm.

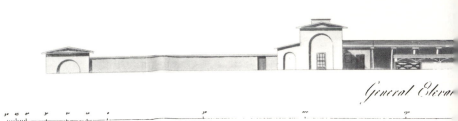

*General Eleva*

*Panoramic view of the Farm, & Far*

*Panoramic view of the farm, farm build*

*Farm Bildings, at Tew Lodge.*

*...ings, at Tew Lodge, taken from the entrance front of the farmhouse.*

*...use, at Tew Lodge, taken from a field opposite the house.*

*The novelty of Loudon's stark, unornamented rendering of his first home in England — Tew Lodge — owes something to the materials he specified: tar-paper roofs for durable, light construction, and floor-to-ceiling windows, or French doors.*
Fig. 30
J.C. Loudon, "Diagonal Elevation of Tew Lodge from the North East."

*Gandy's crisp shadows, stark horizontal forms, irregular massing and picturesque settings may have inspired Loudon's architectural designs at Tew Lodge.*
Fig. 31
J.M. Gandy, "Four Cottages," ca. 1805.

for ten or twenty years.[9] Assuming they were also economical, he specified paper roofs not only for his farm offices and sheep houses but for his own house, as well — where their light weight allowed him to construct thin load-bearing walls and floor-to-ceiling windows.[10]

Loudon's renderings of Tew Lodge (fig. 30) and its farm buildings bear some resemblance to the unornamented, highly abstract architectural designs of J.M. Gandy.[11] In many of Gandy's renderings, there is a strong three-dimensional geometry that Loudon would have found appealing, for he believed that domes and circles were inherently beautiful. Loudon also recognized the economy of geometric forms, for when a structure approximates the sphere or the cube, a large volume can be enclosed within a relatively small "shell," requiring, as a rule, fewer construction materials. In fact, in both of the houses Loudon designed for himself, at Tew and in Bayswater, the main central mass was nearly a cube.

Among the picturesque and symmetrical designs for houses in Gandy's *The Rural Architect* (1805), was one dramatically horizontal design for four cottages in a single structure — which even today seems remarkably "modern" (fig. 31). Loudon may have been intrigued by this design; and he probably admired Gandy's crisp graphic style, which emphasized the bright, sunlit surfaces that projected from the shadows of deep recesses, beneath long, low overhanging roofs. Loudon's own "Diagonal

Diagonal Elevation of Tew Lodge from the North East.

Four Cottages

Elevation" of the farmhouse, glasshouse, and appendages at Tew Lodge is rendered in a similar style, with crisp shadows, projecting masses, unornamented windows, and dramatically horizontal lines (fig. 30). Years later, Loudon alluded to Gandy as a "first-rate architect," but he never revealed the sources of his own architectural designs at Tew.

Loudon's farmhouse was probably without precedent among the houses and cottages of stone, brick, stucco, thatch, and slate that he would have seen during his travels in England and Scotland. (Gandy, a prolific designer, was not given the opportunity to build many of his projects,[12] so Loudon may never have seen any of his realized buildings.) The direct precedents for Loudon's house at Tew were probably in North Wales, among the villas which William Madocks had created for himself and for his friends.

The visual impressions Loudon had received in North Wales during the two Christmas holidays in 1806 and 1807 would have been fresh in his memory when he took up his lease at Tew in September 1808. Madocks's own villa, Tan-yr-allt, was a long, relatively low stone building, enlarged from a sturdy Welsh cottage of stone and slate, sited on an eminence backed by rocky cliffs (see fig. 24). The old and the new parts of the house would have been lime-washed in order to present a white or pastel exterior against the natural grey-green background of mountain ledge and foliage.[13] The modern addition was given a new lightness and openness by the use of long verandas and large, south-facing windows that afforded stunning views of mountain, sand, and sea. The result was a structure that was unique in its environment, where most cottages were small, buttoned-up dwellings, oriented for shelter rather than for views. Yet, as the *European Magazine* observed, Madocks's house, too, was "built more for a convenient residence than for splendour or show."[14] Its massing was simple, pleasing. The home was unadorned with columns, cornices, pilasters, Gothic labels, tracery, or any other stylistic ornaments.

When the traveler Richard Fenton first saw Tan-yr-allt, he thought the house and its surrounding veranda "singular," particularly because of the shallow pitch of the roofs.[15] Madocks had used unusually large, yet relatively light slabs of Welsh slate from Lord Penrhyn's quarries near Bangor. Loudon achieved a similar effect from shallow-pitched roofs at Tew by using large pieces of tar paper of about the same dimensions as the slate used at Tan-yr-allt. Like Madocks, Loudon confined his chimneys, where possible, to the inner walls. He used Madocks's term "lean-to" to describe the veranda at Tew Lodge. And, like Tan-yr-allt, his farmhouse had tall double windows (or French doors), which conveyed some expression of the openness and genial hospitality which he had received at Madocks's home in North Wales.

At Tew, Loudon was not simply copying some verandas, windows, and roofs he had seen over the Christmas holidays. He was designing his first home, inspired by recollections of a house, a gentleman, and a certain style of life to which he might like to become accustomed. At twenty-three, Loudon had been impressed by Madocks, his enterprises, his achievements, his philanthropic spirit, and his friends. Later, Loudon wrote of the "high pleasures of a select society" which Madocks had added to the rural quiet and agricultural comforts of the country. He recalled that Madocks could look out from his front windows, or stand beneath the lean-

*Between the house and the area devoted to kitchen and botanical gardens, Loudon laid out what he had dreamed of creating at Scone — a collection of hardy plants arranged on the natural system of Jussieu. Here the "relative proportion of hardy plants and trees reared in Britain, and in each class and order, is indicated by the size and group devoted to it."*
Fig. 32
J.C.Loudon, "Working Plan of the Gardens and Pleasure Grounds at Tew Lodge," 1810.

to of his mountain retreat, and look down on a prospect of "art, industry and cultivation." Now the young Scottish farmer could look down from his own sheltered hillside home and enjoy an equivalent prospect, more intimate in scale, from Tew Lodge.[16]

Loudon's gardens and pleasure grounds lay on rising ground around and above the house. The working plan shows a basically axial organization of the various specialized gardens with a system of paths oriented along two perpendicular "spines" that visually hold the entire composition of gardens together (fig. 32). At the same time, all the straight lines of the gardens are skew to the main lines of the house. What holds these two large parts together, each organized on its own grid, is the circumferential path that follows a serpentine line near the house, then straightens out as it merges with the gardens. It is a beautiful plan, as a whole, reconciling picturesque and geometric design on paper — although some of the details are somewhat crude. Unfortunately, nothing remains on the site to judge Loudon's efforts to create a sequence of scenes and three-dimensional spaces.

The specialized gardens were all laid out for a display of horticultural treasures, each to be studied as an individual specimen. The stranger could quickly grasp the whole by following the shortest circumferential path. Most views from the house to the gardens were meant to be picturesque, however; and masses of shrubbery screen the bolder geometries — which could only be seen obliquely from the house.

In the foreground, between the house and the specialized gardens, was a lawn where broad, irregular masses of plants and trees were ar-

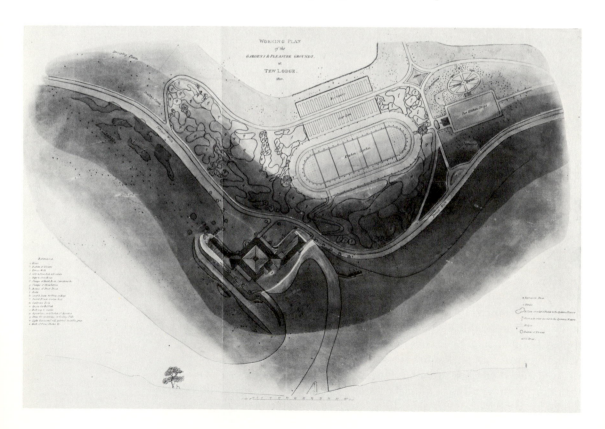

ranged according to the natural system of Jussieu, recalling Erasmus
Darwin's botanic garden at Lichfield, as well as Loudon's previous efforts
at Scone Palace.[17] Here, the *size* of each mass of different plants was
meant to indicate the relative *proportion* of the specimens cultivated in
Britain in Loudon's day. In a landscape much less romantically picturesque, then — with much greater control over the results — Loudon
again tried to create his complete collection of "useful, ornamental, and
curious" plants.

Is it possible that Loudon actually completed these gardens and
pleasure grounds during his two and a half years of active farming at Tew
Lodge? At one time, he had 132 workmen under his direction, some of
whom must have been employed as gardeners. Still, his own description of
the farm and gardens, written in 1811, is impressive enough to raise a few
doubts: Was he describing Tew Lodge Farm of the future, rather than the
place in front of him? He wrote:

Few walks can be more interesting, whether to a farmer, botanist, or admirer
of inland scenery, than the terrace leading from the right and left of the house.
On the one side is this botanical shrubbery, rising on a steep bank of turf, and
every step presenting new dispositions of groups, new shapes of glades and (to
the discriminating eye), new instances of the endless variety of nature. On the
other, a sudden and continued steep, covered or varied, by groups of trees
and shrubs, till it descends to the lake. In the middle distance, the lake, the
buildings, roads, pastures stocked with cattle and sheep, and arable fields,
undergoing the agricultural operations of twenty teams. In the distance, a
continuation of rich pastures, wooded hills, farmhouses, churches and villages;
terminating in woods and hedgerows, which retire from the eye as they
diminish in brilliancy, till they are lost in the mist of the encircling
horizon.[18]

Loudon's renderings of Tew Lodge in its mature landscape setting
must be an idealization of what he actually experienced. In a rendering
called *East Front of Tew Lodge* two men on horseback have paused, and
one gestures towards the cows, the sheep, and the cultivated valley below
(pl. 5). A farmhand leads a two-horse cart loaded with hay. In another
view, the men on horseback take no notice of the gentlefolk strolling along
the grounds of the "garden front." Two individuals gesture toward particular shrubs, while their companions look on. A parson converses with two
women. On the veranda, a young man slips an arm around a young lady's
waist. The setting is faintly Arcadian, but the landscape shows signs of a
new nineteenth-century ideal, as yet undeveloped and unarticulated. In
the background, trees and shrubs are disposed in picturesque groupings,
approximating the chance compositions of a natural landscape. In the
foreground, equidistant circles of flowering shrubs are displayed along
the broad, curving approach road. This obviously artificial planting near
the house would later be considered "gardenesque."

The term *gardenesque* did not appear in print until 1832, when
Loudon first defined it.[19] In 1811 Loudon was still closely following the
lead of Uvedale Price and Richard Payne Knight, particularly in the
extensive gentleman's park and pastures. By this time, however, Loudon
was coming to recognize, and act upon, one commonsense principle of
Repton: that comfort, convenience, and neatness were more important
than picturesque appeal for certain uses and human needs. Loudon had

not yet developed a new manner of landscape design, but with a horticulturist's eye for the beauty of individual plants, trees, and shrubs, he saw the possibilities for modifying the picturesque ideal of rugged, untamed, luxuriant landscapes. As early as 1804, he, like Price, had not fully accepted Knight's ideal of brambles, wild flowers, and overgrown shrubbery brought right up to the house. In contrast to the wild, more luxuriant picturesque setting, Loudon would recommend some "decidedly beautiful" flower gardens and, nearest the house, some well-kept paths and a smooth lawn for relief and repose.[20]

In the larger landscapes of country residences, Loudon would always follow the picturesque principles of unity, variety, harmony, contrast, grouping, the imitation of nature, and respect for the genius of the place. The farm, however, demanded economy, utility, convenience, and productivity. At Tew Lodge, Loudon tried to achieve a balance among all these principles, and he aimed for a degree of refinement which Repton had thought self-defeating on a working farm. Tew Lodge was to be practical and profitable, but to include some glimpses of highly kept gardens and picturesque passages of scenery in the agricultural landscape. Though the different interests of farming, landscape gardening, botany, and horticulture would be served in separate scenes or areas, a few scenes would be visible simultaneously, designed so that their juxtaposition could be harmonious, not jarring. Emerging near the house was the gardenesque, a manner founded in the concerns for use and scientific observation. And Loudon's vision of landscape beauty was expanding — of necessity.

Tew Lodge Farm was also the setting of an educational experiment, perhaps the first of its kind in England.[21] In 1809 Loudon established a small agricultural college where the sons of landed gentlemen and practical farmers could observe "plain northern farming, carried on in an extensive and scientific manner." The prospectus, entitled *The Utility of Agricultural Knowledge to the Sons of the Landed Proprietors of England, and to Young Men intended for Estate Agents* (1809), outlined the types of instruction which Loudon and his bailiff would provide. Students would live on the farm, participate in all the various operations, and keep a daily journal. They would have access to the best authors on rural affairs, gardening, planting, architecture, political economy, and statistics. Loudon would lead field trips to other farms and landscape gardens. He would also give lectures on the site; and he explained his own role: "Like the Druids [the director] would sometimes officiate under a spreading oak, or like the modern field preachers (whom posterity in some future aera may view through the perspective of ages with druidical veneration) under the shelter of a hedge. Occasionally the peripatetic practice would be preferred. . . . possibly on horseback, for a discussion of trees and timber plantations."[22]

Ultimately it was general principles, not simply Scottish practices, that Loudon hoped to infuse into the minds of his pupils. The young men who came to Tew for agricultural studies would see a landscape of small hills and valleys that presented some natural obstacles to cultivation — as well as some natural opportunities for "ingenious design." Loudon's Midlothian methods of farming, developed on more expansive, relatively flat land, could not be imposed directly on this part of Oxfordshire; but some

general principles could be applied. Students would observe, and participate in, a process of subtle and dramatic change on the land. They would
discover for themselves the means of adapting any kind of land for the
greatest advantage, public and private. And they would learn this by
attention to *things*, as well as to words.[23]

Loudon believed that tangible things could be more effective for
teaching than words and images alone — a notion he may have found in
the writings of Count Rumford.[24] Loudon had already used models of
proposed improvements to help persuade a proprietor. Early in 1805 he
had invented a collapsible, three-dimensional model of an estate, in
which the trees, hedges, rivers, roads, and buildings were shown to scale
on a contoured, colored surface. Though it was bulkier than its accompanying working plan, the model was divided into parts that could be
stored in a small chest, then reassembled in a few seconds. Loudon gave
Sir Hew Hamilton Dalrymple one of these models when he recommended
improvements on Dalrymple's estate in North Berwick. Another model, of
Tew Lodge Farm improved, he sent to the National (Royal) Institution,
along with his model of a sheep house covered with tar-paper roofs.[25]

At Tew, Loudon could introduce students to agricultural studies
among the "visible and tangible" implements, machines, buildings, and
vegetation of a modern working farm. There were several places for experimentation, such as in the nursery, where Loudon planted currant
bushes, hoping to make wine. In the botanical garden, he sacrificed some
picturesque effects for the sake of scientific classification. Near the arable
fields, however, he preserved patches of picturesque wilderness wherever
the land was too steep for the plow — in dells, for instance, where the
game could find shelter, and in the furzy knolls, for the fox.

One "old-world" relic he would not preserve: the old pollarded
trees, some infested with vermin, others merely ignoble, deformed by
scars and stumps, fit only for firewood. Loudon began a crusade against
these pollards, which he considered an ugly menace, unless they could be
trained into timber trees. In general, the pollard's prolific roots drew too
much nourishment from the soil of Loudon's model farm. As Noel
Humphreys later explained, Loudon "had thrown all his best energies into
those improvements, and never lost sight of his great principle that 'tillage
should beautify the land' and not disfigure it; in short, that the farmer
should be at the same time a landscape gardener; because, labour being
the highest of all human vocations, it ought to be invested with beauty."[26]

At Tew Lodge Farm, Loudon assumed responsibility for the well-
being of his laborers. Some of the bachelors had high, dry, well-ventilated
accommodations on the farm; their lodgings were on the second floor,
above the new stables. Loudon gave the men milk, vegetables, and oatmeal (if they would have it). After balking at first, several of his young
English laborers learned from their Scottish co-workers and eventually
developed a taste for oatmeal. Then, too, like the Scots, they began to save
their money instead of squandering it on washy beer at the alehouse.
Loudon had set up his own brewery on the farm to supply that wholesome
beverage now so much appreciated: "real ale." Loudon offered to sell his
men sheep at below market prices, and they consumed about one sheep
each week. They began to dress better and read more. All in all, Loudon
could feel somewhat responsible for the development of his laborers'

"whole faculties" of body and mind.[27] Was this the way he was meant to benefit his fellow man? Or, in spite of the satisfactions of farming, could he have been growing restless?

In the prospectus for his agricultural college, Loudon had alluded to the "more active and extensive range of a beloved profession" (landscape gardening) that he apparently had no intention of giving up. Noel Humphreys explains that at one time, while his health was poor, Loudon had planned to sublet his holdings; he would maintain his permanent residence at Tew Lodge. After two and a half years of farming and experimenting, he did sublet some of his holdings, and made a considerable sum. Then General Stratton, hoping to realize a profit himself, offered to buy back Loudon's lease, stock, and total interest. This offer posed a question: Did Loudon still intend to make Tew Lodge his permanent home? Had he planted trees and shrubs in order to enjoy them in his old age? A gentleman farmer's life could be arduous, though agreeable. While Loudon still felt a few pains from his bad left knee, the French horn and the speaking trumpet allowed him to stay on the veranda and call out directions to the bailiff or the laborers in the farmyard below. In the end, however, Loudon accepted Stratton's offer to buy back the lease of Tew Lodge Farm. The agreement was concluded in February 1811 to their mutual satisfaction.[28]

It is not difficult to understand the good relationship between Stratton and Loudon. Both appreciated the utility and beauty intended to be combined on a fairly large scale at Tew. Both were hoping to realize a profit while supplying their warring nation with more grain. In 1810 Stratton insisted that he did not mind the extra expenses that Loudon had incurred for improvements — more than three times Loudon's original estimate of four thousand pounds. He appreciated Loudon's conscientious offer to share more of the expenses than their original contract required.[29] And he shared Loudon's confidence. Neither proprietor nor tenant could have forseen the rapid fall in prices and land values which would begin once the Napoleonic wars ended. In his letter to Sir John Sinclair of 12 March 1810, Stratton was still optimistic and claimed credit only for his perseverance in the face of opposition to his agricultural reforms:

I can only add, that the whole system which I am now pursuing, is entirely owing to the suggestions of Mr Loudon, who has the entire merit of planning it, and to whom I must give the credit of finally opening my eyes to the real value of my estate. . . . the reign of prejudice is rapidly declining in power, and . . . many of my neighbours are rapidly adopting that grand support of Scotch husbandry, the two-horse plough. I begin to feel sanguine hopes that the county of Oxfordshire will, in course of time, be as pre-eminent in agriculture as its university is in learning, and that the rest of the country, following its bright example, will adopt a system of husbandry, which will provide ample resources for its increasing population, without being under the necessity of applying to foreign nations, for their permission to import the first necessaries of life.[30]

Ultimately, Tew Lodge Farm was not a financial success for General Stratton. Looking back in 1825, Loudon admitted that his own efforts at Tew would long (and incorrectly) be remembered in Oxfordshire as a "ruinous project of wild adventurers."[31] He regretted that the amiable and patriotic General Stratton had suffered financial losses, but the stakes and risks had been high. Other proprietors and farmers had suffered, too, during the postwar years.

By surrendering the lease on Tew Lodge Farm in the spring of 1811, Loudon appears to have realized a profit. He never expressed in print, however, what he felt upon leaving his home, his farm, and his gardens. He did note that the principal kitchen garden contained "a specimen of every fruit tree, fruit shrub and culinary vegetable known in Britain, with very few exceptions." Today all that remain of the gardens of Tew Lodge are the exotic evergreen trees and rhododendrons.[32] A noble cedar of Lebanon crowns the hill just above the wildly overgrown site of the vanished farmhouse. One of the few structures that remain, an old stone barn in a hollow, obscured by trees, is not of Loudon's design. Barely rising above the summer foliage, the old barn seems a part of the earth itself.

It has sometimes been assumed that Loudon had a hand in designing the "unforgettable" village of Great Tew, Oxfordshire (fig. 33).[33] Considered one of the most beautiful and unspoiled villages in Britain, with its cottages dating from the sixteenth through the early nineteenth centuries, Great Tew was designated "of outstanding interest" by the Department of the Environment of Great Britain in 1978.[34] To date, no evidence of Loudon's involvement in the village of Great Tew has surfaced. The cottages, however, simple in massing and detail, bear some resemblance to his earliest designs in *Country Residences*. Many are "clothed" in the vines and shrubbery with which young Loudon liked to decorate houses. Their siting would also have pleased him. While a few cottages are free-standing, others are attached, lining a sloping, curving lane. All are nestled, like the remaining old stone barn, in a landscape that has withstood social and economic changes more dramatic than Loudon ever knew.

*Considered one of the most beautiful and unspoiled villages in Britain, Great Tew was designated "of outstanding interest" by the Department of the Environment of Great Britain in 1978.*

Fig. 33
Cottages at Great Tew, Oxfordshire.

# 6

## Architecture and the Beautiful Economy of Nature

Before he ever dreamed of an architecture free of historical styles, Loudon assisted a master builder of hothouses. In time he recognized some intriguing relationships between architecture and horticultural engineering.

While still a schoolboy in Edinburgh, Loudon learned about buildings from two men who were not architects — Sir Uvedale Price, a connoisseur, and John Mawer, a professional nurseryman and hothouse designer. Both men offered valuable lessons on beauty and utility not generally taught in schools of architecture; and, partly from their unorthodox introductions to the subject, Loudon emerged as an outspoken critic and theorist of architecture — independent-minded, but retaining something of Price's broad vision of buildings in the landscape and Mawer's attention to structural and functional detail.

Price assumed an informed, educated, and well-traveled audience when he discussed architecture in his revised *Essay on the Picturesque*.[1] He was less interested in the minute points of style and correct ornament than in buildings that were themselves fine ornaments in the landscape. It was the architecture of Vanbrugh — not of Jones, Wren, or Burlington — that Price recommended for careful study. In spite of Vanbrugh's faults and eccentricities, his buildings — particularly Castle Howard and Blenheim — produced powerful, striking effects in the larger composition of ground, water, and trees. Bold, projecting towers and pavilions, domes and porticoes, and fantastically ornamented chimneys, best seen silhouetted against a brooding sky or tinged with the golden glow of the setting sun: these were the characteristic features of the early eighteenth-century palaces for which Vanbrugh, the soldier, dramatist, and architect, was best known. Vanbrugh regarded architecture with the eye of a landscape painter; and for this reason, above all, Price considered Vanbrugh's buildings eminently worthy of the architect's and connoisseur's close scrutiny.

Price also described the buildings of the great landscape painters, set in the Roman campagna, a Flemish hamlet, or a clearing in an East Anglian wood. Poussin's buildings were firm, solid resting places for the eye, Price observed. Rubens's columns supported profusions of climbing plants; and Claude's ruins, teeming with rich vegetation, gave animation to his otherwise quiet scenes of repose, bathed in the gentle light of dawn or dusk (fig. 34, pl. 1). Rembrandt, Gainsborough, and David Teniers gave important hints for improving cottages and villages. From their works, Price implied, the rural designer could learn to combine neatness

*From Claude's dreamlike scenes, Uvedale Price and his disciple, Loudon, learned to appreciate subtly irregular forms in buildings that were themselves integral parts of a landscape composition. The young Loudon often aimed for the same studied irregularity in the masses of his architectural designs — whether Gothic, eclectic, or without any reference to historical styles.*

Fig. 34

Claude Lorrain, *Landscape with the Voyage of Jacob*, 1677. Courtesy, Sterling and Francine Clark Art Institute, Williamstown, Massachusetts.

with wild luxuriance, humility with grandeur, a secluded setting of homely comforts with a spirited affirmation of human dignity.[2]

Sometime in adolescence, Loudon discovered the writings of Price. At twenty-one, he declared himself Price's "profound admirer and disciple."[3] Thereafter, he would reiterate Price's advice to the young architect: he should study real landscapes in nature, and he should unite the profession of architecture with that of landscape painting. In 1794, however, before meeting Price, Loudon began to receive more practical and technical lessons in building from John Mawer, generally considered among the best hothouse designers in Britain.[4]

Mawer's practice demanded little attention to the aesthetics of composition in wood, brick, and glass. Unlike recognized "architecture," Mawer's buildings were simple, utilitarian structures. For melons and cucumbers, he used pits with sunken floors and glass roofs, dug into sloping ground; for peaches and apricots, he built traditional hot-wall structures with steeply sloping, south-facing, wood-framed glass façades and hollow brick or stone walls that encased flues for circulating the smoke from a single stove. Grapes and pineapples required their own houses, heated by the smoke and steam of several boilers or large stoves. None of these structures were entirely self-contained, internally regulated shelters; even those equipped with furnaces, flues, and pipes required the radiant light and heat of the sun, as well, for the survival of the plants.[5] Thus, the form and orientation of Mawer's structures were determined, to some extent, by the natural environment.

While attending school in Edinburgh, Loudon worked part-time for Mawer, assisting in all the technical operations of constructing and maintaining glasshouses. After Mawer's death in 1798, Loudon became an apprentice to the nurserymen James and George Dickson, and in 1802 he made some alterations of his own on the Dicksons' hothouse.[6] Describing this work three years later, Loudon acknowledged his intellectual debts

both to Count Rumford, for the construction of his furnace, and to Walter Nicol, for general hints on hothouses. The writings of both men, published in the late 1790s, represented the most recent work on the conduction and conservation of heat.[7] Still, Loudon insisted that his first inspiration, and primary source, was Nature. Explaining the principles of his new invention, a portable steamer, Loudon wrote, "The air in hothouses should never be more charged with steam than the open air appears to be charged with dew in the evenings. . . . Nature affords the best examples and instruction for steaming."[8] Loudon also constructed a ventilator to simulate a natural breeze, which made indoor plants more sturdy and healthy looking. These and all other improvements he traced to his patient observation of Nature and her "beautiful economy."[9]

Loudon's first pineries (hothouses for pineapples) were based largely on those of Mawer: long ranges of brick walls heated by flues and flanked by single shed roofs — presumably of glass, in a wooden frame — angled at about 60 degrees from the wall (fig. 35). Loudon's improvements were simple, but effective: He affixed a system of cords and pulleys to his "inner roof," a simple canvas shade drawn beneath the glass roof at night to retain heat. For added insulation, he laid all smoke flues below the level of the walk. To regulate indoor temperatures, he provided separate pipes for releasing hot or cold air into the house. To heat the soil, Loudon invented a way to produce steam below its surface: he poured water through tubes reaching down to a layer of hot stones over the smoke flues. On contact with the hot stones, the water produced steam which permeated the soil with a moist, uniform heat. Most important, Loudon's glass roof was merely a thin wooden frame — sturdy enough to support the expensive glass panes, but not so thick and massive as to block the precious rays of the sun.[10] Some of these pineries were actually built for Loudon's clients in Scotland and England;[11] but it seems he never real-

*This diagram illustrates the larger type of "pinery" which Loudon erected at Prinknash, the residence of J.B.Howell, Esq., in Gloucestershire. Smoke flues (AA) from a nearby furnace and vacuities of hot air (CC) heat the rubble stones (D) which, when water is poured through tubes (GG), produce steam heat. By covering the tubes, one forces the steam to permeate the plant bed.*

Fig. 35
J.C.Loudon, Pine stoves, or hothouses for pineapples, ca. 1805.

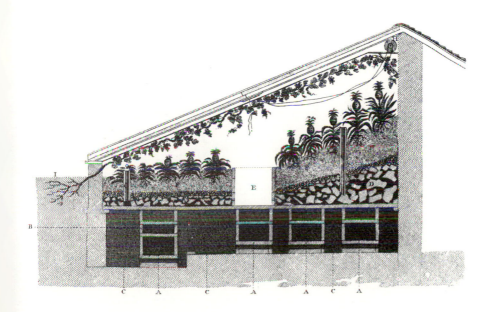

*For a site near London, Loudon designed this two-story house with a central tower, a two-story conservatory, and a one-story vinery. Heat from the house's fireplaces was allowed to enter the glass structures at ground level, then return to the house through second-floor windows.*

Fig. 36
J.C.Loudon, Plan of a house with a large conservatory and vinery.

ized his ideal glasshouse of 1805 — an entirely free-standing house of light wooden construction, its frame painted ivory and its roof and sides constructed as one entire envelope of glass.[12]

Loudon made some tentative applications of hothouse engineering to domestic architecture in the early 1800s, when he was just establishing his practice as a landscape gardener. For one small house near London, without distant prospects or fine views, he designed a two-story conservatory and a one-story vinery, which together ran the entire length of the south front and provided a new kind of verdant "scenery" for the ground-floor windows (fig. 36).[13] The fireplaces of the kitchen wing backed into the vinery, and those of the library, drawing room, and dining room, into the conservatory. Like Rumford's, these fireplaces had inner side walls that angled outward, and back walls that projected forward (from the bottom upward). Loudon also constructed a maze of hot-air passages behind the fuel chamber of each fireplace. Warm air from the base of each fire thus entered the glasshouses through shoulder-high vents over the exterior projections of the fireplaces. When water was poured onto metal plates covering these vents, steam was diffused into the conservatory and vinery.

By this arrangement, glasshouses were to conserve some of the heat that would otherwise escape into the atmosphere through the chimneys and outside walls. Upstairs, all the south-facing bedrooms would also

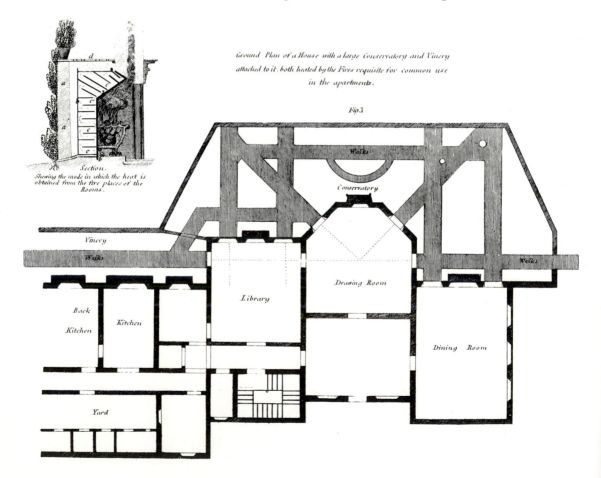

Ground Plan of a House with a large Conservatory and Vinery attached to it, both heated by the Fires requisite for common use in the apartments.

Fig.1

Section. Shewing the mode in which the heat is obtained from the fire places of the Rooms.

have fireplaces that released hot air into the conservatory. The large windows in these bedrooms reached to the floor; when opened, they allowed heat from the conservatory to circulate back into the house. Meanwhile, looking into the conservatory, one gazed upon a scene of potted trees bearing peaches, cherries, and figs; of myrtles, mimosas, succulents, and hardy greenhouse plants; and of mossy paths, overhung with vines and creepers among the rafters. Ivy and creepers would also clothe the exterior walls for a "singular and romantic appearance."[14]

As Loudon's ideas on architecture evolved, romantic imagery would become less important than construction and environmental controls. Even as early as 1806, in aiming to improve cottages, he focused on the most critical concerns of laborers in a temperate, moist climate: heat and food. "The most important improvements," he wrote, "are such as relate to the construction of fire-places, and the adoption of particular utensils for preparing food."[15] Ten years earlier, Count Rumford had emphasized these two improvements in one of his first essays on the domestic conservation of heat, "Chimney Fireplaces."[16] In a later essay, Rumford considered the potential uses of refuse coal dust and reflected on the superiority of coke, hard coal, and "artificial fire-balls" over crude, dirty, powdery sea coal. The mysteries of light and heat, and the practical means of their generation had been neglected for too long: "While the industry and ingenuity of millions are employed, with unceasing activity, in inventing, improving and varying those superfluities which wealth and luxury introduce into society, no attention whatever is paid to the improvement of those common necessaries of life on which the subsistence of all, and the comforts and enjoyments of the great majority of mankind, absolutely depend."[17]

Loudon's improvements on the standard cottage fireplace, meant to obtain maximum heat from a given quantity of fuel, were not entirely original; apparently he had paid close attention to Rumford's essays on heat, fuel, and chimney fireplaces (figs. 37 and 38). Like Rumford, Loudon would avoid large, drafty chimney "canals," which let too much warm air escape rapidly from the room; instead, he would construct a narrow "throat" to make smoke and warm air rise slowly and effectively. Again like Rumford, he advised that the fuel chamber should be kept low and compact, nearly cubic. Most important, as Rumford had observed, the back wall of the fireplace should project forward, from just above the fuel chamber to the chimney's "throat," in order to throw radiant heat into the room.[18]

The floor plan of Loudon's cottage fireplace was semielliptical, and the interior surface was a continuously curving shell, radiating heat into the room from all directions. Rumford had warned, however, that curved surfaces tended to produce eddies in air currents, which would disturb the fire or smoke. Had Loudon foreseen these complications? In *Country Residences*, not all the technicalities of fireplace construction are fully explained. Loudon simply credited his predecessors, Benjamin Franklin and Rumford; explained and illustrated his own successful practices; and emphasized the importance of warm, comfortable cottages for laboring people.

In planning for the cottage's exterior, Loudon was most concerned with construction and materials. Doors, windows, roofs, and chimneys

*Rumford pointed out that large chimney "canals," or flues, were drafty and wasteful of heat. His diagrams for channeling the smoke of a fireplace influenced Loudon's modest efforts to improve cottage fireplaces.*

Fig. 37
Benjamin Thompson, Count Rumford, Fireplace: ground plan, elevation, and section.

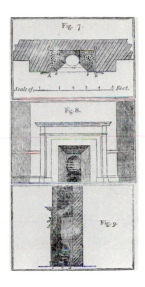

*Loudon's* Treatise on Country Residences *(1806) includes no renderings of interiors, grand or humble. To improve cottages, he focused on what he believed to be one of the two most important concerns of the inhabitant — the construction of fireplaces. (The other was kitchen equipment.)*
Fig. 38
J.C. Loudon, Diagram of an improved cottage fireplace.

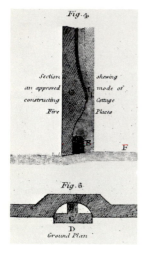

*Attending to massing and details of chimneys, Loudon designed this house with a "picturesque, or perhaps romantic effect." He was not aiming for any particular style, and he claimed to have seen no precedent — though Knight's Downton Castle and Price's Foxley, both of which he had seen in Herefordshire, came close. Many of Claude's timeworn piles of masonry — or certain corn mills and ironworks in Britain — could also have served as inspiration.*
Fig. 39 (*right*)
J.C. Loudon, Elevation of a house to be covered with ivy and creepers.

should be plain, and solidly built. Decorations might include trees in the garden and creeping vines and shrubs against the walls (see fig. 8).[19] He recommended no fancy Gothic bargeboards or tiny diamond-paned windows, however. His cottage façades were as straightforward as those of his controversial contemporary, J.M. Gandy.

In 1805 Joseph Michael Gandy, Sir John Soane's brilliant draftsman, called for a fresh, realistic approach to cottage design. Instead of imitating the chance effects in picturesque, decaying villages — the muted colors, mottled textures, and small, obscured windows — Gandy offered white lime-washed surfaces, and stark, unornamented doors and windows (see fig. 31).[20] While other architects were aiming for the traditional character of old rural cottages — humility, wooded seclusion, and weather-stained, cosy rusticity — Gandy called for convenience, simplicity, and elegance, using abstract, geometrical forms in both picturesque and symmetrical compositions. Today, his multifamily cottages, public houses, dairies, and farmsteads still appear delightfully fresh and modern; but when first offered to the public, they appeared stark, cold. The *Annual Review* of 1805 denounced Gandy's "frigid" and "extravagant" style, just as the *Review* had despaired of Wordsworth's "frigid" and "extravagant" system.[21]

Loudon followed Gandy's lead, to a point.[22] The windows and doors of his "Decorated English Cottage" (1806) are unmistakably like Gandy's, although the rendering is conventionally picturesque. Loudon's house "decorated" with ivy and creepers, also from 1806, is a fantasy of abstract, castle-like forms, which owe something to Gandy and quite a lot to his countryman, Robert Adam, particularly in the three-dimensional composition of masses that advance and recede with a nervous intensity (fig. 39). Loudon had already seen Adam's work in Edinburgh and the Scottish countryside. One of Loudon's client's, the earl of Wemyss, had engaged Adam to design Gosford House, Haddingtonshire, in 1790. No doubt Loudon knew of Adam's ideas about picturesque movement in architecture.

Adam was fascinated by the movement of forms: by the rising and falling, advancing and receding of masses, which he admired in Vanbrugh's work at Castle Howard and Blenheim. Though Vanbrugh's architectural details and proportions were unorthodox, Adam forgave his "barbarisms and absurdities"; he considered the flamboyant Vanbrugh a "genius of the first class." What Vanbrugh had achieved in his own

*Elevation of a House calculated for being decorated with Ivy & Creepers, and adapted to a particular situation, as shewn in Plate VIII.*

eccentric version of the English baroque, Adam would refine, assimilating his architecture into its modern landscape setting: "The rising and falling, advancing and receding, with the convexity and concavity and other forms of the great parts [of a building] have the same effect in architecture, that hill and dale, foreground and distance, swelling and sinking have in landscape: that is, they serve to produce an agreeable and diversified contour, that groups and contrasts like a picture, and creates a variety of light and shade, which gives great spirit, beauty and effect to the composition."[23]

Loudon adopted Adam's principle of "picturesque movement" in his own compositions for buildings, streets, and villages. His rendering of a house decorated with ivy and creepers resembles Adam's Culzean Castle on the western coast of Ayrshire (figs. 40 and 41) — not in architectural detail, but in the mountainous massing of architectural forms, the syncopated skyline, and, most important, in the romantic siting on a wooded promontory jutting into a body of water.[24] On the other hand, Loudon found the architectural details of Culzean Castle and other works by Adam disturbing. He pointed to their useless battlements, a jumble of Venetian and Gothic motifs, and moldings of many different styles. In these works, he believed, the eminent Adam had violated the principle which constituted the essential excellence of architecture: Harmony.[25]

At architectural school in Edinburgh in 1801, Loudon had been taught the "basics": the five orders of classical architecture and, most likely, the fundamental principles of architectural design that he outlined in 1806, including utility, beauty, truth, fitness, symmetry, uniformity, unity, variety, and harmony.[26] In *Country Residences*, Loudon published his first critical remarks on architecture, subjecting even the works of the masters to the scrutiny of rational taste. Now, suppose the stylistic "impurities" of Adam's Culzean Castle could be cleansed and all the component parts rendered useful and correct; then Loudon's chastened ivy- and creeper-covered house might emerge. On its wildly overgrown promontory, this house seems a grand, craggy feature of the natural landscape. Shorn of its vegetation, however — in the starkness of the undecorated version — the house is eerie. If one gazes intently, the dark, spare, punched-out voids begin to assume the strange, anthropomorphic quality of Gandy's fantastic forms. In all their stark simplicity, Gandy's buildings are uncanny — as are Loudon's, until clothed with "decorative" foliage.

At this early stage, probably inspired by Gandy, Loudon was eager to surpass the "mere architect" who ornamented façades with columns and pediments, and reproduced rotundas derived from Greek and Roman models. The rural landscape of Britain already contained better models for study, Loudon believed. True taste in the British "rural style" should be founded on the best of indigenous cottages, castles, and villas. The rural architect should learn to distinguish, moreover, between "that wretched poverty of form, which is the result of necessity, and the more pleasing simplicity, which is the result of contentment and sufficiency."[27]

In 1796 Price had called for more British *architetti-pittori*, like the great architect-painters of the Italian Renaissance: Raphael, Michelangelo, Giulio Romano, Vignola, Serlio, Peruzzi, and others.[28] Loudon went further, asserting that rural architecture should become a special branch of the profession, separate from urban architecture. The rural

J. Loudon del.

J. Greig sculp

*Fig 2. of Pl. 4. put in perspective & adapted to its situation.*

improver ought to combine architecture and landscape design. Having studied the character of landscapes, the nature of building materials, and the principles of composition, he should learn to create an architecture appropriate to the indigenous character of the place, whether it be grand, sublime, beautiful, picturesque, melancholy, gay, romantic, or wild.[29]

At the time he wrote this, Loudon recognized two main styles of European architecture that had enjoyed their moments of perfection: the Grecian and the Gothic. The Grecian, he wrote, was most pure as an architecture of temples only. In time, the structural elements of temples — columns, entablatures, cornices, pediments — were applied indiscriminately to palaces, baths, and other private and public buildings. Once the Romans completed the corruption of this style, Grecian architecture lost its "primitive simplicity and fitness."[30]

Gothic architecture was perfected in what Loudon called the "pointed" style, characterized by the pointed arches of the nave in York Minster and the vaulted roof of Durham Cathedral. In these edifices, as in Westminster Abbey, he appreciated a certain lightness of construction unattainable in Grecian architecture. He was himself more impressed by this pointed Gothic style than by any other, because of its superb construction:

The beauty of fitness is so prevalent, that not one part appears superfluous. . . . By an examination into the mechanical principles which pervade the whole, this fitness is no less apparent than real or necessary; so much so, indeed, that not one single buttress, and in some cases (as in the ribs of open crowns on the tops of spires) not one single pinnacle, could be taken away without injuring that part of the fabric.

Whether we regard the variety in the columns, and the intricacy of the roof from the tracery, the leaves, and other ornaments, or consider the noble perspectives of the middle and side aisles, we must be constrained to say, that the general effect of a cathedral in this style far surpasses that of any Grecian building in producing that exhilarating sublimity which is so analogous to the purpose for which they are erected.[31]

Here, Loudon was looking at architecture in a manner not yet suggested by his acknowledged mentors, Archibald Alison and Sir Uvedale Price. Alison, a philosopher of the fine arts, was not concerned with the details of building construction, and Price merely offered a few warnings. For instance, he recommended sparing use of columns: "To make columns support some trifle, merely to have an excuse for them, is to degrade a member of such great and obvious use, to a mere gewgaw."[32] Thus forewarned, Loudon pointed out the architectural deformities of columns engaged in, or barely distinct from, a wall. Intended for noble purposes, columns should be erected for necessary support and significant shadow, not applied gratuitously to façades. Loudon's main criterion for aesthetic judgment of architecture was the degree to which the various elements were used for constructive purposes such as support or shelter.

Who were Loudon's teachers of architecture in Edinburgh? One wonders how much his emphasis on construction is derived from books, and how much from instructors, or from original observation. He openly disagreed with Sir William Chambers, who had defended the virtues of Roman, versus ancient Greek, architecture in his *Treatise on Civil Architecture* (1759).[33] Concerning painting, Loudon tended to agree with Sir

*In its commanding site overlooking the sea, this castle designed by Robert Adam bears some resemblance to Loudon's design for a house on a promontory (fig. 41). Ironically, Loudon was sharply critical of Adam's mélange of Gothic and Grecian ornament at Colzean (or Culzean) Castle.*

Fig. 40 (*opposite*)
W.H.Bartlett, "Colzean Castle, Ayrshire."

*Overhung with vines and creepers, Loudon's asymmetrical house takes on the "intricacy and richness" that he believed other designers tried to achieve by applying ornament.*

Fig. 41 (*opposite*)
J.C.Loudon, Perspective view of a house covered with ivy and creepers, adapted to its particular site.

Joshua Reynolds, whose *Discourses on Art,* based on lectures given at the Royal Academy in the 1770s and 1780s, also contained observations on architecture. Like Price in the 1790s, Reynolds viewed architecture with a painter's eye and praised Vanbrugh as one who knowingly broke some of the rules of the ancients, yet clearly understood the "general ruling principles" of architecture and painting.[34]

Decades earlier, Marc-Antoine Laugier had viewed architecture rationally, with a builder's eye, in his *Essay* (1753) and *Observations on Architecture* (1765). From these works, Loudon would have gleaned some understanding of the constructive origins of architectural elements. Though he disclaimed any interest in "original huts" (Laugier had tried to deduce their construction), Loudon would surely appreciate Laugier's emphasis on the logic of a constructive system and his attacks on excessively thick walls and useless pilasters and pedestals — faults which Loudon enumerated in his own *Country Residences.*

So much for the eighteenth-century theorists that Loudon acknowledged: Chambers and Reynolds in 1806; Laugier later, in 1832.[35] But what of Loudon's contemporaries? Just as he quoted familiar eighteenth-century poets when he first set forth his own views on landscape design — but did not mention his controversial contemporary, Wordsworth — so the twenty-three-year-old Loudon acknowledged several eminent eighteenth-century architectural writers, yet neglected not only Laugier but also contemporaries whose controversial views he shared. Both Thomas Hope and J.N.L. Durand are cited in Loudon's mature architectural writings of the 1820s and 1830s.[36] Were their early works too recent, or too radical, in 1806, to support Loudon's first statement of architectural principles?

In 1804 a controversy had erupted over the architectural style to be adopted in the new buildings for Downing College, at Cambridge. James Wyatt, surveyor general and comptroller of the works, had proposed a composition of classical buildings reminiscent of Sir Christopher Wren's Chelsea Hospital and Wyatt's own earlier work at Oxford.[37] Thomas Hope, a young member of the Society of Dilettanti (a genial circle of well-traveled connoisseurs of art), objected to Wyatt's work in a letter to Francis Annesley, Esq., M.P., published as *Observations on the Plans and Elevations . . . for Downing College* (1804). If Loudon had read this celebrated pamphlet, he would have found timely support for his own reflections on Grecian versus Roman architecture. "I could wish that instead of the degraded architecture of the Romans, the purest style of the Greeks had been exclusively adhibited," Hope had written, in what could be considered a manifesto.[38] As David Watkin has observed, Hope was the first critic in Britain to express the "full revolutionary doctrines of French Neo-Classicism as enunciated in their most austere form in the pioneering works of the Abbé Laugier."[39]

Loudon's *Country Residences* was still in progress in March 1806, when the Grecian design of Hope's favored architect, William Wilkins, was selected for Downing College. If this choice did not represent the "triumph" of Grecian over Roman architecture, at least it suggested that a purer, simpler form of classicism — Greek classicism — was coming into favor. Loudon himself had not taken a side in this controversy; perhaps he did not care to defend the virtues of one style over another in the unfamiliar context of the English universities. By the 1830s his attitude toward the styles would be clearly impartial: the fitness of a style and its characteristic forms for a particular use were more important than the style per se. Then, too, in 1805–06, he may have been too preoccupied to follow the Cambridge competition. At any rate, years later, Loudon enthusiastically praised Thomas Hope for his knowledgeable, discriminating taste in sculpture and the "ecstatic" architectural creation of Deepdene, Hope's country home in Surrey (fig. 42).[40]

By the early 1800s Loudon probably knew of Durand's writings, which emphasized the nature of materials in relation to proportion and construction. In his *Encyclopaedia of Architecture* (1832–33) and elsewhere, Loudon cited the later editions of works by Durand, a professor of architecture at the Ecole Polytechnique in Paris.[41] But how soon did Loudon actually discover Durand's two-volume *Précis des leçons d'architecture* (1802–05)? The *Précis* included Durand's straightforward introduction to the practical goals and general principles of architecture, the qualities of building materials, and the problems of construction. Only after considering these structural issues did Durand treat the aesthetic problems of composition and style. The three main problems of architecture, he noted, were *decoration, distribution* (the arrangement of the various parts, according to use), and *construction*. Of these, only *construction* was a fundamental problem of all building types, however simple or conventional.

These observations appeared in volume 1 of Durand's *Précis* (1802). Loudon's similar observations first appeared in 1806.[42] Though he acknowledged his debts to Alison and Price, however, Loudon made no reference to Durand. Was this an oversight? Just a few years before Loudon suggested in print that proportion should be related to the nature of building materials (not to ancient rules), Durand had amassed and published a wealth of technical evidence in support of his argument that forms and proportions must be derived from the nature of materials. Alison had made similar suggestions — but without the solid conviction of an engineer.[43] Again, before Loudon first emphasized the original structural purposes of ornaments such as pilasters, columns, and cornices, Durand had explained these structural purposes in minute detail.

In 1829 Loudon, the fastidious critic, had little to do at Deepdene "but to walk round and admire." The Germans, he noted, would consider the place "ecstatic" in architectural style. Because of its rich variety of classical forms, combining the "landscape architecture" (a new term) and sculpture of Italy, Louaon believed Deepdene would delight his mentor, Uvedale Price, and Gilbert Laing Meason, the author of On the Landscape Architecture of the Great Painters of Italy (1828).

Fig. 42
"Deepdene," the residence of Thomas Hope, Esq., in Surrey.

Before Loudon publicly objected to "blind prejudices" in favor of a particular style and "servile imitations" of ancient models, Durand had exposed these errors by challenging both the ancient rules of Vitruvius and Laugier's theory of the "primitive hut."[44] Most significant, before Loudon demonstrated the "beauty of fitness" in pointed Gothic architecture, where no single element was structurally superfluous, Durand had made the same observations on the "beauty of sufficiency" without specifying a style: "When an edifice has everything it needs, and only what it needs, and when all necessary parts are disposed in the most economical way — that is, the most simple way — the edifice has the type and degree of beauty which is fitting; to add anything else, besides the ornaments of painting and sculpture, is to weaken and sometimes even to destroy its style, its character, in a word, all the beauties which one tries to give to the edifice."[45]

If, as the evidence suggests, Loudon had known of Hope's and Durand's writings soon after they were published, then he would have been reassured by the congenial views of a well-traveled connoisseur, Hope, and a professional architect-engineer, Durand, before submitting to public scrutiny his first essay on architecture, *Country Residences*. Ironically, British reviewers did not pay much attention to Loudon's principles of architecture.[46] Perhaps they found his ideas on landscape gardening — his main subject in that work — disturbing enough! English critics would no doubt be wary of a self-assured Scot who expressed his unorthodox views on many subjects in an occasionally pretentious, irreverent prose. Still, more than one reader must have been intrigued by an author who could recommend weedy, wild luxuriance and romantic imitations of nature's careless ways in lawns and flower gardens, yet criticize such well-known monumental buildings as Sir John Soane's Bank of England and Robert Adam's Register House in Edinburgh for the most trifling and conventional breaches of "truth" in construction or "purity" of style.

As a critic, Loudon had an uncompromising, purist streak. More than a critic, however, he was an inventor and a designer who questioned the authority of the ancients. Mechanically inventive in the design of hothouses and romantically inventive in the design of landscape gardens, the young Loudon could already conceive of an architecture for which the rules were not written in stone. In the early 1800s Loudon imagined buildings entirely free of historical styles. And, he felt that exhilarating sense of independence that comes from questioning the rules.

These were the years of Loudon's headstrong, self-assured outbursts, the time of his youth and early manhood, when he tended to trust his own eye and his instincts before reason and common sense. At that time, Loudon wrote with a flourish and sketched with ease. Still possessed of a good right arm, he did not yet have to employ a draftsman, and he could hardly speak with the subdued voice of experience. Swept away by his own enthusiasm, he would write of the expressive "finishing touches" of an ash or an elm, and the proper mixture of light and shade, mass and void, color and texture, which would render a pile of masonry worthy of the name *architecture*.[47]

As he gained more practical experience, Loudon would give more thought to the homes of the "great mass of society," for whom dry floors, warm air, and daylight were more important than the quality of shadow cast by a pilaster projecting so many inches from a façade. His penetrating gaze may have always detected the most minute "deformities" of architectural design. But in time, he wrote less often about these peccadilloes, and instead focused on the more sobering lack of light, heat, or air in a dwelling. If there was no single, decisive moment of change in Loudon's thinking about buildings and people — no sudden flash of insight or revelation of a new architectural mission in life — Loudon did leave evidence of his growing fascination for the comfortable, well-tempered building, with or without any "pretension to style." Though his earliest writings tend to differentiate "architecture" from utilitarian barns, stables, and hothouses, he was already, in the early 1800s, beginning to recognize that the "beauty of fitness" could ennoble any structure.

Two buildings that seem to bridge the gap between "architecture" and "mere building" are Loudon's proposed conservatories of 1811 and 1812: both plain, well-tempered environments for plants, meant to accommodate — and delight — people. In December 1811, as a fellow of the Linnaean Society, Loudon read before his colleagues a paper entitled "Hints for a National Garden," his proposal for a "living museum" containing every species and variety of the vegetable kingdom (fig. 43).[48]

*Believing British botanical gardens of interest only to scientists, Loudon conceived of this national garden for some site near London. It was designed to include not only medicinal or curious plants — but also fruits, vegetables, flowers and grains. The outer circle of his central glass structures would be large enough for a carriage drive and climate-controlled for "perpetual verdure, bloom and fruit, jets of water, singing birds . . ."*

Fig. 43
J.C.Loudon, Design for a Botanic Garden, ca. 1811.

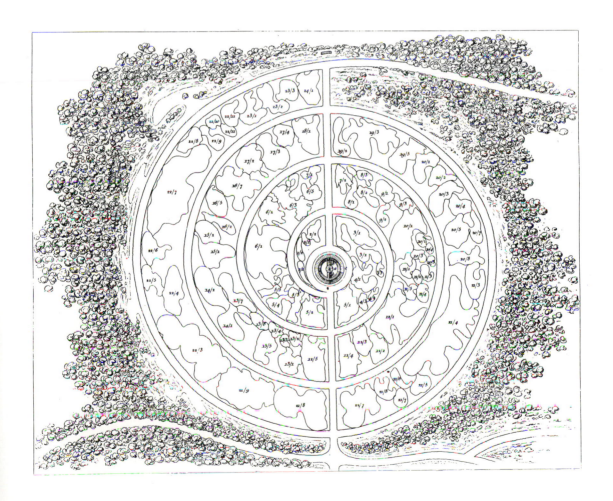

*Dedicated to the Prince Regent (with his permission), Loudon's* Hints on Gardens *(1812) included this conservatory, to be constructed of copper sashes and cast-iron framework. Ideally, four glass trellises would lead straight to the conservatory, and a canal with fountains, fish, and exotics would run down the center.*

Fig. 44
J.C.Loudon, Design for a conservatory, sited in the center of a flower garden: sections, elevations, and plan.

Ideally, the hothouses and greenhouses would form two concentric rings, connected by four radial wings; and the outer ring of glasshouses would be large enough to contain a circular carriage drive. "The effect," he predicted, "would surpass anything of the kind hitherto known but in the regions of Romance."[49]

In 1812, just before leaving for Sweden and Russia, Loudon published his *Hints on the Formation of Gardens and Pleasure Grounds*, which included a large rectilinear conservatory, sheathed and roofed entirely with glass, meant for the center of a geometrical flower garden (fig. 44). In plan, the conservatory is composed of two intersecting rectangles, with an interior straight canal running down the center of the longest rectangle. In section, the gabled roof above the canal is supported by pillars, rafters, and trusses of cast iron. The elevations reveal a subtly irregular grid of glass set in copper sashes. Glass verandas, or trellises, cover the four paths leading to the four entrances, each dignified by a plain pediment.[50]

Instead of wood, Loudon recommended cast iron and copper for the frames and sashes of this conservatory because the metals would last longer and, requiring less mass than wood, they would admit more light. This change of structural materials from wood to metals he considered "the greatest improvement hitherto made in horticultural architecture."[51] And with this phrase, perhaps for the first time, Loudon suggests that these well-tempered, utilitarian yet elegant structures should be considered "architecture."

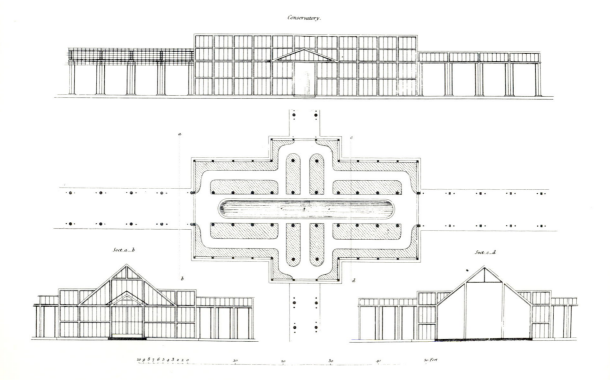

Conservatory.

Sect. a...b                                    Sect. c...d

7

# Engineering for Splendor
# and for Health

One of Loudon's most significant contributions to architecture — the invention of the means to build curving glass-and-iron conservatories — owes something to his Russian sojourn in the winter of 1813–14.

Russia! Endless flat, snow-blanketed steppes; forests of onion domes and spires; the piercing stares of stern, glittering madonnas; log cabins, palaces, and the charred remains of an ancient capital . . . One can only speculate about the notes that filled Loudon's journals during his nineteen-month journey through northern Europe in 1813 and 1814, before the Napoleonic Wars had ended. Though he never published a complete account of these travels, years later he did recall things that had impressed him in Russia, including the profusion of pineapples, magnificent buildings marred by poor workmanship and ephemeral materials, small double-glazed windows in a serf's cabin, and the lack of ancient ruins. [1]

Loudon's backward glances are cool, somewhat clinical—as if the lapse of time had drained his memory of vital first impressions. Still, the recollections must be pieced together in order to understand two of the most remarkable efforts of his career: constructing well-tempered environments for plants — his curvilinear hothouses, and designing equally well-tempered environments for people — his centrally heated multistory dwellings for the poor. As Loudon focused on these projects soon after his return from Russia, his experiences there may hold clues to his development both as an engineer-architect and as a compassionate human being.

During seven months of the bitter cold winter and spring of 1813–14, Loudon lived in two great Russian cities. Moscow, the ancient capital, had lately been devastated by the fire of September 1812, which had driven out Napoleon's troops (fig. 45). St. Petersburg, the new capital, was flourishing, with handsome stone buildings, some soberly neoclassical, some exuberantly baroque. [2] There Loudon was impressed by the bazaars, with their broad paved walks sheltered by colonnades and their central courts open to the sky. He appreciated the variety in the so-called English line of townhouses, and he admired Thomas de Thomon's new Exchange, one of the finest public monuments to rise during the reign of Czar Alexander I. Begun in 1805, this great Tuscan Doric building commanded a direct view up the Neva, with oblique views north and south across the river to the old island fortress of Peter and Paul, the Hermitage, the Winter Palace, and the Admiralty, then under construction. [3]

St. Petersburg's renewal also left impressions of skillful engineering. Loudon admired the magnificent embankments along the Neva, and he inspected projects for a new bridge to span that great river. Later he published one of his own designs for a suspension bridge over the river Mersey at Runcorn, Lancashire.[4] He also inspected the ingenious centrally planned, efficiently supervised panopticon workhouse, or prison, in St. Petersburg, originally designed by Jeremy Bentham and executed by Bentham's younger brother Samuel for Catherine the Great.[5]

In Russia, Loudon must have made a few friends — though one wonders if he ever penetrated the social and cultural barriers in that foreign land. As he had been elected to the Imperial Society of Moscow, among other institutions, he must have carried impressive letters of introduction — possibly from the eminent naturalist, Sir Joseph Banks, president of the Royal Society, who furnished letters for Loudon's southern European tour in 1819.[6] With such letters, Loudon would have had entrée into the professional and social circles in which distinguished foreign visitors tended to mingle. As the German traveler Chrétien Müller explained, any stranger who arrived in St. Petersburg carrying proper letters of recommendation would be graciously received by noble and well-to-do families.[7] British visitors were especially welcome. Russia, traditionally a friend to Britain, was also her strong ally during the Napoleonic Wars. As John Quincy Adams, the United States ambassador, noted, the Russians were "Anglomanes," partly by habit, partly on account of their long-established commerce.[8]

Finally, one must assume that Loudon had few problems of communication in Russia. His command of French would have been useful in "polite" society. He could have spoken English or German with the head

gardeners. And, as he could converse in Italian, he became acquainted with two architects — Giacomo Quarenghi, court architect to Catherine the Great, Paul I, and Alexander I; and a Signor Camporezi, who had designed buildings for Petrowsky Razumowsky at Petrowka, a country seat near Moscow.[9] To Loudon, only the great mass of Russian people— servants and peasants — would have been incomprehensible. These people he respected for their diligence, endurance, and "perfectly good-hearted" nature, while he abhorred their condition of near-slavery.

Russian serfs typically lived in bleak wooden huts. Some better-off peasants and impoverished noblemen lived in large wooden cottages, but, as Loudon discovered, there was no Russian middle class of any consequence. In St. Petersburg most of the merchants were British, and most innkeepers German, French. or Italian. Artists and architects tended to be foreigners, though some were Russian serfs trained in Italy. German and British stewards and head gardeners usually managed the noblemen's farms, gardens, and hothouses, producing, mostly under glass, luscious pineapples, grapes, peaches, apples, pears, cherries, and plums. Meanwhile, the Russian serf had not even the smallest patch of a kitchen garden. No flowers graced his door, and the only fruits he ate were wild pears, strawberries, and cranberries.[10]

Recalling such contrasts in 1835, Loudon observed that Russia was lowest, among all the Continental states, in the scale of civilization.[11] As society progressed, he believed, the contrasts of wealth and poverty would be lessened, and inequalities would tend to level off — but not disappear altogether. This belief permeates all of Loudon's mature writings. But did he always judge a civilization in such frankly socioeconomic terms? Madame de Staël, then exiled from her beloved France by Napoleon, predicted "great things" for Russia because of the striking contrasts in the *character* of the Russian people. Among all classes, from the distinguished nobility to the graceful female peasants of the Ukraine, singing as they left the fields, she found a people who were alternately impetuous and patient, melancholy and gay, as well as utterly fearless and tireless. Only superior beings possess opposing qualities, she reasoned; the masses are, for the most part, of a uniform color. As a champion of civil liberties, however, Madame de Staël could never be reconciled to the slavery of the Russian people. She noted, too, that the songs of the Ukraine celebrated love and liberty with a kind of melancholy, something touching upon regret.[12]

While other Europeans were mystified by the culture and sensibilities of the Russian people, Loudon focused on their technical achievements, particularly their ability to survive in a hostile environment. Snow covered the ground for five or six months a year, and thick clouds often blocked the sun; yet winter in St. Petersburg was the season for balls, festivals, concerts, and daily promenades along the banks of the Neva or in the park of Prince Strogonof. In the countryside, even the poor could survive a Russian winter. Whenever Loudon stopped in a posthouse or a log cabin, he observed the economy and efficiency of the Russian stove. It was built of nonconducting materials such as sandstone or glazed earthenware, which retained heat better than iron. The fuel chamber and flues were contained entirely within the house, not against an outside wall — so that all the heat was diffused slowly into the room, for periods of up to forty-eight hours between fires.[13] In the humblest cottages, windows were small — sometimes boarded up, not glazed. Again, heat was conserved, but the lack of light and ventilation Loudon found intolerable. Back in London, Loudon would try to improve the dwellings of the poor, focusing on heat, light, and air.

On the whole, what Loudon found most intriguing in Russia was imported advanced technology, and traditional means — such as the earthenware stoves — used for appropriate ends. He regretted the lack of antiquity and diversity in the landscape. Looking back in 1835, he recalled that Russia had seemed a vast country, rather new and unvaried. There had been few hills, mountains, or rocks and few ancient buildings, save for the Kremlin and a few churches. In a country of extreme heat and cold, he reasoned, buildings hastily erected of brick, wood, and plaster could not last. He concluded,

A country without venerable architectural ruins conveys the idea of one where human society is in a state of infancy. The sight of ruins, on the other hand, carries us back to past ages, and seems to show us that previous generations have existed on the land; that men have lived and made progress, and have given way in order to make room for others to make farther progress. In short, they show the age, growth, and the power of mankind. A country of ruins is a country full of ideas; and one without them is a blank, except to the naturalist.[14]

Traveling for the first time outside his native British Isles, Loudon had regretted that Russia offered him no "readable" landscape, nothing man-made that could communicate the ideas of an ancient, gradually progressing people. Even the vast natural landscape of snow-covered steppes and half-frozen rivers could not speak to him. Beauty and meaning lay elsewhere, in the hilly or mountainous, wooded and luxuriant British countryside, punctuated by the occasional ruin of a castle or monastery, yet neatly maintained for the most part, productive, and humanized by cheerful cottages and farmhouses.

Loudon understood the language of classical architecture in Russia, but Russian Gothic baffled him. Though the skylines of domes, towers, and spires had dazzled the travelers Madame de Staël and Sir Robert Ker Porter, Loudon was appalled when he looked inside the structures. Wrought-iron tie rods sticking out in all directions revealed to him the builders' inability to construct columns and supporting walls properly. "The Gothic style," he remarked, "is not adapted to a rude and unscientific people."[15]

Attending to technical faults, Loudon seems to have missed much of the enchantment and poetry of the man-made Russian environment. Even man-made scenes of nature could not delight him, though they charmed other Europeans. In St. Petersburg, Ker Porter found the conservatory at the Taurida palace a summery paradise in the midst of winter (fig. 46): "Trees, fruits and flowers, fill up the fragrant assemblage, and court you into walks winding through many a luxuriant maze of oranges, myrtles, and clustering vines. Whilst straying in so delicious an atmosphere, and surrounded by the foliage of a hundred groves, flowers springing at your feet, and scenting a perfume which *takes the captive soul and laps it in Elysium*, how are the senses dissolved!"[16] Loudon did enjoy this scene, illuminated at night. By day, however, he noted the gloomy interior of this

semicircular appendage to the palace; the ceiling was opaque, and the
granite colonnade blocked light from the windows. Since plants could not
grow naturally inside, they had to be raised in glass sheds, then carted into
the conservatory and sunk into the ground.[17]

However awkward or inappropriate their construction, some Russian glasshouses did offer a splendid display. Loudon particularly admired the magnificent hothouses at Gorinka, the seat of Count Alexy Razumowsky, near Moscow, where more than three English acres were
covered by structures of glass. These included a 980-foot ensemble of the
main house and two lateral, curving wings of glasshouses fronting the
lawn. Terminating each wing was a pavilion: one, a museum of natural
history; the other, a theatre that could be used as a ballroom, concert
room, tennis court, or riding house — as at Versailles.[18]

On April 20, 1814, Loudon found the imperial hothouses at
Tzaritzina, near Moscow, full of ripe apples, pears, cherries, plums,
gooseberries, raspberries, and strawberries, along with parsley, lettuce,
carrots, turnips, potatoes, and other roots and legumes. Outside, the
ground had been covered for five months with a blanket of snow. By May
the ground was bare, then two inches of snow fell on the eve of June first—
the eve of Loudon's departure from Moscow.[19]

After a summer of travels in Poland, Austria, and northern Germany, Loudon returned to London at the end of September in 1814.
Discovering that a banker had mismanaged his hard-earned fortune,
Loudon fell ill. By 1816 he had moved from Newman Street, Holborn, to a
small house in Bayswater, The Hermitage, where he welcomed his wid-
owed mother and two of his sisters, Mary and Jane.

Still recovering from his illness, Loudon, now thirty-three, returned
to the interest he had first developed as an eleven-year-old part-time
nurseryman's apprentice: the design of hothouses. Working on some experimental glasshouses at home, he received a few words of encouragement from the Horticultural Society in London. But equally inspiring must
have been the memory of the magnificent Russian hothouses and of the
persistence of the gardeners in that country of pale, fleeting winter sun. In
1817 he mused, "If, in such a climate, the art of forcing is so far advanced, what may not be done in this country, where we have so much
more sun during our short winter?"[20]

In London, Loudon's fellow members of the Horticultural Society
had been encouraged to improve their own plant houses by Thomas Andrew Knight's 1808 reading of a paper on the forcing of grapes. Imbued
with the same persistent, probing spirit that had led his brother, Richard

*"Too gloomy for the growth
of plants," this elegant col-
onnaded conservatory pre-
sented the contradiction
Loudon tried to resolve in
1817 and 1818. By experi-
menting with lighter structures of glass and iron, he
hoped to achieve an en-
vironment equally elegant,
but better adapted for
plants.*

Fig. 46
Conservatory of the Taurida
palace, St. Petersburg.

*These sketches were the catalyst for Loudon's invention of a curvilinear wrought-iron sash bar. In turn, his sash bar made possible the construction of the billowing glass-and-iron conservatories that we now call "Victorian."*

Fig. 47 (*opposite*)
Sir George Stuart Mackenzie, Proposal for an Improved Forcing House: elevation, plan, and section, 1815.

Payne Knight, to enquire about the subtleties of picturesque landscapes, T. A. Knight mused over the varieties of plant houses and their designers' various claims of superiority. Given the same fruit, climate, and seasons of the year, Knight reasoned, there must be one form of plant house that could best produce an excellent grape. "In our climate," he wrote, "where sunshine and natural heat do not abound, that form, which admits the greatest quantity of light through the least breadth of glass, and affords the greatest regular heat with the least expenditure of fuel, must generally be the best."[21]

Knight's paper was not published until 1812, the year in which Loudon left Britain to travel in northern Europe and Russia. There he saw some of the most extensive glasshouses in the world. Still, Knight's concern for economy and efficiency seems to have stimulated Loudon as much as the Russians' splendor and display. In 1817 when he published the first results of his own hothouse experiments in Bayswater, Loudon noted that Knight (now president of the Horticultural Society) had given an important stimulus to horticultural improvement.[22]

By this time, however, another stimulus appeared — Sir George Stuart Mackenzie's open letter of August 1, 1815, to Sir Joseph Banks, in which he tried to determine the optimum form of a hothouse, having calculated the quantity of the sun's rays that would strike an exterior glass roof and walls at optimum angles throughout the day and at different times of the year. His calculations yielded a "semi-dome," or quarter of a sphere, which could be constructed, he believed, with curving ribs of cast iron and then set up against a plain brick wall. Above the wall would be a plain pediment and, above that, an urn (fig. 47).[23]

Mackenzie's design was a strange hybrid of classical architecture and horticultural engineering. T. A. Knight was intrigued, but felt the proportions were wrong. Anticipating that the plants would be shaded by the cast-iron ribs' converging at the top, and concerned about the rainwater that would collect outside on the relatively flat top of the semidome, Knight suggested some changes in form and materials. He read another paper before the Horticultural Society in April 1817; and in August, writing from Downton, in Herefordshire, he added that iron sash bars of less weight than cast iron but equal in strength could be used, attributing the idea to Mr. Loudon, "to whose practical skill and extensive observation," he noted, "much attention is due."[24]

Loudon proposed to improve Mackenzie's semidome by "acuminating" the form, that is, by shaping the longitudinal ribs into a slight peak at the top that would shed rain. Instead of the semidome attached to a brick wall, Loudon preferred a free-standing dome, or acuminated structure, entirely of glass, for elegance and a maximum of light (fig. 48, no. 254).[25] To reduce the structural framework to as thin a skeleton as possible, he would use wrought iron instead of wood or cast iron. To make the framework curvilinear, he had invented a wrought-iron sash bar, which could be bent and curved without losing its strength. This sash bar could be used to improve traditional conservatories and hothouses, but its most exciting application would be to create forms as yet unknown in the garden. "Imagine," he wrote, "instead of a row of glazed sheds, a row of detached sections of spherical bodies of an almost perfect transparence — the genial climate and highly coloured productions within, obtaining during the whole day the unobstructed influence of the sun's rays, and the con-

## Elevation of the Front.

### Fig. 1.

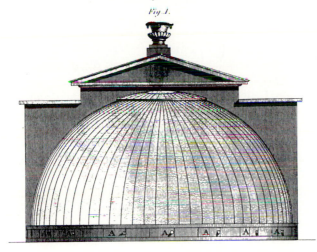

A — *Sliding shutters in low wall to admit Air.*

B — *Shutters along the top of back wall to open and shut on pivots with a cord. Larger openings may be made by means of windows in the back wall.*

C — *Half the plan of the glass cover formed of cast iron astragals 2¾ inches from front to inside and ⅜ inches thick on which the glass is fixed thus — Glass.*

D — *Half the plan shewing the flue F going round to B and out at the vase at top.*

G — *Treillage for vines with an opening in the centre 6 by or 3 to allow a person to pass.*

H — *Cast iron astragals glazed.*

## Plan of the House.

### Fig. 2.

*The roofs of the Porch Furnace will be about 8 feet from the ground.*

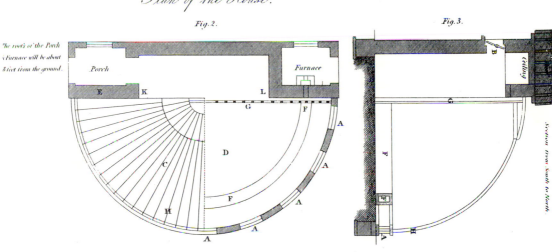

Porch

Furnace

### Fig. 3.

*Section from South to North.*

### Fig. 4.

struction of the edifice combining the greatest strength and durability —
what will be the expression?"[26] In envisioning circular towers and Eastern
domes of glass, Loudon was seeking more than a technical solution to the
problem of forcing fruits and vegetables. He longed for the elegant effect
of Russian glasshouses, which had made British hothouses seem scattered
and disconnected, if more durable and efficient. Again, beauty and utility
had to be reconciled.

At that time, Loudon's spherical glasshouses attached to brick walls
were being built by Messrs W. and D. Bailey, who had acquired the rights
to Loudon's sash bar. Loudon was still thinking of liberating these sections
of spheres from the wall, to create the more elegant free-standing structure
entirely sheathed in glass that he had imagined in 1805.[27] Essentially, he
wanted to liberate the horticultural structure from its dependence on the
architectural tradition of massiveness, which Reyner Banham has discussed in *The Architecture of the Well-Tempered Environment* (1969).
"Architecture came to be seen as the conscious art of creating these
massive and perdurable structures," Banham explains — structures of
stone and earthy substances that tend to absorb and store heat and to
conserve valuable building materials, because they are built to last.[28]
Loudon's curvilinear glass and iron structure would be relatively durable
and lightweight. It would admit a maximum amount of sunlight. To make
up for the loss of heat through its shell, it would depend on artificial modes
of heating, but Loudon tried to reduce the need for fuel (and for the human
labor of tending the furnaces) by doubling the roof with a second layer of
glass or with a covering, erected of canvas or boards.[29]

The utility of these structures was undeniable — but their beauty?
Most people, Loudon reasoned, would now agree that edifices could be
beautiful without displaying any features of the Grecian or Gothic styles.
Nearly thirty years earlier, Archibald Alison had observed that the sublimity or beauty of forms arises from their evocative associations and
expressive qualities.[30] If the arguments in Alison's *Essays on Taste* were
still valid, perhaps new transparent curvilinear forms, arising from a need
for more light and space, could express something more dignified than the

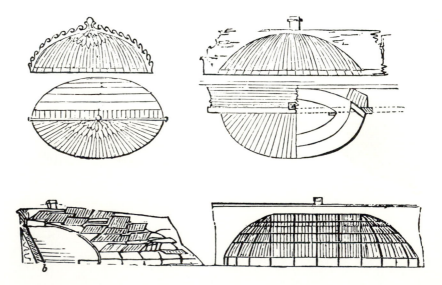

1609. *The general form and appearance of a ridge and furrow house* ( *fig.* 259.) is not materially different from that of others. Where the curved end is adopted, it will not be necessary to deviate from the common mode of glazing in these parts of the roof, unless with a view to resist a weight of snow. While the parallelogram part of the roof, therefore, is ridged ( *fig.* 260. *a, a*), the ends will present a smooth surface ( *fig.* 260. *b, b*).

1610. *The polyprosopic hot-house* ( *fig.* 261. ) resembles a curvilinear house, but differs in having the surface thrown into a number of faces, the chief advantages of which are, 1. That by hinging all the different

These sketches include Loudon's semiellipse (fig. 255), his polyprosopic hothouse (fig. 261), *his ridge-and-furrow (or "double meridian") hothouse* (figs. 259, 260), *the conglomeration of several types of glasshouses at his home in Bayswater (fig. 253), and his acuminated semidome (fig. 254).*

Fig. 48
J.C.Loudon, Sketches of curvilinear hothouses.

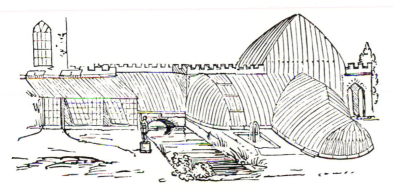

260

faces at their upper angles, and by having rods connecting the lower outside corners of the faces terminating in chains which go over pulleys in the top or above the back wall, the whole roof, including the ends, may be opened or raised sympathetically, like Venetian blinds ( *fig.* 261. *a.* ), either so as each sash or face may be placed in the plane of the angle of the sun's rays at the time, or to the perpendicular, to admit a shower of rain.

1603. *Some forms of hot-houses on the curvilinear principle* shall now be submitted, and afterwards some specimens of the forms in common use; for common forms, it is to be observed, are not recommended to be laid aside in cases where ordinary objects are to be attained in the easiest manner; and they are, besides the forms of roofs, the most convenient for pits, frames, and glass tents, as already exemplified in treating of these structures.

1604. *The acuminated semi-globe.* ( *fig.* 254.) The most perfect form of a hot-house is indisputably that of a glazed semi-globe. Here plants, as far as respects light, would be nearly in the same situation as if in the open air; and art, as already observed, (1592.) can add heat, and all the other agents of vegetation, nearly to perfection. But in respect to excluding the rain, the semi-globe is too flat at top,

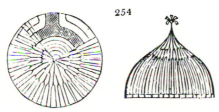

254

and requires to be acuminated; and in regard to economy, the first cost and expense of maintaining an artificial heat against its constant abduction through a thin medium, exposed to the north winds, would, for most purposes, be a great objection.

1605. *An acuminated semi-dome*, or a vertical section of the last figure, placed against a wall built in a direction from east to west, removes a great part of the objection as to heat, and will still admit an adequate supply of light to plants kept constantly in the same position, or turned very frequently. This, therefore, may be reckoned the second best form for a plant-habitation for general purposes, and without reference to particular modes of culture.

old hothouse shed. What new associations, Loudon wondered, what new trains of thought, might arise from the sight of curvilinear glass forms? Wherever strength, lightness, permanence, and security were needed — whether in skylights, shop fronts, warehouses, churches, hospitals, homes, or offices — Loudon recommended the use of his wrought-iron sash bar for glazing, whether planar or curved.

In his Bayswater garden, Loudon continued to experiment with new forms and systems. He compared different types of glass and iron construction for their various effects on the plants inside. He built traditional greenhouse sheds attached to a curvilinear pyramid of glass. He erected convex curvilinear walls with ridge-and-furrow (or "double-meridian") glazing, originally designed to let the sun's rays strike at favorable right angles twice a day — in the morning and afternoon, when the sun's rays were generally less powerful, instead of just once, around noon, when the intense rays could scorch the leaves of plants closest to the glass. The combination of curvilinear ribs and ridge-and-furrow glazing, he noted, tended to equalize both the amount and the intensity of sunlight that plants received during several hours of the day. His "polyprosophic house" had curving glass roofs composed of flat sashes that could be opened simultaneously to admit fresh air, breezes, rain, or direct sunlight.[31] The indoor artificial climate was further regulated by an apparatus that automatically controlled heat and ventilation. Near the steam boiler Loudon set up Kewley's "alarum thermometer" and "automaton gardener," which, working together, would open and shut the moveable glazed sashes with the rising and falling of the indoor temperature. (This subtle, continuous motion Loudon found fascinating.)[32]

The visual result of all these experiments in Bayswater was a curious mixture of traditional sheds, Gothic imagery, and unprecedented forms that spread out in all directions like some prehistoric "presence," rearing its battlemented backbone of brick and cast iron, or like some prophetic being, a strange new transparent beast slouching toward London (see fig. 48). Its first progeny, however, were the elegant glass ranges constructed by W. and D. Bailey from Loudon's designs, including the 120-foot north stove and 50-foot south stove at Chiswick; T. A. Knight's 50-foot hothouse for pineapples at Downton, Herefordshire; and, for M. P. S. De Caters de Wolfe, of Antwerp, two curvilinear structures for grapes and pineapples, 33 feet long, 15 feet wide, and 16 feet high.[33] All these ranges had curvilinear roofs, although some still stood against a massive brick wall. Later in the century, some free-standing glasshouses, such as Mrs. Beaumont's conservatory at Bretton Hall, Yorkshire (1827), were built according to Loudon's designs.[34] Richard Turner's Palm House (fig. 49) at Kew Gardens (1845–58) and Sir Joseph Paxton's Crystal Palace at the Great Exhibition in Hyde Park (1851) were both influenced by Loudon's combination of the curvilinear sash bar with ridge-and-furrow glazing.[35] Sadly, his finest glass designs, for a great circular range of hothouses in the Birmingham Botanical Garden (1831) were never realized—possibly because of the expense, probably because of their unprecedented half-doughnut or beehive-shaped structure (see figs. 78 and 79).

As Loudon had observed in 1822, most people's idea of a glasshouse was still the traditional eighteenth-century greenhouse, with its stone piers or columns, its cornices and entablatures — even though the rules of classical architecture were no more relevant to the design of a hothouse

PALM HOUSE. KEW.

BRIDGE AND

CARNIVORA CAGES. ZOOL. GARDENS.

WINTER GARDEN R.B.

KNIGHT'S CYCLOPÆDIA
OF
LONDON.

NO. II. GARDENS.

than to the design of a ship or a fortress![36] Unlike Le Corbusier, however, Loudon never imitated the forms of a ship.[37] He simply insisted that any structure for raising plants in an artificial climate should be judged by its ability to supply heat, light, air, and water. By the same criteria he judged the quality of houses for people, especially for the poor. It cannot be a coincidence that his last paper on curvilinear hothouses (1818) was published just two months before he devised a scheme of multifamily housing for the poor in London.

From the time of his return from the Continent in 1814 until he settled in Bayswater, Loudon had lived for a couple of years in his old neighborhood, on Newman Street — just a few blocks west of the infamous "rookery," or slum, of St. Giles's Parish, Holborn (the site of the recent Centre Point development on New Oxford Street).[38] Apparently he did not ignore his near neighbors, for he alluded to their wretched living conditions when he proposed better dwellings and tried to find someone to build them.

At the time, no one was building housing expressly for the poor in London.[39] So-called third- and fourth-rate row houses were beginning to appear in areas like Somers Town, east of Regent's Park, disconcerting those who wanted to maintain the property values of the first-rate houses in Regent's Park.[40] Yet even these humble row houses were beyond the means of London's poorest inhabitants, who tended to drift into the cramped quarters of older dwellings converted to tenements. For these people, overcrowding, filth, disease, and epidemics were the norm.

Appalled by these conditions, Loudon was convinced that "the advantages of steam and gas may be enjoyed by the lowest classes of society, at an expense less, or at least not more, than what they pay for miserable lodgings, or small houses in unhealthy lanes and courts of the metropolis."[41] Thus, in May 1818 Loudon drew up his first multifamily housing scheme, "Colleges for Working Men," and showed it to Sir Joseph Banks. Unfortunately, nothing came of it, and Loudon became ill soon afterwards. A year later he was in southern Europe, gathering additional material for the first edition of his *Encyclopaedia of Gardening*, and the housing project was forgotten. (Sir Joseph Banks died in June 1820.) In the next several years, Loudon was preoccupied with writing the encyclopedia, laying out grounds of country residences, building his own home in Bayswater, and editing his new *Gardener's Magazine*, in which he discussed housing for gardeners and agricultural laborers. Then, in December 1831, "Junius Redivivus" proposed a scheme for urban housing in the *Mechanics' Magazine*. Intrigued, Loudon immediately contributed his own design for working men's colleges, somewhat revised. On February 4, 1832, Loudon's design appeared on the cover of the *Mechanics' Magazine* (fig. 50).

Thus Loudon and Junius Redivivus (actually William Bridges Adams, the railway engineer and inventor) began to share their congenial views on economical housing. Both had utilitarian sympathies and were apparently aware of the centrally planned Panopticon workhouse scheme of Jeremy Bentham.[42] Junius wrote occasional anonymous articles in Bentham's *Westminster Review*, where Loudon's books and his arboretum in Derby received long, sympathetic reviews.[43] Both Junius and Loudon were accustomed to solving the technical problems of construction and mechanical services. Junius, for example, saw no great difficulty in hous-

# 𝕸𝖊𝖈𝖍𝖆𝖓𝖎𝖈𝖘' 𝕸𝖆𝖌𝖆𝖟𝖎𝖓𝖊,
## MUSEUM, REGISTER, JOURNAL, AND GAZETTE.

No. 443.]  SATURDAY, FEBRUARY 4, 1832.  [Price 8d.

## COLLEGES FOR WORKING MEN.

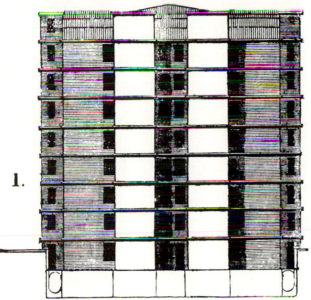

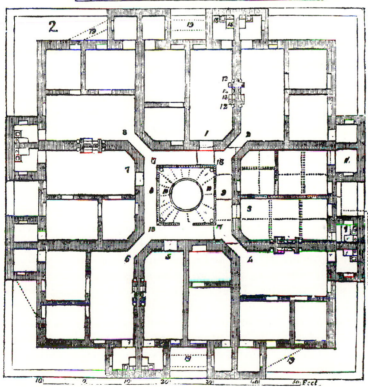

*First conceived in 1818, this scheme for unsubsidized housing in London was discussed in the parliamentary report on the* State of Large Towns *(1844), but never built. Quintessentially urban, the scheme was intended to provide working men's families with the basic spatial and technological requirements of any social class in a densely built environment. For suburban or rural sites, Loudon always insisted that dwellings have land attached, for gardens, orchards, bees, and so forth.*

Fig. 50
J.C.Loudon, Elevation and plan of colleges for working men.

ing hundreds of families under one roof, so long as a favorable indoor climate could be maintained and individual privacy preserved. "Children, in warm climates, thrive best naked," he reasoned. "In cold and variable climates they will not bear it. Make then an equable artificial climate, and the difficulty will be removed. Children may then be reared as easily as grapes and pineapples. . . . What an advantage would it be to the poor children, to need no more sleeping potions of gin and Dalby's!"[44]

Junius's proposal was straightforward: let some entrepreneur erect a building 350 feet square, composed of a basement and five stories, with a central courtyard. Each two-room apartment would open onto courtyard galleries on each floor, as in an old-fashioned inn. The cast-iron construction should be fireproof, and lighting could be centrally regulated by a gasometer. Heating would be provided by a combination of individual fireplaces and a system of pipes to collect and redistribute all surplus heat from the public laundries, baths, and kitchens located on each side of the building. These cooperative features implied no utopian dream, Junius asserted; they simply offered a practical means of improving the lives of people who had few, if any, material comforts. No philanthropy was expected. The builder should realize his 5 percent, or more. And working people should learn to be good citizens — particularly from the civilizing influences of nurseries, warm baths, and schools within the building. The essential ingredient was cooperation.

Junius also anticipated the need for flexibility, in order to accommodate individual tastes and needs. Although all bedrooms would face the street and all sitting rooms would face the galleries and courtyard, some apartments might be joined together for larger families. One apartment might be shared by unmarried women, another by unmarried men. Furniture, built-in closets, a lending library, and space for lectures might be provided. Given these opportunities for warmth, cleanliness, and nourishment for the mind, the poor should gradually give up the vices to which they were especially prone, such as drunkenness, a kind of environmental palliative. "In a short time," Junius reflected, "the influence of the virtuous part of such a community would either reform the vicious, or drive them to seek refuge elsewhere, and either would be a gain."[45]

Loudon's plan, left uncompleted in 1818, focused on the technical and spatial problems of housing. His building of seven stories and a half-basement would measure 65 feet square and house only sixty-four families, not Junius's four hundred. In place of Junius's four corner-staircases, Loudon proposed a central inclined plane, or spiraling ramp, which would rise at a rate slightly greater than that of Holborn Hill in London (which has since been nearly leveled by the Holborn Viaduct, built in the 1860s).[46] Thus, the ramp would not be too steep for pedestrians, barrow-women, and "go-carts," Loudon reasoned. Each apartment would be entered from the galleries surrounding the central spiraling ramp. The hollow core of the building would be roofed over — presumably by a skylight — and centrally heated by steam. Walls would be of brick and floors (large slabs of Arbroath pavement) would rest on brick walls or on cast-iron rafters.

The simplicity and modernity of Loudon's design is remarkable. In fact, the elevation resembles an apartment building that Skidmore, Owings and Merrill have recently completed near Harvard Square in Cambridge, Massachusetts.[47] Loudon used no ornament and made no reference to the historical styles. On each façade, the two projecting "towers," banded by continuous string courses, may be the first service towers ever conceived for an apartment building. Designed with side windows and a blank wall facing the street, the towers would supply each apartment with a so-called sink-stone, a water-closet, and a water supply cistern. The façades reveal few windows, although those that exist are relatively large. (In 1818 there was still a duty on glass and a tax on windows.)[48]

For low-income units, to be let at market rates, Loudon's proposed accommodations were remarkably generous. Each family would have three rooms and two or three exposures. Every room had a window facing the street or the galleries. Each large family room, ten feet by twenty feet, contained an open fireplace. On an inside wall, recessed steam tubes were connected to an apparatus for cooking, washing, and central heating. Each family could regulate the temperature of its own apartment by opening or closing the various sections of a tripartite door enclosing the recessed steam tubes. Laundry lines could be hung on pulleys stretching between some of the windows (as indicated by dotted lines on the plan). Within the central spiraling ramp would be a rubbish chute. (Here Loudon's manuscript broke off.)

Although this housing scheme was tucked away and forgotten for many years, Loudon kept up with all the latest inventions and new materials. When his housing scheme was finally published in 1832, Loudon added an account of Frost's new fireproof floors made of hollow earthenware tubes imbedded in Frost's own mixture of cement. Loudon also included a description of Witty's improved furnace, in which coal was first carbonized into coke, then burned. Within this furnace, smoke was efficiently consumed, emitting no smell or soot to pollute the air.[49]

Junius Redivivus was delighted with Loudon's housing scheme, accompanied by notes on fireproof floors and improved furnaces — although he still preferred his own open, angular courtyard and stairwells to Loudon's spiraling ramp.[50] The two men spoke the same technical and humane language. They saw the possibilities for extending the benefits of technology, initially devised for utilitarian factories and splendid plant houses, to houses for the working classes. In turn, they would confidently recommend the benefits of cooperation, not only to the poor, but to people of other socioeconomic classes. Junius recalled the boarding houses of New York, for example, where the rich and the middle classes lived comfortably, side by side; the lawyers' chambers in the Inns of Court; and the lofty buildings of Edinburgh, where some families lived on single stories, rather than in individual homes.[51]

In his *Encyclopaedia of Architecture* (1832–33), Loudon pointed out that his cooperative scheme for "Eighty dwellings of the humblest class" could be altered to suit the needs of any income group (Fig. 51).[52] Given a limited budget, a quadrangle could be composed of one-story cottages with concrete floors, plastered earthen walls, and thatched roofs. Fronting onto its own flower garden and orchard–pleasure-ground, each cottage would also overlook the central public gardens and playgrounds. With more ample funds and sturdier materials, Loudon suggested, a two-story quadrangle could be erected, perhaps surrounded by relatively smaller private gardens and a second, larger quadrangle — indicated by dotted lines on his plan. (This plan may have inspired Colonel Edward Akroyd's

*First published in 1832–33,
this plan may have gener-
ated other housing schemes,
such as J.S.Buckingham's
projected "Victoria" (1849)
and Colonel Edward
Akroyd's Akroydon, in
Halifax, built in 1861–63.
Both Loudon and Buck-
ingham served on the Com-
mittee of the Metropolitan
Improvement Society, Lon-
don, formed in January,
1842.*

Fig. 51
J.C.Loudon, "Eighty dwellings
for the labouring classes,"
plan.

model village in Halifax — Akroydon [1861–63] — designed by George
Gilbert Scott and W. H. Crossland without Loudon's centralized public
facilities and buffer of private gardens between the concentric quadrangles.)[53]

Whatever their scale, Loudon's proposed quadrangles would be
centrally heated by steam or (preferably) by hot water, conducted to each
dwelling from the central facility that also housed a public kitchen and
bakehouse, two dining rooms, a laundry, drying room, brewhouse, library, infant school, and Lancasterian schools for both boys and girls. If
money were no object, the wealthy occupants of such quadrangles could
enjoy stables, coach houses, assembly rooms, a theatre, walled gardens,
conservatories, hothouses, pleasure grounds, and a park. "The principle
is the same in all," Loudon observed, "—that of producing in masses, by
machinery, and by a division of labour, what has hitherto been effected in
scattered fragments, by manual labour, and by every individual family for
itself."[54] Through cooperation, each individual could enjoy more comfort
and enjoyment for a given sum or amount of labor than he ever could
independently. For further suggestions, Loudon referred to Robert
Owen's cooperative schemes for people with incomes of £500 to £1,000 a
year.

Junius thought Owen's schemes pleasant, but unrealistic. A truly
cooperative system would succeed only among people of comparable
property, health, and intellect—and even relative equality in such matters might take centuries to achieve.[55] Loudon was more optimistic.
*Education* would prepare the rising generation for living in working men's

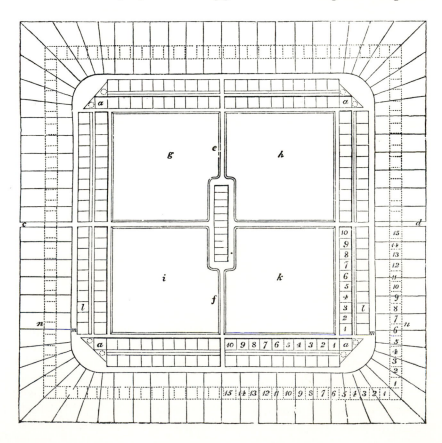

colleges. "The first step towards living together in communities," he wrote, "is being educated together in infant and Lancasterian schools."[56]

Loudon was continually striving to educate the new generation of architects who would design these new communities. In his gardener's and architectural magazines, with their discussions of heating, fireproofing, ventilation, construction, and new materials, he informed architects of the technical innovations that were changing the nature of their profession. With Frost's fireproof cement slabs reinforced by iron or hollow earthenware tubes, for instance, terrace gardens could be created on flat roofs. Witty's smoke-consuming furnaces could help to eliminate smoke in the atmosphere. Someday, Loudon noted, "London might become a city of flat roofs covered with gardens of pots."[57]

At that time, smoke was coming to be recognized as a serious environmental problem—not only in cities, but in gardens where glasshouses were heated by burning coal to produce steam or hot water. Perhaps the sun itself could be relied upon to provide a cleaner source of artificial heat, Loudon mused, even in the often overcast isle of Britain. In September 1827, he gave an account of Robert Gauen's experiments with solar heating in an orchard at Millbrook, near Southampton (fig. 52). Gauen, a gardener, had constructed a cluster of glass lenses and focused them on a hollow cast-iron ball set on a pedestal. As the sun's rays were concentrated on the ball through the lenses, the air inside the ball was heated, rose through a tube, and diffused through a long horizontal tube with vertical "branches" of different lengths—a sort of giant hot air comb, with hollow, uneven teeth. Eventually the heated air rose through the vertical "branches" and escaped among the leaves and blossoms of the adjacent fruit tree.[58]

*In 1827 the* ne plus ultra *of hothouse gardening, in Loudon's view, would have been the application of Gauen's forcing apparatus and Kewley's "automaton gardener," a regulating thermometer, to Loudon's own "polyprosopic hothouse" (see fig. 48). Here, in the open air, Gauen's apparatus distributes hot air from the cast-iron solar collector (the ball on a pedestal), through tubes, to the leaves and blossoms of fruit trees.*

Fig. 52
Robert Gauen, Apparatus for forcing fruit trees by concentrating solar energy on a hollow cast-iron ball.

" . . . what would be the
effect on the climate of the
whole world, supposing it
were practicable for all its
seas, rivers, and lakes to be
covered with solar con-
centrators?" (Loudon, 1828).

Fig. 53
J.C.Loudon, Proposed apparatus for warming the earth by
solar concentration.

In January 1828, Loudon proposed a solar heating system based on elements of various schemes published in his *Gardener's Magazine.* Gauen's hollow cast-iron ball; Thomas Tredgold's experiments with heat, moisture, and evaporation; and William Atkinson's method for controlling humidity and ventilation in hothouses.[59] With a siphon connected to a hollow, presumably metallic, ball, Loudon proposed to heat underground water and thereby to heat the interior or exterior atmosphere (fig. 53). This was his suggestion:

Sink wells or cisterns, at regular distances, all over a garden or a country, and place over each a concentrating apparatus, so contrived as to operate on a ball. This ball being connected with a pipe, the change of temperature of the water in the ball would cause the water to ascend in successive portions, and thus the pipe would act like a syphon, and draw up the water from the bottom of the well or tank, to be heated in the ball, and return it to the top of the well or tank, there to give out its heat to the earth above.[60]

Just as Britain was kept unusually warm for its latitude because of water heated largely in warmer regions, he reasoned, so hothouses are kept warm at night by water which has been heated during the day. He then speculated on the effects of heating a garden over a cistern, or a whole countryside near a lake, or of heating all the lakes, ponds, canals, wells, and tanks in England, or of heating all the seas, rivers, and lakes of the world! What might be the effect on the climate of covering these portions of the earth with solar concentrators? Without pursuing the idea of altering the climate of the globe, Loudon was content to make one practical suggestion: that solar concentrators be placed on the roof of a church. "There would at least be enough of sunshine during the week to produce heat for Sundays," he observed. Thus one could heat the immersion tanks of Baptist chapels, or perhaps public and private baths. Machinery would have to be designed to keep the solar concentrators perpendicular to the sun's rays. And someone would have to fund the project.[61]

The cost of this, or of any other, complex scheme might be prohibitive—in the short term. But Loudon and colleagues such as Junius Redivivus were also thinking of the long-term effects of advanced technology, on the one hand, or of stagnation, on the other. Junius was disgusted with the smoke-polluted air of London and the rude state of domestic architecture in Britain in general. In spite of the advances in heating and fireproofing found in industrial buildings, dwellings were still being erected and maintained by mere expedients, "as though we were willing to increase, to the greatest possible extent, the labour of our servants."[62]

The implications were clear: while labor remained relatively cheap and architecture was still considered an exercise in the decoration of a shell, living conditions inside were likely to remain in a rude state. Loudon, although he could appreciate a beautiful shell, was equally interested in its construction, its materials, and the mechanical services inside. The young architect, he realized, must not neglect any of the sciences of building; nor could he assume that the *art* of architecture was independent of these concerns. The progressive architect, in Loudon's mature view, must be something of an engineer, as well as an artist.

# 8

## Progressive Architecture

Loudon's mature writings
on architecture are
prophetic. He emphasizes
function and expression of
function rather than style;
and he favors the Pro-
gressive, not the Stationary,
"School" of architecture.

When Loudon introduced the first number of his *Architectural Magazine*, in March 1834, he himself needed no introduction. He had just completed the twelfth and final segment of the *Encyclopaedia of Cottage, Farm and Villa Architecture and Furniture*, a popular work that had already begun to encourage better construction in the cottages and farm buildings of the British Isles, Australia, and America.[1] To this encyclopedia the *Architectural Magazine* would be a monthly supplement. Loudon and his contributors would continue to discuss the technical, aesthetic, and social aspects of design, but the scope of their discussions would be broader than the encyclopedia's, encompassing public and private buildings, both urban and rural. Loudon's goals were also more ambitious. With the *Encyclopaedia* he had hoped to diffuse an informed taste for architecture among a wide audience so that, ultimately, the dwellings of the great mass of society would be improved. With the *Magazine*, he would pursue this goal on a higher plane, "by rendering [architecture] a more intellectual profession, by recommending it as a fit study for ladies, and by inducing young architects to read, write and think, as well as to see and draw."[2]

Loudon's *Architectural Magazine* was the first periodical devoted to architecture in the English language.[3] In its pages Loudon reported on new inventions and building projects and featured essays on aesthetic or technical issues, with relatively few illustrations. In contrast, his *Encyclopaedia* was a profusely illustrated compendium of ideas and general principles of architecture, rural and suburban, which encouraged potential homeowners to formulate their own ideas before conferring with an architect or builder. The *Architectural Magazine* provoked and accommodated more diversity of opinion, but in both works, a liberal exchange of information and opinion was essential to Loudon's purposes. He welcomed contributions from architects, engineers, artisans, and amateurs, for he wanted his readers to exercise their critical judgments on designs of varying quality. In fact, Loudon believed that a student could learn more from analyzing a poor design than from gazing upon a beautiful one.

Given this conviction, Loudon could not continue in the pattern-book tradition of Serlio and Palladio, the sixteenth-century Italian architects who had also compiled designs for a variety of building types and patrons.[4] Both had maintained a consistently high quality and personal style, but Loudon included a variety of designs contributed by others. In the *Encyclopaedia*, he mingled the fanciful and the straightforward, the extravagant and the humble, the ridiculous and the sublime. In the *Magazine*, however, he included fewer architectural designs; and these were generally of higher quality.

Loudon was aware that many architects looked upon his architectural publications "with anything but a favourable eye." Some feared that his diffusing architectural knowledge to a wide audience would have a depressing effect on their profession, as laymen would come to believe they could do without the services of a professional. Loudon disagreed. He maintained that men of wealth and taste would always demand first-rate architects. In fact, as people became more enlightened in architecture — as they had in public health, law, education, and gardening, for example — they would create a greater demand for the professional's services. Loudon continued to urge that carpenters, masons, builders, and laymen — particularly women — study the principles of architecture and make some effort to improve the common dwellings of the country. Some of their modest efforts might be considered "incorrect" or lacking in taste. But Loudon was convinced that faults, once recognized, would lead to better buildings; "in the path of improvement," he wrote, "anything is better than standing still."[5]

Loudon must have been encouraged by the strong support he received from the press. Though they expressed an occasional reservation, the *Westminster Review*, the *Athenaeum*, the *Penny Magazine*, the *New Monthly Magazine*, and even the *Annales* of the Paris Horticultural Society praised Loudon's architectural works for their undisputed utility. In 1839 the London *Times* wrote of the *Encyclopaedia*, "no single work has ever effected so much good in improving the arrangement and external appearance of country dwellings, generally."[6] In 1841 Alexandre Poiteau, writing for the *Annales* in Paris, recognized the author of the *Encyclopaedia* as a "friend of humanity," who was continually trying to improve the relations between master and servant by informing the one and elevating the feelings of the other.[7]

Loudon's *Encyclopaedia* made such a solid contribution to the well-being of cottagers that only a few reviewers even mentioned the issues of taste and quality of design. Poiteau appreciated Loudon's critical commentaries, the result, he believed, of "deep reflection" on the art of architecture. The *Gentleman's Magazine*, judging the collected designs as a whole, noted, "The publication of Mr. Loudon's will, we hope, be the means of banishing this spurious taste [for Carpenter's Gothic] from our land; and if it does not display absolute purity in all the designs, it possesses the merit, that a contrast may be made between the good and the bad, the chaste and the flimsy, and, being published in a periodical form, admit of improvement as the work proceeds to a close."[8]

Whether Loudon was correct in holding that the architectural student could best learn to design by sharpening his critical skills on a variety of images, the chaste and the flimsy alike, is still open to question. Does the sight of perfection intimidate — or stimulate? Is a principle of design best instilled by rational argument — or by a beautiful image? And how important is a first impression? A century earlier, Joseph Addison had suggested that ideas first enter the mind through the sense of sight, that "most perfect and most delightful of all our senses." On June 23, 1712, he had reminded the readers of the *Spectator* that "there is nothing that makes its way more directly to the soul than beauty, which immediately diffuses a secret satisfaction and complacency through the imagination and gives a finishing to any thing that is great or uncommon. The very first discovery of it strikes the mind with an inward joy, and spreads a cheerfulness and delight through all its faculties."[9]

Addison's emphasis on the power of visual beauty could hardly have escaped Loudon's attention, for these remarks appeared in Addison's well-known essay "On the Pleasures of the Imagination," in which Loudon found some of the earliest and most endearing arguments for including views of pastures and cultivated fields in the landscape garden.[10] He would certainly agree that images were a powerful means of conveying ideas. In his own earliest writings, Loudon had furnished clear technical illustrations to instruct workmen, along with more evocative renderings meant to persuade prospective clients. As noted earlier, he had even invented a portable, three-dimensional model to explain visually his ideas for improving a gentleman's estate.[11] Still, decades later, Loudon's *Encyclopaedia* displayed flawed images before the untrained eye of the general reader. Apparently he was confident that reason — his own discussions and the reader's critical response — could overcome the power of the faulty image, which assailed the beholder at first glance.

Unfortunately, the casual browser in the *Encyclopaedia* who skipped Loudon's rational discussions and remembered only the fanciful images, could easily come away with some vague notion that architectural design was merely a matter of historical style (cross sections of buildings and diagrams of heating systems notwithstanding). Only the close reader would detect Loudon's personal preference for simplicity of form and economy of means, whatever the architectural style. After describing a design, Loudon often proposed changes, such as adjustment to a floor plan or refinement of proportions. Granted, a great architect would have scrapped a poor design and begun again, intending to create a thing of beauty. But Loudon, as critic and editor, was trying to stimulate the critical faculties of his readers; he wanted them to become their own critics and, ultimately, to think for themselves.

As a mature writer, Loudon meant "to instruct and not to lead." If his architectural publications reflect his own taste and aspirations, this is most evident in the text, not in the images. Having lost his right arm in 1825, at the age of forty-two, Loudon required draftsmen and engravers to give form to his ideas for design. His sisters and assistants made woodcuts from some of his earlier sketches and copperplate or steel engravings, but for the most part he depended on the talents of his contributors, eminent or obscure.[12] After his marriage in September 1830, Loudon also relied on the manual and editorial skills of his young wife Jane, whose cheerful assistance and good common sense contributed something to the tone of Loudon's later works. On the whole, his mature architectural publications reflect the tastes and tempers of his collaborators, and his images reflect the tastes of the age.

Who were some of these tastemakers? Perhaps the best-known contributor to Loudon's *Encyclopaedia* was Sir Charles Barry, who, with A.W.N.Pugin, designed the new Houses of Parliament (1835–60). The

*Before he became involved with A.W.N.Pugin on the new Houses of Parliament, Barry contributed some revised elevations in various styles to Loudon's Encyclopaedia of Cottage, Farm, and Villa Architecture. As far as comfort and convenience were concerned, Loudon thought the Grecian, Gothic, and Italian styles equally appropriate for villas; the differences lay mainly in men's minds and in historical associations — not in the forms themselves. His leading principle would still remain "fitness for the end in view."*

Fig. 54
Charles Barry, Revision of the northwest façade of the *"Beau Ideal Villa"* by Selim.

*Encyclopaedia* contains Barry's design for a faintly Jacobean, faintly Tudor-Gothic parsonage, with fenestration and details resembling those of Hatfield House, in Herefordshire (ca. 1611). Barry also produced Italianate and Tudor-Gothic elevations for the circular stables which Loudon designed and built in 1809 at Garth, in Montgomeryshire. Charles Fowler, architect of Covent Garden Market (1828–30) and the conservatory at Syon House, in Brentford (ca. 1830), supplied a suburban villa in the "Old English" manner. John Robertson, Loudon's draftsman and, later, Sir Joseph Paxton's assistant, contributed many of his own designs for cottages (see fig. 61). And Edward Buckton Lamb, architect of the two pavilions in Loudon's arboretum in Derby (see fig. 87), prepared designs for a school, a country public house, several villas, domestic interiors, and furnishings.[13]

For the *beau idéal* of an English villa, "Selim," an amateur architect from Wiltshire, contributed the original design and text. At Loudon's request, Barry furnished the revised Elizabethan elevations (see fig. 54), which were reminiscent of Hatfield; of Burghley House, Northamptonshire (ca. 1575); and of Anthony Salvin's Harlaxton Manor, Lincolnshire (1831). The time for building such grand "villas" was rapidly passing, Loudon admitted; for as civilization progressed, the wealthy were no longer elevated so "immeasurably" above the rest of society. Still, Loudon believed that, someday, architects would look back on such villas for ideas when building smaller homes and "inns of recreation."[14]

While many of the architectural designs in Loudon's *Encyclopaedia* seem quaint today, the technical material is straightforward, often prophetic. The engineers Robert and William Mallet, of Dublin, contributed plans for a complete kitchen, or "culinary laboratory," equipped with gas ranges and a refrigerating apparatus that ran on the principles of cooling by evaporation and conduction by cold water. From Count Rumford's *Essays* Loudon extracted long passages on the arrangement of kitchens; and he reproduced the plates and text describing the extraordinary kitchen that Rumford had designed for the Baron de Lerchenfeld, Munich (fig. 55). The surveyor William Laxton submitted his suburban public house (or "pub"), featuring a bar with a "six-motion beer-machine" that would draw beer and ale of varying age and quality from butts stored in the cellar.

The carpenter-builder William Manning offered his design for prefabricated portable cottages, which he manufactured in packages of interchangeable parts in London, then shipped to the Australian colonies for rapid construction by a method resembling our now familiar "balloon frame" (fig. 56). And John Robison, secretary of the Royal Society in Edinburgh, contributed remarks on the merits of cast-iron construction, of gas lighting, and of hiring fire-fighting policemen in cities. [15]

As editor, Loudon often pushed a contributor's idea or principle a few steps further. Travelers, for instance, might purchase some of Manning's portable cottages, fit them with wheels, and convey them to camps by the sea or among the lakes of Cumberland and Westmoreland. By fitting each cottage with pipes coupled in series, families could enjoy hot-water heat from a single fire and fresh water from a single cistern. If cottages were aligned in a row, their projecting roofs would form a continuous veranda. In these ways, travelers might enjoy some of the benefits of society, as well as the freedom of mobility. [16]

Loudon's most significant and influential contribution to the *Encyclopaedia* was his model cottage, first published in his *Gardener's Magazine* for 1830 (fig. 57). [17] "Combining all the Accommodation and Conveniences of which human Dwellings of that description are susceptible," Loudon established a high minimum standard for a simple rural dwelling. In such a cottage every laborer *ought* to live, and any nobleman *might* live. (The necessities and basic comforts of life were relatively few, Loudon believed; and they were within reach of a far greater portion of

*Although the elegance of the engraving was lost, the ideas on kitchen engineering were retained in an engraving made of this scheme of Rumford's and published in Loudon's Encyclopaedia of Cottage, Farm and Villa Architecture.*

Fig. 55
T. Webster, "Perspective view of the Kitchen of Baron de Lerchenfeld at Munich," designed by Benjamin Thompson, Count Rumford.

*Perspective View of the Kitchen of Baron de Lerchenfeld at Munich*

*In* The Mummy *(1819), Mrs. Loudon (then Jane Webb) had imagined houses rolling down the street. In 1832–33 Loudon published an illustration of one of Manning's portable cottages and added some hints for cooperation among their transient or vacationing owners.*

Fig. 56 (*see also p. 144*)
William Manning, Prefabricated portable cottage for the Australian colonies.

mankind than one might imagine!) For a laborer, his wife, and their children of both sexes, Loudon proposed a one-story three-bedroom cottage, 24′ × 23′ in plan, with a hipped roof extended in the back to shelter cows, ducks, geese, fuel, and two separate lavatories: one for men and boys, entered from the back yard, and one for women and girls, opening off the girls' bedroom.

For economy of space, the cottage had no halls. The two front rooms — a combined kitchen and living room and a parlor — contained fireplaces. Hot air flues from the basement oven also heated the ground floor.[18] Next to the oven was the washing area and bath. A cistern over the projecting roof in the rear collected fresh water, which was filtered and piped to a basement storage tank. A manually operated "rotatory pump" after Siebe's design drew water to the ground floor. Each room had at least one sash window (the parlor had two); and the kitchen was equipped with a ventilating flue running up through the attic loft. For added insulation, the double brick walls were partly hollow, containing two-inch-wide air pockets along the inner sides of the stretchers and between the headers. Built into the exterior side wall of the kitchen-living room were a dovecot, a few shelves for beehives, and a dog kennel. Finally, swallows, those useful destroyers of winged insects, were allowed to build nests in the ample cornice surrounding the chimney tops and the kitchen air flue.

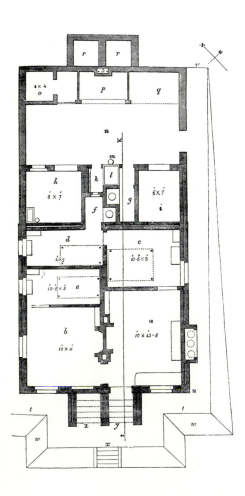

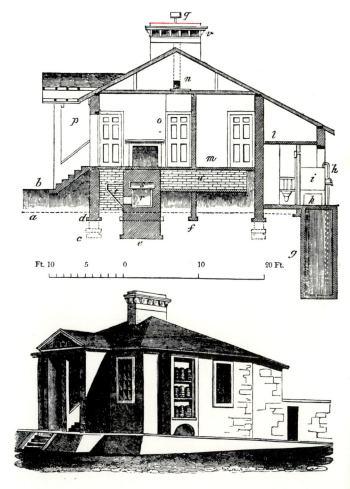

Loudon noted that his model cottage had no pretension to architectural style. It simply expressed its purpose: to house a fairly self-sufficient rural family of modest means. Ideally, the cottage was meant to be oriented so that the diagonal of the main structure ran north and south, and the entrance porch faced southeast. Thus, the sun's rays would strike all sides of the cottage in the course of a day. The terrace was designed to keep the ground floor dry, to provide a comfortable place to walk, and to elevate the character of the cottage — ensuring more dignity than would be found in most laborer's dwellings.

Loudon suggested a few desirable additions to this model cottage: hedges or dwarf walls; espaliered fruit trees; and climbing, flowering plants and vines; with perhaps an ivy-covered trellis over the roof, to retain some of the heat within the cottage. These embellishments recall Loudon's earliest ideas for improving cottages (in *Country Residences*), but in the later work he cautioned against excessive vegetation, which might shelter flies and produce dampness.[19] Two features clearly distinguish Loudon's model cottage from most "pattern book" cottages of the day — the terrace and the front porch. Like the idiosyncratic architect Gandy, Loudon refused to emphasize the cottage's humility and obscurity; he stressed the dignity to which even the poorest cottager could aspire.

The "Principles of Criticism in Architecture" were reserved for the very end of Loudon's *Encyclopaedia*. Only after the reader had been gradually introduced to plans, elevations, and design criteria did Loudon offer a systematic explanation of abstract principles. As in his confessedly "juvenile effort," *Country Residences*, Loudon's architectural principles were still divided into two main categories: utility, or convenience; and beauty, or ornament.[20] In the *Encyclopaedia*, however, he emphasized utility. "Fitness for the end in view" was Loudon's most important principle of architectural design. Second in importance was "the expression of the end in view." Both principles, as George Hersey has shown, are derived from Archibald Alison's *Essays on Taste* (1790).[21]

"The expression of some particular style" is Loudon's third principle, comprising all aesthetic concerns. The phrase is misleading, however; for in Loudon's view, the use of historical architectural styles is not essential to the achievement of beauty in architecture. Moreover, "beauty" is subdivided into two kinds: *accidental* and *universal*. Accidental, or historical beauty — the non-essential kind — is expressed by traditional elements of style, such as columns, pediments, entablatures, arches, and battlements. To achieve accidental beauty, the architect must have a sound knowledge of the traditional styles — their rules, principles, and customary applications. The other, *essential* kind of beauty — universal or inherent beauty — is expressed by the abstract qualities of composition, including unity, variety, harmony, regularity, ornament, and character. Thus, in Loudon's view, a building can be considered inherently beautiful without elegant columns, pediments, moldings, and so forth; the only essential considerations are abstract qualities of design.[22]

Today, one might well ask whether, by recognizing a kind of beauty not conditioned by the traditional rules or orders of architecture, Loudon was opening the door to a whimsical playing with the stylistic elements of the past, therefore auguring the even more whimsical or anarchic assemblages of recent "postmodern" architecture. On the contrary, as will

*When Loudon reproduced these plans in 1832–33, some ideas from his original lengthy article had to be omitted — among them, the notion that "all useful knowledge, and all useful food, lodging, and clothing, are surely destined to be common to all men."*
Fig. 57 (*opposite*)
J.C. Loudon, "Model cottage for a Country Labourer," plan, section, and perspective.

become clear, Loudon wanted to "read" the logical, believable story of a
building's construction on its façade, and he was not amused by little
tricks or conceits that defied conventional laws of gravity or propriety.
Moreover, he insisted that all ornament should be applied according to a
logical hierarchy based on fitness:

For example, in a very plain elevation of a house, without facings to the
windows, or a porch to the door, or a terminating cornice to the wall, it would
be an improper style of decoration to add vases or statues. The first step in
ornamenting such an elevation would be, to add facings or architraves to the
door and windows; next a porch, and a cornice under the roof, or near the top
of the walls. After this was done, if a degree higher in the scale of ornament
should be considered desirable, perhaps vases might form terminations to the
supporting pillars of the porch, or projecting balconies might be added to
some of the windows.[23]

To conclude this discussion of ornament, Loudon strongly recommends
that the young architect consult Quatremère de Quincy's *Essai sur l'imitation* (not yet translated into English in 1833) and Percier and Fontaine's
*Décorations intérieures*.[24]

Beauty, the ultimate aim of architecture viewed as a fine art, always
remained ineffable for Loudon, a matter of subtle, metaphysical speculation. As a mature writer, he revealed a sound, rational approach to design
and well-developed sensibilities. But the discussion of aesthetics and
metaphysics he left to others for elaboration. In his *Architectural Magazine*, he included articles by the architects George Wightwick, George
Godwin, and Charles Fowler, and the laymen Henry Noel Humphreys and
Thomas Sopwith. The magazine also contained several essays by
W. H. Leeds, or "Candidus," who championed the German neoclassical
architects, Karl Friedrich Schinkel and Leo von Klenze; articles by von
Klenze himself; and excerpts from Friedrich Weinbrenner's *Architek-
tonisches Lehrbuch* (1810–19).[25]

The *Architectural Magazine* also contained, in serial form, Thomas
Hope's *Historical Essay on Architecture*, Quatremère de Quincy's *On the
Principles of Taste*, and John Ruskin's *The Poetry of Architecture*.[26] To
young Ruskin, Loudon was particularly encouraging and receptive.

Loudon was the first to publish Ruskin's prose. Ruskin's speculations on the causes of the color of the water of the Rhine, written when he
was fifteen, appeared in Loudon's *Magazine of Natural History* in 1834;
three years later, his *Poetry of Architecture* appeared in Loudon's *Architectural Magazine*. Here Ruskin, the Oxford undergraduate, announced that
"no man can be an architect who is not a metaphysician. . . . Architecture is, or ought to be, a science of feeling more than of rule, a ministry to
the mind, more than to the eye."[27] At this, Loudon might smile and reflect
on his own youthful impatience with rules. But even as a young man,
Loudon had believed that the eye and the mind (or understanding) should
operate together in judging such qualities of a building as proportion.
Loudon assumed that architecture was more an art of reason than of
imagination, or feeling.

As Ruskin further developed the *Poetry of Architecture* in the fifth
volume of Loudon's *Magazine*, he wrote of the gentleness and humility of a
typical mountain cottage in Westmoreland: "It can never lie too humbly in
the pastures of the valley, nor shrink too submissively into the hollows of

the hills; it should seem to be asking the storm for mercy, and the mountain for protection; and should appear to owe to its weakness, rather than to its strength, that it is neither overwhelmed by the one, nor crushed by the other."[28] Gainsborough might have painted that scene. Price would have described the cottage in all its picturesque detail. Both might have tinged the humble scene with grandeur and affirmed the human dignity of the cottager. But Loudon, in his mature years, would have felt *obligated* to affirm that human dignity: to make the cottage more comfortable and to elevate its visual character. Ruskin shuddered at the "horrors of improvement" evident in the Lake District — typically along the public roads frequented by tourists.[29] Loudon generally welcomed improvements, however — material, technical, intellectual, and artistic. Improvements in political and social spheres were, in his view, inevitable; and personal improvement was necessary for one's own survival.

On principle, then, Loudon would resist the warnings that could already be detected in the 1830s in the writings of young Ruskin, Thomas Carlyle, and A.W.N.Pugin. In their disdain for an increasingly materialistic culture, these men were beginning to call for a halt to the incessant striving after progress, and to question the underlying values of a civilization based on continual change. Loudon not only welcomed change as a precondition for any kind of improvement — social, political, or artistic — he also warned that architects who resisted change and ignored improvements in the building trades did so at their peril. Some architects, favored by the old system of patronage, could perhaps afford to ignore technical improvements in heating, fireproofing, insulation, and construction. But, Loudon observed, "in this progressive age, a man who has the means of existence to procure by his labour or his talent ought to be learning every day of his life. If he stands still for a moment, the world will march on without him."[30] Today this warning about a relentlessly marching world seems ominous. Loudon, having always made tremendous personal efforts to "move forward," could perhaps never appreciate the anxiety that might haunt individuals who did remain stationary. Not to make progress was to be left behind—somehow to fail—yet the very standards of success were no longer fixed, but shifting, apparently rising with expectations. Loudon was, of course, alluding to the upward mobility of the intellect, or the "March of Mind," not only to social and economic advancement. Still, this constant intellectual striving was just one component of an emerging new economic, political, and social order; and, in spite of all its failings, Loudon considered this order progressive, superior to any preceding order. He continually professed his faith in liberalism, laissez faire, free trade, democracy, a gradual decrease in the vast gulf between the very rich and the very poor, and a gradual diffusion of opportunities for self-cultivation and self-advancement among the different classes of society.

These were the ideological roots from which Loudon's understanding of "progressive" architecture developed over a lifetime. This was his vision of an evolving, progressive society, one which he welcomed while some of his contemporaries were beginning to resist its momentum. Carlyle, for one, recognized the overwhelming necessity for a lifelong personal, spiritual struggle, but he recoiled from that struggle which was imposed on the individual by social and economic pressures. His own vision of Hell on Earth (or Hell in Britain) was "the Hell of not making money." In the first seven weeks of 1843 (the year in which Loudon succumbed to illness, exhaustion, anxiety, debts, and death), Carlyle wrote *Past and Present*, a devastating critique of his times — a period in which a man was driven by the irresistible momentum of progress to "make money and advance himself."[31] Carlyle was repelled by the cash-nexus, the only bond left between man and man, born of supply-and-demand, profit-and-loss, laissez faire, free trade, and competition. Midas-eared Mammon was steadily, and surely, destroying the nobility and dignity of labor.

Carlyle was a critic of society and civilization, not of architecture and the fine arts. He did, however, observe that "The civilized man lives not in wheeled houses. . . . He builds stone castles, plants lands, makes lifelong marriage-contracts; — has long-dated hundred-fold possessions, not to be valued in the money-market; has pedigrees, libraries, law codes; has memories and hopes, even for this Earth, that reach over thousands of years."[32] In short, the civilized man was a landed gentleman, an enlightened lord of the manor, who provided honorable labor for his cottagers. He was the benevolent steward of the land whom Loudon had described, with some lyrical embellishments, at the end of *Country Residences*.[33] In 1843, however, Carlyle's civilized man was an endangered species. Crying out in the wilderness for the preservation of this civilized man and his complement, the noble laborer, Carlyle turned to the middle ages for an idealized version of society. If *Past and Present* was not able to convince all progressive men to join him in turning backwards, at least the work lent substance and extraordinary literary power to the more simplistic arguments of A. W. N. Pugin's *Contrasts*.

In *Contrasts*, first published in 1836, Pugin called for nothing less than a return to the social order, the spiritual fervor, and the architectural fabric of the fourteenth and fifteenth centuries; for the architecture of the present day was in a "wretched state," mirroring the degraded condition of religious belief and social relations. When Loudon reviewed *Contrasts* in March 1837, he reprinted long excerpts to give a clear idea of the work, as it had been largely abused or overlooked by the critics. Loudon agreed with Pugin that the decay of religious devotion must necessarily lead to a certain "decay" in religious edifices.[34] But he also welcomed the current shift towards simplicity in all building types. As religions and modes of living became simplified, Loudon reasoned, gorgeous buildings would naturally pass away. He predicted, however, that beautiful architecture would not cease to exist; rather, it would cease to be so rare. "[It] will be universal in every dwelling house, from the cottage upwards, in every street, and in all public buildings. . . . [In fact] a higher degree of science and of taste may be displayed in a modern dwelling-house, taking the interior, as well as the exterior, into account, and including the furniture and the architecture, and also the mode of warming, ventilating, and lighting, than in any cathedral, Gothic or Grecian, that ever existed."[35]

In 1837 the future of architecture looked bright. Within another generation, Loudon believed, all members of civilized society would learn to draw as soon as they learned to write. Museums of the fine arts would be established and opened to all. Inevitably, a better-educated public would create a greater demand for good architects — those of the caliber of Charles Barry, for instance, or Anthony Salvin. In time, modern architects would far surpass the ancients, given the benefit of far greater "means of intelligence," or accumulated scientific knowledge.[36]

For all his impatience with the trammels of ancient rules and precedents, however, Loudon did not renounce the historical styles altogether. He was a champion of liberalism, not only in political economy, but in the arts. He recognized a certain lingering appeal, a certain beauty of association, that could be achieved by imaginative new combinations among the elements of Greek or Roman architecture. Even the "correct" application of the rules and orders of architecture could be pleasing, if not progressive, for it could achieve a kind of beauty dependent on mind and memory, and on the degree of sensitivity and learning of the beholder.

Having learned in his youth to distinguish subtleties among the historic architectural styles, Loudon personally found those styles a continuing source of pleasure. In the summer of 1840, for instance, on his last visit to Paris, he spent an afternoon at Fontainebleau (fig. 58) with his distinguished horticultural colleagues, P.P.-A.de Vilmorin and Poiteau.[37] As they examined parts of the château and the chapel, Loudon could immediately recognize the different periods represented — Louis VII, Louis IX, François I, Henri IV, Louis XIV, and so forth. He could distinguish restored segments from the original fabric of a building, and he could understand why the architect adopted a particular plan, given the site and the circumstances. Poiteau, who had spent years at Versailles as royal botanist before becoming an editor of *Le Bon Jardinier*, was amazed to discover that Loudon, a fellow scientist of monumental accomplishments, had such a deep appreciation of the fine arts as well. "Many people are involved with the arts," he observed, "but few know how to 'purify' in the crucible both genius and meditation."[38] This insight into Loudon's aesthetic sensibilities is rare, for Loudon's own writing rarely conveys the quality and intensity of his perception of beauty — only the fact.

When Loudon recommended some particular style of architecture, it was usually for practical reasons. For public buildings, he preferred a

*When Loudon visited Fontainebleau for the last time, Alexandre Poiteau was amazed by his ability to recognize the various architectural styles of the château. Loudon's own account of the visit focuses on the trees in the famous forest, however — the beeches, oaks (*Quercus sessiliflora*), and occidental planes—as well as on the forest management schemes and the excellent cherry liqueur (from* Cerasus Padus *and* C. Mahaleb*), which he sipped at the table of M. Marrier de Bois d'Hyver, Inspector of the forest.*

Fig. 58
A.Pugin, Jr., "Fontainebleau: view toward the gardens."

version of "classical" architecture, for he believed relatively simple, classic forms had a more public, or universal, character than the various Gothic styles.[39] Given the site of the new National Gallery — the urban, densely built-up area of Trafalgar Square — Loudon believed the essentially one-story Greek style was less appropriate than the style of the Roman buildings of Florence and Rome.[40] For domestic architecture in democratic countries like America, Loudon recommended the Italianate styles because the relatively inexpensive finishings and decorations were well suited to a people in moderate circumstances. Italianate houses, moreover, were not symmetrical, but irregular, in their massing — so they could easily accommodate the later additions one might expect from such a "prosperous and improving people."[41]

Making no apologies for the stylistic eclecticism of his day, then, Loudon continued to emphasize that new building types and materials might suggest new combinations of forms, whether derived from past styles or purely inventive. In 1834 he recognized three great opportunities which had not yet been exploited and which called for "original genius" on the part of the architect: first, the plant house, or winter garden, which required a controlled summer climate throughout the year and an unprecedented quantity of glass as a building material; second, the use of cast iron for construction; and third, the design of suspension bridges.[42] In all three cases, references to historical styles were not necessary; but even in the design of plant houses, Loudon did not entirely rule out all allusion to past styles.[43]

Loudon was not so insistent as E. E. Viollet-le-Duc, the French architect and theorist who, in the 1860s, would call for the adoption of one style as *the* style for the epoch. The style that Viollet-le-Duc demanded, as the only one worthy of his scientific age, was the Gothic of the thirteenth century. This architecture, with its eminently rational construction, was the very form of Gothic that Loudon had most admired, for the same reason as Viollet-le-Duc, ever since his earliest architectural writings in 1806. But Loudon never insisted that this, or any single style, be used exclusively. In 1817 he had designed curvilinear glasshouses, dependent on no historical style whatever; and he had delighted in imagining an architecture which, from its perfect fitness for new uses, could stimulate new associations in the mind of the beholder.[44] Yet he would never quite renounce the pleasures of the old styles and old associations.

Loudon never saw the worst of mid-Victorian architecture, some of it arguably the progeny of his own *Encyclopaedia of Cottage Architecture*. But Viollet-le-Duc saw, and was horrified. By the 1860s he was convinced that architecture itself was dying. In his view, the successive imitations of architectural styles had produced only debased monuments — "bodies without souls, the fragments of some departed civilization, a language incomprehensible even to those who employ it."[45] If Loudon had not despaired, this was partly because, in his lifetime, the *language* of architecture was not yet incomprehensible. He was still able to "read" a particular kind of architectural language — one that remained legible insofar as it remained true to the system of construction that apparently sustained the building.

In the *Architectural Magazine* of January 1835, Loudon discussed this "language," explaining that all elements of a façade need not express, in a literally truthful way, the actual means of support employed. But all the architectural elements — whether structural or purely ornamental — should "read" as component parts of a unified system of construction. Apparent truth was sufficient:

A pilaster, for example, represents a square column or pillar, supposed to be of the thickness of the wall in which it is placed, and to be of a much stronger and more durable material than the wall itself. The wall, indeed, is supposed to be merely the filling in of the intervals between the pillars, from the ground to the architrave, adopted originally to keep out the weather, and of no use whatever with reference to supporting the roof. . . . This is the fiction of Classical architecture, but the reality of it is, that the pilasters and the wall are generally of the same material; and that the former, with their architraves, are merely projections from its surface, of little or no real use, but as supporting the fictitious idea intended to be conveyed.[46]

Once this apparent, or fictive, truth of construction was accepted, one could begin to appreciate the architecture of any country or age, regardless of style and regardless of his own personal preferences, Loudon argued. He was reconsidering, without denying, his earlier notion of truth, expressed in 1806: that a building should appear to be simply what it is — a barn, a church, a house. He now thought of truth in a relative sense. And he was intrigued by new artificial materials such as papier-mâché — which had been used as a substitute for plaster work in the temporary rebuilding of the Houses of Lords and Commons after the great fire in 1834 — and Coade stone, a type of cast stone invented in the 1770s and widely used for ornaments in Loudon's day.[47]

Loudon's views on the apparent truth of construction and on artificial materials would have disturbed Pugin, Ruskin, and, to some extent, Viollet-le-Duc, all of whom demanded a more literal truth in construction and materials.[48] These uncompromising writers judged the moral fiber of a people, and of their civilization as a whole, by the demonstrable "truth" of their built environment. But Loudon's system of truth was no less valid, no less "moral," just because it acknowledged the artificiality of the very nature of art. As a critic, Loudon was neither complacent, nor permissive. Having accepted the fictive truth of the system of construction adopted for a particular building, he expected all the structural elements in that building to be consistent within that system — whether the elements were truly structural, or simply ornamental expressions of some aboriginal structural purpose. Here is the way Loudon applied his theory of "fictive truth" in 1835 (fig. 59):

In the interior of the Pantheon Bazaar in Oxford Street [London], the system pursued is that of piers and arches, and the effect, looking at the sides and roof, when entering from Oxford Street, is harmonious and beautiful; but, on arriving at the opposite end, if we turn round, and look up to the gallery, we are shocked by a square opening with coupled pilasters on each side, surmounted by an architrave, without any connection whatever with any part of the prevailing system.[49]

This is a prophetic vision of a new kind of rational architecture, one in which the elements could still be derived from the classical language of architecture, and still tell a story, though the message would be concerned with the process of building, not with mythology. Here one detects a faint premonition of Louis Kahn, whose wooden beams and reinforced concrete piers, he says, want to cry out, "Let me tell you about how I was made."[50] (In Loudon's ideal case, the elements would cry, "Let me tell you a *story* of how I was made!")

Exactly how Loudon developed his theory of the "fictive truth of construction" is not clear. He himself was an amateur engineer-architect of houses, barns, and hothouses, and he probably learned something in his later years from engineer-architects such as T. L. Donaldson, founder and secretary of the (Royal) Institute of British Architects (IBA), and William Hosking, Professor of the Arts of Construction at King's College, London. Loudon's *Architectural Magazine* regularly covered the IBA's meetings and *Transactions*, and by 1833 Loudon had read Hosking's "excellent" *Treatise on Architecture and Building*, a rational anti-Vitruvian statement of principles.[51] More important, by the early 1830s Loudon knew of Quatremère de Quincy's ideas on the "fictive," or artificial, aspects of all works of art.[52]

If, in fact, Quatremère de Quincy produced the seeds of Loudon's theory of the "fictive truth of construction," another French writer may have nourished them. In January 1840 Loudon reviewed a new French journal, the *Revue générale de l'architecture et des travaux publics*, begun in 1839 by the architect César Daly.[53] Daly was also the eloquent spokesman for what Neil Levine has lately described as the "readable" architecture of Henri Labrouste.[54] Now, could it be that, sometime before 1835, Loudon was aware of Daly's views and those of the independent-

minded Labrouste, whose flouting of the rules and precedents of Roman classicism had begun to alarm the professors at the *Ecole des Beaux-Arts* in the late 1820s? The published accounts of Loudon's horticultural tour of Paris in 1828–29 included no discussions of architectural theory per se.[55] Still, it is remarkable that Loudon's criticism of the Pantheon Bazaar in 1835 is so similar to Daly's criticism of Barry's Travellers' Club in 1840.

Having toured in England for nearly five months in 1839, Daly published his impressions of British architecture in the *Revue générale* of June 1840. In London he had greatly admired the Travellers' Club (1829–32); he reproduced plans, elevations, sections, and details along with a complete description of the building. His only reservation was that Barry's apparent system of construction was not consistently followed on all four sides of the building: "Thus, in the principal façade, the decoration of the [square-headed] windows is perfectly motivated, as if directly resulting from the construction; while the decoration of arches, used as borders around the windows on the back of the building, seems to be an annoying fantasy, in complete contradiction with the principle which M. Ch. Barry has obeyed in the rest of his composition."[56]

Much as he, too, admired Barry's work, Loudon would have had to agree. His mature architectural criticism has always this same "constructive" foundation, a rational, principled basis for ascribing praise or blame. His eye is a reasoning, thinking eye, which cannot easily become lost, as Pugin's could — "lost in the intricacies of the aisles and lateral chapels of a Gothic Cathedral," lost among the sacred, mysterious lights and shadows, tombs, tapers, and golden doves.[57] While Pugin reflected on the faith and altruism of the medieval craftsmen as expressed in their glorious churches, Loudon would appreciate the sublime expression of the whole, as well as noting, in the *construction* of the Gothic cathedral, the unity of system, a system in which no part of the whole was superfluous.

Loudon could also admire the poetic vision of the eighteen-year-old Ruskin. But apparently he could not pass on to the young literary genius any interest in structure, new materials, and "original genius" (that of the architect-engineer). In 1840 Loudon praised Rouen's new cathedral spire, with its interior staircase, the whole constructed entirely in open-work of cast iron.[58] In 1849 Ruskin insisted that Rouen's spire was not "architecture" at all. "True architecture," he explained, "does not admit iron as a constructive material."[59] Disdaining new materials and suspicious of "progress," Ruskin emphasized "Obedience," "Unity," "Fellowship," and "Order." "The forms of architecture already known are good enough for us, and for far better than any of us," he wrote in *The Seven Lamps of Architecture*, "and it will be time enough to think of changing them for better when we can use them as they are."[60]

No doubt Loudon occasionally disagreed with Ruskin's more conservative opinions. But in the penultimate issue of his *Architectural Magazine*, in December 1838, Loudon recommended Ruskin's series "The Poetry of Architecture," completed in that issue. He recognized the young man's genius, and he could appreciate the general principles that Ruskin had derived from his close, sympathetic study of European and British cottages and villas. Then, too, as the *Architectural Magazine* was drawing to a close, Loudon may have sensed a passing of the torch. At the end of November 1838, he wrote to Ruskin's father, "Your son is certainly the

*The poetic vision of Ruskin's original drawing is lost in this woodcut from the* Architectural Magazine, *but the text of Ruskin's "Poetry of Architecture," which it accompanied, remained intact. There he delighted in the sensuous appeal of cool, dark grottoes and trees of "dark leaf and little color." Apparently Ruskin appreciated these trees more for their "free touches of shade" than as trees per se.*

Fig. 60 (*below*)
"Bellaggio, Lago di Como," woodcut after John Ruskin's original drawing.

*Such picturesque designs from Loudon's* Encyclopaedia of Cottage, Farm, and Villa Architecture *established the standard for "Loudonesque" dwellings still to be found in various parts of the English-speaking world.*

Fig. 61 (*opposite, left*)
John Robertson, "Cottage in the Old English Manner."

greatest natural genius that ever it has been my fortune to become acquainted with, and I cannot but feel proud to think that at some future period, when both you and I are under the turf, it will be stated in the literary history of your son's life that the first article of his which was published was in Loudon's *Magazine of Natural History*."[61]

Ironically, the mature architectural writings of Ruskin have little in common with those of his first editor. As Ruskin went on to explore the metaphysics of architecture, developing the sensibilities of his eye, his mind, his heart, and his social conscience, he led architectural thought and practice in a direction quite different from Loudon's. Whereas Ruskin would insist on the most traditional of building materials — wood, stone, and clay — and would admire truthful, massive construction, Loudon recognized the beauty of glass and iron, materials which suggested new, equally "truthful," but lighter, more elegant construction. In *The Seven Lamps of Architecture* and *The Stones of Venice* (1851–53), Ruskin led the way toward an architecture of exquisite impressions and rich historical associations, an architecture in the service of painting and sculpture, an architecture of imagination, intimacy, and emotion.[62] But as early as 1805, in his *Remarks on the Construction of Hot-houses*, Loudon had envisioned an architecture of reason, free of the constraints of the ancient orders, original in its use of new materials, and appropriate for its intended use.

Although they appealed to somewhat different audiences of laymen and professionals, Loudon and Ruskin each had a pervasive influence for several generations on both sides of the Atlantic. Much of their popularity was due to purely visual imagery. Ruskin's delicate sketches, which had suffered when reduced to woodcuts in the *Architectural Magazine* (fig. 60), were most effective when reproduced as lithographs — shadowy, vague, highly evocative; expressive of life, organic growth, and endless

possibility. Loudon offered other possibilities in his *Encyclopaedia:* hundreds of woodcuts and a treasury of ideas and ideals.

Today there is scarcely a nineteenth-century town or village in the English-speaking world that shows no trace of Loudon's or Ruskin's influences.[63] In Britain, perhaps Ruskin's most sympathetic interpreters among architects were the distinguished Irish firm of Deane and Woodward, whose Oxford University Museum of Physical Sciences (1855) is a masterpiece of what Eve Blau has defined as "Ruskinian Gothic."[64] The Oxford museum is a massive polychromatic stone edifice with a low, barely projecting central tower; middle-pointed arched windows; and richly ornamental details reminiscent of a fifteenth-century Venetian palace. Loudon had no close disciples among British architects, but "Loudonesque" cottages and villas, derived from the designs he gathered from Barry, Lamb, Robertson, W. A. Nesfield, Richard Varden, John Perry, and others, were erected throughout the British Isles, as in parts of Australia and America (fig. 61).

In America the writer who most faithfully disseminated Loudon's ideas on architecture (and gardening) was Andrew Jackson Downing, of

*While Loudon began to concentrate on useful features, such as interior toilets and large windows, Downing emphasized the deep yearning for beauty and tranquility in the American home. Loudon demanded clarity in his woodcuts—so faults could not be disguised; Downing tended to offer vignettes of embowered homes in the country.*

Fig. 62 (*below, right*)
Andrew Jackson Downing, "Symmetrical Cottage."

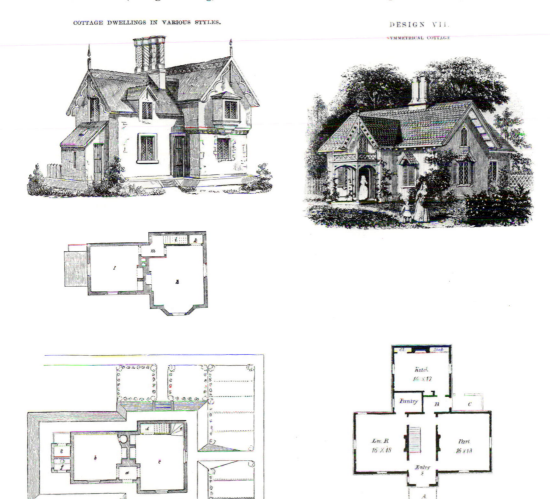

COTTAGE DWELLINGS IN VARIOUS STYLES.                                DESIGN VII.

SYMMETRICAL COTTAGE

Newburgh, New York, a landscape gardener who contributed to Loudon's *Gardener's Magazine*. Downing and his architectural collaborator, Alexander Jackson Davis, adapted Loudonesque Gothic and Italianate cottages and villas for the particular materials, climate, and clients of America (fig. 62). In his *Cottage Residences* (1842), Downing reiterated Loudon's three main architectural principles: fitness, expression of purpose, and expression of style. Like Loudon, Downing furnished elevations, plans, sections, and details of a variety of dwellings, furnishings, and mechanical services. Later, in *The Architecture of Country Houses* (1850), Downing devoted a whole chapter to "Warming and Ventilating." The architect should never neglect utility for beauty, Downing advised; utility should be elevated and ennobled by beauty.[65]

Thus far, Downing followed Loudon; but he did not adopt Loudon's "fictive truth of construction." As Vincent Scully has pointed out, Downing's notion of truth in architecture was derived from Pugin and Ruskin.[66] Like Ruskin, Downing carefully distinguished "mere building" from architecture, and the Useful from the Beautiful. "There are many to whose undeveloped natures the Useful is sufficient," he explained; "but there are also, not a few who yearn, with an instinct as strong as for life itself, for the manifestation of a higher attribute of matter — the Beautiful."[67]

In these writings there is a gentleness and a softly ingratiating tone that suggests Ruskin's influence, while the appeal of Loudon's matter-of-fact arguments was waning. Even Downing's architectural imagery suggests Ruskin's influence. Though unmistakably Loudonesque in massing and detail, Downing's perspectives do not exhibit the stark clarity that Loudon had required of illustrations for his *Encyclopaedia* in order that no defect of architectural design should be obscured.[68] Downing instead presented his cottages and villas as charming vignettes and picturesque renderings, enhanced by framing foliage, clinging vines, foreground trees and shrubs, domestic animals, and people. These images, suggesting idyllic rural retreats, were meant to stir the emotions and captivate the imagination — not to instruct the reasoning mind. In time Loudon's influence waned, as readers in both Britain and America sought a more lyrical and soothing refuge from the strange new structures and urban environments of the later Victorian era.

Ultimately Downing and his contemporaries, as well as succeeding generations, could hardly resist the spell of Ruskin's words and images. No one had ever looked so intensely at venerable buildings in the landscape — buildings as grand canvases for painting; as environments for sculpture; as exquisite assemblages of isolated, beautiful ornament; worked by the hands of craftsmen to whom labor was full of dignity and joy. When Ruskin gazed upon a building he wanted to penetrate its soul and find Poetry. When Loudon confronted a building, he wanted to read its façade, understand its structure and mechanical services, and recognize Progress.

One of the few buildings that Loudon found truly progressive was London's Covent Garden Market (1828–30), designed by Charles Fowler and built by William Cubitt (fig. 63). Soon after its opening in June 1831, Loudon wrote that he was both impressed and encouraged. Such a building, he observed, could mark the beginning of a "new school" in architecture, the "School of Reason and Progression" (as opposed to the prevailing

"School of Authority" — the "Stationary School").[69] Loudon admired the efficient planning and logical order of the market, as well as the mechanical services and the original composition. Tuscan colonnades, rusticated corner pavilions, plain balustrades and pediments, and roof garden promenades were combined with an elegant conservatory of copper and cast-iron construction. "By what cause has it come to pass," Loudon wondered, "that the pillared grandeur and temple-like magnificence, which in former and no distant times were exclusively devoted to the edifices consecrated to the gods or occupied by princes, are now judged appropriate to the scene of humble industry and the abode of every-day people?"[70] (See figure 64.)

Loudon attributed this change to the "principle of commerce, or civilization," which could be understood only in its historical context, as an evolutionary, dynamic, progressive force. He also offered a classic liberal interpretation of economic, social, and architectural history — in retrospect, an intriguing alternative to the more familiar radical and yet reactionary views of Pugin, Ruskin, and Viollet-le-Duc. In the last issue of the *Architectural Magazine* (January 1839) Loudon offered his most comprehensive statement of progressive architecture.[71] More than an architectural history, this is a brief summary of human progress in the Western world — past, present, and to come.

Loudon began in antiquity with Greek temples and Roman palaces and villas. Gradually these edifices were destroyed by hardy barbarians. In the dark ages, only the churches, convents, palaces, and castles were magnificent; most other structures were merely temporary, until the rise of commercial towns: "These towns constituted a new power in society, and gave birth to that principle of modern commerce, or, in other words, of civilisation, which has since gradually developed itself, and produced, in towns and cities, market-places, piers, quays, exchanges, and other public buildings." Tracing this "principle of civilization," Loudon noted the gradual shift in the basis of wealth from land and vassals to movable goods and commercial enterprises, the gradual appearance of beauty in ordinary civic buildings, and the gradual diffusion of useful knowledge and rational taste. Someday, Loudon predicted, the only magnificent buildings would be public ones; castles, palaces, and convents would disappear, along with wretched hovels. In the rising nation of America, one would find no cathedrals and few private palaces to rival those of Europe—but he would

*Loudon believed that this market signaled the beginning of a new school of architecture — the School of Reason, or the Progressive School — as opposed to the School of Authority, or the Stationary School. Drawing freely from past styles and orders, Fowler here created a functional and attractive new synthesis, following sound general principles, not ancient rules of design.*

Fig. 63
Covent Garden Market, London, by Charles Fowler: bird's-eye view.

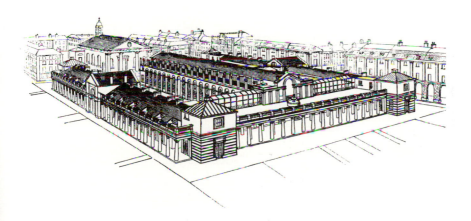

find markets, colleges, schools, and public gardens unprecedented in "real grandeur and beauty."

In the architecture of his own time, Loudon recognized two "schools" of architecture (and agriculture); one he called stationary, the other rational, or progressive:

The Stationary Schools . . . were very good schools when mankind were in more danger of retrograding in arts and civilisation than of advancing. Where all are not enlightened, the many must be led by the few; these few, whether in politics or in the arts and sciences, form the Stationary School; and the principle of self-preservation will render that school jealous of its power, and consequently, adverse to all innovation or interference. There is, however, no Stationary School in nature; and, taking a general view of past ages, mankind have always been progressing, however slowly, towards something better. In modern times, the ratio of this progress has greatly increased, and the School of Reason is now everywhere in conflict with the School of Authority. . . . the first assault upon the Stationary School of architecture was the employment of cast-iron; first in bridges, and afterwards in houses, gates, and fences. A cast-iron bridge is an abomination to the Stationary School of architects.

Loudon's sympathies were clearly with the progressive school, or school of reason, and he singled out one of the few contemporary architects belonging to that school — Charles Fowler — for designing buildings on fundamental principles, not "antiquated rules and precedents."

Fowler's Covent Garden Market, just north of the Strand in London, has been restored recently and once again is used for commercial purposes. There, with Loudon's *Architectural Magazine* in hand, one may still trace for himself the progress of architecture — and of civilization.

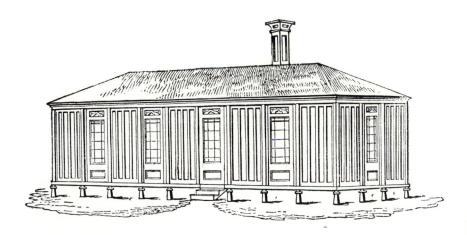

# 9

## Progressive Gardening

Loudon believed that progress in gardening depended on the liberal and professional education of gardeners. Accordingly, his *Gardener's Magazine* informed them of the technical, aesthetic, and economic aspects of their trade — including wages, hours, and living conditions.

In 1822, after nearly twenty years of practice as an "architect of gardens," Loudon brought out an encyclopedia that covered the history, science, theory, and practice of gardening more comprehensively than anyone had done before. His avowed intention was simply "to combine as far as practicable the whole of this knowledge, and arrange it in a systematic form, adapted both for study and reference."[1] The scope was unprecedented, the utility unquestionable, and the tone remarkably objective for a man of strong opinions.

In the grand old tradition of horticultural treatises, Loudon began the *Encyclopaedia of Gardening* with a cosmic perspective: "The earth, as Herder observes, is a star among other stars, and man, an improving animal acclimated in every zone of its diversified surface. The great mass of this star is composed of inorganic matters called minerals, from the decomposing surface of which proceed fixed organic bodies called vegetables, and moving organic bodies called animals."[2] Having identified the three great kingdoms of the earth, Loudon proceeded to examine the vegetable kingdom, beginning with the garden of Eden and the landscapes of the gods and gradually descending to such particulars as the nomenclature, quality, use, and improvement of soils; the use of raspberries and strawberries to dissolve tartar on the teeth; and the pedestrian's loss of expansive views and spaces as Regent's Park became a haven of private houses and gardens. Such details were included within the 1,469 pages of the first ponderous, somewhat thinly illustrated, but magnificently organized edition of the *Encyclopaedia of Gardening*.

The arrangement of the *Encyclopaedia* was as comprehensive and logical as the natural system of classification that Antoine Laurent de Jussieu had formulated for the whole vegetable kingdom, a system that Loudon highly recommended in the section of the book dealing with taxonomy. Just as Jussieu had determined the classes, orders, genera, species, varieties, and subvarieties of plants, so Loudon offered an encyclopedia subdivided into parts, books, chapters, sections, subsections, and numbered paragraphs. Part I featured "Gardening considered in Respect to its Origin, Progress and Present State among Different Nations, Governments, and Climates"; Part II, "Gardening Considered as a Science"; Part III, "Gardening as Practiced in Britain"; and Part IV,

"Statistics of British Gardening," including its present state and future progress.

The *Encyclopaedia of Gardening* was a popular, critical, and financial success, running through several editions and revisions over half a century. The *Gentleman's Magazine*, for one, envied Loudon the serene nature of his pursuits. While other men were plodding along the dusty, dirty roads of life, they wrote, preoccupied with writs, pleas, navy five percents, block tin, pit coal, gin, molasses, or broadcloths and kersemeres, Loudon — the Columella of the modern world — was soaring and fluttering, sipping the nectar of wisdom and delight from the gardens of the Elysée Bourbon and Bel Respiro.[3] The *Literary Gazette* came straight to the point. The *Encyclopaedia* was a valuable reference work, logically arranged and energetically written, bearing an urgent message to gardeners, particularly the young: gardeners should be constantly improving their minds, their skills, and their characters, unwilling to rest and be satisfied until they feel they are making progress.[4]

Loudon's ominous warning would not be generally appreciated until the 1830s, when jobs for the young gardener would become increasingly scarce and insecure. Today it is not often recognized that British horticulture suffered an economic recession in Loudon's lifetime. Both commercial and private horticultural collections were being dispersed, some nurserymen went bankrupt, and head gardeners as well as apprentices were losing their jobs. In Loudon's view this recession challenged the very survival of landscape gardening as a profession, as it was interdependent with the survival of commercial suppliers, experienced head gardeners, and sympathetic employers. In response, he urged that more thought and resources be given to the general education and professional training of young apprentices, for on them, he believed, the progress of gardening ultimately depended.

As early as 1821, in his prospectus for the *Encyclopaedia*, Loudon began to draw attention to the young gardener's course of training and living conditions — not only in Britain, but on the Continent, where he expected to (and did) find a significant audience for his work.[5] In a thick pamphlet written in both English and French, Loudon outlined a proposal for a section of the encyclopedia to be devoted to gardening as practiced around the world in the past and present. Assuming an objective stance, he acknowledged the skill of two contemporary landscape designers in France, Gabriel Thouin and Thomas Blaikie; the excellence of French public gardens; and the absence of smoke in French cities. He was sufficiently impartial, however, also to point out a few unpleasant facts about gardening in France, where, for the most part, ordinary working gardeners were badly trained, poorly paid, and overworked. Moreover, they were generally ignorant, and they received no apprenticeship. In Germany, Loudon observed, the working gardener usually served an apprenticeship of three and a half years, during which time he proved that he could read, write, draw, and understand the "written secrets" of gardening. Then, as a journeyman, he was allowed to wander from town to town, looking for work, while he lived in gardeners' lodging houses. There he would receive food and pocket money until he moved on, free to roam the entire German empire if he wished, as well as parts of Denmark and Holland, all at the "general expense." This probation period ended when the journeyman accepted a situation as a master gardener. He could also aspire to become an artist or architect of gardens — a *Land Baumeister*. Or he might be sent by a nobleman to visit the best gardens in England, Holland, or France for a year or two, before returning to assume his new position as a *Garten Baumeister*.

Three important conclusions may be drawn from Loudon's prospectus. First, he was confident that the progress of gardening would be accelerated by the liberal and professional education of working gardeners. Second, he believed that progress would depend, to some extent, on the effectual demand for good gardeners. In a country like France, he reasoned, where there were at the time relatively few extremely wealthy men, there would be few first-rate gardeners. Third, in assessing a country's general level of civilization, Loudon considered not only the grand horticultural establishments of the wealthy, but cottage gardens, too. In the south of France, where cottage gardens were not well tended, he considered the level of civilization low. In northern France, the evidence of neat kitchen gardens with flowers and fruit trees near the cottages indicated a much higher degree of civilization. (By their gardens ye shall know them.)

An article in the *Quarterly Review* of January 1821 entitled "The Rise and Progress of Horticulture" contains so many ideas embodied in Loudon's prospectus and *Encyclopaedia* that it reads like a preamble to the mighty tome Loudon published in 1822.[6] The author has remained anonymous, and it is tempting to believe that Loudon wrote the article, collaborated on it, or at least shared with the author the fruits of his own work and thought over the previous eighteen years. After perusing the *Transactions* of the London Horticultural Society and the *Memoirs* of the Caledonian Horticultural Society (Scotland), the *Quarterly* writer called for both improvements in British horticulture and ornamental gardening, and the diffusion of the comforts of horticulture among the lower classes. His specific recommendations included the provision of commodious, comfortable cottages with attached gardens for rural laborers, improved professional education for gardeners, and the study of vegetable physiology as part of the science of gardening. "Accustomed to abundance, and to procure everything by money," the reviewer noted, "we feel little want of science. Our resources are in our purses rather than in our heads, and we blunder on without regarding expense till we attain our object."[7] Most of this article was devoted to the "astonishing progress" made in Britain since 1724, the publication date of Philip Miller's monumental *Gardener's Dictionary*, which had inaugurated a new era in gardening. That progress was furthered by the development of better hothouses, which, in turn, fostered a new spirit of improvement on scientific principles.

Loudon was clearly of the same mind. Ten years later, he referred to this article in the *Quarterly*, along with his own *Encyclopaedia*, in a discussion of the four "species" of the "genus" Gardening: horticulture, ornamental gardening, arboriculture or planting, and landscape gardening. Both the *Quarterly* and the *Encyclopaedia* included discussions of ancient Roman pits for forcing fruits and vegetables, notes on the importance of climate and geography, facts about the cultivation of the pineapple (the subject of a treatise by Loudon in 1822), and a rambling history of British and Continental gardening, noting in particular the produce of Russian hothouses.

As early as 1817, Loudon had already expressed one candid opinion concerning horticultural scholarship which the *Quarterly* confirmed: although the *Transactions* and *Memoirs* of the horticultural societies tended to advance scientific knowledge, they had little practical value in themselves. Rather, these splendid volumes, or "costly quarto[s] for the rich," tended to make gardening a fashionable pastime. In turn, gardening became a science worthy of patronage and a means of employment for highly skilled workers. Ultimately, the benefits of producing hothouse luxuries such as grapes and pineapples for the wealthy would benefit other classes by providing better-paying jobs and by improving the standard fare of the great mass of society.[8] This "trickle-down" theory was hardly new at the time, but the demystifying language, devoid of deference, was bold.

These and other insights into the social and economic significance of gardening had appeared, and would continue to appear, throughout Loudon's writings. A case in point was the decade-long series of misunderstandings between Loudon and Thomas Andrew Knight, president of the Horticultural Society of London, over the value of the society's *Transactions* and of Knight's own papers in particular. In March of 1820, Knight read a paper before the horticultural society in which he explained his own method of cultivating the pineapple, a method so simple that, in his absence, even his illiterate laborer could carry out the whole procedure. Loudon protested: Did not Knight's comment suggest that the clever employer can make do with any illiterate gardener — and that employers thus might consider lowering the wages of their present gardeners? And what unfortunate effects might this kind of thinking have on the education of gardeners?[9]

Eight years passed. In June of 1828, Richard Williams, a gardener of T. A. Knight's, read before the horticultural society an account of an easy method of destroying caterpillars. Loudon reported this fact in the August issue of the *Gardener's Magazine* and added with pleasure that Knight apparently now believed it worthwhile to employ a gardener who could read and write. If Knight would only demonstrate the utility of a good, general education for gardeners, Loudon continued, and if he would only advocate the formation of garden libraries (as Loudon had already recommended, with gratifying results), then Knight could "do more for the advancement of horticulture, than by all the practical papers that he has ever written, or ever will write."[10]

Knight and his colleagues were indignant, and the controversy deepened. In September, Loudon was in Paris, enjoying celebrity as the distinguished author of the *Encyclopaedia of Gardening* and as a new foreign member of the Horticultural Society of Paris. Meanwhile, his amanuensis was refused access to the minutes of the meetings of the Horticultural Society of London. Icy letters flew back and forth across the English Channel between Loudon, a fellow of the society, and Knight, its president. Meanings were misconstrued and motivations suspected. It was several years before Loudon returned to the good graces of Knight and the London Horticultural Society. Knight graciously agreed to make some corrections for a new edition of Loudon's *Encyclopaedia;* and Loudon recorded his gratitude to the "much esteemed and venerable President of the Horticultural Society, who may be truly called the father of scientific gardening."[11]

In spite of all the furor, however, Loudon continued to advance the cause of the young gardener's education — liberal, moral, and professional. He endured a savage, though humorous, attack on his educational views from *Blackwood's Magazine* in 1834, and he replied with equanimity.[12] As Alexandre Poiteau, an editor of *Le Bon Jardinier* in Paris, once remarked, "A thousand times [Loudon] has spoken about those things he found lacking in the instruction of gardeners in England, whom he regarded as his children — and they themselves revered him as a good father; he wished that, by their education and their feelings, they would render themselves worthy of the consideration which society is disposed to accord them; and his counsels, his precepts, have already brought the fruits which honor those who are benefiting from his efforts."[13]

On another occasion, Loudon had the opportunity to *defend* the London Horticultural Society. Perhaps antagonizing some colleagues and readers once again, he openly defended the society's right to enjoy an annual fête in their own garden. On July 23rd, 1827, the Horticultural Society gave a public breakfast for fellows of the society and their families and friends in the society's gardens at Chiswick. Tickets sold for a guinea and 2,843 persons attended, including an unprecedented number of fellows, accompanied by elegant ladies of "beauty, fashion and rank." Refreshments proved insufficient for such a crowd, but no plants were damaged, and the society realized a considerable profit. Still, the event caused friction in the society — and in Loudon's *Gardener's Magazine*. One Fellow wrote that the fête constituted a misappropriation of the Horticultural Society's garden, a form of pandering to the "sickly appetite for amusement of the fashionable world." In his view, such fêtes would only degrade an important botanical garden to the rank of a public amusement park. Another critic insisted that the society remain devoted to science, while a third questioned the price of tickets for ladies.[14]

Loudon's response was, for once, a model of diplomacy: The experimental gardens at Chiswick should not be used as a public promenade, but an annual festivity would be harmless — even useful (fig. 65). Hor-

*Although some members of the Society objected to its first public fête, claiming that such gatherings had nothing to do with the advancement of horticultural science, Loudon countered, Must gardeners be less gallant than other men?*

Fig. 65
The London Horticultural Society's gardens at Chiswick during an exhibition.

*Loudon greatly admired his "excellent friend," Sou-lange-Bodin, a man of science, an educator, tradesman (or nurseryman), and landscape gardener. "It is one of the finest moral features in France," Loudon observed, "that most gentlemen are either manufacturers, tradesmen, or farmers; and that nearly all of the persons practicing these professions are, in education and manners, gentlemen."*

Fig. 66
West bank of the Seine at Ris-Orangis, France, formerly the site of the Horticultural Institute of Fromont, directed by the chevalier Etienne Soulange-Bodin.

ticulturists need not be less social and gallant than other men. Moreover, "fashion" could help to support institutions; and, in turn, institutional gatherings would tend to "generalise" manners, feelings, and taste. "If the difference in society in these matters were less," he observed, "the moral strength and happiness of society would be greater."[15]

A few months later, Loudon recorded another horticultural fête, one which proposed to become an annual event, at the Horticultural Institute of Fromont, south of Paris (fig. 66). Though he did not himself attend the fête, Loudon published details of the elegant proceedings, including the solemn high mass, the concerts, the ball, the horticultural banquet graced by rare plants, and the toast to the King, and described the fountains and serpentine paths of the garden. The host was the Chevalier Etienne Soulange-Bodin, proprietor of the institute, and formerly superintendent of the Empress Josephine's gardens at Malmaison.[16] Hybridizer of the *Magnolia Soulangeana*, Soulange-Bodin was perhaps Loudon's closest counterpart in France, in his capacity as editor of the *Annales* of Fromont, as an ardent instructor of young gardeners, as a horticulturist, and as a designer of picturesque landscape gardens. At Fromont, seventeen miles south of Paris, Soulange-Bodin combined an institute for young gardeners, a commercial nursery, and an elegant hundred-acre garden with rare trees and picturesque views down the gently sloping west bank of the Seine.[17]

Within a year after the fête, Loudon visited Fromont and met its proprietor. Thereafter he enjoyed the friendship of the eminent Soulange-Bodin, a gentleman, a tradesman, and a man of science.[18] In turn, Soulange-Bodin appreciated the good intentions and talents of J.C. Loudon, "one of the most enlightened and at the same time, the most generous men that we have the pleasure of knowing personally, and whose most technical writings shine with the most gentle philosophy."[19]

In 1826, three years before the *Annales* of Fromont appeared, Loudon had begun his *Gardener's Magazine* as a sequel to the *Encyclopaedia*

of *Gardening* (see figure 67). He had two "grave objects in view; — to disseminate new and important information on all topics connected with horticulture, and to raise the intellect and character of those engaged in this art."[20] The magazine was a success on several counts for many years. Still, Loudon frequently printed the plaintive remarks of readers. A discontented reader from Sussex wrote that the *Gardener's Magazine* was not

*By his own admission, Loudon was personally responsible for all unsigned articles in the* Gardener's Magazine *— and it is here, often in the smallest typeface, that one can best find the cumulative revelation of Loudon's mature character, beliefs, and optimism for the "rising generation."*

Fig. 67
The *Gardener's Magazine* 5 (1829), title page.

THE

# GARDENER'S MAGAZINE,

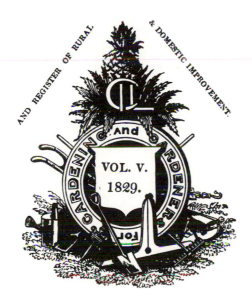

AND REGISTER OF RURAL & DOMESTIC IMPROVEMENT.

GARDENING and GARDENER for

VOL. V.
1829.

CONDUCTED

## By J. C. LOUDON, F.L.S. H.S. &c.,

AUTHOR OF THE ENCYCLOPÆDIAS OF GARDENING AND OF AGRICULTURE, AND
EDITOR OF THE ENCYCLOPÆDIA OF PLANTS.

LONDON:

PRINTED FOR

LONGMAN, REES, ORME, BROWN, AND GREEN,

PATERNOSTER-ROW.

1829.

adequately serving the needs of a popular audience. Though valuable and "singularly liberal," much of the magazine was becoming unintelligible to conscientious flower-loving amateurs. Britain was a nation of gardeners, the reader agreed, but "we are not a nation of *scientific* gardeners," he insisted, calling for more practical information on horticultural matters.[21] Another reader, an Irish woman, agreed. "I have made a large collection of valuable shrubs," she wrote, "and have been guided chiefly by your Magazine, &c; which has of late become so scientific and aristocratic that it fails to assist me."[22] To these and other bewildered readers, Loudon explained that his magazine would not repeat what could easily be found in more elementary, popular works, such as Thomas Mawe's *Every Man his Own Gardener* and William Cobbett's *English Gardener*. The *Gardener's Magazine and Register of Rural and Domestic Improvement* would remain essentially a repository for what was new, or less generally known.[23]

Still the pleas for less technical and scientific, more practical, information kept arriving in the post. In March 1831, an Ipswich reader planning to move south for his health asked if Loudon could advise him on some particulars of life in Dorset, Devonshire, or Cornwall. Could he tell him the rent required for a house with four rooms on the ground floor, besides a kitchen and wash house and six bedrooms, with a garden and five or six acres of land in a dry airy place, either in a village or within five miles of a market town? Could he also comment on the nature of the soil; the wages of farmers, carpenters, and bricklayers; the price of such a freehold estate; the poor rates; the price of meat, and of coals or firewood; the mean temperatures of each month; the general face of the country; and other matters?[24]

One "would-be Suburban Gardener" had a number of specific queries:

Now, I live close to the city; but, Sir, what we wish most to be informed of, is as follows: How to get the *Rosa indica* higher than 2 ft.; how to make the various fuchsias flower in the open border. Query, by thinning the shoots? this I have done, but to no purpose. How to get good georginas. Mine, as soon as they are budding are eaten to a cobweb, yet no insect can I see, except once or twice a green fly.[25]

These amateur gardeners had come to rely on Loudon for horticultural information and advice, for, at that time, his magazine was the only gardening periodical in Britain which attempted to assimilate working plans and horticultural practices, new scientific discoveries, technological improvements, aesthetic theories, and elements of garden and landscape design. Many subscribers assumed that Loudon's magazine was meant primarily for amateurs like themselves — townhouse dwellers in Chelsea, country clergymen in Warwickshire, architects, doctors, engineers, the "Suburbanus Oxfordiensis," and fellows of the Horticultural, Linnaean, Geological, and Royal societies. These people sent articles, queries, and the occasional compliment to Loudon, the editor. They, as well as the professional head gardeners, curators of horticultural collections, and landscape gardeners, would naturally expect to find their "two shillings' worth" in each issue.

Two shillings, however, was about a day's pay for a young gardener employed at a gentleman's or nobleman's country seat, and more than a day's pay for an unskilled or semiskilled gardener in a nursery. These lads had to *borrow* issues of the *Gardener's Magazine*, yet it was precisely for these gardeners of the "rising generation" that Loudon had the most sanguine hopes, and to them that he spoke most sympathetically in his editorials. He wanted to instill in their minds some curiosity, some habits of observation and reflection, something of his own fascination for order and comprehensive understanding of the natural world.

But before these young gardeners could begin to observe and reflect, they had to survive! Loudon persistently argued that a gardener, like any other self-respecting artisan or professional, deserved fair wages, a few hours a day for leisure and study, and decent living conditions. He began a series of articles on the design of gardeners' cottages, seeking to improve upon the familiar "holes in the wall," typically sheds on the north side of a hothouse wall where gardeners lived in relative dampness and darkness (fig. 68).[26] Loudon also printed first-hand accounts of gardeners' working conditions.

*A London architect, T.A., erected this gardener's house on his own grounds and sent Loudon the elevation and plans. Seated in the center of the living room (a), with bedroom (e) and scullery (f) doors open, a person could survey the entire garden enclosed by the walls adjacent to this corner house.*

Fig. 68

T.A., Plan and elevation of a gardener's house designed to serve as a watchtower.

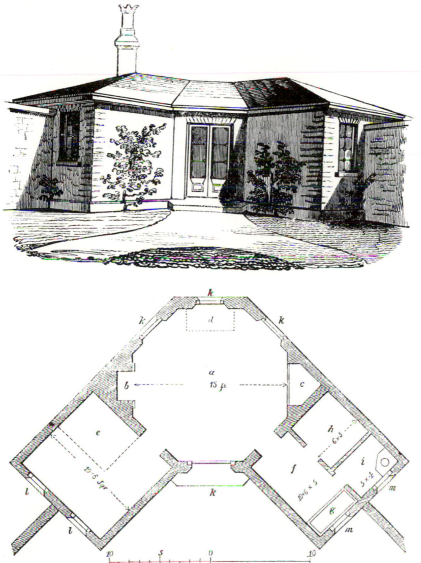

In 1826 "Sensitivus," a root-grown gardener from Yorkshire, traced the cause of gardeners' low wages to nurserymen who treated the hired gardener as a troublesome weed, grudging him his week's pay of nine shillings or ten and sixpence. Paid only this subsistence wage, the gardener tended to slack off. Shown no respect, roughly handled, he soon became demoralized. Then, desperate, he would accept much less than he deserved to work as a gardener for a private gentleman.[27]

Another reader, Archibald M'Naughton, had initially tried to avoid such servitude — only to learn that pride and ambition did not pay. After leaving Edinburgh in 1777, he had worked as a nurseryman's assistant, a gentleman's gardener, an independent jobbing gardener, and a partner in a nursery business. Having experienced bankruptcy, a robbery, the deaths of his partner and his wife, and prejudice against the Scots, in 1825 M'Naughton was nearly seventy and again a jobbing gardener. His advice was to stick with servitude and avoid the "greater slavery" of his own lot in life.[28]

I.P.Burnard, an architect from Holloway, North London, wrote indignantly, "There is no class of servants so ill paid as gardeners, and none, who from their general good conduct, and the long study and attention required to excel in their profession, deserve to be so well paid." An illiterate bricklayer's wages were about five to seven shillings a day. A journeyman gardener who had studied geometry, land surveying, and botany, and worked in a good nursery received no more than two shillings, or two and sixpence, a day. In fact, Burnard knew of one exceptionally intelligent Scottish master-gardener (married, with three children) who had created a vast park and pleasure ground for one of the wealthiest men in England, yet was paid a mere forty pounds a year — about two shillings, sixpence a day, plus lodgings.[29] A journeyman gardener wrote to assert that he and his fellows deserved at least "pay for their labour at the same rate that other journeymen tradesmen are paid for theirs."[30]

Such statements in the *Gardener's Magazine* did not endear Loudon to some employers. At least two announced that they were cancelling their subscriptions to avoid placing the seeds of discontent into the hands of their gardeners.[31] Ironically, Loudon had deeply wished to promote harmony between employer and gardener. In the spirit of free inquiry, he printed letters defending both sides of the wage disputes. (After all, in Bayswater he was himself an employer of gardeners.) He recognized a mutual obligation between landlord and farmer, farmer and laborer, master and gardener. His own obligations as editor involved keeping his magazine solvent, yet, in spite of the cancelled subscriptions of irate employers, Loudon continued to print the plaintive letters of working gardeners. "The fundamental causes of these grievances lie wide and deep," he observed in 1832; "and [they] apply to every other class who live by their bodily labour."[32]

Loudon tried to help personally. He would mention by name a diligent, intelligent gardener lately unemployed, or "out of place." He wrote thoughtful obituaries of men such as Charles Davidson, formerly a gardener at Loudon's home in Bayswater, and Alexander M'Leish, who had helped Loudon lay out gardens in Oxfordshire and Norfolk. For the poor widows of these gardeners, Loudon established a fund, and he promised to publish a list of contributors on the cover of the *Gardener's Magazine*.[33]

Over time, the whole spectrum of a gardener's life was considered in this magazine. One reader suggested that horticultural societies should publicize not only the winning fruits and flowers at an exhibition, but also the gardener who had produced them.[34] Loudon agreed; such notices would help the gardener to establish solid credentials. Nonetheless, every gardener should draw up his own "professional character," or résumé, of which Loudon gave a sample:

JAMES GREEN. *Prof. Char.* Author of papers on turnips, peaches, and ferns, in *Caledon. Trans.*, vol. i and ii.; on pompions, in *Lond. Hort. Trans.*, vol. iv.; on celery, endive, laying out a garden, and the Carolina poplar, in *Gard. Mag.*, vols. ii, iii, iv., in which also the essence of his other papers are given. . . .

*Moral and Biog. Char.* Born in Dundee, 5 ft. 10 in. high, healthy and vigorous, 45 years of age, 15 years married, three children; apprentice at Red Hill; two years in the Edinburgh Botanic Garden, head-gardener in four places in different parts of the country, with a good character for sobriety, integrity, and industry from his last place.[35]

In reflecting on his own accomplishments and moral character, Loudon believed, a gardener would recognize his limitations and try to improve himself. Likewise, in assessing the characters of their different masters, gardeners might learn something about human behavior.

This was not the advice of some remote, kind-hearted philosopher. Loudon lived, quite literally, in a world of gardeners, masters, nurserymen, and knowledgeable amateurs. In Bayswater, part of his own garden was leased from Hopgood's nursery. Nearby were the Conduit nursery and Kensington Gardens, with kitchen gardens and stables west of the present boundary. A neighbor, the comte de Vandes, had one of the most splendid horticultural collections in the metropolis. In 1831, after one of the comte's gardeners, a man named Mowbray, had moved on to become curator of the Manchester Botanic Garden, Loudon was pleased to examine Mowbray's decent housing for his journeymen gardeners. In Bayswater, the comte de Vandes had provided only a "wretched stokehole" of a dwelling, where, on winter evenings, Mowbray had had to read by the light of the furnace door. This fact might explain why Loudon never alluded to the comte more warmly than as "a neighbour." Mowbray he was proud to call a friend, adding, "there is no man for whose independence of character we have more respect."[36]

If Loudon's magazine was truly "aristocratic" then, it presupposed an "aristocracy of the spirit," a respect for excellence, which, Loudon believed, was in the reach of all who made a whole-hearted attempt to attain it. "The grand drawback to every kind of improvement is the vulgar and degrading idea that certain things are beyond our reach," Loudon advised young gardeners, as well as farmers. "There are many things which it is not desirable to wish for, and which are only desired by men of extraordinary minds; but let no man fancy *anything* is impossible to him, for this is the bane of all improvement."[37]

One reader from Doncaster clearly understood the spirit of the *Gardener's Magazine* and responded to the first three volumes with some of the excitement that Loudon, too, must have felt: "Sir, It must be truly gratifying to the lovers of the science of gardening, to witness the long list of practical gardeners who have taken up the pen to contribute to your excellent Magazine, and who had never written before in any publication. The great utility of your work . . . is obvious to the meanest capacity. It might indeed, be expected that every gardener would eagerly approach to it, as he would to a feast after enduring a famine."[38]

Loudon's feast included "An account of grafting the peach, nectarine and apricot on stocks of their own kind," by Daniel Cameron, of late gardener to Admiral Sir George Cockburn, at Highbeach, Essex; the design of a gardener's house, adapted for the south wall of a kitchen garden by Loudon's draftsman, John Robertson; a catalogue of 350 species of *Ericae*, or heaths, from the botanical collection of George Dunbar, professor of Greek at the University of Edinburgh; a paper on the relation of heat, moisture, and evaporation in natural and artificial atmospheres by Thomas Tredgold, a civil engineer; an account of the construction of a double-roofed hothouse in Vienna, by Charles Rauch, court gardener in Laxenburg; "Observations on the Landscape-Gardening of Germany, as compared with that of England," by the Chevalier Charles Sckell, Director-General of the Gardens of the Kingdom of Bavaria; and a hitherto unpublished manuscript by the late Thomas Whately, "Observations on Windsor Castle."[39] The *Gardener's Magazine* was indeed a feast, even for the most knowledgeable professionals, yet it was comprehensible to any patient, literate gardener.

Loudon was particularly anxious to reach the young gardener who lived and worked in relative isolation, far from London, or removed from regular contact with others in his profession. Communication was essential. If there was to be any significant permanent improvement in horticulture, ornamental gardening, and landscape gardening, Loudon believed, such young gardeners must be made aware of all advances in the arts and sciences relevant to his profession. Like the young architect, the young gardener had to keep pace with the rapid changes taking place in the world around him. As the previously mentioned reader from Doncaster observed, gardeners tended to be among the most conservative of workmen,

. . . held in chains by old customs, and fettered even in opposition to their own best interests. . . . But happily there are others better disposed; and to such the *Gardener's Magazine* is a treasure. These are minds of a superior order; they are now bursting their chains, and loosening themselves from the trammels of authority. A spirit of improvement, a passion for experiment, and a liberal curiosity, prompt them to quit the old beaten paths, and to explore untried ways; to disdain the bondage of prescription, and to seek to acquire wisdom by experience.[40]

This Yorkshireman wrote about education and scientific experiment in the language of a political revolutionary — and outside the garden, signs of rebellion could hardly be more clear. Discontented laborers in other trades were discovering their own strength through "combinations," or unions. In December 1829 the Grand General Union of Operative Spinners organized members from all quarters of the United Kingdom.[41] If education, improvement, and reform were to enter the domain of the working gardener, could discontent and insubordination be kept out?

Loudon had already seen the sort of places in which British laborers lived and worked, and he recognized some conditions that might well lead to discontent, as well as others that were cause for some hope. In the summer of 1831, while traveling from London to Manchester with his wife Jane, he passed through the Midlands and Lancashire, and noticed that the conditions of the laboring classes in the towns had generally improved since he had passed through the region in 1806. People seemed to be better informed, he reported: "Labouring men now consider themselves as citizens, with certain rights natural and civil, as well as their superiors; they are capable of acting with more independence, and in concert, with a view of effecting permanent advantage for themselves and their descendants."[42] The rural population, however, especially in Buckinghamshire, was generally destitute. Many of the working people in large towns also still lived in wretched conditions. Anticipating Friedrich Engels's conclusion by more than a decade, Loudon remarked, "There appears to be a tendency in the present state of society to separate producers into only two classes; capitalists and labourers. The labourers, therefore, must necessarily be more or less at the mercy of the capitalists; whether the latter be possessors of land, money or machinery."[43]

Much as he hated monopolies, Loudon reasoned that a monopoly of employers must be met by some kind of "counter-monopoly" of laborers — a combination to support the price of labor. Combinations could be effective only when the laboring classes were better educated and fit to "comprehend and cooperate for their true interests." Like many middle-class "radicals" — John Bright, Richard Cobden, Francis Place — Loudon was opposed to the formation of trade unions of unskilled and uneducated laborers, who could be easily swayed, they argued, by the passionate speeches of revolutionaries.[44] Loudon believed in a fundamental harmony, not antagonism, of class interests. At the same time, he acknowledged that some struggle between the classes, some effort to redeem workers' rights, was inevitable and just.

Loudon wrote no inflammatory tracts urging gardeners to break their chains, however. He never attempted officially to "organize" them, for he trusted that his magazine was a means of vital communication, informing gardeners of the wages and conditions they could justly expect. There was already a "tacit combination" among gardeners, Loudon observed. "There is not one of them about London, who ranks beyond what is considered in the profession a gardener's labourer, who would accept a situation as a master at less than 50 pounds a year, with a free house or lodging, and vegetables." A good footman earned more, Loudon admitted. But this differential was, in effect, something a gardener could be proud of. "The time will come," he predicted, "when professions of learning and leisure will be worse paid than those of severe bodily labour, watching and fatigue."[45]

From this philosophical perspective, gardeners might take some comfort. Meanwhile, they must make every exertion to acquire deeper and broader knowledge in the several branches of the science and art of gardening. For, if the present tendencies continued, Loudon observed, gardeners in England would have to be as resourceful as their Scottish counterparts, who often served as foresters or as general managers of estates.

Not surprisingly, Loudon's magazine was particularly well received and well read in Scotland. After his garden tour of northern England and

Scotland in 1831, Loudon reported that the *Gardener's Magazine* was read by every gardener, and many farmers, in the west of Scotland. Wherever he went in the region, gardeners and their employers assured Loudon that the magazine had contributed to spreading a knowledge of horticulture and to raising the character of gardeners. Public dinners at Ayr and Kilmarnock were held in Loudon's honor. He was flattered, but he could not count on such a sympathetic audience — and such financial success — forever.

During that journey in 1831, Loudon came across a new gardening periodical that, in time, would break the "monopoly" of the *Gardener's Magazine* and reduce the annual income of £750 that Loudon had realized from the magazine in its early years.[46] While suburban gardeners were asking about georginas and the green fly, and journeymen were demanding fair wages, the new *Horticultural Register* would respond more sympathetically than Loudon's magazine to the queries and interests of the amateur. The editors were the young Joseph Paxton, gardener to the duke of Devonshire at Chatsworth, in Derbyshire; and Joseph Harrison, gardener to Lord Wharncliffe at Wortley Hall, Yorkshire.

Loudon spied the first issue of the *Horticultural Register* in Chester, in July 1831. Three months later, in a nine-page review, he gave the outline and long extracts from the *Register*, noting that this new work was intent on reporting, more comprehensively than had any periodical before, the progress in horticulture, natural history, and other aspects of rural and domestic economy, and for a low price. Loudon noted a few flaws, such as faulty accentuation of botanical names, and he detected a certain lack of understanding of the aesthetics of garden design. "It would indeed be, perhaps, too much, to expect practical gardeners to excel in this department of the art," he observed, "with their present degree of school education, and their want of leisure which is necessary to enable any one to acquire an artist's eye and hand. The period will come, however, when taste in a practical gardener will be considered as necessary as a knowledge of culture; and the requisite education and leisure will of course follow."[47]

Beneath the characteristically prickly surface of this note is the familiar substance of Loudon's words, calmly arguing for the benefits and rights of gardeners. He concluded by wishing success to Paxton and Harrison's periodical, which ought to do some good, he thought, in part because it would tend to generate further interest in his own magazines on gardening and natural history.

Paxton, an inventive and energetic young gardener, achieved his greatest fame after Loudon's death; he was knighted for his creation, in 1851, of the Crystal Palace.[48] Paxton was first a good-natured rival to Loudon, then a friend. After Loudon's death, Paxton generously assisted his widow and daughter. But in the early 1830s there was apparently some friction between the two horticultural journalists.

By 1834 Paxton had begun a new periodical, the *Magazine of Botany and Register of Flowering Plants*.[49] His *Horticultural Register* had become broader in scope under the new editorship of James Main (one of Loudon's contributors). The *Register*'s "Letters to a Friend in London," for instance, considered such matters as propriety, fitness, harmonious plans, botanical variety, and the "Recognition of Art" in the landscape:

all among Loudon's most characteristic and widely publicized principles
of design. Of course, Loudon had no monopoly on principles of design, but
he was, no doubt, chagrined to find that, in the *Horticultural Register,* his
theories were rendered less precise — if more ingratiating. The comparative appeal of Loudon's and Paxton's magazines would vary, according to the reader's particular interests in gardening, his training, his
intellectual curiosity, and his political views.

In 1834 Loudon bowed to the pressure of readers' requests for
monthly issues rather than an issue every two months. He also reduced the
price of an issue to one shilling, sixpence. (In 1827 a bi-monthly issue had
sold for three shillings, sixpence.) The quality of the material remained
high — although there were some utterly chaotic designs for flower gardens, which Loudon had included for the purpose of exercising the reader's critical judgment. He continued to print controversial letters and
articles. And his own critical eye remained sharp, while his temperament
mellowed somewhat, ripening to a state of tolerant — even gracious —
acknowledgment of others' tastes and opinions.

During the 1830s severe economic pressures in the horticultural
world were forcing Loudon, Paxton, and later entrants into the field of
horticultural journalism to compete for readers. This was a time when
splendid private gardens were beginning to be broken up, and their
collections auctioned off for a pittance; when head gardeners, journeymen, and apprentices were being laid off; when bankrupt nurserymen
were letting seedling larches and Scotch pines go for a mere sixpence a
thousand. Apparently no longer wanted for the vast forest plantations of
landed proprietors, these seedlings were now being sold for kindling![50]
Meanwhile, nurserymen were facing new competition from the nobility;
for, as one outraged reader of the *Gardener's Magazine* reported in 1834,
noblemen and gentlemen were now selling their forced fruit in the marketplace: "That noblemen should degrade themselves by sanctioning
such a practice, is really extraordinary. Conceive a noble duke, or a royal
one, if you please, sending his forced fruit and vegetables to Covent
Garden market. The aristocracy expect the people to respect them, and to
consider them as something superior to the rest of the community; but, if
they lower themselves by becoming traders, how is it possible for them to
command respect?"[51]

This was also the time when, as Ray Desmond has lately shown,
gardening periodicals were beginning to proliferate and to prosper.[52] The
simultaneous depression of the nursery business and increase of horticultural journals may seem to be an economic contradiction, particularly
in Britain, a country of gardens, where never before had there been so
many enthusiastic amateur gardeners and consumers. Loudon offered one
plausible explanation for the depression: This was a temporary, though
painful, period of transition. The taste for rare plants and exotic trees
would continue, but the business of nurserymen and the profession of
gardening would never be what they once were. Now that methods of
propagation were generally well known, head gardeners were acquiring
new plants and trees for their employers, then propagating them for the
employers' friends and neighbors. This practice was reducing nurserymen's profit on rare specimens, encouraging them to stock only the
most popular, such as pelargoniums and camellias. A second factor was

that the financial incentive for landed gentry to undertake vast forest plantations had diminished, as war-inflated prices for timber had fallen and private fortunes had dwindled. "In short," Loudon explained, "capital employed in the nursery business returns at present perhaps less than capital employed in any other trade." The nurseryman who propagated rare plants no longer held a monopoly over his skills. "That monopoly is now gone for ever," Loudon concluded, "as other monopolies have gone, and as all will go."[53]

Though a liberal and a strong supporter of free trade, Loudon could not explain this vanishing monopoly and the temporary economic depression which followed without some regret. He sympathized with the nurserymen and had even greater compassion for their working gardeners, many of whom had not the youth nor the skills to adapt to changing conditions. Nevertheless, Loudon believed in the progress of liberalism, and he had to accept some of its casualties. A monopoly of skill, like any monopoly of capital, opinion, taste, or means of education, was abhorrent to him. Progress in gardening could only come gradually, inevitably, by propagating the plants and diffusing the skills and scientific understanding that had once been accessible only to a few. Convinced that the future would bear out his predictions, Loudon tried to help quicken the pace, and ease the pains, of that inevitable development, progress.

Two severe casualties of this kind of progress in gardening occurred in 1832 — the year of the Reform Bill, which had seemed so promising for the political life of Britain. In Bayswater the superb horticultural collection of the comtesse de Vandes was auctioned off after her death in that year. In Paris the splendid horticultural collection contained in the commercial nursery garden of M. Boursault was broken up following Boursault's death (fig. 69). Horticulturists on both sides of the English Channel had good cause to mourn the loss of these collections, which would probably not be matched for many years to come, if ever.

Loudon knew both gardens intimately. He had visited Boursault's two-acre garden in the rue Blanche four times since 1815 and had always found it exceedingly well maintained. Greenhouses, hothouses, a conservatory with a removable roof, choice collections of herbaceous plants, masses of *Magnolia grandiflora*, handsome cedars of Lebanon, and hundreds of rare, beautiful plants made Boursault's garden "one of the prettiest town gardens in France, unequalled by any of the kind in Britain."[54] Loudon also knew well the garden of his neighbor in Bayswater, the comte de Vandes — one of the founders and administrators of the London Horticultural Society. He had hoped someone might preserve the comte's two-acre horticultural collection and maintain it as a subscription botanic garden. However, on August 13th, 1832, the rare plants and trees were auctioned off, many for a tiny fraction of their worth.[55]

Perhaps no one was more distressed by the loss of this garden in Bayswater than the chevalier Soulange-Bodin. In the spring of 1824 he had visited his friend, the comte de Vandes, and had marveled at the evidence of so much human industry and care given to the plants in this unusually rich collection. In 1832 Soulange-Bodin still recalled his impressions of London as a "village of glass," so numerous were the greenhouses and conservatories in Bayswater and other parts of the metropolis. Sadly, the situation was even more grave in Paris; the need for well-maintained scientific collections was much greater there. Now M. Boursault's garden in the rue Blanche could never offer the attractions it had once held for botanists, painters, and foreign visitors — even for *les gens du monde*. As Soulange-Bodin explained, "Even the single glimpse of those collections, changing curiosity into admiration, elevated and ennobled a hundred times a day the amusements which are necessary for polite society and which, after the return from an enchanting promenade among the most frivolous circles, helped another species of thoughts to flourish."[56] Thus a commercial establishment in Paris and a private collection in London, both of which had helped to refine the tastes and interests of all who visited, were no longer.

Loudon shared something of Soulange-Bodin's sense of loss. In return, his French colleague acknowledged Loudon's more philosophical "elevated philanthropy." He had read Loudon's conclusion in the *Gardener's Magazine* that times were changing and the monopoly once held by wealthy individuals over taste and connoisseurship was being broken by associations. "Degeneracy," some would cry; but Loudon judged this state of affairs by the standard of the greatest happiness of the greatest number. He regretted the dispersion of the comte and comtesse de Vande's collection (which few were ever permitted to see); still, he was delighted that another botanical garden might be formed on Primrose Hill, just north of London, "to which all the world may have access."[57]

And what if the fashionable world would not join "all the world" on

*Both Loudon and Soulange-Bodin regretted the breaking up of this garden in 1832. At a meeting of the Paris Horticultural Society in 1828, Loudon had heard M. Boursault's arguments on the beneficial influence of gardening on society generally, but Loudon needed no convincing.*

Fig. 69

"*Serre Ornée,*" or ornamented conservatory, in the commercial botanic garden of M. Boursault, in the rue Blanche, Paris.

**SERRE ORNÉE**

Plate 1
Claude Lorrain, *Landscape
with the Voyage of Jacob*,
1677. Courtesy, Sterling and
Francine Clark Art Institute,
Williamstown, Massachusetts.

Plate 2
Thomas Gainsborough, R.A.,
*Woody Landscape*. Courtesy,
Wadsworth Atheneum,
Hartford. The Ella Gallup
Sumner and Mary Catlin
Sumner Collection.

Plate 3
J.C.Loudon, "Scone," ca.
1811.

Plate 4
J.C.Loudon, "Garden Front of
Tew Lodge," ca. 1809–11.

Plate 5
J.C.Loudon, "East Front of
Tew Lodge," ca. 1809–11.

Plate 6
J.C.Loudon, Panoramic view in
the grounds, illustrating his
proposals for Bullmarsh Court,
Berkshire (1818). Courtesy,
Yale Center for British Art,
Paul Mellon Collection.

Plate 7
John Constable, R.A., *A View
on Hampstead Heath with Figures in the Foreground*, 1821.
Courtesy, Yale Center for British Art, Paul Mellon
Collection.

Plate 8
J.C.Loudon, "Vertical Profile
of Bullmarsh Court," Berkshire
(1818). Courtesy, Yale Center
for British Art, Paul Mellon
Collection.

Primrose Hill? Loudon did not linger over this prospect, but looked to those who would surely carry on the progress of gardening, including the Messrs. Loddiges at the Hackney botanical garden and a Mr. Campbell, the late comtesse's curator, "than whom there is not a more amiable and worthy man, or a better gardener."[58] Ultimately, even the most knowledgeable nurserymen, horticulturists, and designers could not, however, ensure the progress of gardening. These specialists could not be expected to exert their skills and talents to the utmost — nor could they be expected to survive in a free-market economy — without a public who appreciated their services and who would recognize excellence in a garden. Loudon was convinced that "in landscape gardening, therefore, as in every thing else, the only certain mode of insuring the progress and the durability of improvement is, to enlighten the people generally, and to create in them a superior degree of knowledge and taste; in short, to make all men critics, in all that concerns the general improvement and ornament of the towns and the country, and the comforts and enjoyment of the great mass of society."[59]

Plate 1

Plate 2

*Plate 3*

*Plate 4*

*Plate 5*

*Plate 7*

*Plate 6*

*Plate 8*

Plate 9

*Adesmia Loudonia.*

*The botanist John Lindley named this newfound plant from Chile after his colleague John Claudius Loudon, observing that Loudon's horticultural works were "well known in every part of the civilized world."*

Plate 10

*Benthamia fragifera.*

*Named for George Bentham, secretary to the London Horticultural Society, this hardy evergreen shrub would always remind Loudon of the secretary's uncle, Jeremy Bentham. "The greatest happiness for the greatest number" had been Bentham's — and then Loudon's — standard for assessing change.*

Plate 9

Plate 10

# 10

## Art and Science in the Landscape

While collections of colorful exotic flowers became increasingly popular, Loudon recommended a more permanent embellishment of the countryside: the planting of trees. As guides, he offered the *Arboretum Britannicum* and his theory of the gardenesque.

Every one feels that trees are among the grandest and most ornamental objects of natural scenery: what would landscapes be without them? Where would be the charm of hills, plains, valleys, rocks, rivers, cascades, lakes or islands, without the hanging wood, the widely extended forest, the open grove, the scattered groups, the varied clothing, the shade and intricacy, the contrast, and the variety of form and colour, conferred by trees and shrubs? A tree is a grand object in itself; its bold perpendicular elevation, and its commanding attitude, render it sublime.

    J.C.Loudon
    *Arboretum et Fruticetum Britannicum*

Throughout his life, Loudon was fascinated by trees. He looked at them with the eye of an artist; he understood them with the mind of a botanist. Like a connoisseur of anything rare and vulnerable, he longed to see the objects of his interest assembled by discriminating collectors, carefully maintained, and magnificently displayed. And, like a radical reformer, he ardently wished to make these objects, native and exotic trees — for centuries the objects of exclusive possession — accessible to all. These facts are all made explicit in the *Arboretum et Fruticetum Britannicum; or, The Trees and Shrubs of Britain* (1838), Loudon's most universally satisfying work.

    Many of the sentiments expressed in this work were not Loudon's at all, but those of predecessors, colleagues, and friends, among them John Evelyn, Geoffrey Chaucer, William Shakespeare, Virgil, William Wordsworth, Sir Humphrey Davy, the chevalier Soulange-Bodin, David Hosack, Joseph Paxton, the duke of Northumberland, and the archbishop of Canterbury. Among their facts, figures, prose, poetry, and portraits of trees and shrubs, Loudon sifted and selected to produce four volumes of closely printed text and four volumes of plates (woodcuts and lithographs). The result, published serially between 1834 and 1837, was a visual and literary treasure, prepared without subsidy but dependent upon the generous cooperation of hundreds of individuals on several continents. It was generally acclaimed as a monumental work; it was also, in a sense, patriotic — for Loudon's greatest hope was that his readers, especially the landed gentlemen and noblemen of Britain, would come to know, love, and *plant* a great variety of fine trees and shrubs, to make a permanent contribution to the beauty and utility of the British countryside.

In the *Arboretum Britannicum* Loudon revealed himself in print to be what he was, by all accounts, at his own dinner table in Bayswater — a genial storyteller with a vast mine of amusing, as well as scientific, facts to offer. How many landed gentlemen were aware, for instance, that the Three Shire Oak at Worksop Park sheltered parts of Yorkshire, Nottinghamshire, and Derbyshire, its beneficent branches shading a total of 777 square yards? The oldest park in England, once seized by William the Conqueror, he informed them, was Clipstone Park, seat of the duke of Portland. At Welbeck, "the Duke's Walking Stick," an old oak that had survived until the 1790s, had once stood higher than Westminister Abbey.[1]

Loudon's tales of druids, sylvan spirits, pagans, and Christians included the supposed origin of decking English halls with boughs of holly. He also quoted a few stanzas of an English carol dating from the time of Henry VI that proved the holly's superiority to the ivy:

> Holy hath byrdys, aful fayre flok,
> The nyghtyngale, the poppyngy, the gayntyl lavyrok.
> Good Ivy! what byrdis ast thou!
> Non but the howlet that shouts 'How! How!'[2]

Delving into legends, carols, and the plays of Shakespeare, Loudon searched for whatever was known about a tree or shrub; for he believed that popular, historical, and geographical associations (for instance, those attached to the roses of Paestum or the cedars of Mount Lebanon) helped to form the character of a plant. Each tree or shrub might well have a fascinating biography, drawn from its local or universal associations. And most would deserve their own portraits, like the hundreds drawn from life in different parts of the world expressly for the *Arboretum Britannicum* (fig. 70).[3]

To organize the contents of the eight volumes, Loudon chose the natural system of Jussieu — the system of classification he also recommended as a guide for planting trees and shrubs. Since the mid eighteenth century, British botanists had typically used Linnaeus's artificial system, which identified and classified plants according to their means of propagation (that is, the number, union, and grouping of stamens and pistils, or carpels). This was a fine system with which to begin the study of plants, Loudon observed, but he found it ultimately unsatisfying. Derived from an essentially abstract system, the Linnaean classes contained "a crowd of unconnected images and facts," not segments of a naturally harmonious whole.[4]

Over the centuries, several botanists (Linnaeus included) had already made efforts to classify plants according to a more "natural" system.[5] The culmination of their efforts was the refined natural system of Jussieu, established in 1789, which grouped plants according to the greatest number of their natural similarities of form. These were to some extent visible to an untrained eye; they were also naturally harmonious.[6] As early as 1803, Loudon had proposed a flower garden designed according to this natural system at Scone Palace, Scotland. Since then, he had been advocating Jussieu's system rather than that of Linnaeus, in part for

the design potential inherent in the former system. For instance, the
natural system might be used as a guide for laying out the pleasure ground
and park of a country seat, using both exotic and indigenous materials.
The actual groupings of the trees and shrubs need not be much different in
character from the customary picturesque groupings of an eighteenth-
century landscape garden. The designer who was also a poet or a painter
could still follow his fancy. But, with a keen understanding of the physical
needs of plants and a mastery of the order implicit in the natural system,
the designer would be able to lay out a botanically interesting sequence of
plants in loosely grouped masses, taking care to provide the natural
conditions for their growth to perfection.

These arguments were first made tentatively in the *Treatise on Scone*

*Pópulus monilifera*.   The necklace-bearing, *Canadian, or Black Italian*, Poplar.

Full-grown tree at Syon, 102 ft. high ; diam. of the trunk 4¼ ft., and of the head 96 ft.
[Scale 1 in. to 12 ft.]

(1803), then expressed confidently in the *Arboretum Britannicum* and throughout the pages of the *Gardener's Magazine*.[7] In effect, Loudon wanted to lead "science," gently but with discipline, out of the walled garden and secluded arboretum, and into the landscape garden, the hedgerow, and the sides of public roads in town and countryside. He hoped that, if he was successful, one would someday find throughout the landscape, in public and private places, a wealth of species and varieties representing all the trees and shrubs hardy in the climate of Britain.

This introduction of scientific interests to the English landscape garden was a most delicate matter, particularly in a country where poets, philosophers, and painters had originally led the way towards the currently accepted, more or less picturesque, manner of gardening. Naturally these innovators had had to know something about plants — but they had tended to acquire practical knowledge, not scientific understanding. (The Reverend Dr. Erasmus Darwin, a poet who laid out his picturesque garden in Lichfield according to the Linnaean system, was a rare exception in the eighteenth century.)[8] Then, too, these innovators were amateurs. Brown and Repton, the two best known professionals, had combined a painter's vision with a practical gardener's skill — but not with the scientist's curiosity. Moreover, the followers of Brown and Repton were not equally competent, as artists or as practical gardeners. As the *Quarterly Review* pointed out in a sympathetic article on Loudon's *Arboretum Britannicum*, the first landscape gardeners did not really know their trees: "It is astonishing how little even the landscape-gardeners of the old school knew about the different forms and colours of trees; they directed plantations to be made to hide some objects and to shelter others, but in general cared little of what trees their plantations were composed."[9]

While compiling his definitive work on trees and shrubs, in part for the benefit of professional gardeners, Loudon had received the generous cooperation of their employers, the nobility and the gentry. The duke of Northumberland had granted Loudon and his botanical illustrators and artists complete access to his splendid collection of exotic trees at Syon, in Middlesex, and had underwritten the expense of drawings and engravings of more than a hundred of the largest and rarest trees. The countess of Bridgewater had provided Loudon with portraits of the gigantic beeches at Ashridge, in Hertfordshire. And Lady Grenville, assisted by her able gardener, a man named Frost, had supplied Loudon with information on the magnificent specimens in her pinetum at Dropmore, in Buckinghamshire.[10]

Since the early 1830s, Loudon had sent out over three thousand questionnaires, seeking information on interesting trees. When filled out by a knowledgeable head gardener or proprietor, these forms constituted a major source of reliable information for the *Arboretum Britannicum*. Loudon also received personal letters from justly proud proprietors, revealing their hospitality, their generosity, and their respect for Loudon's skills and taste in arboricultural matters.[11]

Lord Harrington, for instance, wrote that he would be "exceedingly happy" to see Loudon at Elvaston Castle, in Derbyshire, should he ever find himself in that part of England. The earl of Caernarvon likewise said he would be greatly pleased to receive Loudon at Highclere, in Hampshire — particularly after having read Loudon's "very able article," a fifteen-page analysis of the fine natural landscape and botanical riches on the earl's estate.[12] Other gracious letters arrived, by mail or by hand delivery, from such men as Sir Robert Peel, Thornton Leigh Hunt (son of the poet and journalist), and the duke of Devonshire.

The earl of Coventry's letter to Loudon revealed the kind of personal pride and public spirit with which some noblemen directed the management of their gardens, parks, and plantations. While his head gardener, William Clarke, was preparing the questionnaire for Croome, his seat in Worcestershire, the earl wrote to Loudon, "I am happy to find that a person so intelligent as yourself should hold so high an opinion of the plants and shrubs at Croome; I have great pleasure in keeping them up in the highest perfection, and it was a great delight to me this year to receive a letter from Mr. Forbes, the Duke of Bedford's head gardener at Woburn, to say he had paid Croome a visit, and that my place and plants 'were an ornament to the Country.' "[13]

This allusion to public ornament in the planting of fine trees and shrubs was precisely the result Loudon had aimed for. He was looking beyond the splendor of private arboretums and horticultural collections to the public collections of the future in all parts of the world. Referring to the potential for great public gardens in New York, Charleston, and Washington, D.C., Loudon observed, "The time for believing that the exclusive possession of any benefit contributes to the prosperity or happiness of nations is gone by; and the principles of free and universal exchange and intercourse are found to constitute the surest foundation for the happiness of nations."[14] Eventually, Loudon believed, civilization throughout the world would be "comparatively equalized"; and the trees and shrubs of one region would someday be generally distributed among other regions of similar climates. In the meantime, Loudon hoped his *Arboretum Britannicum* would be useful in contributing to this spread of the earth's treasures around the globe.

British reviewers of the massive *Arboretum Britannicum* did not challenge Loudon's opinions on free trade, exclusive possessions, or the equalization of civilization. Generally, they were impressed, even moved, by the enormous amount of care, scientific knowledge, and artistic skill that had gone into Loudon's work.[15] Some were aware, too, of the outstanding debt of ten thousand pounds that Loudon had personally incurred, and at least a few reviewers must have known of the physical sufferings Loudon had endured during the last year of the work's production (1836–37). At any rate, they did not choose to discuss Loudon's political views or his fascination for something called the gardenesque.

Loudon's notion of gardenesque design, a departure to some extent from the picturesque principles of Gilpin, Price, and Knight, stemmed not from any grand personal ambition to be original or to subvert the old order of landscape gardening. Rather, the gardenesque emerged from Loudon's profound interest in trees as living things of great beauty. He realized that the splendid exotic trees and shrubs still being introduced into Britain could be truly appreciated only if each specimen were planted in relative isolation so that its natural form could develop to perfection. Some compromise with picturesque principles, which called for dense masses of trees, therefore would be necessary, and Loudon turned to a recognized authority on aesthetics for support.

From Sir Joshua Reynolds's *Discourses on Art* (1769–90), Loudon had learned that the painter should never attempt to imitate the accidental effects or deformities of nature; rather, he should strive for a "higher" beauty, nature's *ideal*. In 1806 Loudon had reiterated this advice for students of landscape painting.[16] In 1838, again citing Reynolds, he applied the same principle to landscape gardening in the gardenesque mode: the designer should lay out trees and shrubs so that each could realize its own *ideal* nature under conditions as nearly perfect as possible.[17]

Loudon was delighted to observe the beauty of each individual young plant as it made daily progress towards its ultimate perfection of form. He was also fascinated by the "beauty of system" that Jussieu had perceived within the whole vegetable kingdom. Loudon explained in 1831 that "the true beauty of plants, as of everything else, lies in the mind."[18] He himself had a well-trained, rational, ever-probing mind that could not tolerate a merely superficial acquaintance with a subject. He was driven to keep searching for fundamental principles to explain whatever phenomenon he chose to study. Given his lifelong fascination for trees, then, Loudon could not be satisfied with an artist's view. He needed a scientist's understanding. In 1827 he commented, "The mind must always remain in the dark respecting any subject which it cannot comprehend as a whole, and be in a state of distraction respecting any science the facts of which it cannot associate according to some leading or connecting principles."[19] Such a mind needed a rationale for recommending a new mode of gardening — the gardenesque — without denying the charms of the more traditional mode, the picturesque.[20]

Loudon never expected or wanted picturesque landscape gardening to wither away like some faded flower or some political system that had served its purpose. Rather, he considered it part of the whole spectrum of possibilities for the landscape designer. In 1835, for instance, he alluded to the potential for what William Robinson would later popularize as "wild gardening." In picturesque scenery, Loudon observed, any herbaceous flowers introduced should be "allowed to run wild," on uncultivated ground. In gardenesque scenery, however, only those flowers which could thrive to perfection in a particular plot of well-cultivated ground should be planted there.[21] Loudon had acknowledged other possibilities for designing with trees and shrubs as well as flowers: Those who had developed a taste for landscape scenery and who had several acres to adorn could indulge in picturesque landscape gardening. Ornamental gardening was accessible to anyone, no matter how small his plot of ground. And those who had little land, but keen botanical interests, could enjoy "scientific ornamental gardening . . . and of this species is the variety known to botanists as the Jussieuean or Natural System."[22]

With a botanist's love of system and comprehension, Loudon classified not only the different "genera" of gardening practices, but also the families, or orders, of all works of art. A simple comparison with Jussieu's system may be helpful: Jussieu had classified the vegetable kingdom by creating three grand divisions, or "primitive classes": acotyledons (or cryptogams), monocotyledons, and dicotyledons. These divisions were derived from the functions of seeds and embryos in the reproduction of plants. Similarly, Loudon classified all works of art according to three basic divisions: the useful arts, the arts of imitation, and the mixed arts.

These divisions Loudon derived from the needs of the body and the mind. He maintained that the useful arts, such as baking and brewing, primarily serve physical needs. The fine arts — or arts of imitation — such as music, painting, and poetry, primarily serve spiritual or intellectual needs: "A fine art . . . may be said to be a creation or composition intended, through the eye or the ear, to please the mind . . . to satisfy the reason or the judgment; to awaken the sentiments of approbation, of love, of reverence, or of admiration; to surprise, delight, astonish or wholly absorb the attention and the imagination."[23] The mixed arts, such as architecture and landscape gardening, serve the needs of both body and mind, and they are governed by the leading principles of both the useful arts ("fitness for the end in view") and the fine arts ("expression of the end in view" and "expression of some particular style").

Given this straightforward division of the three kinds of arts, Loudon believed that gardening could never aspire to the heights of imitative beauty which painting, poetry, music, and other "purely imitative" arts could attain. Though Whately, Alison, and Girardin had insisted that landscape gardening could transcend the beauty of painting — even of nature itself — Loudon had somewhat more modest expectations for his art. He reasoned that the landscape painter, in imitating nature, had more control over his materials than the landscape gardener. The painter could improve on what he found in nature, seeking that higher ideal of which Reynolds had spoken. What is more, once the painter laid down his brush, his work was complete. The gardener, on the other hand, had only limited control over many accidental circumstances which would affect his garden — the given site, the immediate environment, the climate, the weather, the practical needs of the client, and so forth. Further, Loudon reasoned, when the gardener lays down his tools, he must wait for the slow growth to maturity that only time and favorable conditions can bring about. He concluded that Horace Walpole had been right all along: the gardener must be "proud of no other art than that of softening nature's harshness and copying her graceful touch."[24]

This was Loudon's view of his own role as a landscape gardener, first expressed in the *Encyclopaedia of Gardening* in 1822, and never struck out or revised in the later editions of that work. By 1832, however, in the *Gardener's Magazine,* and by the 1835 edition of the *Encyclopaedia,* Loudon began to include discussions of a few ways in which the gardener might do something more than "soften nature's harshness." In 1832, he observed, "There are various other beauties besides those of the picturesque, which ought to engage the attention of the landscape gardener; and one of the principal of these is, what may be called the botany of trees and shrubs. . . . Mere picturesque improvement is not enough in these enlightened times: it is necessary to understand that there is such a character of art, as the gardenesque, as well as the picturesque."[25]

Here Loudon appears to have used the term *gardenesque* in print for the first time. He did not claim to have invented the term, however. It was probably derived from the French expression *jardinique,* coined sometime in the 1820s to indicate a work of landscape design conceived by an artist, not by a "mere" gardener. M. Viart, the designer and proprietor of the celebrated landscape garden of Brunehaut, may have been the first to use the term *jardinique* in print when, in 1827, he inserted it into the second edition of his theoretical work *Le jardiniste moderne*.[26] Loudon had known of Viart's book in its first edition (1819) before his own *Encyclopaedia of Gardening* appeared in 1822, and he had learned of Viart's second edition by the summer of 1828.[27] When Loudon arrived in Paris that autumn for a professional tour of gardens, apparently the term *jardinique* was "in the air." Three years later, when Soulange-Bodin gave a long, thoughtful review of Loudon's *Encyclopaedia of Gardening*, which had been abridged and translated into French in 1830, he briefly considered the terms *jardinisme* and *jardinique* as inconvenient neologisms. Though one of the most progressive horticulturists of his time, he preferred the old, familiar English expression "landscape garden" (or *jardin paysager*).[28]

Loudon was not simply trying to introduce a new word into the English language, however; he was formulating a new theory that would offer, he believed, a rationale for the design of gardens in various styles throughout the ages in all parts of the world. In light of his fascination for comprehensive theories of classification, including his determined efforts to popularize the system of Jussieu, it is not surprising that Loudon should keep searching for a comprehensive theory of gardening.

Ultimately, it was the French Academician A.-C. Quatremère de Quincy who offered Loudon the most important clue to something which every scientist, if not every artist, craves: a theory based on "eternal principles." In his essay "Imitation in the Fine Arts" (1823) Quatremère de Quincy attempted to establish a general principle that would hold true for all the fine arts. He believed that, though each art was governed by a particular theory and set of principles, all the arts were united essentially by a few common principles. All artists strive to create the *semblance* of reality, not a facsimile. To produce this semblance, or imitation, of nature, the materials of the work of art must be in some way different from the materials of the model. The painter reproduces three-dimensional scenes on a two-dimensional canvas. The sculptor models three-dimensional forms in clay or stone. In all cases, the artist never intends to deceive the beholder.[29]

Quatremère de Quincy went on to reject the English landscape garden from the realm of the fine arts, or arts of imitation. Unlike such arts as poetry, drama, music, painting, or sculpture, the English garden imitated nature by employing nature's own materials: trees, plants, shrubs, flowers, water, turf. Further, he observed, the true merits of this style of gardening consisted in concealing all artifice, such that a landscape might be mistaken for a work of nature. The true merit of all arts of imitation, however, consisted in the avowal of artifice, such that the poem, the dance, or the painting might be compared and judged in relation to nature — and therein lay the pleasure of beholding a work of art.[30]

Loudon acquired a copy of Quatremère de Quincy's essay as soon as it appeared in Britain. By 1834 he had asked his friend J.C. Kent to translate it into English. Reviewing Kent's translation in 1837, Loudon found it contained "the rudiments of the only satisfactory theory of gardening, as an art of imagination, that has yet appeared; and we freely acknowledge ourselves more indebted to it than to all the other works on landscape gardening, or the fine arts, put together."[31] A year later, Loudon wrote that it was to Whately and Price and a few others that he was indebted for "all we know of landscape gardening."[32] This was no contradiction.

If the British writers had given Loudon a sound practical and philosophical foundation for his work as a landscape gardener, Quatremère de Quincy offered something entirely different, something Loudon's logical, orderly mind craved: the basis of a *theory* embracing all works of art and, in particular, all styles of gardening, ancient and modern. Nevertheless, Loudon believed the French writer had made one grave error, that of assuming that the English landscape gardener aimed for results which might be mistaken for natural scenery. Shenstone, Price, and others had made the same error, Loudon maintained; for they had not recognized that the effort to imitate nature must be subordinated to a more fundamental principle, one he called the "Recognition of Art." By not insisting on the recognizable distinction between nature's model and art's re-creation, they had tended to encourage a literal imitation of nature — whereas Quatremère de Quincy had insisted upon the element of "fiction" in any work of art. He had wanted to "extend" the truth of nature, not to mimic nature.[33]

Loudon's solution was to encourage a freer imitation of nature, with a greater variety of plants than nature would have provided on a particular site. He would blend native plants with exotics, or he would arrange native trees and shrubs in open, airy groves, rather than in dense masses. In certain places an entirely geometric garden might be appropriate; elsewhere, the contours of the ground, the character of distant scenery, the style of the house, or the temperament of the proprietor might suggest a more picturesque treatment. As in architecture, so in gardening, Loudon would recommend no particular style apart from its context. He desired the pleasure of recognizing the work of art as art, whatever the style.

In emphasizing artifice in a garden, Loudon was not recommending that lawns be haphazardly sprinkled with whatever was rare, colorful, or bizarre. He was not inviting anarchy or chaos into the landscape. Rather, he was making a theoretical statement about the very nature of art. When he recommended that Quatremère de Quincy's essay on imitation be read by every landscape gardener, Loudon hoped to spread "more liberal and enlightened ideas on the different styles of landscape gardening," including the "much desired ancient style" (fig. 71).[34] This appreciation for the ancient, clearly artificial garden, expressed in 1837, was hardly original; Loudon was echoing sentiments expressed by Sir Joshua Reynolds in 1786, by Sir Uvedale Price in 1794, by Thomas Hope in 1808, and by Sir Walter Scott in 1828. As Reynolds had observed in his Thirteenth Discourse, the art of gardening is a "deviation from nature; for if the true taste consists, as many hold, in banishing every appearance of Art, or any traces of the footsteps of man, it would then be no longer a Garden."[35]

Among Loudon's predecessors who emphasized artifice in gardening, perhaps Sir Walter Scott was the most winsome. Scott had appealed to national pride and nostalgia as he wrote of the old long, straight walks between hedges of yew and hornbeam; of trellis walks and flower parterres; of brick walls seen through a veil of green boughs; and of other

*Vue du grand Jet a S.<sup>t</sup> Cloud.*

features in the gardens created during the reigns of Henry VIII, Charles I, and Queen Anne. Deploring the bare grounds near the house in a "modern" landscape garden, Scott called attention to the flower garden, then suffering in exile, concealed from the view of all decent society:

If the peculiarity of the proprietor's taste inclines him to the worship of Flora or Pomona, he must attend their rites in distance and secresy, as if he were practicing some abhored mysteries, instead of rendering an homage which is so peculiarly united with that of the household gods.[36]

Rather than champion ancient or modern gardening, Loudon tended simply to appeal to common sense and tolerance:

Whoever will reflect on the two styles without prejudice, must allow that, in any given space, the geometrical style is capable of producing a more grand and magnificent effect than the natural style; while, on the other hand, in the same space, the natural style will produce more grace and variety.[37]

Ironically, there was so much renewed interest in ancient gardens and artifice in the 1830s and 1840s that Loudon had to warn against the proliferation of acute-angled flower beds and other isolated splashes of color on the lawn — which reminded him of "Maltese crosses, stars, darts, commas, figures like saddle-bags, kidney potatoes, leeches, tadpoles, worms, anemone or ginger roots, pincushions, cloak-pins, . . ."[38] There would be nothing but confusion, he explained, if grounds were "covered a little more in some places than in others, but not sufficiently uncovered in any place to produce repose or breadth of effect, that is, masses of light or masses of shade."[39] His concerns were still those of a painter, as he confessed in 1840: "It is lamentable to see the pleasure grounds of some of the finest old places in England spoiled by the introduction of these angular beds, in the most romantic or otherwise strongly marked scenes, that no man of taste would dare to touch."[40]

Distressed to find that the general increase in horticultural knowledge had not led to a diffusion of good taste in gardening, Loudon was continually emphasizing principles of design, both the philosophical and the practical. His most concise summary of these principles appeared in his "Remarks on laying out Public Gardens and Promenades" (1835): First, the most universally applicable principle in laying out any garden is that, "as every garden is a work of art, Art should be everywhere avowed in it," and the result should never be mistaken for nature itself.[41] Second, "Unity of Expression" requires that whatever meets the eye at a single glance, or in a single scene, must be composed as a picture; it must form a unified composition, a whole. Otherwise, the mind would be "deprived of that repose which is essential to comprehension and enjoyment."[42]

Loudon's third principle is Variety; and the fourth, Relation, or Order — which involves the sequence of scenes in a landscape garden. He could not have foreseen the possibilities which celluloid film would offer to film directors of a later age. However, working in the greatest visual medium of his time for creating scenes — landscape gardening — Loudon was thinking and designing in kinetic terms. Music, another lively art, also provided clues for design in this "cinematic" art form:

Scenes in a garden should not succeed one another at random, but according to some principle of succession . . . [which] should be recognisable from the

*Believing, with Stephen Switzer, that water is "the very life and soul of a garden," Loudon regretted the decline of waterworks in eighteenth-century Britain. In the Gardener's Magazine of 1833, he reproduced a woodcut of this jet at St. Cloud, near Paris, along with some British designs, to illustrate his article on the construction of and new materials for fountains.*

Fig. 71 (opposite)
Baltard, "View of the great jet at St. Cloud," ca. 1815.

*Loudon never recommended the design of the parks of Paris for emulation in Britain, where topography, climate, culture, and tastes were quite different. He did believe, however, that "the Parisian populace owe a part of their urbanity and politeness to their familiarity, in the public and royal institutions and gardens, with the rarest and finest productions of nature and art."*

Fig. 72
J. Nash, "The Gardens of the Tuileries: View from the grand entrance."

first by the spectator in the same manner as the first strain of music enables the hearer to form some idea of what is to follow. The spectator ought never to be taken violently by surprise; for that is the character of the lowest degree of art. . . . Where there are remarkably fine points of view, the walk should be so directed, and its margin so planted, as not to exhibit the view till at the most favourable situation for seeing it to advantage; and it should then be continued in a straight direction for a short distance, with the prospect full in front, in order to prolong the enjoyment of it.[43]

Having stated his main principles, Loudon offers further hints for public promenades, parks, and scientific gardens; for landscape gardens, gardens for recreation and refreshment, and gardens for burial. Whatever the purpose or the scale, however — and whether his plan be garden-esque or picturesque in character — Loudon emphasizes the spatial qualities of planting design. He would allow few closely planted masses in the interior of a park, for instance, for these would diminish the sense of space and limit broad vistas. To create the effect of a mass, he preferred to plant groves or groups of trees which, when viewed from a distance, would appear to combine as a whole. His main spatial concern in designing a park was to offer the greatest possible "depth of view" across the property while screening distant roads and boundaries.[44]

In this summary of his mature views on landscape design, Loudon only briefly alludes to "geometrical scenery," such as was found in most public and private gardens from antiquity to the early eighteenth century — the finest of which include the Tuileries (fig. 72) and the Luxembourg gardens in Paris; Schönbrunn in Vienna; and Peterhof, near St. Petersburg. Offering no rhapsodies on the beauty of these geometrical gardens, Loudon simply recognizes their potential for grandeur, public

utility, and enjoyment. On one occasion, he witnessed the "magnificent sight" of the fountains at Versailles, but he thought the gardens dreary when not filled with people. Another time, having seen an old plan of Fountainebleau and having experienced the gardens as transformed by Le Nôtre, Loudon paid his greatest compliment to France's greatest garden designer: Le Nôtre had "simplified" the design.[45]

The greatest pleasure Loudon ever expressed after visiting the Tuileries, the Luxembourg, and other great French gardens had nothing to do with aesthetic beauty; he was simply charmed by the very existence of these gardens as healthful retreats and as cheerful scenes of people. At Sceaux, a vast park some six miles south of Paris, he was particularly interested in a small section now completely covered by houses and private gardens.[46] In 1828 it was a public park where, on Sundays and holidays, people danced and indulged in other forms of "festive enjoyment." Sceaux, Loudon recognized, was appropriately laid out in straight lines and geometrical forms. Necessarily lacking the "variety and intricacy of natural scenery," it was a place where masses of people felt welcome to disperse into smaller spaces near the broad central spaces — much as people might pass into smaller apartments near the great living rooms of a house. Such public functions were best served, Loudon believed, by the "architectural style" of gardening, appropriate because of its "determinate forms and its direct, compressing, and systematic disposition of those forms."[47] He concluded that Sceaux, a park meant for festive enjoyment, was "perfect of its kind."

Writing as an observer of people, not as a connoisseur of works of art, Loudon praised French gardens in 1831: "The public gardens of recreation in and around Paris are numerous, and they are all of them more conspicuously, and perhaps more truly, scenes of enjoyment than the public gardens of England; because the French are more gay and social in their enjoyments than the English. The Garden of the Tuilleries, once called royal, is, taking it altogether, perhaps the most interesting public garden in the world."[48] As a designer of *gardens*, however, Loudon never considered these or any other geometrical gardens inherently more beautiful than the picturesque landscape gardens of his native Britain. His notions of natural landscape beauty, deeply ingrained from childhood, had been formed in the wilder, more romantic parts of Scotland. His taste in landscape gardens, as he revealed in 1841, had been formed on the "secluded lawns and glades of English pleasure grounds; such as are met with, for instance, at Kenwood near Hampstead [fig. 73], at Pain's Hill [in Surrey], and a few first-rate places."[49] These were the gardens that stirred Loudon's deepest emotions, and elicited his greatest admiration, as works of art.

As a designer of public parks, Loudon tried to reconcile the needs of large groups of people with his own instinctive love of quieter places for solitude, reflection, and repose. His inclination was to provide some areas for the kind of social interaction that had pleased him so much in the Luxembourg and the Tuileries — some broad, straight walks and other opportunities for people to meet and mingle. (Frederick Law Olmsted and Calvert Vaux's "Mall" in Central Park, New York, would be America's most famous mid-nineteenth-century equivalent.) Loudon would also offer something of the "grace and variety" of the picturesque, so appealing

*Over time Loudon learned to appreciate a degree of beauty and utility in formal French gardens, but his affections and his most acute feelings for beauty in a garden were aroused by the pastoral and woodland scenes of such places as Kenwood, then the seat of the earl of Mansfield. Today, as a result of public purchase and private gifts, Kenwood, known as the Iveagh Bequest, is fully open to the public, a fact that would have delighted Loudon.*

Fig. 73 (see p. 190)
"Kenwood, View on Entering the Gates," near Hampstead Heath, London.

to his own tastes and those of his countrymen. Finally, wherever appropriate, Loudon would try to stimulate the curiosity of even the most casual
observer by placing botanical labels in front of the trees and shrubs. And
most trees would be arranged in a light and free imitation of nature — in
the true spirit of the gardenesque.

Equipped with some understanding of Loudon's attempts to unite art
and science in the landscape, one can appreciate his principles of design
in two late commissions: one for the Birmingham Botanical Garden (1831)
and the other for Coleshill House, Berkshire (1843). These were modest
projects, not so grand as the estate of Scone nor so small as the flower
gardens and squares that Loudon had designed in and around the metropolis.[50] Neither plan was fully realized, and the definitive history of the
Coleshill project remains to be written. Both plans, however, show Loudon's characteristic attempts to bring into harmony the specimens of
interest to botanists and horticulturists, and the picturesque compositions
traditionally of appeal in Britain.

The Birmingham Botanical and Horticultural Society required a
scientific garden, an ornamental garden, and a reserve ground in which
they could raise plants for sale to help defray expenses (fig. 74).[51] The site

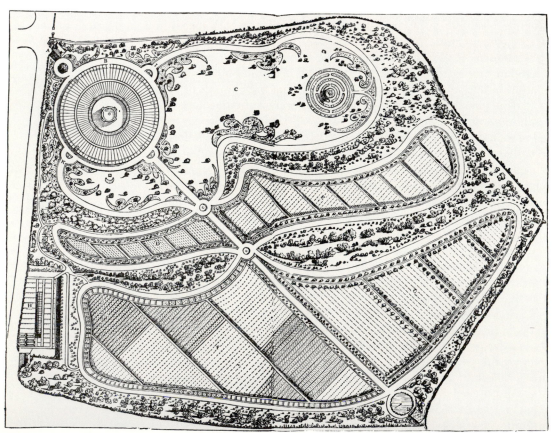

A, The main entrance.                    B, Circular terrace walk surrounding the hot-houses.
C, Pleasure-ground.          D, Floricultural garden.                    E, American garden.
F, Kitchen-garden, and agricultural garden.        G, Orchard.        H, Experimental garden.

The remainder of the ground is occupied with the arboretum and the herbaceous arrangement,
as before explained, commencing at I, and ending at K.

included sixteen acres of partially sloping ground (B and K in figure 74) and a lower, flat ground (F and G). Rather than separate the various functions, Loudon integrated several, partly because of the contours of the land. To lay out walks that must descend from a plateau to lower ground, he chose a convenient, flowing, transverse pattern of circulation. This, in turn, suggested that the arboretum should wind around and through the site, along the paths.

Given this complex program, Loudon devised a unified plan that shows his characteristic integration of picturesque and geometrical elements of design. A central straight walk is crossed at intervals by the meandering peripheral walk. At each intersection is a jet of water. On the highest ground is the grand feature — a circular range of glasshouses (B), reflected in the circular rose garden at the far end of the largest lawn. On the lowest ground are the orchard (G) and the kitchen gardens and "agricultural" gardens (F), planted in straight rows with parallel and perpendicular divisions. These gardens, like the others, are enclosed by a serpentine walk planted as an arboretum. All the trees, shrubs, and arabesque borders have been laid out according to the picturesque principle of connection (that is, they are not randomly "dotted" about). The overall planting design is gardenesque, however, in that each item within a group, or mass, has an immediate environment of inviolable space around it. In this way, the individual plants are given room to grow to perfection. They also contribute to the general effect of the whole — a light, free imitation of nature, recognizable as art.

The degree to which Loudon integrated geometry and irregularity into a unified whole is remarkable. Aside from the small experimental garden tucked away on the lower left, each element has an organic relationship to the other elements and to the whole; if any one element were removed, it would be obvious (at least on paper) that something was missing. This unity of plan becomes clear when one compares the Birmingham plan with one of John Nash's plans for a larger site, Regent's Park in London (fig. 75).[52] At first glance, there is a similarity of circular forms and straight paths in the midst of picturesque masses of plants, trees, and shrubs. On the ground, the effects of these two plans of different scales, contours, functions, and environments would deserve more investigation than is possible here. In plan, however, the main difference is that Nash has assembled *all* the elements into a picturesque composition. Even though certain geometrical elements are aligned on axes and perpendiculars, the effect of the whole is more like a collection of fragments brought together over a period of time. In contrast, Loudon's plan is an organic whole, so designed that, even allowing for later alterations or for casual wandering, the visitor could recognize a sense of structure and logical progession from the beginning of one's journey to the end.[53]

These observations based merely on two-dimensional plans imply no value judgment on the overall quality of the designs, of course — for a landscape design must also be assessed on the ground and in relation to actual or intended effects, visual, psychological, social, environmental, or otherwise. Still, the plan is a visual record of an approach to a design problem, and in this case, Loudon's plan is a clear display of the mind that conceived it: a logical, orderly mind with some inclination to be lyrical and romantic.

Fig. 75
John Nash, "Plan of an Estate belonging to the Crown called Marylebone Park Farm [now known as Regent's Park]" (1812).

This combination of traits can rarely be found in the plans of the so-called Loudonesque or gardenesque gardens designed by others and published in the *Gardener's Magazine*.[54] Something of this order and freedom, discipline and ease can be recognized, however, in two plans that Loudon knew well, by designers for whom he had great respect. The first is Gabriel Thouin's design for a "Jardin fantastique anglais," of 1820, which Loudon reproduced in a tiny woodcut (upside down and without identification) in the *Encyclopaedia of Gardening* (fig. 76).[55] This imaginary garden, its kitchen garden surrounded by curvilinear borders and penetrated by a short, straight path, seems to contain the germ of Loudon's plan for the Birmingham garden. In both, a broad open space is provided, and a sense of unity and balance among the elements on either side of the imaginary main axis is preserved. Both also contain picturesquely grouped single trees, an effect that Viart would describe as "masses of isolated trees" when discussing his own designs, in his *Le jardiniste moderne* (1819). But Viart, like Thouin, set these masses against denser masses of trees.[56] In Loudon's more gardenesque plan, there are no dense masses — only the lightly grouped trees and shrubs that would characterize all his garden-

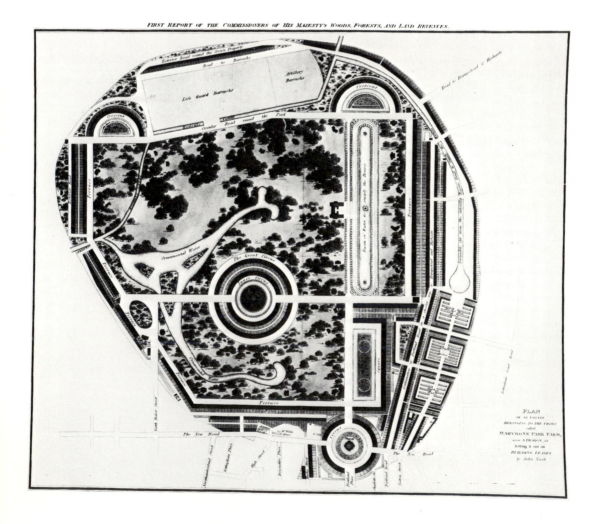

FIRST REPORT OF THE COMMISSIONERS OF HIS MAJESTY'S WOODS, FORESTS, AND LAND REVENUES.

esque designs. Then, too, Loudon's long, straight path is more prominent than Thouin's, serving as a kind of spine — or suggesting the trunk of a tall tree from which graceful branches grow. Years earlier, Loudon had laid out a similar straight path at Tew Lodge, Oxfordshire. In Birmingham, however, for a semipublic garden, his straight path was a broader, bolder element of the grand whole.

   F. L. von Sckell's plan for the Nymphenburg gardens, near Munich, embodies this integration of geometry and the picturesque on a magnificent scale (fig. 77). Loudon had seen these gardens in 1828, and, in publishing the plan in 1833, noted that Sckell was "the father of landscape gardening" in Germany. Though, partly due to climate, there was not a great variety of trees at Nymphenburg, Loudon considered the

*With this project for a garden, Thouin, a designer whom Loudon greatly admired, may have set the precedent for Loudon's integration of a utilitarian reserve ground within the larger scheme of picturesque gardens in Birmingham.*

Fig. 76
Gabriel Thouin, "Jardin fantastique anglais," ca. 1819.

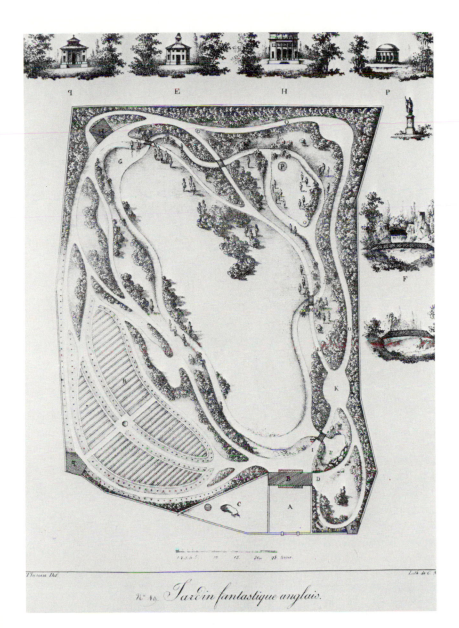

Jardin fantastique anglais.

Fig. 77

*Loudon considered this one of the greatest and most successful gardening efforts in Germany. He appreciated the "beautifully massed" trees which allowed a breadth of lawn and depth of view. Impressed, too, by the magnificent jets of water along the central axis, Loudon seems to have adapted them, on a much smaller scale, for his central axis in Birmingham. There he attempted an integration of axial and picturesque design similar to Sckell's in principle.*

Fig. 77
F. L. von Sckell, Plan of the Nymphenburg Gardens, near Munich.

project "one of the greatest and most successful gardening efforts in Germany." He went on to say, "The trees, it will be seen from the plan, are beautifully massed and grouped; and, at the same time, breadth of lawn is preserved and depth of view maintained. The straight walks, on both sides of the central canal, are lined with large orange trees in the summer season. . . . As far as art is concerned, the late M. Sckell and his successor have done every thing that modern skill in planting, and in artificially undulating the surface, could suggest."[57]

The plans for Sckell's Nymphenburg gardens and Loudon's Birmingham garden both include a long, straight path, or avenue; a few jets of water on axis; and clear divisions of beginning, middle, and end. In both there is a strong axis of symmetry, yet the two sides of the axis do not exactly correspond. This is an example of what Loudon called "cultivated and refined symmetry," suggesting an equilibrium, or balance of forms and masses, without a mirror image on either side.[58]

The circular range of glasshouses is the glory of Loudon's plan for Birmingham (fig. 78). Designed to be built in stages, it would cover 1¾ acres eventually, including an underground system of steam pipes heated by two central boilers (each of which alone could heat the whole structure if the other broke down). For service access, an inclined plane would

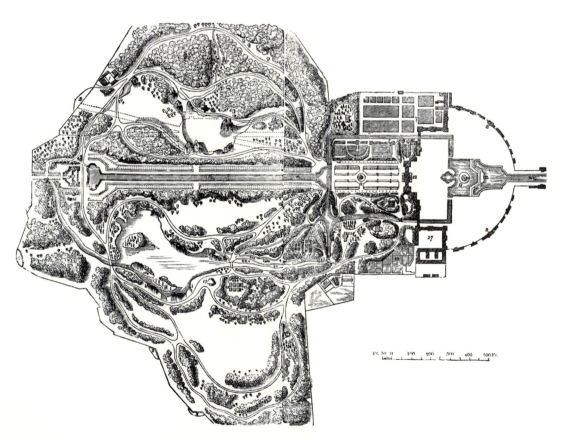

Ft. 50 0  100  200  300  400  500 Ft.

1, Aviary and cottage.
2 2 2, Sunk fence, in order to admit of a view beyond the boundary.
3, Garden pavilion.
4, Statues.
5, Covered seat or alcove.
6, Range of hot-houses in the botanic garden.
7, Kitchen-garden.

8, Buildings connected with the palace, for different officers, troops, &c.
9, Cascade.  10, Straight canal.
11 11,*Jets proceeding from rocks, which throw the water, in hollow columns nearly 9 in. in diameter, upwards of 80 ft. high.
12, Centre of the palace.
13, Cascade.  14, Straight canal.

15, Small temple.  16, Grecian temple.
17, Garden pavilion, containing pictures, statues, china, &c.
18, Place for beavers.
19, Gamekeeper's cottage.
20, Pheasantry.  21, Engine-house.
22, Bridge and water-wheel.
23, Banqueting-house for the use of the public.

24, Private flower-garden and summer-house.
25, Private flower-garden and open bower.
26, Private garden and entrance to the palace.
27, Quadrangle of buildings for the officers of the court, and their establishments.
28, Small gardens for the officers of the court.
29, Poultry yard, sheds, and keeper's cottage.
30, Shelters for game.

descend from a point near the center of the floor to a tunnel connecting with the main road. Rising straight up through the center were eight Tuscan pillars supporting the cistern that supplied the hothouses and jets with water. At the lower end of the long, straight path would be an overshot wheel, which would work as a forcing pump to keep the water in circulation.

Given a more generous budget, Loudon added, the hothouses could be erected in the form of a great dome, or beehive (fig. 79). The ground

*The Birmingham Commit-tee's rejection of these hothouses, in favor of more conventional (and surely cheaper) straight ranges of glass, was a bitter disap-pointment to Loudon.*

Fig. 78

J.C.Loudon, Circular range of hothouses proposed for the Bir-mingham Botanical Garden (1831).

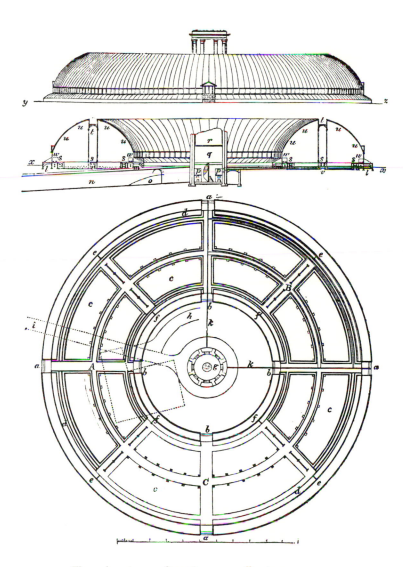

*a a a a,* The main entrances from the surrounding terrace.
*b b b b,* Corresponding entrances from the interior area.
*c c c c,* &c., Beds for large specimens to grow in the free soil.
*d d d,* &c., Shelves for plants in pots.
*e e e e,* The exterior pit, in four divisions.
*f f f f,* The interior pit, in four divisions.
*g,* Central tower, in which is contained the steam or hot-water apparatus in the cellar story, a potting-shed on the ground floor, and in the upper

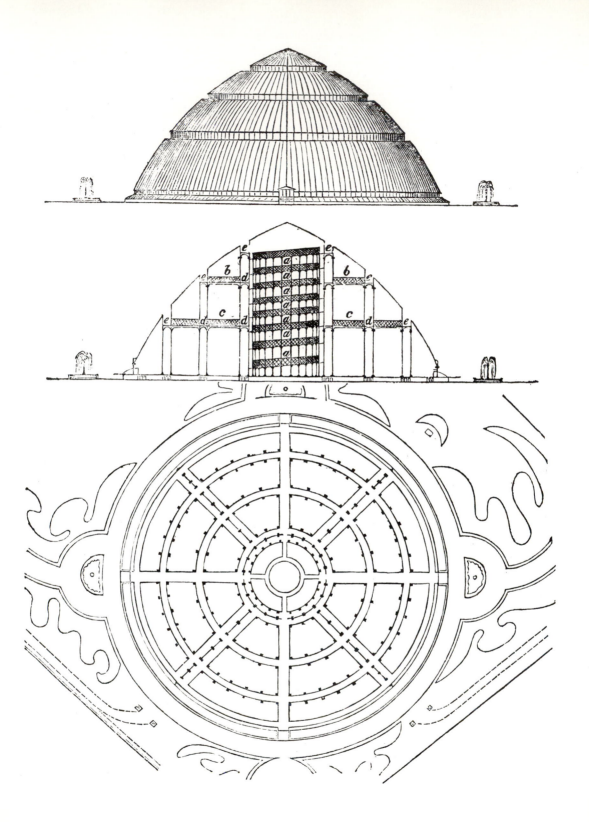

would be laid out in radial and concentric paths, with four grand quadrants to house four different climates. In the center, a cylindrical space sheathed in glass would shelter the most rapidly growing and tallest tropical trees, their branches clothed in epiphytes and climbing plants, and the ground covered with ferns. A spiraling ramp would ascend the interior of the cylinder — prefiguring Frank Lloyd Wright's ramp in the Guggenheim Museum, in New York (1946–59). Loudon's galleries would radiate from the spiral on two levels (whereas Wright's ramp is itself a gallery).[59] Vines and creepers might wrap around the railings of the inclined plane and pathways of Loudon's domed hothouse, and the tropical division could be hung with epiphytes.

Unfortunately, the Birmingham committee believed both versions of circular glasshouses would prove too expensive — even though Loudon had given detailed instructions for constructing the glasshouses in stages, as funds became available. This was not the first time that Loudon's fondest schemes had been rejected by a client; he had known the same frustrations in his early career as a landscape gardener. A client's hired gardener, for example, would disregard his instructions to plant trees of a single kind in masses, one mass blending into another, as in natural forests.[60] But in Birmingham, on a semipublic project, the frustration was particularly acute. Loudon's only consolation was his belief that someday truly public institutions would give designers even greater opportunities:

When towns and their suburbs are legislated for and governed as a whole, and not, as they are now, in petty detail, by corporations and vestries; and when the recreation and enjoyment of the whole of society are cared for by their representatives; public gardens, with hothouses of this sort, or even of far greater magnificence, will be erected, for the general enjoyment, at the general expense.[61]

Joseph Paxton, Frederick Law Olmsted, and others would one day realize Loudon's hopes. At least in his lifetime, Loudon would have the opportunity to realize his designs more fully in two small public gardens — the arboretum in Derby and a garden for some unnamed town.[62]

For one of the finest country houses in England, Loudon produced one of the most satisfying landscape designs of his late career — perhaps his finest. Coleshill House, in Berkshire, built in 1650 by Roger Pratt (possibly with the aid of Inigo Jones) was a handsome foursquare pile of fine proportions and graceful classical detail (fig. 80).[63] Faintly recalling the villas of Palladio and Serlio, Coleshill was admirably adapted to the British climate and temperament. With no extraneous pilasters or columns, the house rose from a low, rusticated basement and two full stories of nearly equal height to an attic with dormer windows, a hipped roof, a crowning balustrade, and central cupola. As Sir John Summerson has written, "Massive, serene, thoughtful, absolutely without affectation, Coleshill was a statement of the utmost value to British architecture."[64]

In its landscape setting, Coleshill was a classic image of country life in England, refined through centuries of responsible tenure and gradual change. In 1801 the house commanded a gentle view of undulating ground that, from the entrance front, sloped gradually down, then rose up to the public road. From the garden front, the land sloped gently

Fig. 80
J. Storer, engraving of Coleshill House, Berkshire, formerly a residence of the earl of Radnor.

down to the rivulet Cole, beyond pastures and woodlands to the south and west. In the distance were views of the village of Highworth, in Wiltshire, and the distant Cotswold Hills. One of John Britton's engravings of Coleshill features two cows lying in dappled sunlight, apparently free to wander as far as the outward-curving balustrade of the entrance-front steps. At that time the grounds had lately undergone alterations in keeping with the "modern" taste in landscape gardening.[65] When William Cobbett visited Coleshill in 1826, he praised the beautiful locust clumps and well-equipped farmyard. He also found the laborers well treated: "Here all are comfortable; gaunt hunger stares no man in the face."[66]

Since 1799, Coleshill had been the seat of William Pleydell-Bouverie, Viscount Folkestone and member of Parliament for Downton, Wiltshire. Folkestone was also a reader of Adam Smith and Jeremy Bentham, and an advocate of free trade, repeal of the Corn Laws, Catholic emancipation, and Parliamentary reform. According to Ronald Huch, his biographer, for nearly half a century Folkestone was considered "the most radical and reform-minded aristocrat in England."[67] In 1828 he succeeded his father, becoming the third earl of Radnor, and continued to advocate reform in the House of Lords. From then on, though his primary residence was Longford Castle, Wiltshire (seat of the present earl of Radnor), the third earl spent many summers at Coleshill and erected a school in the village. He died at Coleshill in 1869.

Loudon had at least two opportunities to serve Lord Radnor at Coleshill. First, in 1814, he designed a ducted hot-air heating system in the basement of the house, with circuitous iron smoke flues and an underground hot air shaft 300 feet long.[68] In the spring of 1843, the last year of his life, Loudon produced a series of plans for improving about 50 acres of the grounds.[69] Each plan was successively more complete, with an increasing richness of detail. In each, rectilinear terrace gardens surround the house, and the entrance court is approached by a straight avenue of cedars. These features would tend to restore a typical seventeenth-century

setting for the house (though the choice of cedars reflected Loudon's own particular fondness for evergreens).

The second and third alternative plans for Coleshill include a sequence of specialized gardens, all relatively secluded within the woods bordering a pasture that slopes down from the terrace on the garden front. (Grazing animals could be kept out of the gardens by means of a "strained wire fence" around the pasture and a sunken fence, or ha-ha, around the woods.) The plans were meant to speak for themselves; Loudon's *Report* gave only his itemized expenses. The plan Loudon considered superior, No. 3, would have required an outlay of some £10,200 and a staff of one gardener, one groundskeeper, and three laborers (fig. 81).

Loudon's image of Coleshill improved has a delightful sense of ease and openness in the landscape beyond the house, terraces, and offices. Much of the rural simplicity of the fine seventeenth-century stone house is preserved in its productive, mainly pastoral, landscape. Close to the house, the flower gardens are disciplined rectilinear plots of low-growing plants, embellished by three quatrefoil pools, each of which contains a fountain. The largest flower garden fills a slightly sunken terrace, adding subtly to the apparent height of the house. Viewed from the open lawn, this terrace would be barely visible; and as one descended the slope, the terrace would recede and disappear (see fig. 82 for a similar landscape treatment). One main sweeping graveled path would allow visitors a glimpse of several specialized gardens: the rosary, the American garden, the spiraea garden, the thornery, the botanic flower garden, the winter garden, the heathery, and the pinetum. A public footpath would skirt the gardens on the south, and a proposed bridge would cross over the public road to the new farm offices on the west.

Further research may reveal that some of Loudon's plans for Coleshill were actually realized. Loudon's plans, the neat graphic work of a skilled draftsman, were dated April 1843 and signed May 2, 1843. During that summer, the earl of Radnor was engaged in helping James Wilson establish a new political journal, the *Economist*, which, after a first few troubled years, has managed to survive to the present day.[70] Sadly, Coleshill House has not. It was gutted by fire, then demolished, in 1952.[71] The memory of the house is preserved in photographs and engravings. Loudon's elegant proposal survives in his plans and elevations. At Coleshill there remain two handsome stone gate piers along the road to Farringdon, two stone piers near the stables, and a charming stone village of model cottages. Finally, the landscape remains: a frame of low hills, woodlands, pastures, and magnificent, lightly grouped single trees, which may owe something to Loudon's presence in 1843.

The specialized gardens do not compete for attention. Laid out in a chain of secluded scenes, they are planted out, or screened, from the broad views of pastures and fields, in keeping with Loudon's earliest aspirations at Scone Palace, forty years before.

Fig. 81
J.C. Loudon, "Design for Rearranging the Pleasure Grounds at Coleshill," 1843.

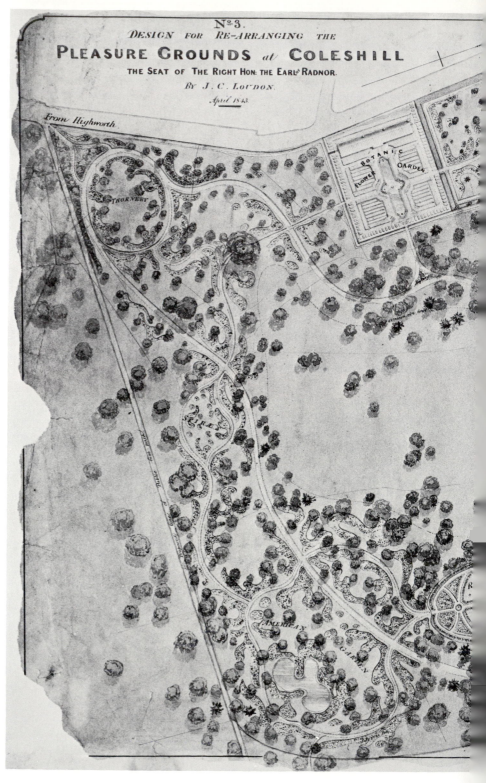

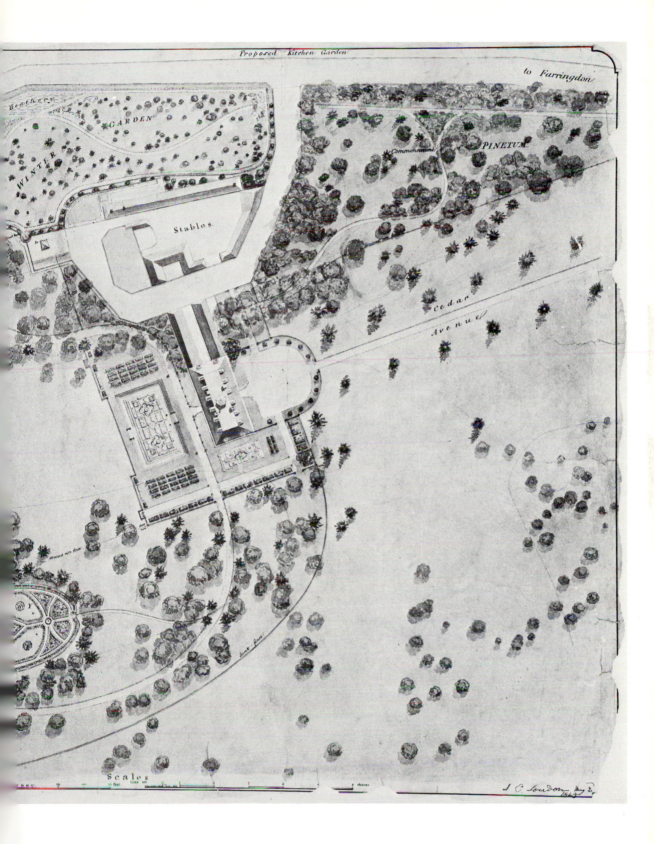

Proposed Kitchen Garden

to Farringdon

Heathery

GARDEN

WINTER

PINETUM

Commencement of

Stables

Cedar

Avenue

Scales

J C Loudon May 2
1845

*In 1843 Loudon's design for
Coleshill would have al-
lowed a depth of view from
the house, similar to that
achieved here at White
Knights, also in Berkshire.
Familiar with this cele-
brated place since 1804,
Loudon always admired the
rare trees and shrubs while
lamenting some faults in
maintenance. In 1833 he
suggested that, if it were
ever offered for sale, the
town of Reading should
purchase White Knights and
open it as a public garden.*
Fig. 82
T.C.Hofland, "View of White
Knights from the New Gar-
dens," ca. 1820.

VIEW of WHITE KNIGHTS from the NEW GARDENS.

View of Kenwood (Fig. 73)

# 11

## The Derby Arboretum

The Derby Arboretum offered Loudon his finest opportunity to combine the art and science of gardening for public enjoyment. Some criticized its design; others recognized its social and scientific values.

In the spring of 1839, less than a year after completing the *Arboretum et Fruticetum Britannicum*, Loudon accepted what he considered to be the most important commission of his design career — laying out the Derby Arboretum.[1] This first of England's parks designed for public use, a small (eleven-acre) arboretum, was to be located just south of the smoky industrial town of Derby (fig. 83). The immediate environment was not particularly inspiring, but not far away were some of the most beautiful hills and mountains of England.

Derbyshire: peaks, valleys, picturesque rivers, and streams came to mind when this midland county was mentioned in Loudon's day. The well-traveled, or well-informed, would know of Matlock, a secluded village some fifteen miles north of Derby which lay deep in the romantic, rock-faced, pine-clumped, windy dale (fig. 84). There summer residents danced in the old assembly rooms and drank drafts of mineral water. North of Matlock, at Chatsworth, the seat of the duke of Devonshire, was an

*When Dr. A.B.Granville toured the spas of England in 1839–40, he passed through Derby and remarked on its change from quiet county town to bustling railway junction. He also recognized advances in the cultivation of the useful and the "polite" arts. Largely responsible for these changes was the former mayor, Joseph Strutt, who had opened his picture gallery to the public and was about to present the town with its first public park.*

Fig. 83
"The Town of Derby, viewed from the Southeast," engraving, ca. 1840.

extensive park laid out by Capability Brown, a variety of specialized gardens, and Joseph Paxton's awesome, billowing, curvilinear conservatory — itself a mountain of glass in a mountainous land.

The road leading down from Chatsworth and Matlock to Derby was one of the most wildly picturesque in the region, following the course of the Derwent through gorges and past white cliffs, slipping by the occasional cotton mill and column of black smoke toward the rich agricultural lands around Milford, and finally ending at Derby. Once a sleepy, sepulchral town, now the junction of three railway lines, Derby had suddenly become a bustling, expanding, improving city.

Such is the picture of Derby and environs in 1840 given by the genial A. B. Granville, M.D., as he toured the spas of England.[2] In passing, he paid tribute to the benevolence of Joseph Strutt, formerly mayor of Derby, who had donated to the town a new arboretum laid out, Granville noted, by Loudon, the well-known author of useful books on agriculture and gardening. The educational value of the arboretum was self-evident; Granville simply emphasized that the working people of Derby could now enjoy this useful and beautiful public place for their health, their pleasure, and the cultivation of their taste.

As a landscape garden, the arboretum was not all that Loudon could have wished. "I should have made certain hollows and winding hollow valleys," he wrote, "as well as the hills and winding ridges."[3] He would have liked to evoke something of the spirit of Derbyshire, where William Gilpin had studied the winding river Wye before it joined the sweeping river Derwent between Matlock and Chatsworth and had gazed upon the sheer cliffs of rock and hanging wood high above the murmuring river Dove (figs. 84 and 85).[4] Gilpin's published tours had helped to spread the renown of this romantically picturesque scenery. As a boy, Loudon had read about it; later, as a young landscape gardener, he had explored it.

This was scenery that industrial workers in Derby rarely, if ever, saw. The millhands, lace workers, silk weavers, stocking makers, china workers, brush makers, and foundrymen worked long hours, six days a week; kept the Sabbath, if they were devout; married young, and died young. (In 1845 the average age at death of the laborers and artisans of Derby was twenty-one.)[5] Many of these people would never have known the ravines and crystal streams just a few miles to the north, in another world.

It was not just a love of specimen trees that kept Loudon from creating a more romantically picturesque park. Nor was it just the change in popular taste from the subtle imitations of nature in a landscape garden toward something more highly polished and artificial that induced Loudon to be content with introducing only a few undulating mounds along his sinuous paths. Although these were factors in his decision, there was another, more fundamental, reason: the site and its nearby industrial town desperately needed drainage.

Both the park and the town were located on relatively flat ground. The soil was retentive, and all streams were used as open sewers. According to J. R. Martin, a parliamentary commissioner who contributed to an inquiry in 1845, these sewers gave off "offensive emanations" in all quarters of the town.[6] Since 1801 Derby had more than tripled its population — to a total of 35,000 people in 1844 — and the town had been allowed to grow without a proper drainage plan. Sewers ran close behind rows of small terrace houses, and some private back gardens remained permanently saturated with sewage. In some areas, typhus fever was a constant plague. Furthermore, given the smoke of the factories and the narrow streets that trapped the air, Derby was often suffused with an atmosphere of tainted, dull fog.

The site of the arboretum was flat and badly drained, with loamy soil and a subsoil of gravel and loam. A belt of mature trees nearly surrounded the site. The prediction — a correct one — was that soon it would be entirely surrounded by buildings, as well. Therefore, though Loudon provided almost a mile of drains below his straight and winding paths; he did not create deep ravines and hollows, which would collect the foul waters and fogs from the encroaching town. He had previously seen a site where sooty fog was trapped by high walls, trees, densely planted shrubberies, and an artificial mountain — at Buckingham Palace in London![7]

*"It is impossible to view such scenes as these, without feeling the imagination take fire" (William Gilpin, at Matlock, 1786).*

Fig. 84
William Gilpin, "Matlock [Derbyshire]."

*About twenty miles from the hosiery and silk factories, copper- and wrought-iron works of Derby, were these gorges and streams, in a wilderness the well-traveled had come to appreciate. Loudon had admired the scenery of Dove Dale as a young man, yet he would not recall any of its romantically picturesque features in the Derby Arboretum.*

Fig. 85
W. Westall, A.R.A., "View in Dove Dale, Derbyshire," 1829.

Drawn by W. Westall A.R.A.                                                    Engraved by E. Finden.

VIEW IN DOVE DALE, DERBYSHIRE

There was another fundamental reason for Loudon's less-than-romantic landscape design in Derby. The eleven-acre site was meant to accommodate not only one thousand different kinds of trees and shrubs, to be examined for their individual characteristics, but also hundreds of people and thousands on festive occasions. The only other public open space was located north of town on a poorly drained fifteen-acre patch of ground known as Chester Green. Surrounding this remnant of common land were ditches that were periodically flooded by the river Derwent, as it spilled what was then thought to be "malaria" onto the shrunken green. Sadly, no open land or playgrounds were attached to Derby's schools. Before the arboretum was created, the working people of Derby would congregate in market places or pubs for relaxation; their walks were confined to the public roads and footpaths along the Derwent and its dependent canals.[8]

In other midland towns as well, open space was meager, and the Derby Arboretum had to serve as a regional public park for some years. On Sundays people would arrive in Derby by train, having traveled up to sixty miles or more in third-class railway carriages — from Nottingham, Sheffield, Birmingham, or Leeds — just to enjoy an afternoon in the arboretum.[9]

In the early 1840s, as Parliamentary commissions made exhaustive investigations into such matters as water supply, drainage, smoke nuisance, street cleaning, schools, hospitals, and birth and death rates, very few provincial towns, such as Derby, Newcastle-under-Lyme, and Shrewsbury reported having public parks or other open spaces. Birmingham, Wolverhampton, Manchester, Liverpool, and Leeds had no public parks, as such. In some cases, a quarry, a quay, a well-kept cemetery, or a private horticultural garden maintained by subscriptions and admission fees provided an open space for repose or mild exercise.[10] After 1837, largely due to the exertions of Joseph Hume in the House of Commons, all parliamentary enclosure acts were required to contain provisions for some public open space. But as late as 1845, no towns — not even the most prosperous municipal corporations — were yet empowered by a general act of Parliament to raise their own funds in order to create and maintain public walks and parks.[11]

As if anticipating that his design would set an important precedent for future public parks, Loudon published a complete report of his plan with its planting and management scheme, along with an explanation of the design principles behind the Derby Arboretum. This report appeared in the October 1840 issue of the *Gardener's Magazine*, and large extracts, accompanied by the plan, appeared in the appendix to Edwin Chadwick's *Parliamentary Report on the Sanitary Condition of the Labouring Population of Great Britain,* of 1842. Chadwick's comment was brief: Loudon's plan deserved "particular attention." An even larger extract from the report, including the plan and several renderings, appeared in the *Westminster Review* of April 1841. W.E.Hickson, the *Review* writer, was extravagant with both space and praise: Strutt's gift to the town of Derby was one of the "noblest benefactions of modern times."[12]

The plot of land was oddly shaped — like a leg of mutton — with a slight inclination from the northeast to the southwest (fig. 86). Loudon had been asked to retain many of the existing trees along the margins, as well as the existing flower garden, the cottage, an ivy-covered toolshed (if possible), and an ivy-draped oak near the main entrance that had been planted by one of Strutt's ancestors. Loudon was then to lay out the walks; make a planting design; and provide designs for two entrance lodges, each containing toilet facilities and a room to accommodate the general public. Visitors would be welcome to bring their own refreshments and, for a small charge, would be provided with knives, forks, crockery, and hot water for tea. Loudon was also to reserve several open spaces where, for celebrations, tents might be pitched to shelter bands, dancing, and spectacles.

The main organizing element of the plan was the broad, straight central walk, or spine, reminiscent of Loudon's main walk at the Birmingham Botanical Garden. Given the odd shape of the site in Derby, the fifteen-foot wide straight walk had to be deflected at an obtuse angle and crossed by another straight walk. At the intersection, Loudon designed a circular space for a central fountain or statue. "A straight walk without a terminating object is felt to be deficient in meaning," he explained.[13] Around this central object he recommended curved stone seats, which would form four segments of either a circle or an ellipse.

A system of serpentine paths provided the peripheral route around the arboretum. They ran between the raised mounds and the old belt of mature trees, lately thinned according to Loudon's directions. Among the trees that were to remain, Loudon specified evergreen shrubs — including rhododendrons, kalmia, laurustinus, holly, box, and mahonia — along with arborvitae, cedar, cypress, silver fir, hemlock, spruce, and evergreen oak.

Just as the straight paths required terminating objects, so the meandering paths required reasons for their various curves and shifts in direction. Pre-existing trees, natural irregularities of ground, new plantations,

*Of all his works of landscape design, Loudon was most proud of the Derby Arboretum, because it was to be a public garden where anyone could enjoy the grounds and learn about trees and plants. As he had once remarked in the* Jardin des Plantes *in Paris, "The most indifferent cannot see so great a variety of natural objects without having his views of nature enlarged and his mind expanded."*

Fig. 86
J. C. Loudon, Contour plan of the Derby Arboretum, 1839.

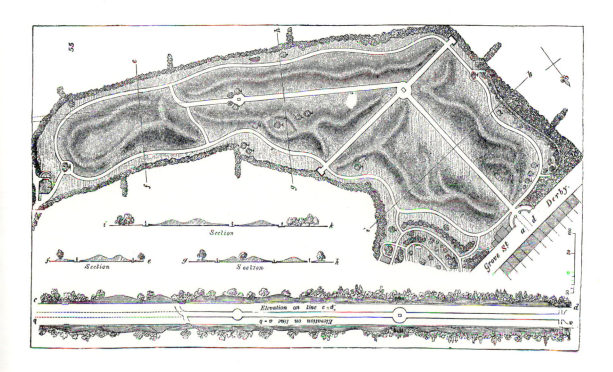

Fig. 87
Pavilion in the Derby Arboretum, designed by E.B.Lamb "in the style of James I."

and the new mounds all contributed to the apparently logical direction of the winding paths (fig. 87). The six- to ten-foot mounds provided some intimacy for the winding walks and screened the boundaries of the small arboretum, giving the suggestion of spaciousness beyond. Beneath the network of more than a mile of paths was nearly a mile of underdrains, consisting of semicylindrical tiles laid on flat tiles, running along the center of each walk. Cross drains led from the central drain to the edges of the walk, where there were cast-iron gratings set in stone. The walks were covered by rolled, hard-packed gravel, leaving the surface "dry, comfortable, durable and agreeable." In carrying out his design, Loudon was assisted by one Mr. Rauch, who supervised the formation of the mounds and the planting of all the trees and shrubs.[14]

This collection of plants was assembled from nurseries in Canterbury, Exeter, Hereford, and elsewhere. A few plants were supplied by the London Horticultural Society's garden at Chiswick, some grown from seed, some planted as saplings. All were arranged according to the natural system of Jussieu; numbered; and identified on glass-covered brick tallies with botanical name, common name, place of origin, height of the mature specimen in its native habitat, and date of introduction into Britain. For further details, the visitor could purchase Loudon's pamphlet *The Derby Arboretum*, which included a history of the arboretum, details of the opening days' celebrations, a proposed management scheme, and a complete catalogue of the more than one thousand numbered and labeled specimens, enriched with the kind of anecdotal information found in the *Arboretum Britannicum*.

The pamphlet also suggested a tour of the arboretum's treasures in proper sequence. Beginning at number 1, along the serpentine path to the right of the main entrance, the visitor might pause before several species and varieties of *Ranunculaceae*. Consulting the pamphlet, he would learn that these shrubs grow well in cool, damp soil, hence the name of the order, derived from *rana*, meaning "frog." The visitor might also recog-

nize some varieties of clematis — "Virgin's Bower," named for Queen
Elizabeth I, as it was introduced from southern Europe during her reign.
Loudon reminded the pamphlet's readers of Cowper's lines

> Why should not the virgin's friend
> Be crown'd with virgin's bower?

Nearby was the *Clematis Vitalba* — the White-Vine Clematis or "Traveller's Joy," sometimes known as "Old Man's Beard." Shepherds and
schoolboys in parts of England and Germany used to cut off pieces of the
old wood of this plant, light them at one end, and smoke them like pipes.
The flowers of this clematis, Loudon explained, are greenish-white, with a
fragrance like almonds, "much sought after by bees." As seasons passed,
the attractions of the plant changed: "The seeds have long, feathery, wavy
silky tails, which form beautiful tufts during the months of October and
November, and often remain on, all the winter."[15]

Pausing to read these amusing notes, parents and their children
could spend a long time making the circuit of Loudon's small arboretum.
As they followed the serpentine path and gazed to their left, they would
notice peonies and magnolias, then a tulip tree, berberry shrubs, the
mahonias, hibiscus, and various limes and maples. Stopping at one *Acer*,
the mock plane or sycamore, they would be reminded that this tree shadows the grave of the poet Cowper, in the churchyard of Dereham in
Norfolk. If the poetry and Jussieu's system of classification was of less
interest than fresh air and exercise, the family could leave the pamphlet in
the lodge and stroll down the main path towards the fountain where the two
main straight paths intersected. On the right were the clematis and magnolias; on the left, the evergreens: juniper, cypress, cedar of Lebanon,
Deodar cedar, Chilean pine, silver fir, Douglas fir, spruce fir, Weymouth
pine, stone pine, and Scotch pine. Some visitors might never quite learn
the distinctions, but would be content simply to breathe the refreshing
fragrances and enjoy the songs of birds.

Loudon calculated that a head gardener, or curator, and two assistants could maintain the Derby Arboretum in good condition during the
spring, summer, and fall. In winter, only one assistant would be needed.
Year-round duties would include mowing the grass, weeding the walks,
wiping the seats, and, during the summer, arranging flowers in the vases
on pedestals at the intersection of certain walks. If possible, these flowers
might be lent by local nurseries or horticultural societies, labeled, then
put in concealed pots inside the vases. They would be replaced by new
species each week. At a minimum expense, then, fifty vases might exhibit
more than five hundred different varieties during a ten-week summer
season.

This arboretum was just the kind of garden, on a more modest scale,
that Loudon had recommended for the London metropolis as early as
1811 — a "living museum."[16] In Derby each specimen was scrupulously
kept separate from the others, and the placement and management of
specimens was admittedly artificial. The climbing plants, for instance,
were trained on iron rods with "expanded umbrella-like tops." Loudon
explained, "The lower end of the iron rod [was] leaded into a block of
stone, and the stone [was] set in mortar on brickwork, so that the upper
surface of the stone appears 1 in. higher than the surrounding surface." In

this way, he emphasized the plant's "artistic" (that is, not naturalistic) appearance while protecting the iron rod from excessive dampness.

The trees were somewhat less artificially maintained. Each was to be allowed "as perfect a freedom of growth as if it were in its native habitat." Pruning would be prohibited, and no decaying leaves or ripe fruit were to be cut from the tree. If natural growth included throwing up suckers or rambling shoots, these were to remain, as well. The main surface roots of trees were to be left exposed, rather than covered with soil and turf. As Loudon hated the appearance of trees that resembled posts driven into the ground, he insisted that, for the benefit of its roots, each young specimen be planted on a low, carefully weeded hill. When mature, the tree would display its main branch roots. These precautions were taken for the health of the tree and to achieve "truth to nature."

Other practices, however, would prevent young trees in the Derby Arboretum from appearing entirely natural. The small hills around each tree were to be covered by newly mown grass and dead leaves to provide compost for the soil. Loudon added, "When at any time the leaves laid at the roots of the plant are blown off by the wind, they must be swept on again; and this practice must be continued till the leaves have so far rotted as to adhere to the surface of the soil."[17]

As we have seen, Loudon's principles of the gardenesque required that trees and shrubs be laid out so as to form groups. When viewed at a distance, the groups should appear connected; but on closer inspection, the branches of any individual tree should never be seen to mingle with those of another. Each tree must receive the necessary sunlight and space to grow uninhibitedly and to display its natural form at all times. Applying these principles to the small Derby Arboretum posed serious conflicts of space, however, as more than a thousand species and varieties of trees and shrubs approached full maturity. Loudon's solution was bold: when a tree became forty or fifty feet tall and its branches began to mingle with those of neighboring trees, that tree was to be cut down and replaced. Otherwise, as Loudon observed, the rapidly growing large trees would dominate and soon destroy the trees and shrubs that were more delicate and slower-growing.

In the 1830s many new species and varieties of plants from all parts of the globe were still being introduced into Britain. Aware that the collection he had amassed for the arboretum would someday lack scientific interest, Loudon suggested that no additions be made to the arboretum for fifteen or twenty years. Then the whole collection might be taken up, and replanted with the latest exotics available. He continued,

The most effective mode of increasing the number of species would be, — 20, 30 or 40 years hence, to take up the trees and shrubs of the belt, as well as all the other trees and shrubs; to reduce the whole to a *tabula rasa;* to surround the whole with a boundary wall; to form a narrow border and a walk within this wall; to plant the wall with select kinds which would not grow so well in the open ground; and to include the remaining part of the ground occupied by the belt in the present Arboretum. . . . In this way the Arboretum might be arranged every 20, 30 or 40 years, for an indefinite period; always maintaining its original character of entertainment and instruction, and always kept up to the existing state of knowledge and arboricultural riches.[18]

This proposal to tear up and replant the entire arboretum every twenty to forty years may seem startling or wildly extravagant for a public park. Even the suggestion to thin the existing belt of trees irked Joseph Strutt, who had originally planted most of it. But Loudon, the designer of a "living museum," was thinking no more radically than the directors of other kinds of museums, who continually rearrange their galleries and replace exhibitions. At any rate, the Derby Arboretum was never entirely torn up and replanted. Over time, certain specimens could not withstand the smoke of the encroaching town. As the more delicate specimens died, hardier and more common trees were chosen to replace them, piecemeal, with the financial resources at hand.

Joseph Strutt, one of three sons of the wealthy industrialist Jedediah Strutt, had not hesitated to spend some ten thousand pounds on the arboretum before he donated it to the town; yet he left no endowment. Instead, he entrusted his gift to those who would enjoy it and profit by it — the Corporation of Derby and, by extension, the people of Derby. At that time, as Strutt acknowledged, the English were typically reluctant to open museums and other institutions to the public for fear of property damage.[19] But his advice was to solicit kindness with kindness, to wean people from "brutalising pleasures" by offering them new forms of "rational enjoyment." Assuming that people would care for something they considered their own, Strutt believed he would preserve his property by making it public.[20]

Ironically, it was not until 1882 that the Derby Arboretum could be maintained "at the expense of all, for the enjoyment of all," as Loudon had expected. In the early 1840s, because municipal corporations were not yet empowered to tax themselves to maintain public parks, the new arboretum had to generate its own income. Initially, on five days a week, admission was open to subscribers who paid an annual fee of 10 shillings 6 pence for a family and to visitors who paid an entrance fee of 6 pence for adults, 3 pence for children. Perhaps Strutt should not have condoned these rather steep charges, determined by a committee. In any event, he did insist that the new park be open free of charge at least two days a week — on Sunday afternoons and on Wednesdays, from sunrise to sunset.

The opening of the Derby Arboretum was greeted by a three-day celebration, on the 16th, 17th, and 19th of September, 1840. Twelve volleys of cannon were fired the first morning, and rumblings echoed throughout the day. The Derby town council and fifteen hundred invited guests celebrated a private opening with a tea dance and a procession to the home of Joseph Strutt, whose gift was favorably compared with that of Julius Caesar. But, whereas Caesar had died before leaving his gardens and orchards to the Romans, Strutt gave the arboretum to the people of Derby in his lifetime. That evening, choruses of "Old English Gentleman" and the national anthem filled the air.

The next day, the working classes had their own celebration. Church bells proclaimed a holiday that rainy morning, and by noon the skies had just about cleared for the procession to the arboretum. The Loyal Prudence Lodge, No. 117, of the United Ancient Order of Druids led the way, followed by the Loyal Duke of Devonshire Lodge of Druids, the Rechabites, the Odd Fellows, the Independent Brush-makers' Society, and other associations. The workers, apprentices, and managers of the Derby

China Manufactory proudly displayed silk flags bearing the crest of Joseph Strutt; a scroll, representing his deed to the arboretum; and the motto "Deeds are preferable to words." And in a bower of flowers and ever-greens, the workers had set two splendid china vases featuring views of two great Derbyshire estates: Chatsworth, seat of the Duke of Devonshire; and Kedleston Hall, seat of the Right Honourable Lord Scarsdale. One rose-covered banner read, "The Gift is noble, don't abuse it."

Bands played and windows were full of spectators as the working people of Derby marched through crowded streets, displaying their grati-tude, their delight, and their self-respect. Some artisans simply carried the tools of their trade as they marched in uniform. Others, like the mechanics, carried elegant silk banners bearing such phrases as "Seek Truth," "Honour Science," and "From Art and Science true Contentment Flows." Asserting their own critical participation in the greatness of Great Britain, these artisans fitted out a horse-drawn cart with a model of a steam engine, a pair of globes, a telescope, the national and union flags, a royal crown, and the queen's arms.[21] The printers and bookbinders marched beneath proclamations such as "The Press, the Palladium of the Liberties of the People — the Terror of Bad Governments." Meanwhile, from their printing press, elevated on a decorated horse-drawn cart, two workers were pulling off copies of Joseph Strutt's speech to the town council. It ended: "As the sun has shown brightly on me through life, it would be ungrateful in me not to employ a portion of the fortune which I possess in promoting the welfare of those amongst whom I live, and by whose indus-try I have been aided in its acquisition. (Tremendous cheering.)"[22]

Although an estimated nine thousand people filled the arboretum on that second day, not a single tree or shrub was destroyed. Hearing this report, Loudon remarked, "Such a population is worthy of the noble gift."[23]

On Saturday afternoon, September 19, another six thousand people attended the Children's Celebration. A band marched into the arboretum playing "God Save the Queen" as the gates were thrown open. Parents strolled while children scampered along the walks, some heading for a nearby field, where there were games of leapfrog, thread the needle, and drop the glove. Tea was served in the pavilion for a charge of one shilling for adults, six pence for children. Two or three thousand people danced quadrilles. At 7 P.M. the national anthem was sung with great enthusiasm and the crowds dispersed, "as orderly and quietly as if they were retiring from a place of worship."[24] Some thought this the happiest of the three-day celebration. Others said it was the "pleasantest" day of their lives.

Was the Derby Arboretum a "critical," as well as popular, success? As a horticultural collection, or as an edifying, civilizing influence, cer-tainly; as a work of art, possibly. It appears that British observers were most concerned with the social implications of the arboretum, not with the art of landscape design. A.B.Granville, for instance, said he would not quibble with the "well-known skill and taste" of the designer. Instead, Granville wrote of the arboretum's "noblest combinations of artificial gardening," and considered Loudon "the only man whom the government might have placed with confidence in the management of all the royal and public parks and gardens, if they were desirous of seeing them always in their best attire and most favourable conditions."[25]

When W.E.Hickson, a retired manufacturer and a champion of national education, commented on the Derby Arboretum in the *Westminster Review,* he did not dwell on beauty. It was the nobility and utility of Strutt's gift that he found gratifying. Here was an institution, a public park, that would neither "pauperise industry" nor induce the poor to trust the bounty of the rich. Like Loudon, Hickson was looking ahead to the time when towns would be legally able to create their own parks and support them by public funds. Thus, with delicate hesitation, aware that largesse was not the ultimate solution, Hickson observed that a permanent endowment from Strutt could have kept the grounds open every day of the year, free to all, from the start. In a country where sunshine was a fleeting pleasure, he reasoned, the people must try to make the most of whatever pleasant weather should appear, even on days other than Wednesday and Sunday.[26]

Concerning the design and planting of the arboretum, Hickson had no reservations. Loudon had proven himself "eminently fitted" for his task, "and we cannot but lament," Hickson added, "that it is not to men of equal taste and judgment, and known ability, that the Commissioners of Woods and Forests entrust the management of the vast domains for which they act as trustees for the Crown and the public."[27] What was needed in the London metropolis, he added, was the adoption of one general system for all the parks and gardens. There was enough variety of soil and aspect among them that they could display fine specimens of all the different kinds of trees and shrubs that would grow in the climate of Middlesex County.

Implied in Granville's and Hickson's views was the notion that the beauty of the arboretum emanated from two primary considerations, social well-being and scientific interests. Others tended to agree. William Jerdan, editor of the *Literary Gazette,* described Loudon's "little Derby domain" as "the very treasury and epitome of the wide world's natural wealth."[28] Charles Mott, an assistant parliamentary commissioner who prepared reports on the sanitary conditions of several midland counties, observed that Strutt's "princely" gift to the people of Derby was "beyond all praise."[29] Two years later another commissioner, J.R.Martin, described the arboretum as an aesthetic and scientific achievement, "tastefully laid out in grass intersected by broad gravel walks, and planted with a great variety of trees, shrubs and flowers, botanically arranged." In the four years since its opening, he maintained, the park had already served the humanizing purposes of Loudon and Strutt. Martin concluded, "The Arboretum, as these gardens are designated, is much frequented, and has already produced a perceptible effect in improving the appearance and demeanour of the working classes, and it has, doubtless, conferred an equal benefit upon their health."[30]

Happily, Loudon was able to see something of the results of his labors in Derby (where he had extended himself on "the most liberal terms," because it was a public work). Writing in her own *Lady's Magazine of Gardening,* Jane Loudon told of their visit with Strutt in June 1841. As the three were strolling through the grounds of the arboretum, a light rain began to fall, and they entered one of the lodges. Seated inside was a party of 250 people who had come by train from Nottingham to take tea in the arboretum. When they saw Strutt, they all rose and, with one voice, thanked him for the great pleasure he had afforded them. Loudon may have felt some gratification, too. "I never saw anything more affecting," Jane Loudon wrote, "though it was but for a moment."[31]

The real beauty of the Derby Arboretum lay not simply in the eye of the beholder, but in the mind, and was dependent on an understanding of the site, the program, and the people of the town; and on intellectual curiosity, scientific education, and awareness of the larger environment. A copy of Loudon's catalogue of the trees and shrubs would surely pique the curiosity of a visitor — botanist or layman — with its scientific and anecdotal account of the specimens. The catalogue could also inform the stranger of the social value of the arboretum, for it gave a complete account of the three-day celebration marking the opening of this park. Through the vivid details of balloons, cannons, fireworks, processions, church bells, shouts of joy, and general euphoria, the stranger would learn something of what the arboretum meant to the people of Derby. But the visitor would have to penetrate the town, finally, to appreciate the park.

The working people and indigent poor of Derby commonly lived in back-to-back houses in alleys and back courtyards whose only communication with the outside world was via long, narrow tunnels through masses of buildings.[32] As William Baker, a physician and parliamentary commissioner observed, these back-to-back houses, with indoor privies and pigsties, were not limited to relics of a past unenlightened age. Some back-to-back houses had recently been built by landlords whose object was to maximize rents for a given plot of land. One of the worst properties was called Robinson's Yard, a narrow, hidden cul-de-sac and a haven for typhus fever, where a row of tiny two-story cottages faced a row of privies and the two-story walls of nearby slaughterhouses.[33] Those who knew intimately these sights and smells of Derby's back alleys and courts could, from 1840 onwards, find relief only a few miles away in the Arboretum, where a band might be playing while adults sat sipping tea and children romped. There saplings grew, unharmed and well labeled, in the light and airy spaces provided for them among undulating mounds and infant shrubs.

A stranger whose background was quite removed from Derby and the industrial midlands might experience the arboretum quite differently, however. In the autumn of 1844, Charles Mason Hovey, the proprietor of a splendid nursery in Cambridge, Massachusetts, and the editor of the Boston-based *Magazine of Horticulture*, came to the Derby Arboretum well prepared to appreciate its treasures. Hovey had used Loudon's magazine as the model for his own periodical, originally named the *American Gardener's Magazine*. He frequently reprinted, with due credit, articles by Loudon and his correspondents; and he generally adopted Loudon's aesthetic principles, including the recognition of art in the landscape and the importance of "high keeping" (or a high degree of neatness and careful cultivation) in pleasure grounds near the house. He had already seen the plan and catalogue of all the trees and shrubs in the arboretum, and he had marveled at Loudon's *Arboretum Britannicum*. He was clearly delighted to see the Derby Arboretum, by far the best he had seen on his tour of Scotland, England, and France. It even surpassed the arboretum at

Chatsworth (which was not so well maintained at the time). "Why not such an arboretum in America?" Hovey asked.

Few of our cities or large towns have done anything towards establishing places for the health and recreation of the inhabitants. Boston, with its beautiful common, and Philadelphia, with its elegant squares, stand before other cities, but in the newer towns which have recently sprung up, there have been scarcely any which have made provision for gardens or grounds, where the public could resort and breathe the fresh air. We know no object so well deserving the attention of men of wealth than the formation of public gardens *free to all* in crowded towns or cities.[34]

Hovey was impressed by the neatness of the arboretum. There were no weeds, and the flower garden was flourishing. The brick tallies, with their botanical information, were in good order. Hovey listed about fifty trees in the arboretum which he would recommend for American villa gardens, including varieties of elms, ashes, oaks, aspens, maples, and cherries. He was disappointed only by Loudon's undulating mounds, which he believed were not large enough to look "natural," (fig. 88). A dense plantation of evergreens here and there might have improved the general effect, he suggested.

Hovey's countryman Andrew Jackson Downing would agree. A nurseryman as well as an architect and landscape designer, Downing had recommended a variety of ornamental trees, both native and foreign, for use in American landscape gardens (although lately he had begun to emphasize native species). In 1839 he had expressed profound admiration for Loudon's *Arboretum Britannicum*. In fact, Downing was indebted to Loudon for much of the horticultural and architectural matter in his own writings. Like Loudon in England, Downing was a strong advocate for public parks and rural cemeteries in America. He was thus prepared to appreciate the Derby Arboretum on several counts when he arrived in the

*Early views show how effectively these mounds once screened the views of one path from another. Over time, the mounds have settled. Restoration will be a complex task, but Loudon's plans, planting lists, and guide for management are available.*

Fig. 88
View of mounds and a winding path in the Derby Arboretum.

summer of 1850, having just seen and admired Chatsworth. By then the arboretum was freely open to the public five days a week, instead of two. Downing found the trees and shrubs well labeled in Strutt's "noble bequest," clearly one of the most useful and instructive public gardens in the world.[35]

As a work of art, however, he thought it somewhat disappointing. Though he recognized that Loudon's intention had been to create a fine horticultural collection, not a simple pleasure ground, Downing wished that Loudon had more "cleverly planted the groups of trees and shrubs in thicker masses, so as to blend with all the "ease of nature." A more beautiful example of a small garden of scientific interest, in Downing's view, was the botanic garden in Regent's Park, London, with its extensive velvet lawn, its noble conservatory, and the thickets of foliage that amply concealed its boundaries and gave the suggestion of much great extent beyond. In effect, this botanic garden seemed more "natural," therefore more beautiful.[36]

This preference for a subtler imitation of nature's careless ways — for softening, camouflaging or otherwise concealing the traces of man in the landscape — looked back to the eighteenth century and forward to the later nineteenth century. Though true to their characteristically "American" instincts for simplicity and unadorned nature, these visitors to the Derby Arboretum were hardly recommending anything new. Downing had learned from the best eighteenth-century British writers on gardening, from Addison, Shaftesbury, and Pope — the same authors whom Loudon had read and appreciated as a young man. Nor could Downing and Hovey help being influenced by "modern" British writers who discussed use and beauty in the landscape, among them, Repton and Ruskin.

At that time, Britain was, by and large, the immediate source of philosophical ideas on the art of gardening for Americans living and working along the eastern seaboard. But Hovey and Downing, two leading tastemakers in America, were both somewhat disappointed by the visual qualities of the Derby Arboretum, though it had been laid out by the arbiter of taste for both Britain and America. These American gardeners were not satisfied by the overall effect of the scenery in the Derby Arboretum. In fact, it was not scenery at all. The young specimens stood alone, each in its well-tended space. They neither fought among one another for the essentials of light, air, and nourishment, as they would in their true "state of nature," nor did they project beyond the undistinguished mass of vegetation that always served in the great royal parks and country seats of Britain as a supportive, comforting frame for foreground plants and distant scenery. Loudon's young specimens stood alone, open to all the sun that would ever appear in Derby, open to the fleeting moments of intense radiant energy, open to the wind and rain, open to view.

Loudon cared about these specimens as few, if any, landscape gardeners had ever done before. Perhaps only to his exceptionally curious, disciplined, and well-trained mind were the young saplings worth the absence of more conventionally picturesque scenery. Viewed as the object of the good gardener's infinite care, the sapling would mature, developing a personality of its own as it grew into a fine specimen. The gardener, and any frequent visitor whose curiosity was piqued, would be

excited to watch its development under nearly ideal conditions, as it
received attention and encouragement that it would never have received in
nature. With the ingenuousness of a child — curious, trusting — Loudon
believed that others naturally would share his excitement. They had only
to be introduced, early on, to habits of observation and enquiry. "The
taste must be originated in youth," he explained.[37] Aiming beyond the
limits of present possibilities, Loudon always looked to the rising generation with hope.

After several generations, times and tastes have changed. Today the
iron railings that once surrounded the Derby Arboretum are gone. The
eastern gate lodge has been dismantled, and one of the pavilions has been
replaced by a public lavatory. In 1981 a neo-Jacobean covered garden
seat of ivory-painted brick still had a vandal-proof iron grill across its
arcade, and the curved stone seats that had marked the intersection of the
straight main walks were gone. Victorian terrace houses, along with rows
of modern brick dwellings, completely surrounded the arboretum.

Partly because of the smoke from domestic and industrial coal-
burning in the late nineteenth century, many of the original species of
trees have been lost. For the most part, they were replaced by common
sycamores. The arboretum now resembles a reasonably well kept park,
with its mature trees far exceeding Loudon's recommended forty- to fifty-
foot limit. To many, this little haven of green, with its beds of flowers and
common trees, is pleasant enough even without the original labels inscribed with botanical information. J.W. Allen, a local historian, has
observed that "the Arboretum is rather a place to walk through than walk
in."[38]

For anyone familiar with Loudon and his times, however, the Derby
Arboretum is a memorable place to walk in. The present writer, a stranger
to the town, wishes every success to the people of Derby who are trying to
conserve and restore what they have.[39]

# 12

# Metropolitan Improvements

Loudon was twenty years old when he first saw London in 1803. For most of the next forty years, the metropolis would be his home. His address would change as he gradually moved westward, however, from humble to relatively prosperous neighborhoods — Holborn and Soho to Pall Mall.[1] By 1816 he was living in Bayswater, just north of Kensington Gardens. Loudon was then thirty-three. Thereafter, until his death at age sixty, Loudon would be a resident of Bayswater and, in spirit if not in fact, a citizen of the metropolis (fig. 89).

Not until 1889, when the London County Council was formed, could anyone be considered a true "citizen of the metropolis"; for no local governing body had such a broad jurisdiction until then. Still, in Loudon's lifetime, Londoners were beginning to recognize some civic responsibility for the vast, ever-increasing mass of buildings and streets spreading from the centers of London and Westminster. In just three decades from 1801 to 1830, the metropolitan population jumped from 865,000 to 1,500,000.[2] (Compare figures 90 and 91.) For some, metropolitan living centered around the seat of national government, the royal parks, the fashionable shops and promenades; for others, it consisted of crowded tenements and dark, filthy alleys; some form of labor; and the solace of the public house, or "gin temple." William Cobbett, the political journalist and gardening writer from Hampshire, cursed London as "the all-devouring Wen."[3] James Grant, the Parliamentary reporter, was exhilarated by London's infinite variety and possibility and called it "the Metropolis of the World."[4]

Loudon viewed London as a vast, diverse landscape — buildings and roads, one great river fed by streams and open sewers, many gardens and squares and a few great parks, and considerably more people than cows and sheep. Nonetheless, when he first arrived, grazing animals and windmills were still visible near the periphery of the built metropolis — just north of the New Road, for instance, on the future site of Regent's Park. Hammersmith and Hackney were then famous for their nursery gardens. Islington, like Bayswater, was a rural village. And Vauxhall was not yet an underground station — but still a public garden![5]

Loudon also viewed London with the eye of a town planner; and in this respect he was no more remarkable than another horticultural writer,

*St. Paul's, the centerpiece of this montage, was also the conceptual center of Loudon's most important plan for metropolitan improvement.*

Fig. 89
St. Paul's Cathedral, Ludgate Hill, by Sir Christopher Wren, centered in a montage of London buildings.

John Evelyn, who had proposed an early greenbelt scheme for London after the Great Fire of 1666.[6] From that time, England's traditions of town planning had mingled increasingly with those of gardening. In 1779 Capability Brown proposed to alter the course of the river Cam and to unify its backs (or banks), thereby reshaping the landscape of Cambridge — not just the colleges but also the urban fabric.[7] John Nash had learned about landscape design through a commission for Sir Uvedale Price and a brief partnership with Humphry Repton, before becoming architect to the Prince Regent, later King George IV. Though primarily an architect, Nash

KNIGHTS CYCLOPÆDIA OF LONDON.

achieved a remarkable fusion of architecture, landscape gardening, and town planning in his work during the first two decades of the nineteenth century in Regent's Park and St. James's Park in London, and at the Brighton Pavilion.

Sir John Summerson described Nash as an architect-entrepreneur who stood at the end of a tradition of town planning — one in which the coordination of social, economic, political, and aesthetic concerns was largely intuitive.[8] Nash's most impressive feats of town planning — the creation of Regent's Street and Regent's Park — were personal triumphs over all the usual obstacles to any improvements involving street widening, demolition, and new communications between parts of a built environment. His aims and achievements in urban design were dramatic, but not truly metropolitan in scope. He worked mainly in the West End, on projects that were practicable, financially and politically. As Summerson concluded, Nash was "most essentially *of* his generation."[9]

Loudon, on the other hand, looking beyond the immediate future towards a distant ideal, often conceived plans for several generations hence. Even before a new "tradition" of town planning emerged, Loudon anticipated it and urged changes that seemed inevitable to him, though sometimes farfetched to others. As an editor, writer, critic and activist —

*When Loudon first arrived in London, he found a metropolis of some 865,000 people. Edinburgh, his own native capital, had a population of about 100,000.*

Fig. 90
"Cary's Actual Survey of the Country 15 Miles round London," June 1800, detail, the cities of Westminster and London.

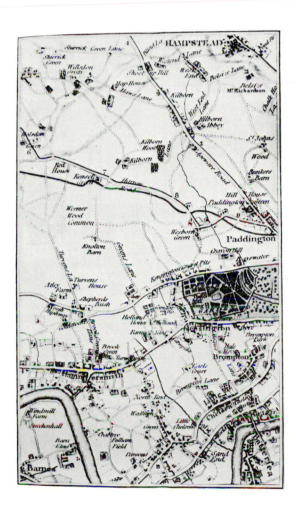
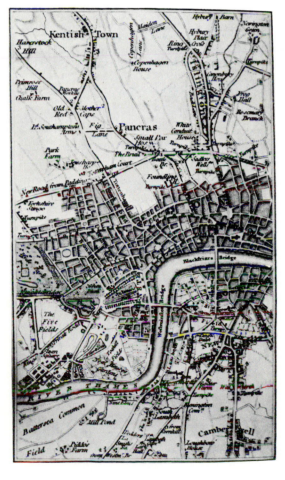

*By 1830 London's popula-*
*tion had jumped to about*
*1,500,000. Paris had about*
*a million people; Edin-*
*burgh, 170,000; New York*
*(in 1820), 123,000.*

Fig. 91
"Cruchley's New Plan of London (1830), Shewing all new and intended improvements to the present time," detail, West End with Regent's Park and Hyde Park.

and occasionally as a designer — Loudon had some influence in shaping the metropolitan landscape; but he was more a guardian of the public interest than a physical planner.[10] His self-appointed task was to arouse public concern over such matters as speculative building in Kensington Gardens, open sewers in Hyde Park, and the need for truly comprehensive planning in the London metropolis.

Loudon always wanted to grasp the whole of any system, whether it be the tempered environment of a hothouse, the construction of a building, or the links between the members of the vegetable kingdom. To

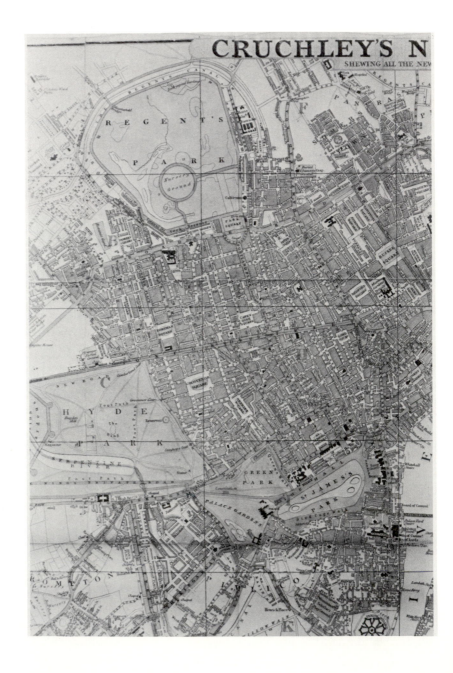

satisfy his intellectual curiosity, he had to analyze the whole of any phenomenon, classifying and reassembling the parts, in order to understand the structure of things which were commonly considered incoherent — if considered at all. Similarly, the new tradition of town planning that emerged in the later nineteenth century would be based on an understanding of system: of structure, function, and interaction among the complex parts of a whole. As a "process of analysis leading to a corresponding synthesis," in Summerson's words, this new tradition could not depend primarily on the intuitive artist-architect-entrepreneur.[11] Somehow the scientist would have to emerge, some latter-day Christopher Wren, with a compassionate understanding of social relations and a keen awareness of political processes, as well as an eye for beauty and a mind which could perceive (or elicit) order. Such a person, in any age, would be rare. Loudon was a likely candidate, but his ideas were often too far in advance of his times. As he once admitted, "no man can steal a march on his age. All improvement is more the result of the general mind of society, than of the mind of the individual, who is the immediate instrument."[12] Loudon was himself an instrument of planning — not always successful in his immediate efforts, but effectively a forerunner for others who would come along years later and, unawares, carry out his suggestions.

Loudon's first proposal for metropolitan improvements, in December 1803, focused on London's residential squares.[13] In a letter addressed to the editor of the *Literary Journal*, he regretted the lack of evergreen shrubs in the squares — particularly of those shrubs that "diffuse the most delightful perfume all around" in early spring and late autumn. Walks would be more pleasant if their edges were softened and their surfaces kept nearly level with the lawn; harsh, "edgy" lines of turf and deep ruts for drainage were unnecessary. Planting should be more natural, as well, with masses of trees, shrubs, and plants grouped so as to unite and harmonize among themselves. As in a natural wood, masses of one kind should be allowed to blend gradually into masses of another kind. Something to "interest and relieve the eye and satisfy the mind" was needed: a sense of progression and variety rather than the usual repetitious, indiscriminate mixing of trees throughout the squares.

The choice of trees could be more interesting, too. Instead of an arbitrary collection of expensive tender specimens that could not long survive the smoky London atmosphere, Loudon recommended "common sorts, singular for beauty, fragrance and luxuriant growth," such as the Mezereon, the almond, the snowdrop tree, the laurustinus, and the arbutus. Botanical labels could be placed before various specimens for the amusement and instruction of the public. Clearly, Loudon was alluding to the public square rather than the private square, with an iron-rail fence and a locked gate enclosing it (fig. 92). Walks, he observed, should be laid out in accordance with the streets leading into the square and with the buildings surrounding it. The planting design should not be so dense as to obstruct the circulation of air, but it should provide handsome foregrounds to the streets and buildings, as viewed from within and without the square. These improvements to the squares would contribute, Loudon believed, to the beauty of the metropolis, the health of its inhabitants, and "even, in some degree, to the honour of the British nation."

Loudon's suggestions in that article have been followed, to some

*In 1803 Loudon recom-
mended that the planting of
London squares follow the
principles of natural scenery: one kind of tree should
predominate in one place,
gradually giving way to
other kinds. These trees
should be chosen, he be-
lieved, not for their rarity,
but for certain sensuous
qualities — beauty, fra-
grance, and luxuriant
growth.*

Fig. 92
Soho Square, ca. 1840.

extent, in parts of Russell Square, Lincoln's Inn Fields, and Soho Square
— all precious islands of trees, shrubs, and turf in the parts of London
where Loudon first found lodgings as a young landscape gardener. A later
scheme, one presented to the Linnaean Society in December 1811, never
materialized. This was Loudon's proposal for a "living museum," a garden
of about one hundred acres, to contain every species and variety of the
known vegetable kingdom. The arrangement of specimens would vary.[14]
In one area, the Linnaean system of classification would prevail; in another, the system of Jussieu. In some sections, the Chinese style of
gardening would be featured; in others, various modes of English landscape gardening would be displayed. The vast circular glasshouses for
this scheme were never realized in their original form. However, the
Archimedean spiral of Loudon's proposed path system for this garden was
actually used in the arboretum of the Loddiges' Botanic Nursery in
Hackney, East London.[15] And much of what Loudon had hoped to see in a
national garden near London — including a research library and a collection of plants and trees arranged so as to interest the general public as well
as the scientist — has been realized at Kew (see fig. 43).

When he settled in Bayswater, in 1816, Loudon was far enough
removed from the built metropolis that he could, if he cared to, concentrate on his own back garden, his hothouses, and the local surroundings — agricultural fields and hedgerows, nursery gardens, villa gardens,
and the gardens of Kensington Palace. Instead, he appears to have gained
just enough distance from the metropolis to gain a certain perspective on
the whole. In May 1818, Loudon proposed two improvements (neither
ever adopted), that looked beyond his immediate neighborhood: One was
a design called "working men's colleges," a seven-story apartment building for families, proposed as an alternative to the miserable tenements of
London's East End (see chapter 7). The other improvement initially

[Soho Square.]

focused on the western suburbs, but ultimately involved half the metropolis, from Rotherhithe in East London to Chelsea on the west. This was Loudon's plan for a complex, useful, and ornamental extension of the Regent's Canal.

At that time, the Bayswater brook (or rivulet), which flowed near Loudon's house and fed the Serpentine River in Kensington Gardens and Hyde Park, was an open sewer (fig. 119). Eager to eliminate this nuisance, Loudon suggested, in a letter to the *Gentleman's Magazine* dated May 12, 1818, that the stagnation and stench of both the Bayswater brook and the Serpentine River could be relieved by extending the Regent's Canal at the point where the brook passed under the Paddington Canal.[16] A balance coffer, like those designed by one Mr. Fulton (Robert?) could be employed to lower vessels ten feet to the level of the Serpentine. The canal would then follow the brook's course into Kensington Gardens, where vessels would be guided along the Serpentine by a chain moored to a line of posts along the center. In the lower reach of the Serpentine, in Hyde Park, another balance coffer would lower vessels to an underground channel, which would have openings for wharves at Knightsbridge and in Chelsea and would end at the Thames, between the Vauxhall and Battersea bridges.

In 1818 canals were still a vital means of cheap transportation (see fig. 93).[17] The steam locomotive on rails had not yet doomed the inland waterways to picturesque idleness. Work on the Regent's Canal had lately recommenced, though it was undergoing a brief suspension due to lack of funds at the time Loudon proposed his scheme.[18] In recommending the extension of this canal, Loudon noted that it was a profitable public facility. Public health, however, was apparently his main concern. The canal would deepen, widen, and lower the Bayswater brook, thereby eliminating the damp and dry rot of the houses (including his own) sited along its banks. The canal would also partially dilute the noxious wastes of Paddington. A further advantage, Loudon observed, was that Hyde Park and Kensington Gardens would be made more attractive once the two

*To animate the "dull" grounds of Kensington Gardens, Loudon suggested that the two reaches of the Serpentine be joined to form one long "river" (which has been done) and to introduce canal boats from a new extension of the Regent's or Paddington Canal (a hint not taken).*

Fig. 93
Thomas Shepherd, "Junction of the Regent's Canal, at Paddington," ca. 1829.

JUNCTION OF THE REGENT'S CANAL, AT PADDINGTON.

reaches of the Serpentine were joined on one level to form a more natural-looking river. Canal boats would then animate an otherwise "dull," characterless stretch of parkland.[19] The unsightly sunk fence then separating Hyde Park from Kensington Gardens should be removed, Loudon urged. He suggested planting the banks of the newly formed river with masses of trees — particularly oaks — and shrubbery. Finally, the elders and the "common rubbish" of trees behind the greenhouse near Kensington Palace should be removed, to reveal the ancient cedars, hollies, and yews planted by the landscape designers George London and Henry Wise a century earlier.

Eight years passed. The commissioners of woods and forests were just beginning to repair some of the roads and walks in Hyde Park and to construct lodges at some of the gates. In 1826 Loudon was living in the new three-story semidetached house he had designed and built at numbers 3 and 5, Porchester Terrace. His own house at number 3 faced south; so he had at least a partial view across the Uxbridge (now Bayswater) Road, toward the brick wall that rose from eighteen to twenty-five feet high, enclosing Kensington Gardens.

Loudon detested that wall. He thought it was an eyesore, a dirt and rubbish collector, and a blemish along that potentially handsome entrance into the metropolis. In the first number of his *Gardener's Magazine*, for January 1826, Loudon urged that the wall be torn down and replaced by an open palisade. The mass of elms and poplars along the Uxbridge Road should be removed or thinned. Then a broad margin of evergreen shrubs could be planted — hollies, box, yew, laurels, junipers and cedars — preserving some privacy for the interior gravel road and walk, yet offering a pleasant foreground to Kensington Gardens, as viewed from without.[20] For a better connection between the northeastern and southwestern parts of London, from Islington to Piccadilly, Loudon proposed that certain existing roads be linked to a new road that would run along the northern boundary of the Serpentine in Hyde Park. Once again, Loudon urged that the two reaches of the Serpentine be joined. Fresh water could be fed into the Serpentine from the northern boundary of the park, where it would cascade over a ten-foot rocky cliff in a densely planted wood. (Loudon's friend, the painter John Martin, later proposed a similar, romantically picturesque setting for the source of the Serpentine; his published sketch, of 1828, reveals that he and Loudon shared the same romantic vision of this site[21]) [fig. 94].

By means of this verbal sketch in the *Gardener's Magazine*, as well as his letter to the *Gentleman's Magazine*, other letters to the editors of local newspapers and journals, and several petitions, Loudon may have been partly responsible for the appearance of Hyde Park and Kensington Gardens as we know them today.[22] In 1855 Leigh Hunt observed:

The late public-spirited Mr. Loudon, who had a main hand in bringing about the recent improvements of this kind [labeling trees, shrubs and flowers in the southeastern part of Kensington Gardens] . . . got the old wall in the Bayswater Road exchanged for an iron railing, which gives the wayfarer a pleasant scene of shrubs and green leaves as he goes along, instead of dusty old brickwork; and though too many of the shrubs and new trees, in the line of the railing, are not yet sufficiently grown to keep up the old sense of seclusion, and so render the walker in the gardens equally content with the change, a few years will restore his satisfaction.[23]

Loudon himself was never entirely satisfied with the appearance of Hyde Park and Kensington Gardens, however (fig. 95). Instead of the great bridge of five stone arches spanning the Serpentine, Loudon would have preferred a light footbridge or a low bridge of many arches, like those in paintings by Claude Lorrain.[24] Today the head of the Serpentine is not wildly picturesque, with a cascade such as Loudon and Martin had dreamed of — but somewhat Italianate in character, with four octagonal basins, jets of water, balustrades, nymphs, urns, and fountains. Not far away, however, near Victoria Gate along Bayswater Road, is a pictur-

*Both Loudon and his friend John Martin, the painter, envisioned a rustic cascade as the source for the Serpentine in Hyde Park, and both published schemes to conduct pure water into the metropolis via this secluded spot — which is today the site of sunny Italianate pools, fountains, and sculpture.*
Fig. 94
John Martin, Rendering of a proposed waterfall at the head of the Serpentine River in Hyde Park, ca. 1828.

*Here Loudon would have preferred a simple foot-bridge, or a low stone bridge of many arches — as in many of Claude's land-scapes — rather than the grand bridge with five arches, built in 1828 by John Rennie.*
Fig. 95
View of Kensington Gardens, looking east to the Serpentine River.

esque brick and stone cottage ("Westbourne," 1858), fulfilling Loudon's repeated requests for heated gate lodges to shelter the park keepers.

One of Loudon's earliest ideas for an improvement that would materially affect the entire metropolis was his proposed metropolitan boulevard, or "promenade," of 1822.[25] Like his canal scheme, this plan improved communications, creating links between areas that had as yet no civic identity as parts of a greater whole. The metropolitan boulevard was also based on the same general principle of continuity that underlay Loudon's plans for the flow of fresh water and carriage traffic through Kensington Gardens and Hyde Park. Even the route would be similar. Encompassing many existing roads and leaving most private property intact, the boulevard would proceed from Regent's Park to Kensington Gardens; through Hyde Park Corner and Piccadilly to Knightsbridge; crossing Vauxhall Bridge to Kennington, Blackheath, and Greenwich Park. Beyond Greenwich Hospital, it would cross the Thames over a cast-iron viaduct (high enough for ships in full sail to pass below) and then, joining the City Road with the New Road, circle back to Regent's Park.

It may be that the idea for this metropolitan boulevard, published in the several editions of Loudon's *Encyclopaedia of Gardening*, inspired Sir Joseph Paxton's similar, but more elaborate, scheme for the "Great Victorian Way," of 1853, which included elevated railways and a continuous iron and glass arcade.[26] Both projects were conceived, in part, as embellishments to the metropolis; but, unlike Paxton's boulevard plan, which included houses and shops, Loudon's relatively modest thoroughfare was intended mainly to direct the eye outward, to the varied landscapes beyond. By leaving the boulevard from time to time, Loudon suggested, one could spend a day gathering fine impressions of London: in Kensington Gardens; the Hammersmith Nursery; the King's Road gardens; the Chelsea Garden; the Loddiges' nursery and arboretum in Hackney; Highgate; Hampstead; and Regent's Park.

Evidently Loudon was thinking of the stranger's view: that of families visiting from distant counties, the foreign tourists, the professional gardeners and amateurs — all of whom would be grateful for the glimpses of fine gardens and buildings round the metropolis. This concern for the stranger's view was not an uncommon one at the time. During the years following Wellington's decisive victory at Waterloo, the question was often raised: "What can we show to foreigners that is truly worthy of our capital, our nation, our wealth, our civilization?" Would-be planners were often well-traveled themselves, and their plans for metropolitan improvements were often nourished by memories of foreign lands. They had seen the palaces of Versailles and Fontainebleau; the public buildings of Munich, Karlsruhe, and St. Petersburg; the boulevards of Paris; and that monumental approach to Berlin, Unter den Linden. They admitted, with embarrassment, that several capitals on the Continent far excelled London in the overall quality of their urban architecture. Thus the "Architectural Monstrosities of London" were decried and defended.[27]

A.W.N.Pugin was not impressed by modern architecture at all, whether abroad or at home in Britain. Upholding the architectural standards of medieval England, he detected in modern buildings a lack of soul, too much mask, too much mechanism — in a word, vulgarity.[28] Other critics, like Charles Fowler and A.W.Hakewill, were confident that

London's architecture could indeed display the wealth and power of the nation with refined taste and grandeur, and that London could outdo her European rivals in both quantity and quality of monumental public buildings.[29]

Loudon was deeply concerned about both architectural and environmental quality. He discussed the public utility of the Regent's Canal and Regent Street; the quality of Wilkins's new National Gallery and of the architecture along Regent Street; the style and, more important, the site of the new Houses of Parliament; and the condition of the old slaughterhouses in Smithfield Market. However, compared with the mass of angry, or whimsical, or brilliant criticism of the day, which disparaged the tasteless mediocrity and superficiality of the age, and clamored for improvements in palaces, museums, and shop fronts, Loudon's own remarks seem modest, reasonable, restrained. It was a critical age. As William Hazlitt, one of Loudon's favorite essayists, wrote in 1823 of literature and the arts: " 'We are nothing if not critical.' Be it so: but then let us be critical, or we shall be nothing."[30]

In 1825 a critic signing himself "An Admirer of Good Taste, and Lover of my Country" published an open letter to the Right Honorable Sir Charles Long (Lord Farnborough, a well-known arbiter of taste), in which he complained about the dusty, unpaved avenues that formed the approaches to London. The nation's capital was so destitute of fine buildings that it appeared merely a "vast overgrown town." Surely some of the mean houses near Hyde Park Corner might be torn down, he suggested, and some fine monumental buildings, commemorating the nation's recent victories in war, might be erected along Piccadilly, to form one grand entrance to the metropolis from the west.[31]

In 1827 a writer for the *Mechanics' Magazine* noted with regret that the English monarch had a mediocre residence in London. "The sovereigns of this first of nations have long been confessedly the worst lodged in Europe," he wrote. " 'Hospitals like palaces, and palaces like hospitals,' we have been content to see ranked as among the most remarkable of our national distinctions."[32] In criticizing the siting and design of Buckingham Palace, the writer agreed with Loudon, the "intelligent editor of the *Gardener's Magazine*," that, although the garden front of the palace was attractive, its site and the treatment of the grounds were unfortunate (fig. 96). The writer then quoted Loudon at length:

Had the problem been proposed to alter Buckingham-House and gardens, so as to render the former as unhealthy a dwelling as possible, it could not have been better solved than by the works now executed. The belt of trees, which forms the margin of these grounds, has long acted as the sides of a basin, or small valley, to retain the vapours which were collected within; and which, when the basin was full, could only flow out by the lower extremity, over the roofs of the stables and other buildings of the palace . . . between the stems of the trees which adjoin these buildings, and through the palace windows.

Now, all the leading improvements on the grounds have a direct tendency to increase this evil. They consist in thickening the marginal belts on both sides of the hollow with evergreens, to shut out London: in one place substituting for the belt an immense bank of earth, to shut out the stables; and in the area of the grounds forming numerous flower-gardens, and other scenes with dug surfaces, a basin, fountains and a lake of several acres. The effect of

John Nash's west (or gar-
den) front was grand and
elegant, Loudon thought,
but he deplored the damp,
low-lying situation of the
palace, surrounded by high
walls and thick plantations,
and suffused with fog and
smoke pollution. A palace
with hanging gardens high
above the Thames would
have been more "healthful."
Fig. 96
Jonas Dennis, "View of the
West Front of Buckingham Palace, ca. 1835.

all this will be a more copious and rapid exhalation of moisture from the
water, dug earth, and increased surface of foliage. . . . The garden may be
considered as a pond brimful of fog, the ornamental water as the perpetual
supply of this fog, the palace as a cascade which it flows over, and the
windows as the sluices which it passes through. . . . The only question is,
how far this vapour is entitled to be called *malaria*.[33]

Rather than subject the monarch to the foggy atmosphere of this low-lying,
damp situation, Loudon would have preferred to see him lodged in a
palace elevated above the banks of the Thames, with several tiers of
gardens reminiscent of the hanging gardens of Babylon. For "recluse
enjoyment," the monarch could retire to one of the royal palaces in the
country. The grounds of Buckingham Palace could then be united with
Green Park and thrown open to the public.

These thoughts are typical of Loudon's criticism of metropolitan
improvements. His humor was perhaps a little drier than that of most wits
of his time. His architectural criticism was more consistently rational, and
therefore less entertaining, than the impassioned or ludicrous remarks of
others. Loudon's main interest, of course, was usually in the land: in its
qualities as a healthful, attractive, and potentially beautiful setting, appropriate to the needs of people. The royal parks, gardens, squares, and
other open spaces in the metropolis, Loudon considered too precious to be
covered with buildings, except under extraordinary circumstances. Thus,
when he proposed that the new Houses of Parliament be removed to a more
elevated, healthier site (Lincoln's Inn Fields, Soho Square, or Leicester
Square), he would reserve an equivalent amount of land as open space, in
compensation for the public's loss of the square.[34]

This recognition of the need to preserve open space in the metropolis and any notion that the public had acquired a customary right to enjoy a given piece of land, or its equivalent, regardless of whether it was actually public — was absent from many contemporary schemes for metropolitan improvements. Consider the proposal of one anonymous member of Parliament in 1825: The King should be given a splendid new "Palace of St. George," to be built at the eastern end of Hyde Park, facing Park Lane. The Crown could pay for the palace with the revenues derived from converting parts of Kew, Richmond Park, Bushey Park, and Hampton Court to private villas. These parks could be bordered with "decorative masses of buildings," as in Regent's Park; and certain royal structures could be torn down. St. James's Palace could be demolished for some handsome new houses. And Hampton Court could be converted into a university or, perhaps, a lodging house for the "female branches of the less affluent nobility."[35]

This member also recommended that an architectural planning board be formed. An unpaid commission, composed of leisured gentlemen, should control all matters of taste in public buildings, though they would have no control over finances. These men should not be ministers or public officials, but simply men of independent means, whose amusement was the pursuit of taste. "Taste is not a commodity to be bought," the writer explained; "it is rather the fruit of a cultivated idleness, or the recreation of an unoccupied mind."[36]

Loudon once recommended that a committee of taste be formed for the town of Southampton, following the example of Philadelphia. He was not thinking of "leisured gentlemen," however, but of local architects, engineers, and amateurs who would be willing to consult with outside professionals from time to time. The committee would review all designs for proposed buildings, discuss their reservations with the interested parties, and consider alternative designs.[37] For the London metropolis, Loudon repeatedly urged that a representative municipal body be formed, with the necessary political power and financial controls to oversee not only public buildings, but also canal and sewer construction; street widening; and the planning, design, and maintenance of public parks and gardens. He was also intrigued by the proposal he believed had first been suggested by J. M. Gandy (or some other "first-rate architect"): that a board of building inspectors should investigate matters of health and safety.[38]

In 1834 Loudon proposed that the metropolitan government he envisioned should supervise building and planning not only in the parishes of London and Westminster, but also in the suburbs, nearby villages, and adjacent undeveloped lands. He suggested it have jurisdiction within a radius of five miles from St. Paul's, with powers of extending that radius. At the time, the initial jurisdiction would have included the open fields of Hampstead and Highgate on the north, Shepherd's Bush on the west, Clapham and Dulwich to the south, and Greenwich and West Ham to the east — roughly the same boundaries as those of the London County Council, which was created half a century later (1889), after most of this area had been built up.[39]

In 1830 Loudon had listed the features of an effective metropolitan planning board: Its proceedings should be open, like those of the House of Commons. Its plans should be reported in the newspapers and subjected to public criticism. Its actions should conform to some general system or principles.[40] Up to that time, improvements had been initiated and stalled for unexplained reasons. Vast sums of public money had been spent on hastily conceived projects, and private interests had thwarted plans for public improvement. Those who directly profited from Smithfield Market, for instance, repeatedly opposed measures to remove that crowded and unsanitary market from its location in a poor, densely populated neighborhood in East London. Meanwhile, men continued to drive cattle and sheep through the city streets every Sunday night, with torches blazing, dogs barking, beasts wailing, and pedestrians scattering. Adding to the general chaos, the drovers shouted as they beat the frightened beasts into submission. Loudon observed:

It is surely disgraceful that such a place as Smithfield and the scenes to which it gives rise on market days, should be continued in the centre of the most wealthy and populous city in Europe. But nothing on earth is so difficult to move as John Bull; and when he is baited into motion, it is more by the influence of main force, than by the machinery of general system or principle. One person or party takes up the idea of a cemetery, another that of a market; and, after years of perseverance in beating down prejudices and opposing interests, one of the parties becomes fatigued, and the objects are obtained or lost as it may happen.[41]

With rational planning, sufficient power, and enlightened public opinion (which might challenge that power), Loudon argued, metropolitan improvements should no longer be so fragmented or arbitrary.

Like many of his contemporaries, Loudon was encouraged by the existence of some well planned cities on the Continent. Returning from his third journey abroad, in January 1829, his mind was stored with new impressions of buildings, towns, landscapes, and people. In his own words, "as a botanist would examine and describe a plant," so Loudon had studied the particulars of France and Germany.[42] He had examined Leo von Klenze's handsome new Glyptothek, or sculpture gallery, in Munich (1816–34); the plain stone benches for pedestrians on the public roads in Bavaria; and the orderly system of abattoirs, or slaughterhouses, in the outlying districts of Paris. He had also enjoyed the exhilarating prospect of an unenclosed wheat field seen from the elevated open road between Dieppe and Rouen. (The prospect is still exhilarating today.)

While abroad, Loudon had always made comparisons, instinctively, with his native Britain. By this time, however, he observed with an open mind, free of chauvinism. Evidently he had shed the half-conscious assumption that everything in Britain must reflect a level of culture and civilization superior to that of all other nations. "Nations, like individuals, can only know themselves by comparing themselves with others," he reflected, as he compared the conditions of Great Britain, France, and Germany. He began, naturally, with the differences in soils, climate, atmosphere, natural contours, modes of cultivation, division of property, gardening, and architecture. He also considered cooking and domestic economy, manners, education, government, and general level of civilization and the spirit of improvement, all of which he believed to be interrelated.[43]

Like the botanist searching to distinguish plants by their essential, structural characteristics, Loudon tended to look for causes or first prin-

ciples. In Europe in 1829, he found two: the degree of education among
the people, and the character of their government. The "friends of France
and of humanity" were establishing a permanent system of education,
which would be applicable to every male and female child born in
France.[44] In Bavaria, Württemberg, and Baden, the effects of a high level
of general education among all the people could already be observed, to
Loudon's amazement. More clearly than ever before, he recognized that
education was the foundation of the kind of government he ardently hoped
to see in Britain. His ideal was a representative system of "self-government," an expression he had borrowed from Thomas Jefferson.[45] Self-
government, Loudon believed, should prevail at all levels, local and
national. Both of these ideals, for education and government, were being
realized in Bavaria, and Loudon was delighted to report that landscape
gardening was more encouraged there than in any other German state.[46]
The Bavarian government had formed a standing commission made up of
counsellors, engineers, architects, and the landscape gardener Charles
Sckell, Director General of the Court Gardens. This commission was
empowered to improve the management of canals, bridges, public buildings and gardens, national forests, and public roads. The roads were lined
with ornamental trees, fruit trees, mulberry trees (cultivated for the silk-
worm), or forest trees, depending on local conditions. Guideposts were
standardized, and around milestones were semicircular seats of turf or
stone. In Württemberg and Alsace, Loudon noted:

Stone benches are placed along the roads, at different distances, near the
large towns, as seats, with elevated benches adjoining them, of two different
heights . . . [which allows] persons carrying heavy baskets to market on their
back or head, to stop, set down their baskets, rest themselves, and take them
up again without assistance. These stone benches and the turf steps indicate a
most humane attention to the labourious classes, and to the very poorest
people, on the part of the government, and must greatly attach the inhabitants
to their rulers.[47]

Along the country roads of Germany, these seats and milestones surrounded by poplars and fringed by neat grass margins were not the result
of whim or chance (as one might find in Britain), but the logical outcome of
systematic management by the government.

     Arguing that Britain should initiate such a system, Loudon envi-
sioned the whole country laid out with roads as fine as in a gentleman's
park. National roads, county roads, and parish roads should all be subject
to one general law, which would regulate the slopes of roads; the erection
of guideposts, milestones, and lamps; and the planting and management
of the trees and hedges in the margins. Each level of government should
employ its own engineer; and road improvements should be planned many
years in advance. Thus, whenever unemployment was high, Loudon observed, able-bodied men, who would otherwise be dependent on the poor
rates, could be usefully employed on road and railway construction.[48]
     Loudon was enough of a realist to foresee difficulties in the estab-
lishment of a truly comprehensive road system in Britain, a nation where
individual liberty was highly prized. He conceded:

The roads of Britain are characteristic of the people and the government; their
irregular natural-like direction, bold and free, and yet sometimes constrained

and awkward, is a consequence of the independence of local legislation, and of the security and inviolability of individual property. Till lately some of the principal roads were crooked, of irregular widths, and circuitous in their direction, even in the neighbourhood of the metropolis; and the manner of forming and repairing roads differed in almost every district. The reason is, these roads have risen, like the English Constitution, by degrees, out of the wants of the people, in their progress from a rude state to that of regular civilisation.[49]

Like landscape gardens and buildings, roads should be appreciated in their context — political, topographical, cultural, economical. A straight road over a flat country was no more economical or convenient, Loudon reasoned, than a sweeping, curving road following the contours of a hilly landscape. He could appreciate the grandeur of the straight, tree-lined roads crisscrossing the flat countryside of France, while, at the same time, he cherished the simple beauty of the English countryside, with hedgerows and trees lining roads that wound around hills and dipped into valleys. The British government, he believed, should consider the merits and failings of various systems of road design and management, and adopt the most appropriate features of each.[50]

At a time when the profession of planning did not yet exist, Loudon was one of those citizens who freely publicized their own proposals, hoping for some positive response. In 1834 he found some congenial ideas in Sydney Smirke's *Suggestions for the Architectural Improvement of the Western Part of London*. Smirke, an architect, called for the systematic management of streets and roads; the formation of wide, commodious avenues; the provision of clean air and proper drainage; and the formation of a permanent board, or metropolitan commission, which should direct these necessary improvements, superseding any local ordinances as well as the antiquated Building Acts.[51] Like Loudon, Smirke suggested that the planning commission should consider the regulations enforced in Continental cities, as well as in all parts of Britain, and that some code of metropolitan improvements ultimately should be enacted, to ensure the symmetry, beauty, convenience, security, and health of the city.

Loudon briefly but firmly disagreed with Smirke on one issue: the proposed erection of publicly subsidized villages for the working classes. Smirke suggested that a board of metropolitan improvements could lay out rows of rental dwellings along "wide, clear, regular avenues" just beyond the built metropolis — on waste land beyond Vauxhall Road, or in the open fields west of Edgeware Road and north of Euston Square. (For the destitute poor, each parish might sponsor the building of a dormitory — something on the order of Chelsea Hospital — containing well lighted, warmed, and ventilated wards with high ceilings, fire-proof floors, and six-foot partitions between the beds. The wards would lie on either side of wide corridors.) Smirke added that the "inmates" of working-class villages should be given their own recreation ground for exercise and "innocent social pleasures" in the evenings and on Sundays and other holidays.[52] Unconvinced, Loudon insisted on the longer-term benefits of political reform. With a metropolitan representative system of government, under which *every* householder could vote in the election of members to a local parliament, he argued, subsidized villages for working mechanics would be unnecessary: "These, and every working class, must be put into a condition to take care of themselves."[53]

Apparently, the responsibility to "take care of oneself" was a matter of degree. Loudon never gave up his hopes for establishing apartment buildings for working people in the city. A manufacturer or group of gentlemen might erect such structures and receive a five-percent return on their capital. In June 1843, testifying as a witness before the parliamentary commissioners on the "State of Large Towns," Loudon explained that he had recently obtained a new estimate on the cost of building a forty-unit quadrangle.[54] (He had originally conceived such an idea in 1818 and had published it in 1832 in the *Mechanics' Magazine*.) In order to "place the poor in all essential respects as to household comforts on a level with the rich," Loudon would provide, in each apartment, gas for cooking or lighting, and hot and cold water. The resident porter could use a "balance bucket," or dumb-waiter, to lift fuel and other bulky items to the apartments. There could also be a common washing-room, drying room, and bakehouse; separate baths for both sexes; a school; and, "if occupants were harmonized sufficiently," a common work room and a dining room.[55]

Loudon's scheme for cooperative living, intermittently revised and refined over twenty-five years, was meant to be integrated into existing urban neighborhoods — not erected on the outskirts of town. If he could not recommend Smirke's well-meant suggestions for subsidized villages and hospital-like wards for the poor, perhaps it was because Loudon was wary of isolating them too much, of making their dwellings and recreation grounds a kind of ghetto. Such projects would tend to encourage what Loudon repeatedly opposed: "keeping (the poor) under, as a distinct class."[56]

For all of Loudon's interest in labeled trees and systems of classification, in the precise definition of objects in the natural world, he did not believe in segregating facilities or areas of the metropolis by class. Nor could he condone public officials' little acts of favoritism that benefited only the well-to-do. In 1829 he had pointed out that views into Hyde Park were being opened up to the grand houses along Bayswater Road through the replacement of a park wall on their side with an iron-rail fence while the high brick wall was allowed to remain opposite the more humble houses in the neighborhood. Thus, the wall was an insult to the poverty of these residents.[57] Loudon was also indignant that anyone should be kept out of Kensington Gardens because of his attire, whether it be the red and gold livery of footmen or the humble clothes of working people.[58]

In his testimony to the parliamentary commissioners, Loudon was optimistic that the poor would act so as to justify every mark of respect and kindness they were being shown now that more parks and museums were being opened to them (fig. 97). Happily, they could now enjoy some "rational amusement" during their few moments of leisure. He explained:

The working classes in and about London have improved immensely within the last 40 years, in consequence of good example, and the more general practice of reading. In the year 1804, it was necessary to have men in Kensington Gardens all the summer, on every Sunday morning as early as four o'clock, to prevent persons from climbing over the walls to gather branches from the trees; but for the last 20 years nothing of the kind has taken place, and there are no watch men on

*Education — not only literacy, but self-cultivation — was essential, in Loudon's view, for any change in the lives of the poor. "Whoever neglects self-cultivation, in every particular matter with which he has to do, is neglecting his own happiness, and trifling with the gift of life" (Loudon, 1831).*

Fig. 97
"Seven Dials," St. Giles's Parish, London.

Sundays, any more than on any other day. I do not believe that there is even so much quarrelling in crowded courts and alleys as there used to be. Even the manners of [the inhabitants of the slums in the parish of] St. Giles's are ameliorated.[59]

As in Munich, Karlsruhe, and Paris, the poor in London could only learn about good conduct and fine manners by observing the people who were presumed to have them. And what could be a better "school" for conduct and manners than a park in which, on Sundays and holidays, people of all ranks tended to mingle?

Loudon was naturally concerned about the park and gardens closest to him in Bayswater. In the last few years of his life, by means of his letters to the editors of the daily newspapers and his editorials in the *Gardener's Magazine*, he tried to prevent development of the land formerly occupied by the kitchen gardens of Kensington Palace. Having heard rumors of contracts for speculative building, he urged that the land be preserved. A few parcels of undeveloped land west of the gardens might be purchased by the government; and, in time, a link of open space might join Holland Park with Kensington Gardens (fig. 98).[60] That opportunity for more continuous open space was never realized, however. Today, the street named Kensington Palace Gardens is lined with imposing Italianate villas of gleaming white stucco and constitutes a haven for foreign ambassadors.

In conclusion, one brief anecdote should illustrate the extent to which Loudon expected a responsive local government to make the metropolis a more pleasant place in which to live, work, and enjoy one's

[Seven Dials.]

leisure time. With the simplicity of a country-bred lad, Loudon mused over the possibility that London might become a haven for those dear friends of Charles Waterton and John Jay Audubon: birds.

At midday on April 23, 1830, as he stood in the office of the *Gardener's Magazine* in his Bayswater home, Loudon dictated a reply to one "R.G." of Sussex, who had reported that the nightingale had been heard for the first time that season on Sunday evening, April 18th, in Regent's Park. Loudon replied that the nightingale had also been heard in Bayswater and Kensington Gardens, on the 18th or 19th — he could not recall which day. As he was dictating, two birds were singing most delightfully in Hopgood's nursery, not far from Loudon's window. He concluded: birdcatchers were probably at that very moment hiding in the lanes, waiting for an opportune moment to strike. The legislature ought to forbid bird catching in London, at a radius of twenty miles from St. Paul's — for the sake of the birds' lovely songs, and to control the population of insects in the gardens.[61]

*In the 1830s Loudon repeatedly objected to speculative development on the site of the kitchen gardens west of Kensington Palace (where ambassadors' residences stand today). His alternative was to preserve the ground for public parkland, someday to be joined, by additional land purchase, to Holland Park.*

Fig. 98
"Cruchley's new Plan of London and environs," 1835, detail, Holland Park and Kensington Gardens.

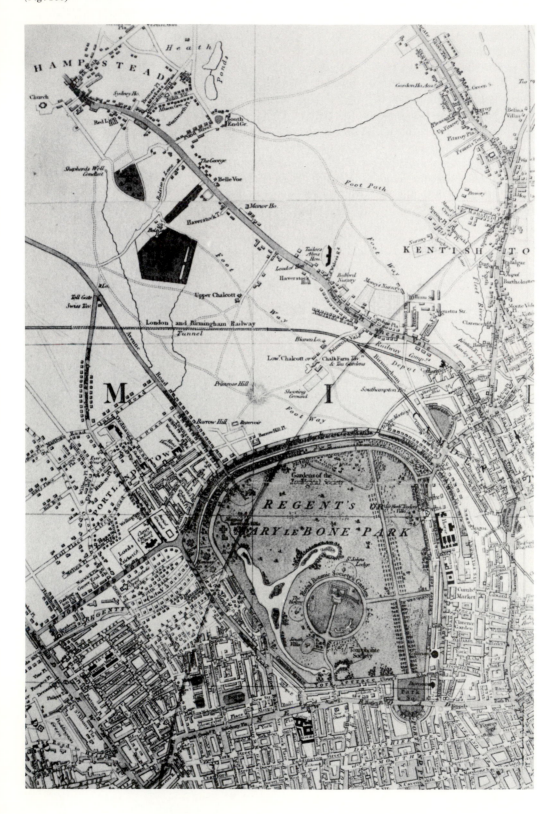

# 13

## Planning for London and the Ideal Capital

In 1829, when Hampstead Heath was threatened by development, Loudon produced his most impressive scheme for improving the London metropolis: a greenbelt plan for containing urban development while allowing for natural growth.

Loudon's plan for London entitled "Hints for Breathing Places" (published in December 1829) was his most comprehensive scheme for metropolitan improvements (fig. 99). In broad outline, it contains the central elements of his vision of the progress and happiness attainable within a society of educated, self-governing people. The Utopian strains are undeniable; and yet, the practical measures for ensuring efficient transportation, adequate fuel and water supply, sewerage, good postal service, clean air, public safety, and other concerns of the modern planner seem quite sensible, somehow possible — to be realized not within Loudon's lifetime, certainly, but sometime in the future.[1]

This is a greenbelt plan, generous enough to allow about one-third of the London metropolis to become open space — for parks, gardens, and public buildings. It is also a plan to allow the metropolis to expand indefinitely — not to contain urban growth, but to *relieve* it, with an unprecedented amount of "country in the city." Appended to this plan for London is a description of what might be considered an *ideal city:* a new capital for an Australian or European nation. The features of both plans are enumerated in a matter-of-fact tone that belies the complexity of all the planning problems involved. The plans are seductive in their simplicity. In the end, the reader might ask, Why *not* such a plan for London, or for a new town?

The mature Loudon had a flair for making his fondest dreams and visions seem inevitable; and at that particular moment in time, December 1829, he had every reason to be optimistic. The *Gardener's Magazine* that month contained the most idealistic and forward-looking collection of writings that Loudon ever assembled between the paper covers of a magazine. His leading article discussed his travels through Normandy in the autumn of 1828, the progress of gardening and general education, and the gradual relative equalization of knowledge and property. Another article considered the possibility that hunger and poverty could be eliminated from the world if only every man and woman would work four hours a day on something useful. One reader suggested that gardeners' and artisans' families, using their own savings and some charitable donations, might join in a cooperative effort to build their own homes. In time, they might determine exactly how many hours per day each adult had to work so that all could have the necessities and comforts of life.[2] Loudon also included accounts of readers' sanguine expectations for steam-powered plows, threshers, and reapers.[3] Most provocative of all was one prospect of improvement that Loudon considered "almost beyond the power of the imagination to contemplate": the combination of steam and rails.

Just two months earlier, on October 14th, 1829, the momentous seven-day competition among steam engines sponsored by the Liverpool and Manchester Railway had come to an impressive end. Outperforming all others, Robert Stephenson's "Rocket" had achieved the extraordinary feat of pulling a cargo of twenty tons at a speed of eighteen to twenty miles per hour. Suddenly, man was given wings![4] Loudon quoted from the magazine the *Scotsman*, which had considered these results the most important impulse to civilization since the invention of the printing press. It explained, "Even steam navigation gives but a faint idea of the wondrous powers which this new agent has put into our hands. . . . The introduction of steam carriages on railways places us on the verge of a new era — of a social revolution of which imagination cannot picture the ultimate effects."[5]

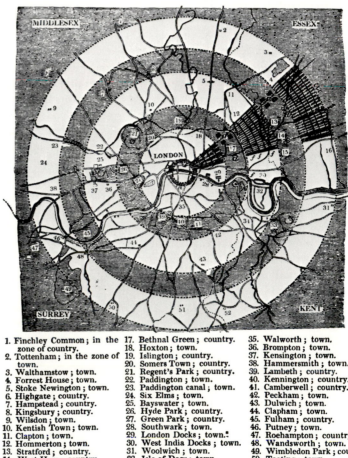

| | | |
|---|---|---|
| 1. Finchley Common; in the zone of country. | 17. Bethnal Green; country. | 35. Walworth; town. |
| 2. Tottenham; in the zone of town. | 18. Hoxton; town. | 36. Brompton; town. |
| 3. Walthamstow; town. | 19. Islington; country. | 37. Kensington; town. |
| 4. Forrest House; town. | 20. Somers Town; country. | 38. Hammersmith; town. |
| 5. Stoke Newington; town. | 21. Regent's Park; country. | 39. Lambeth; country. |
| 6. Highgate; country. | 22. Paddington; town. | 40. Kennington; country. |
| 7. Hampstead; country. | 23. Paddington canal; town. | 41. Camberwell; country. |
| 8. Kingsbury; country. | 24. Six Elms; town. | 42. Peckham; town. |
| 9. Wilsdon; town. | 25. Bayswater; town. | 43. Dulwich; town. |
| 10. Kentish Town; town. | 26. Hyde Park; country. | 44. Clapham; town. |
| 11. Clapton; town. | 27. Green Park; country. | 45. Fulham; country. |
| 12. Hommerton; town. | 28. Southwark; town. | 46. Putney; town. |
| 13. Stratford; country. | 29. London Docks; town. | 47. Roehampton; country. |
| 14. West Ham; country. | 30. West India Docks; town. | 48. Wandsworth; town. |
| 15. West Ham Abbey; country. | 31. Woolwich; town. | 49. Wimbledon Park; country. |
| 16. East Ham; town. | 32. Isle of Dogs; town. | 50. Tooting; town. |
| | 33. Greenwich Park; country. | 51. Norwood, town. |
| | 34. Deptford; town. | 52. Sydenham; town. |

While the *Scotsman* envisioned that steam and rails would make all provincial towns suburbs of the London metropolis, in effect, collecting all the inhabitants of Britain into one great city, Loudon pushed the idea a step further: He predicted that a steam-carriage railway would be constructed between Paris and Peking and that other railways would effectively reduce the vast areas of Russia, North America, and Australia to the size of Britain, so great would be the communications network established round the globe.

The potential of railways to improve the human condition gave Loudon increasing confidence in one of his own most dearly cherished schemes for human improvement, also detailed in the *Gardener's Magazine* that month: a "Plan for a National Education Establishment," devised for the children of rich and poor alike, from infancy to puberty.[6] In a "more perfect state of society than that which now exists," Loudon reasoned, all children, male and female, would receive a high and equal degree of education, at least until age fourteen or fifteen. All would be introduced to the basic arts and sciences, along with natural philosophy, natural theology, political economy, dancing, music, sports (for boys) and domestic arts (for girls). In a more perfect society, everyone would have some understanding of chemistry, agriculture, and gardening, for almost all families living outside large cities would possess a house and land. There would never be absolute equality — but fewer sharp contrasts between rich and poor would remain, as knowledge would no longer be the exclusive preserve of the rich, and ignorance the lot of the poor. "It will be an immeasurable advance in the happiness of the lower classes," Loudon observed, "to know that in the rank of mind they are on a level with the higher classes, or even nearly so. When men once know exactly what they are, they will know what they have a right to expect, and how to realise and maintain these rights."[7]

Loudon's plan for national education did not, by any means, appear in a vacuum. That month, he also noted that the Institute for the Diffusion of Knowledge in Preston was offering public lectures on architectural history. A wealthy manufacturer had just given eighty thousand pounds for the education of poor children in Kirkaldy, Scotland, the birthplace of Adam Smith. In Karlsruhe, in southern Germany, children of laborers and paupers were already receiving a combined liberal arts and technical education in the public schools. And in the United States, every new state admitted to the union was receiving congressional appropriations of land for public schools and colleges.[8]

So much evidence of progress in realizing human and mechanical potential appeared in the *Gardener's Magazine* of December 1829, that Loudon's "Hints for Breathing Places" seem less Utopian in their context, even practicable in many respects. If Loudon was a visionary, his language was plain. He might be a few steps ahead of his time, but he was always conscious of present-day realities. His plans for London and for ideal cities may still be of interest today, in spite of current events that deny us his optimism for all the fruits of a more perfect state of society. His idealistic vision of unity and continuity in the urban landscape — a vision which is generally lacking, if not impossible to achieve, in our time — may still contain some grain of promise.

The immediate catalyst for Loudon's greenbelt plan was the un-

By 1845 the route that Sunday pilgrims followed to Hampstead Heath was increasingly suburban, unless they used the footpaths, which by now have virtually disappeared.
Fig. 100 (see also p. 226)
"Cary's new Plan of London & its Vicinity," 1845, detail, Regent's Park and Hampstead.

named peer who, sometime in the late spring of 1829, leaked the news of Sir Thomas Maryon Wilson's private enclosure bill. Sir Thomas, lord of the manor of Hampstead, was quietly trying to pass a bill in the House of Lords for "improvements" on his common land, Hampstead Heath.[9] Once the secret was out, the bill provoked an urban controversy that lasted nearly half a century. Local residents who protested any building on the heath were joined by editors of the leading newspapers and journals, and by citizens from distant parts of the metropolis. Legally, the complex system of rights to the heath applied only to the lord and local commoners or copyholders; but development of that precious two-hundred-acre stretch of moors, meadows, and woodlands was seen as a threat to the health and happiness of the whole metropolis. If the "brick and mortar demon" was not restrained, London would become what it had once seemed to Wordsworth and would later appear to Dickens — a prison.[10]

By 1829 the open fields of Marylebone, on the northwestern periphery of the metropolis, were already enclosed by the pedimented and pilastered terrace houses of Regent's Park, the first elements of what Sir John Summerson has called a "private garden city for the aristocracy."[11] The *Times*, mindful of the interests of humbler folk, explained that this was no longer a park, but "an irregular polygon of buildings, with grass and water in the midst of it."[12] More rows of terrace houses were being built to the east, south, and west of Regent's Park. Primrose Hill, the open land immediately to the north, was also threatened by enclosure in 1830 (fig. 100). And in other parts of the metropolis, as well, the landscape

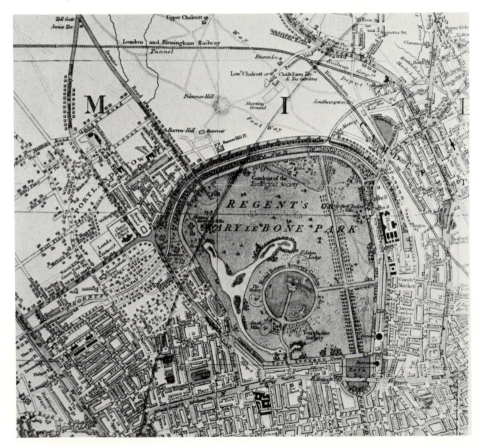

between London and the rural villages that surrounded it was becoming townscape.

The royal parks provided generous open spaces that people in the West End could enjoy daily. But the artisans, laundresses, clerks, and their families who lived in the East End could see green fields only on Sunday; and, for them, Hampstead Heath was practically the only haven of natural wilderness sufficiently high above the smoke and fog to offer fresh air and fine prospects (fig. 101, pl. 7). To protect their customary rights to the heath, Londoners signed petitions and wrote letters to the daily newspapers. In May 1829 a correspondent to the *Times* pointed out that enclosure of Hampstead Heath would be a "serious privation to the inhabitants of the metropolis."[13] Another condemned those who would build on the heath as "ruthless spoilators . . . whose souls appear to be embodied in bricks and mortar." The "great Leviathan" of buildings had already taken away the pleasant fields of Islington and Canonbury on the north (fig. 102); and, south of the river, new construction had turned each peaceful village where "'once the garden smiled'" into a "dusty street." Now that the hills of Highgate and Hampstead were threatened, this reader entreated the government to preserve Hampstead Heath as one of the vital "lungs of the metropolis."[14]

Loudon joined the protest in December 1829 by offering a positive alternative in the *Gardener's Magazine:* a plan to preserve not only the heath, but thousands of acres of undeveloped land in and around the built metropolis. As a diagram, the plan is deceptively simple: a series of concentric white and grey bands (or town and country zones) superimposed on a map of the London region. As a planning concept, it was unique and farsighted in its day. Two major principles are involved: first, the perception of many fragments — the old cities of London and Westminster, the parishes, counties, villages, royal parks, and undeveloped

*A few years after Constable made this oil sketch (looking toward Harrow), the lord of the manor of Hampstead tried surreptitiously to secure development rights on his heath. Londoners were outraged; Hampstead Heath was their weekly retreat from the congestion and smoke of the metropolis.*

Fig. 101
John Constable, R.A., *A View on Hampstead Heath with Figures in the Foreground,* 1821. Courtesy, Yale Center for British Art, Paul Mellon Collection.

Fig. 102
View from Hampstead Heath to the London Metropolis, ca. 1840.

fields and pastures — as one area which ought to be planned and governed as a whole; second, the emphasis on continuity of open space, which is more important than the absolute quantity of open space. A third principle is implicit in the first two: the equality of attention given to all parts of the metropolis simultaneously — rather than the usual concentration on a few major thoroughfares in the City or the West End.

In his diagram (fig. 99) Loudon represents London as an expanding city of concentric town and country zones, which could extend, if necessary, to the sea, some thirty miles away (fig. 103). The plan is geometrically regular, with St. Paul's in the center. Surrounding the cathedral is a circle of lawn and graveled drives, one-half mile in diameter, containing offices of the metropolitan government and administration. The network of existing streets has not been radically affected. The inner zone of town, two to three miles in diameter, remains largely intact. Beyond is a country zone, one-half mile wide, that encompasses the existing Hyde Park and Regent's Park, along with parts of existing urban areas: Somers Town, Islington, Bethnal Green, Camberwell, and Lambeth. A second country zone includes Hampstead Heath on the north and Greenwich Park and Clapham Common on the south. Eventually the metropolis would be contained by distinct alternating zones: one mile wide for town, one-half mile wide for country.

The entire metropolitan landscape would not be geometrically ordered, however, like the ideal plans of Vitruvius, the Renaissance humanists, and the French and English Utopian planners of the eighteenth and nineteenth centuries. Loudon preferred a more economical and "more beautiful" irregular boundary between zones. Country zones would include various kinds of scenery — picturesque landscapes, geometrical gardens (as extensions of some buildings), and simple meadows or

fields — one succeeding the other without harsh contrasts. In town zones the natural topography and existing public buildings, squares, and private gardens would be respected. Thus, the plan would presuppose a great deal of continuity and flexibility.

In conserving current street patterns while planning for expansion, Loudon adopted a traditional British approach to metropolitan improvements. But more radical changes would have to be made to provide for water supply, rubbish and sewage disposal, communications, and, above all, for public open space. Without taking away existing parks or gardens, Loudon was proposing a complete "redistribution" of breathing space, to provide every metropolitan inhabitant access to open land within a half mile or so from his home.

In 1829 such a plan would have called for massive restructuring of local government, which was then complicated by vested interests among boroughs, vestries, boards of commissioners, the Corporation of the City, and Parliament.[15] A new, more powerful local government would have the authority to clear the land for Loudon's inner circle around St. Paul's and for his first country zone. Loudon believed that the many valuable houses and public buildings already existing in his designated country zones should be acquired and razed only gradually, as they became uninhabitable over the course of one or two centuries. Landowners should receive compensation through land exchange. The government thus would have to purchase other land in advance, in designated town zones. Government would also have to juggle extremely long-range goals with short-term priorities, and to deal with the legal complications of entailed property.[16] Clearly, an unprecedented degree of cooperation and centralization of power would be required to carry out Loudon's comprehensive metropolitan plan.

*Projecting the steady development of London in all directions, Loudon proposed that his alternating town and country zones continue until one of them reached the sea — which lies to the east on this map, beyond Gravesend.*

Fig. 103
"Mogg's [map, showing] 45 Miles of the Country Round London," 1831, detail, from central London and Westminster to Gravesend, on the east.

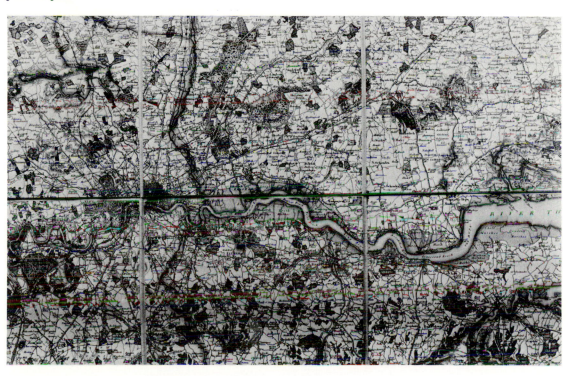

Loudon was optimistic about the kind of improvements that a truly representative metropolitan government might effect, given an initial jurisdiction of a five-mile radius from St. Paul's.[17] He was not discouraged by "temporary obstacles," such as the contemporary lack of a metropolitan planning body. His imagination spanned the chasm between present reality and future possibility like the suspension bridge that he had once designed.[18] In 1809, while living in the country, he had imagined that, someday, female haymakers dressed in silk and muslin might handle the rake with all the grace of delicate, accomplished ladies and might converse on morality, history, and the verses of their lovers.[19] In 1829, while living in Bayswater, he could just as easily imagine a metropolis, well-governed and well-planned, with many generous, continuous belts of open space serving as relief to the network of city streets in a continually expanding metropolis.

It is just a few imaginative leaps from Loudon's practical plan for London to his ideal capital city. To lay out an Australian or European capital, Loudon recommends these principles: (1) All public buildings and governmental offices should be centrally located. (2) The main streets should penetrate the city in all directions in straight lines. (3) The most perfect ground plan of a large town would be a circle, with radiating and concentric streets. (4) Concentric zones of country should be provided, particularly to benefit the health of the poor, whenever rivers, narrow valleys, or sea coasts do not naturally limit urban growth.

This *beau idéal* differs from Loudon's more pragmatic plan for London in specific details. Ideally, the innermost town zone would contain all the government buildings on the periphery and a House of Representatives (not a cathedral) in the center. Between the House and the circle of governmental buildings, the innermost town zone would contain markets, churches, theatres, and houses. The remaining town zones would contain mainly houses and offices, with no squares, market places, burial grounds, or other open spaces. Streets would be broad, and structures close together. The urban fabric would be more regular, less varied, than the existing street pattern that Loudon sought to preserve in London. Some avenues would be specified routes for transporting hay, corn, straw, and livestock to the markets in country zones. Other avenues would be routes for a cheap, efficient postal service. All main radial and concentric streets would be served by public transportation — railway steam carriages or some other vehicles appropriate for the age. A corresponding system below ground would accommodate sewers, as well as water and gas mains. The circulation systems above and below the ground would be specialized and geometrically ordered.

Country zones would offer a greater variety of land uses and building types. Here would be the slaughterhouses, markets, churches, cemeteries, theatres, universities, schools, workhouse gardens, botanical and zoological gardens, public painting and sculpture galleries, national museums, public conservatories, tea gardens, coffeehouses, gasometers, public water works, baths, and swimming ponds. Also located in country zones would be the nongovernmental public buildings and facilities best removed from town, including "sewer works," where solid waste would be strained, compressed, dried, and deodorized, as in the *poudrette* manufactories near Paris. At the same time, liquid wastes would be mechanically filtered and raised to towers, then forced by atmospheric pressure through pipes that would lead to agricultural lands beyond the outermost country zone and provide irrigation.[20]

An indiscriminate blending of these land uses would produce visual chaos. Loudon's vision was essentially kinetic, however, not static. Like a film director, literally a *metteur-en-scène*, Loudon would compose the ideal country zones as a sequence of scenes, each with a particular character, one leading into another without abrupt or violent surprises.[21] Parks and pleasure grounds would gradually merge with wilderness — heaths, caverns, grottoes, ravines, rocks, and quarries. Loudon would create natural-looking bodies of water and lay out roads both straight and winding, open and shady. To complete this ideal, a band of musicians might wander in the parks — as they did in the duke of Baden's park in Karlsruhe, which was open to the public, and in the marquis de Girardin's grounds at Ermenonville, when Rousseau lived there.

After allowing his imagination to wander through his ideal country zone, Loudon abruptly returned to reality:

Though we have not the slightest idea that this *beau idéal* of a capital for an Australian or a European union will ever be carried into execution; and though we would rather see, in every country, innumerable small towns and villages, than a few overgrown capitals; yet we think, that, as there must probably always be some grand central cities in the world, some useful principles for regulating the manner in which each is increased may be deduced from the foregoing hints.[22]

Loudon concluded with one practical suggestion: in all future enclosure bills (or development plans), there should be some provision for public open space — at the least, a village green, a playground, or a garden.

Loudon often laid down principles by which one should judge a façade, lay out a road, or plan a town. His ideal images were merely extensions of his basic principles, such as continuity of public open space. But, eminently practical, Loudon never confused the ideal with reality. He once described nature's *beau idéal* as the tendency in human affairs for things to become equalized: to advance and approach a level. The level would never be reached, however, "because, like still water, it would be inconsistent with that motion and progress which belongs to the constitution of human society."[23]

Loudon offered no visions of a radically new society, such as Thomas More, Robert Owen, St. Simon, and Etienne Cabet proposed; and no detailed models for urban design, such as Frank Lloyd Wright and Le Corbusier conceived. Loudon's plan for London did offer an approach to systematic planning that could be adapted to any real situation. His plan was never realized, nor can it be considered a direct influence on planning and development for London. In Loudon's day, no governmental body existed that could begin to consider a plan of this scale.[24] But like his friend John Martin, the painter, who persistently called for the embankment of the Thames, Loudon was continually trying to implant the desire for public open space and metropolitan government in the minds of the public.[25] He republished his plan for London in his *Architectural Maga-*

*This diagram, conceived over a century after Loudon's own plan, recognizes the concentric patterns of London's growth, and calls for one major greenbelt, several miles from the center of the metropolis.*

Fig. 104
J.H. Forshaw and Patrick Abercrombie, Open Space Plan (1943).

zine in 1836 and cited it in his *Magazine of Natural History* in 1831. These magazines, along with Loudon's books and encyclopedias, received frequent, generally quite favorable reviews in Britain, on the Continent, and in America. Loudon's designs for and writings on public parks, cemeteries, cottages, and multifamily housing also appeared as evidence in parliamentary reports.[26] Finally, though Loudon served barely two years on the Committee of the Metropolitan Improvement Society, just before his death, his fellow professional men and certain members of Parliament continued to advocate the planning, housing, and sanitary reforms that they had recommended to Prime Minister Robert Peel in 1842.[27]

Loudon's ideas did circulate through networks of influence, then, and probably had an indirect effect on national legislation within his lifetime. In 1837, in the House of Commons, Joseph Hume carried a resolution that incorporated the final measure in Loudon's plan for London — that all future enclosure bills should include provisions for public open space.[28] By 1855 London finally had a municipal planning body, the Metropolitan Board of Works, which immediately began to address street improvements and the embankment of the Thames. In 1889 this board was superseded by the London County Council (L.C.C.), which began to control many more public open spaces than its predecessor — including Battersea, Kennington, and Victoria Parks; and, later, Lincoln's Inn Fields, Hackney Marsh, and even, in 1928, Kenwood — that elegant "country" residence of Lord Mansfield that Loudon had hoped to see effectively joined to Hampstead Heath someday.[29]

In our century, London has grown in concentric rings, or zones, and planners have shaped their goals accordingly. Sir Patrick Abercrombie's diagram from his *County of London Plan* (1943) attests to this; and, in his *Greater London Plan* (1944), Abercrombie recognized the "faint indication of structure" of London's growth, in the form of several concentric zones about a dense urban center (fig. 104).[30] Thus he proposed the

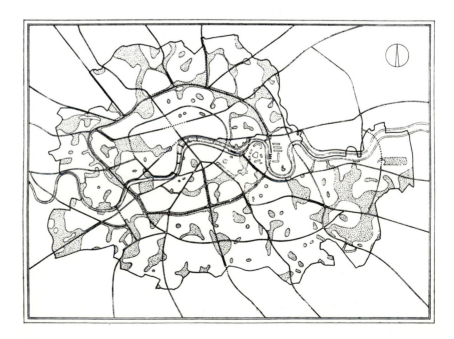

creation of a single greenbelt, about six to eight miles wide, and circular ring roads. Presumably unaware of Loudon's earlier plan, Abercrombie also applied Loudon's principle of continuity of open space, but in a radial, not concentric, pattern, combining the idea of "green wedges" with the radial pattern of parkways.[31]

By the early 1960s, the Green Belt Act of 1938 had enabled some 35,000 acres of open space to be preserved on the periphery of Greater London.[32] And in 1965 the new Greater London Council (G.L.C.) assumed planning authority over an area with a radius of about fifteen miles from Charing Cross, surrounded by and partly including a single green belt about four to fifteen miles wide.[33] Since that time, London has continued to grow, leaping over the metropolitan greenbelt to a radius of about forty miles. Peter Hall, a member of the South-East Planning Council, observed in 1963 that neither the area governed by the L.C.C. nor the area about to be governed by the G.L.C. was large enough to contain, or define, London. Since then, Hall has insisted on the need for planning at the regional scale.[34] As Loudon had expected, London has reached the sea.

In 1829, having accepted London's growth as inevitable, Loudon adopted an uncommonly positive approach to dealing with that growth. The dream of containing London had by then a hallowed tradition, stretching back at least to the time of More's *Utopia*, (1515–16). Queen Elizabeth I had tried to restrict new building construction to within three miles of the City gates; later, Cromwell had urged a ten-mile limit. After the great fire in 1666, Sir Christopher Wren had proposed a twelve-mile limit. And John Evelyn had proposed a greenbelt of gardens and plantations to make London "one of the sweetest and most delicious Habitations in the world."[35]

Exactly a century later, in 1766, John Gwynn thought that the greatest planning mistake committed in London had been to extend the metropolis too far in an east-west direction. He called for growth in a north-south direction, which would make the town more compact and therefore more convenient. However, he would have confined the "rage of building" northward within the new road from Paddington to Islington (now the Marylebone and Euston Roads). Gwynn's great fear was that the hills of Hampstead and Highgate might soon become suburban London.[36]

One eighteenth-century voice which did not cry out for containment of London was James Stuart's. In 1771 he wrote, "On the whole, I look upon the late increase of London as a natural consequence of the prosperity of the nation, and a sure token of its healthy and vigorous state." Stuart's ardent wish was not to contain the metropolis, but to encourage every possible moral, political, and economic improvement. These included canals; embankments; high roads for efficient transport; the widening, paving, and lighting of streets; "nuisance removal;" and any other measures that would contribute to public health and security. Nor were aesthetics to be ignored. Stuart believed that order, decency, and elegance in public places must lead to urbanity in private life — which, in turn, forms the "excellence and bond of society."[37]

Stuart's unusual reluctance to become alarmed by the growth of London was later reflected in Jeremy Bentham's manuscripts on political economy published by Bentham's executor, John Bowring, between 1838 and 1843. "This imaginary evil, the increase of towns, has excited the

Loudon's plan for London
shares with Bentham's panopticon a centralized diagram with radiating
divisions (or avenues) and
comprehensiveness, or attention to all parts of the
whole.

Fig. 105 (below)
Jeremy Bentham, Panopticon,
section and plan.

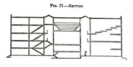

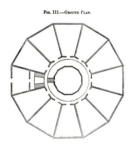

This project, which Loudon
had seen before 1822,
unites centralized, geometric
order and picturesque irregularity — two key planning
elements that Loudon com-
bined in his own scheme for
London. Such a combina-
tion could yield a degree of
freedom and spontaneity,
without creating chaos.

Fig. 106 (opposite)
Gabriel Thouin, "Project for an
experimental farm," ca. 1819.

most extravagant fears," Bentham observed. "Absurdity has been carried so far, as to make rules for limiting their bounds; they should rather have been made for extending them." Bentham reasoned that laws enacted simply to confine growth do not diminish the population of towns; they merely oblige people to heap themselves up within close habitations, amidst disease and foul air: "to build one city upon another."[38]

It is possible that the elderly Bentham shared his thoughts on town planning with Loudon, his younger friend. Loudon's diagram is as centralized and efficient as Bentham's Panopticon (fig. 105) — though the realization of Loudon's plan would entail introducing more variety and irregularity into the urban landscape.[39] In any case, Loudon was inventive, perhaps original, in devising a way to combine the principles of greenbelt containment with unlimited expansion. There was, at the time, no British precedent for this unusual approach to planning for an entire town or capital city — an approach which was conceptually geometric, centralized, and comprehensive, yet which would allow for picturesque landscape and apparently incidental development in the planned expansion of the metropolis. In Bath and in London, for instance, the John Woods (elder and younger) and John Nash had never planned for the whole town or metropolis. Loudon may have picked up a few hints on the Continent.

The towns of Karlsruhe and Chaux (both planned along radial and concentric lines) had already begun to display the semblance of "greenbelt expansion." In 1828, while visiting southern Germany, Loudon had seen Karlsruhe, laid out by the French architect Berceau for the margrave Charles William in 1715. Loudon admired the integrated planning of the park and the town. Nearly surrounded by the duke of Baden's park, the town of Karlsruhe was really an urban "wedge" extending from the palace outward toward the countryside.[40]

Loudon also may have known of Chaux, conceived in 1773–74 by the extraordinary mind of Claude-Nicolas Ledoux. This ideal industrial city, laid out on an elliptical plan for ease of expansion, was never completely realized. But by 1778, half of the inner ellipse was built, and in 1804 Ledoux published his entire vision of Chaux. The director's house was to occupy the center, flanked by the salt factories. Around this "diameter" would be a belt of unornamented Neo-Classical workers' dwellings, with attached gardens behind, in the next belt. Around the gardens would be a road, to be surrounded by workshops, a cannon foundry, and some private villas. These buildings and their gardens would gradually merge with the rural landscape beyond.[41]

Loudon never mentioned Chaux in his published travel journals, but by 1822 he was acquainted with Gabriel Thouin's centrally-planned "project for an experimental farm" (1819).[42] Like Chaux, this proposed settlement was laid out on an elliptical plan, with a double ring of buildings — houses and a hospital — around the central church and straight hedges radiating outwards between the various fields (fig. 106). Thouin's plan is not as purely geometrical as Ledoux's plan for Chaux, however. In the experimental farm, the geometry relaxes more gradually as one moves outwards. Three meandering streams supply the elliptical canal that surrounds the central buildings. From the distant mountains — the sources of the streams — fall cascades, which turn the flour mills. These moun-

Thouin Del.

Im de C.Motte.

N.º 51. *Projet d'une ferme expérimentale de la Zône Torride.*

Had Loudon's plan for London been even partially carried out, the view from Hyde Park Corner eastward toward St. Paul's might look something like this. The palace and the distant villas, apparently floating in a sea of verdure, would be replaced with public buildings, however — museums, theatres, schools, hospitals, and so forth — while private houses would be aligned along the streets of town.
Fig. 107
Sir John Soane, "Design for a Royal Palace [made in] Rome, 1779," proposed for Hyde Park, London, ca. 1828.

tains provide the vast farm with a natural forested belt. Between belt and core are serpentine ring roads that follow the undulating topography and offer distant picturesque views at different elevations, in this Hobbit-like imaginary European colony somewhere in the Torrid Zone.[43]

Such an image — of geometry reconciled with the picturesque, and containment mingled with freedom to expand — could have lingered in Loudon's mind while he was thinking about the need to plan for open space throughout the metropolis. The regional scale of both Ledoux's and Thouin's projects would have been relevant, although their vision of a distinctly new settlement in the hinterland was not so. Loudon's intended town zones would recall the older London streets that we see today, such as the Strand, Ludgate Hill, and "The Avenue" north of Regent's Park. The buildings along these streets are still, for the most part, diverse in style, material, texture, and age, all in some way expressing the unshackled tastes of their builders, owners, or inhabitants.

Loudon's country zones bear some resemblance to Sir John Soane's "Design for a Royal Palace" (1827; based on sketches made in Rome in 1779), exhibited at the Royal Academy in 1828 (fig. 107).[44] Soane's vast palace, an equilateral triangle in plan, with a central dome and six equidistant porticoes, was certainly more grandiose than the precedents Soane acknowledged—including Vignola's Caprarola, the Roman Pantheon, and Hadrian's Villa at Tivoli. The only precedents in urban design were the Woods' circus and Royal Crescent in Bath, and Nash's Regent's Park — all of which Soane surpassed on paper with his bold vision of rural expansion in the metropolis.

In Soane's bird's-eye view to the southeast, the palace appears to be sited in Hyde Park. All other buildings seem to hover, or drift, in a vaguely familiar space, while the palace itself is firmly anchored, as if

DESIGN FOR A PALACE ROME 1779.

moored to an unseen wharf by the curving, sphinx-lined carriage drive. In the miles between the palace's dome and the dome of St. Paul's, private villas, half-hidden in their own bowers, seem to float in an indeterminate greensward that runs from Bayswater to Knightsbridge and eastward, beyond Piccadilly. In the distance, faint traces of the old City of London disappear in the mists that envelop Wren's cathedral. It is as if all of old London is dissolving in verdure and light, as in an early dream of Turner, when distant buildings and trees were just beginning to merge with earth, water, and sky.

Soane's vision of Westminster, with its new royal palace and villas, is much like Loudon's vision of London as viewed from the first country zone. The critical differences are that where Soane has placed embowered villas, Loudon would have public buildings; Soane's palace would be replaced by a university or a museum; Loudon's innermost country zone would be less extensive; and Loudon would preserve the density of familiar London streets.

Because Loudon would have conserved much of the ordinary existing urban fabric, his proposed changes were not dramatic, but systematic. If they were realized, it would be easier for a Londoner to travel from point A to point B; and along the way he would see glimpses of an improved, but still recognizable London. Loudon was not radical at the core. His architectural theories were liberal and iconoclastic; his political views were both liberal and radical; his curvilinear hothouses were revolutionary. Yet his vision for the rural and metropolitan landscape was fairly conservative in visual character. The most significant changes he proposed were political and social: there should be systematic planning and management under a representative metropolitan government; and those represented would be the *educated* "great mass of society."

Loudon's hints for improvements were often casually tossed out, in the hopes that someone with the necessary resources and interests would pursue them. Jane Loudon and Noel Humphreys both observed that many of his plans and designs were frustrated, however, by narrow minds or timid reservations; people thought Loudon's notions were too costly, too impracticable, or too innovative. Then someone might come along years later, and carry through the intended work — perhaps on a different site, or in a different context — and receive the credit for the original idea.[45] Happily, Loudon was not possessive about ideas. As his friend Humphreys later explained, Loudon believed that the person who actually made some invention or idea valuable to the public, or to an individual, deserved more credit than the person who had conceived that idea but never had carried it out.[46]

One wonders if Ebenezer Howard knew of Loudon's multiple greenbelt scheme for London. Some seventy years after Loudon's proposal, using remarkably similar diagrams, Howard introduced a new approach to dealing with metropolitan growth: the creation of garden cities.[47] Such attractive "magnets" would naturally draw population away from London, he believed; for they would combine the advantages of *both* town and country: "beauty of nature, social opportunity; low rents, high wages; bright homes and gardens, no smoke, no slums; freedom, cooperation;" and so on. Ideally, all land would be publicly owned or held in trust for the community. Each garden city, contained by its own rural belt, would be

*Howard may never have known of Loudon's greenbelt scheme, but his diagrams for the containment of small garden cities bear an ironic resemblance to Loudon's plan for the expanding metropolis.*

Fig. 108
Ebenezer Howard, Diagrams 2 and 3 of his Garden City, ca. 1898.

limited to about fifty-eight thousand people; and any further growth would occur by leaping over the greenbelt to start a new garden city, or "satellite" (fig. 108). Meanwhile, London would gradually be transformed, as its population pressures decreased, slums were torn down, and the country "invaded" the town.

To some extent, Loudon's and Howard's values were similar. Both appreciated the merits of small towns, open space, and efficient, modern communications via streets and railways. Loudon also shared Howard's enthusiasm for cooperation, though he never went so far as to recommend public or cooperative ownership of a community's land. What fundamen-

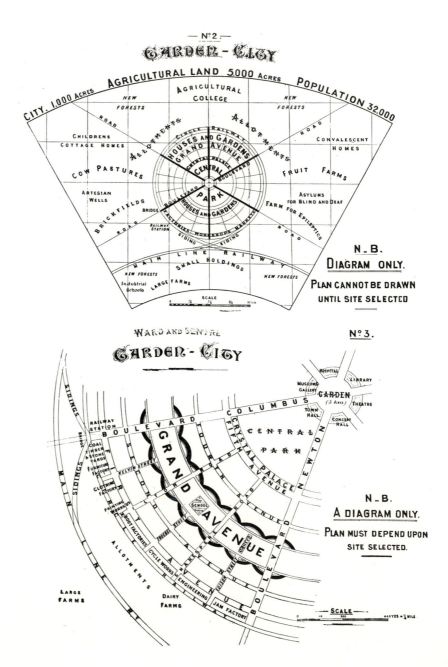

tally distinguishes the two planners was their vision of the London of the future. Howard thought London would decay, sustain a permanent loss of population, and eventually rebuild at lower densities. Loudon believed that London, under a sound, representative metropolitan government, would gradually expand and be renewed.

London, Paris, Venice, Vienna, Munich, St. Petersburg — these were some of the "grand central cities of the world" that Loudon knew and appreciated. He enjoyed the rich variety of architecture; the healthful and useful boulevards (fig. 109); the public parks, pleasure gardens, and botanical gardens; and the mingling of people of all classes, in contrast to the relative seclusion, peace, and lack of social contact in the country. Above all, perhaps, it was the mingling of people, or "intercommunication," which delighted him. Visiting Paris in 1840, Loudon was astonished by the great improvements realized since his last visit in 1828–29 and identified the fundamental cause as intercommunication, which was ultimately the result of cooperation among individuals and organizations.

In Bayswater, Loudon enjoyed the proximity of the city, with its concentration of publishing houses, learned societies and institutions, museums, libraries, and government offices. The metropolis was the "magnet" that attracted the disparate group of Loudon's friends and colleagues who lived in Bayswater, Chelsea, Old Brompton, Hammersmith, Hackney, Hampstead, St. John's Wood, Marylebone, Mayfair, and Westminster. Such frequent interaction among a diversity of people and the high concentration of commerce, cultural activity, government, and industry could not thrive in a garden city as we know it. On the other hand, the concentration, the bustle, and the noise could be tolerated, even enjoyed, because there were gardens *in* the city. These were the essential differences between Loudon's "garden metropolis" and Howard's better-known garden city ideal, which shaped our earliest garden cities.[48]

*This scene in Paris, possibly the Boulevard des Italiens, reveals certain qualities Loudon appreciated in the great European capitals — the breadth and salubriousness of the boulevards themselves (which served as "breathing places," he noted) and the mingling of a great variety of people.*

Fig. 109
J.M.W.Turner, "Boulevards."

Loudon was a realist who believed the metropolis could not be ignored, or diminished, even by creating the magnet of new suburbs. He lived in an earlier age than Howard's, of course, when cities still spread out in horizontal, not yet vertical, directions. Perhaps his concentric country zones would not have withstood the challenges of the elevator, the automobile and airplane. The development pressures on central London, coupled with new, more rapid means of escaping to the distant countryside, might have overwhelmed Loudon's multiple greenbelts. Yet if his "Hints for Breathing Places" had been followed, the result might have been a garden metropolis governed on an unprecedented regional scale.

Unlike today's planners, Loudon never used expressions such as "regional scale," "density control," "zoning," "resource planning," "cost benefit analysis," "housing stock," and "market penetration." "Open space" meant something more specific to him than it does to us today. His breathing places were also to be "civilizing spaces," places where people might gather, mingle, observe the dignified behavior of others, and enjoy the company, or the mere proximity, of people, as he had enjoyed the sights and sounds of people in the Luxembourg gardens in Paris.

In some respects, Loudon anticipated what the landscape architect Frederick Law Olmsted later accomplished in America with his public park systems in New York, Boston, Buffalo, Detroit, Chicago, and other cities.[49] Both men were devoted to the goal of civilizing people in cities and towns. They wanted to see a continuous flow of parkland penetrating the fabric of the town. They hoped to offer people a variety of places for "rational enjoyment" (in Loudon's words) during their moments of leisure. And though they preferred to reserve most of the park for some kind of picturesque scenery, both would lay out some straight avenues — such as the Mall in New York City's Central Park — to accommodate the activities of masses of people. Olmsted referred to this need for "gregarious recreation," in an essay of 1870.[50] In 1831 Loudon had used the expression, "festive enjoyment."[51]

One fundamental difference between the two men as designers was that Loudon tended to use plants for scientific and educational, as well as aesthetic, purposes. Though he never had the opportunity to design a public park on the vast scale of Olmsted's projects, Loudon did reveal, in his small arboretum in Derby and in his botanical garden outside Birmingham, a preference for trees and shrubs loosely grouped and botanically labeled — not densely massed, as they might appear in a more natural-looking composition (fig. 110). Moreover, Loudon was convinced that a certain amount of what might be called "specimen planting" (something Olmsted typically avoided) could stimulate the minds and refine the sensibilities of people who were otherwise unaccustomed to looking intently at plants and natural scenery.

Loudon was not just thinking of mechanics and child laborers, who saw little more than machinery and grim streets for six days a week. He repeatedly emphasized that the minds of all young people — particularly young women — ought to be opened to the intriguing study of botany and other natural sciences. Olmsted's pastoral scenes were meant to soothe the shattered, city-jangled nerves and to *pacify* the mind of the beholder, letting soft pastoral scenery work its magic insensibly, like the elusive power of music. Loudon wanted, instead, to activate the minds of people, young and old; and to awaken in their minds faculties perhaps lying dormant, such as observation, curiosity, and wonder.

Loudon did not envision a truly Utopian transformation for London. His recommendations for parks, public works, and metropolitan government were essentially rational and practical. And yet it was in London, not among the picturesque lakes of Westmoreland or the romantic mountain scenery of his native Scotland or North Wales, that Loudon had a vision of a "paradise" that might be realized on a national scale in Britain. This vision, of arboricultural splendor in public places, came to him as he was visiting a nursery in Hackney, East London. Picture the scene:

It is the twenty-first of June, 1833. Loudon is walking in the arboretum of the Loddiges' Botanical Nursery Garden, which he considers the most interesting scenery about London. The arboretum reminds him of the forests in the panorama of Niagara Falls currently on display in the coliseum in Regent's Park (fig. 111). In Hackney he sees the same birches, maples, and liquidambars, which will turn scarlet, russet, gold, and deep purplish red in the autumn. And he cannot understand why intelligent gardeners continue to plant commonplace shrubberies when such vast botanical treasures are within their reach. Reflecting on his visit, he later writes:

Again we say, that the taste must be originated in youth; but, when once called into action, what a paradise this island will become, displaying, as it will do, all the trees and shrubs in the world which will grow in temperate climates. The time is just commencing for the establishment of public parks, and gardens adjoining towns, in which the *beau idéal* of this description of scenery will be realised, at the expense of all, and for the enjoyment of all.[52]

*Here, in 1850, Frederick Law Olmsted studied the ways in which "art had been employed to obtain from nature so much beauty." After thorough under-draining of the grounds, the three-foot deep "lake" was created and stocked with aquatic plants, goldfish, and swans. In the mid-nineteenth century, the park was not so luxuriantly picturesque and overgrown as it appears today; but, by all accounts, it was more natural-looking than the arboretum in Derby.*

Fig. 110
View in the grounds of Birkenhead Park, near Liverpool, laid out by Joseph Paxton in 1844.

*In 1833 all of the magnifi-
cent trees shown in the
"Panorama of Niagara" in-
side the coliseum — oaks,
maples, birches, liquidambars — could be seen growing in the arboretum of
Messrs. Loddiges in
Hackney, East London.*
Fig. 111
Thomas Shepherd, "The Coliseum, Regent's Park," ca.
1828.

Here is Loudon's vision of an earthly paradise, seen in the gentle light of an English summer solstice. It must have been this, or some such vision, that sustained Loudon as he began, the following summer, to write the eight-volume *Arboretum et Fruticetum Britannicum,* his finest legacy to the nation.

THE COLISEUM, REGENT'S PARK.

# 14

## The Greatest Happiness

Near the camellias, peonies, and roses bordering the path to Loudon's door in Bayswater was a shrub called *Benthamia fragifera*, which Loudon once described to his readers in unusual detail (pl. 10). This "eminently beautiful" hardy evergreen shrub resembled a flowering dogwood, with flowers like those of *Stuartia Malachodendron* and fruit somewhat larger than that of the strawberry tree (*Arbutus Unedo*). "We want words to express our admiration of this shrub," he confessed. It had been named after George Bentham, a distinguished botanist, and secretary to the London Horticultural Society; but Loudon liked to assume the shrub also commemorated the secretary's uncle, Jeremy Bentham, "the greatest benefactor to mankind, in our opinion, that has ever lived since the commencement of the Christian era." Loudon concluded, "We could not have desired a finer plant to perpetuate such a name."[1] And Loudon predicted that this lovely *Benthamia*, so easily propagated, would soon be growing in every cottage garden.

For his life's work, Loudon took on a subject as vast, and as convoluted, as the legal and constitutional codification that occupied Jeremy Bentham. It was the built and the natural environment that nearly monopolized Loudon's long waking hours. Precisely what Loudon learned from his mentor, Bentham, may never be known, for lack of surviving evidence. Still, certain passages in Loudon's own published works and others' memoirs reveal his profound admiration and affection for Bentham, whose "greatest happiness" principle was both an inspiration and a challenge. Loudon frankly avowed his sympathies towards Bentham, the controversial codifier and quantifier of pain and pleasure — even though he was aware that neither the man nor his utilitarian principles were universally respected. In fact, they were sometimes considered philistine, narrow-minded, or dangerous![2] As if his own endorsement were not sufficient, then, Loudon inserted the following note on the *Benthamia fragifera:* "The Rev. W. Fox, in his admirable sermons on Christian Morality, says, 'the late Jeremy Bentham was the ablest expositor of what was really Christian morality, the true law of the Lord as to social duty, that our country or the world has yet produced. The whole of his writings are proofs and illustrations of the position, that we shall find our own greatest happiness in the promotion of the greatest happiness of others.'"[3]

Such is the happiness Loudon sought for himself. To him, Bentham must have been more than an aged mentor, reclusive and whimsical, habitually clothed in black and grey and wearing a broad-brimmed yellow straw hat. Noel Humphreys, a friend who had access to Loudon's journals after his death, relates that Bentham; Sir Joseph Banks, the naturalist; and Sir William Lawrence, the surgeon-anatomist; were among the eminent scientific men who had impressed Loudon as a young man newly arrived in London. The effect of their conversations, writes Humphreys, was "at once most sudden and striking." He described Bentham's influence on Loudon:

From the large-minded Jeremy Bentham, the theoretic politician, who was destined to furnish drafts of free constitutions to so many new States, as in rapid succession they shook off the withering coil and cumbrous trammels of old-world despotisms, young Loudon greedily imbibed those enlarged political and social sentiments which all who knew him intimately so much admired; as in his case they were ever tempered by a benevolence and a general softness of manner and feeling which endowed his conversation, even when expressing his advocacy of the most sweeping and thorough-going progress, with an indefinable charm that seduced even the opponents of his theories; though many of them, no doubt, deemed them wildly extravagant.[4]

Bentham had willed his body to Science, for the benefit of mankind. After his death, in 1832, Loudon attended Dr. Southwood Smith's now-famous anatomical lecture on the philosopher, and Loudon's draftsman later recalled the event in these words:

Just at the moment the lecturer withdrew the covering from the face of the corpse the lightning flashed, and an awful burst of thunder pealed forth —
"Crush'd horrible, convulsing heaven and earth!"
[Loudon quoted from James Thomson, *The Seasons*]

Mr. Loudon, during dinner, gave a most touching, poetical, and graphic description of the lecture, and circumstances attending it; and every one present could see how deeply he felt the loss of his friend Bentham.[5]

Loudon applied Bentham's "greatest happiness" principle as any man who loved trees, plants, and picturesque and pastoral scenery might do: he tried to extend the enjoyment of these things to others, through various schemes of environmental design, including the metropolitan boulevard, which would offer views of some of the finest scenery about London; the multiple greenbelts, or "breathing places for the metropolis"; the circular glasshouses for the Birmingham Botanical Gardens; and some of his designs for metropolitan and national gardens. Viewed as abstract diagrams, these projects had in common a centralized plan with a prominent core and direct communication to a circular periphery. In two-dimensional plan, these schemes resembled the spokes of a wheel or some other mechanical object. Essentially, they were variations on Bentham's centrally planned panopticon, a true Utilitarian symbol (fig. 105). Maximizing the use of a given space and minimizing expense and inconvenience were Loudon's underlying concerns — though not his only ones.

At that time, improvement schemes of Utilitarian origin were often criticized for their mechanical efficiency and cool calculations of rewards, punishments, and degrees of happiness. Carlyle assumed that the schemes of Bentham and his followers had no foundation but logic.[6] Others believed that followers of Bentham, or Philosophic Radicals, had no human warmth, imagination, or capacity for poetry. Even John Stuart Mill, one of the most articulate of Bentham's followers, found it difficult to reconcile Bentham's principles with Wordsworth's poetry. In fact, his reading Wordsworth for the first time, in 1828, was the beginning of Mill's falling away from his cool Utilitarian state of mind. Looking back on his early days with Bentham's *Westminster Review* in the 1820s, Mill admitted that, at the time, he had not cared much for the cultivation of feelings. He had been eager to influence people's minds and actions, but his zeal had not been rooted in real benevolence or sympathy with mankind. "While fully recognizing the superior excellence of unselfish benevolence and love of justice," he wrote, "we did not expect the regeneration of mankind from any direct action on those sentiments, but from the effect of educated intellect, enlightening the selfish feelings."[7]

Loudon, too, as a young farmer addressing the landed gentry and nobility, had appealed to self-interest when he called for rational improvements in agriculture.[8] But Loudon was usually able to achieve a balance between logic and feeling, in part because his love for the beauty of nature, epitomized by his love of trees, was so intense. Later in life, he openly appealed to his readers' feelings of benevolence and patriotism — with the candor of a child, or of a sage. And he nourished a fond hope that the working man could begin to feel sentiments as noble as any man could. In 1828, for instance, Loudon invited young hired gardeners to make the gesture of contributing a few pence to a great public work then in progress (fig. 112).

The Thames Tunnel, a pedestrian subway twelve hundred feet long, which connected Rotherhithe to Wapping in East London, was a feat of engineering comparable to the North Sea oil rigs today — not only for the boost it was meant to give to commerce and industry, but also for the technical difficulties and dangers involved. Begun in 1825 by the French emigré engineer Marc Isambard Brunel, this first passage under the Thames took some eighteen years to complete, during which there were several disasters that cost many lives. Those who benefited initially were the working people of East London — carriageless travelers and commuters whose cross-Thames journey was shortened by four miles.[9] Since the planned access ramps for wheeled vehicles were never constructed, the Thames Tunnel remained, for many Londoners, an unseen monument near the docks and warehouses of the unknown East End. But during its early stages of construction, Loudon urged all gardeners — even the poorest — to contribute, "because there is something grand in feeling an interest and sympathy in public works and national undertakings. . . .

The idea of accomplishing a great national undertaking, at a penny a head, volunteered by men, women and children of all ranks, is sublime. The man who subscribes to a public work for the first time in his life, is using the means for giving a new impulse to the higher order of human feelings. He is adopting a course calculated to impress on the mind the consciousness of sentiments far above those which have reference merely, or chiefly, to self-preservation or advancement in the world; and which, in man, at a certain stage of his progress to intellectual enjoyment, must be hailed as a new

*The monumental project of tunneling beneath the Thames was underwritten in part by public subscription. Loudon encouraged all gardeners — even those earning subsistence wages — to contribute and thus to experience the ennobling feeling of participating in a great national undertaking.*

Fig. 112
Two views of the Thames Tunnel.

[View in the Tunnel.]

sense. . . . It is elevating to feel ourselves connected with our country and mankind by sentiments common to great minds in all ages; and it is ennobling to reflect that the poorest of us may participate in these sentiments as well as the richest.[10]

Charles Darwin was nineteen at the time Loudon offered these informal remarks on one aspect of the origin of species — the evolution of feeling. He was not speaking as a scientist, of course, but as a sympathetic friend who identified with the young men whom he was trying to reach, "men so poor as we gardeners usually are." He continued:

But we should be still better pleased with collections of the smallest coin, and should like to see in the list of subscriptions to the tunnel, published in the newspapers, such items as, "Thirty gardeners out of place, now at work in Lee's nursery at 12 shillings a week, 2 shillings 6 pence." "The Subscribers to the Clapton Nursery Library, collected in halfpence, 3 shillings."[11]

Apparently Loudon's appeal was effective. At Loudon's suggestion, Joseph Thompson, the head gardener at the duke of Portland's seat of Welbeck, in Nottinghamshire, had asked his staff for contributions. The Tunnel enterprise was sent eight pounds, eight shillings by Thompson and the gardeners, farmers, joiners, masons, household servants, the steward, and the clerk of the works.[12] In the end, the tunnel came into being through public subscriptions, government loans, private backing, and individual genius. Apparently Loudon considered it as important a public monument as the bridges over the Thames, the London University, and Covent Garden Market. In 1830 he observed that the age for useless public monuments — such as triumphal arches and metropolitan gateways — was gone. Such architectural extravaganzas led the mind back to the ages of tyranny and slavery, instead of forward to equality and liberty.[13]

When it was finally completed and opened to the public in March 1843 — a few months before Loudon's death — the tunnel became one of the sights of London. For a penny each, fifty thousand people passed through it on opening day. A "Tunnel Waltz" was composed to celebrate it. By 1866, however, the tunnel had been closed to pedestrians and bought by the East London Railway Company, who made it part of the larger system of London's underground traffic.[14]

Loudon did not live to see the great expansion of the metropolis accelerated by the railways above- and below-ground and by steam carriages, or their successors with internal combustion engines. He did, however, anticipate the expansion, and he welcomed its prime movers. He realized that railways could compress the distances between the outskirts and the heart of the metropolis and that they would tend to equalize some of the benefits of metropolitan living. Railways could also help to raise the universal standard of living, especially for people living far from centers of manufacturing or learning, in harsh climates or in smoky environments.

In 1841 Loudon suggested that the bald banks along the new railway lines could be planted with fine trees and shrubs to provide an added stimulation for people traveling at the curiously invigorating speed of twenty miles per hour. If the top soil was preserved during railway construction, the upper slopes of the banks could be planted as gardens and orchards. The following year, Loudon observed that his idea for railway arboretums had been realized — not in Britain, but in Vienna. Pleased to record that ripe grapes recently had come from Boston, Massachusetts, by ship and rail to Chatsworth, in Derbyshire, he mused over the potential of steam and rail to equalize the comforts and luxuries of the world.[15]

Railways did pose one problem, however: they were potential monopolies, a form which Loudon detested. To avert this outcome, government might build the railways and manage them according to the general road system that Loudon had proposed in 1831. In fact, the roads, canals, and railways of the whole island of Great Britain could be unified under one general system of transportation — to include at least a main line from Dover to John O'Groat's house, with branches to Holyhead, Liverpool, Carlisle, Portpatrick, and Aberdeen. Subordinate lines could be maintained by counties and parishes, or by cooperation among different levels of government. Sooner or later, Loudon predicted, the governments of all countries would adopt systems of rail communication from their capital cities to their most distant human settlements.[16]

Loudon expected a humane and enlightened system of self-government to do more than merely defend a people's right to pursue happiness. He frequently urged that institutions such as municipal or national botanical gardens and rural cemeteries be supported, at least in part, by a government of the people. No doubt these refinements of society would come in time, he reasoned. But, as he observed in 1831, a prior duty of government is "to provide the means of subsistence [that is, opportunities for employment] for all the governed; either this is the case, or the government of a country becomes reduced to a mere system of police, whose sole office is to protect the governed from one another, and from foreign aggression."[17]

Loudon was not looking to the government for a panacea, the vain hope that his countryman Thomas Carlyle suspected was the root of all the clamoring for reform in the late 1820s.[18] When Loudon called for reform, he simply assumed that a government which truly represented the people would be responsive to their basic needs. As he pointed out in a pamphlet that he sent to Jeremy Bentham in 1830 (a political tract too controversial even for the finest print of the *Gardener's Magazine*), certain reforms were necessary for the salvation of the country, given the extent of unemployment among agricultural laborers; the vicious circles of poverty, illiteracy, and crime; the high tax on bread corn; and other taxes to support institutions that provided a living to the younger sons of the nobility and gentry. Primogeniture and entail must be abolished, he urged.[19] The government should gradually appropriate the revenues of the national church, the woods and forests, and other crown lands. A fixed income should be set aside for the King. There should be complete freedom of trade. Above all, he desired to see a fair representation of the people, election by ballot, and the establishment of national education in place of the national church establishment. "Freemasonry was the bond of union in the dark ages," Loudon reflected; "and a community of sufferings may operate in modern times as freemasonry did of old. . . . We grow impatient beneath a yoke, from the weight of which we feel that we can be relieved; and we naturally ask why we should endure that, which in the progress of things must soon disappear; but which, unless we make some efforts to throw it off, may yet last long enough to embitter the whole of our existence. Let us not rest satisfied with envying posterity the fruit which will drop ripe at their feet, but let us stretch out our hands to seize our share while it yet remains upon the tree."[20] Finally, convinced that "the strength of every country lies in the mass of its population," Loudon urged that the mass be given a "high and equal school-education"; for without that, "a man or a woman is ushered into society without a fair chance of being able to procure the means of subsistence and of happiness." Such were the great objects to be attained by reform, by union and perseverance, and by every peaceable and lawful means.

With a greater command of language, Carlyle, too, wrote of reform, the Middle Ages, the present, and the bonds that secured sympathy among men. But Carlyle mocked all preoccupation with systems, institutions, and reform of government. First, Reform of Self, he demanded. These are some of the issues on which Loudon and Carlyle were poles apart.

Throughout this study of Loudon's mature work and thought, Carlyle has occasionally appeared as a foil, a man whose deepest feelings were opposed to much of what Loudon valued — including progress, and the individual's constant striving to improve, to succeed in the world. Yet the two Scots had some common social goals and, to some extent, a common intellectual, cultural, and social background. Both were eldest sons of large families. Carlyle's father was a thrifty, prudent mason, considered "prosperous" by local standards; and Loudon's father was an energetic, intelligent, prosperous small farmer.[21] Both Carlyle and Loudon were alert to the profound changes that were undermining the old order of British society. Loudon was alternately impatient for more radical changes and serenely confident that they would occur. Carlyle was more consistently, brilliantly, pessimistic. His optimism was released only in sharp flashes, as in his essay "Signs of the Times" (1829):

There is a deep-lying struggle in the whole fabric of society; a boundless, grinding collision of the New with the Old. (P. 459)

and

Doubtless this age is also advancing. Its very unrest, its ceaseless activity, its discontent, contains matter of promise. Knowledge, education, are opening the eyes of the humblest — are increasing the number of thinking minds without limit. This is as it should be. (P. 458)

Loudon was the older, by twelve years. Carlyle began to publish his best-known works of political history and social criticism in the late 1830s, just as Loudon's most prolific period was ending. Carlyle's *Past and Present* appeared in 1843, the year Loudon died. Thereafter Carlyle would focus on the moral condition of his age, disdaining preoccupation with material conditions, which Loudon had struggled to improve in the company of utilitarians such as Sir Edwin Chadwick; Joseph Hume, M.P.; and Dr. Southwood Smith; and of more conservative reformers, including Charles Kingsley and the earl of Shaftesbury.

Carlyle lived nearly forty years after Loudon's death; ultimately he speaks for a different age, the High Victorian era. Yet their chance collision of attitudes, expressed in the 1820s and 1830s, justifies the comparison of Loudon's mature thought, a mixture of what were then liberal and radical ideas; and Carlyle's early epigrammatic essay, a heady blend of radical criticism and nostalgic idealism that defies all familiar political labels.

In 1829 Loudon published his plan for the controlled growth of London and reiterated his appeals for representative government, national public education, garden libraries, and public open space in towns and villages.[22] Also published in that year was Carlyle's anonymous "Signs of the Times," which expressed his disillusionment not only with reform of government, but also with the force of public opinion, the age of machinery, codification (the hallmark of Jeremy Bentham's legislative efforts), and the art of adapting means to ends. In later years, seeking more positive guides for moral conduct than mechanistic metaphors and faith in the free market, Carlyle would look back to the twelfth century; but in 1829 he demanded no more nor less than an honest assessment of the present. He lamented the moving of mountains and the smoothing of highways: "We war with rude nature; and, by our resistless engines, come off always victorious and loaded with spoils." Wealth was increasing, but so also were the gaps between the rich and the poor. And thus the old social relations were strangely altering.

Loudon was no less saddened to see some of these altered relations. But he believed that the poor could enter into new and more dignified relations with their "betters," given the chance. Because his hopes for bettering the conditions of the working classes rested with working people themselves, he advised young gardeners, agriculturists, and others to cultivate their own abilities — to join subscription libraries, for instance — but not to look to benevolent societies for charity. For the unemployed and disabled poor, temporary measures for relief would necessarily depend on the benevolence of others; but Loudon tried to discourage even the most well-meant paternalism — any measure which, incidentally or by design, tended to "keep [the poor] under, as a distinct class."[23] Rather, the poor should be put into a condition to help themselves, an end which Carlyle also sought, by his own maverick means.

Societies, unions, and cooperation were signs of the times which Carlyle mocked and Loudon generally welcomed. Loudon did believe, however, that cooperation could offer real benefits only among people with a certain degree of education. To cooperate effectively, people must learn to recognize their essential equality — as human beings with common rights — with other people who, by chance or ability, occupied different ranks of society. Loudon's social views were not quite egalitarian. He believed that inequalities in character, ability, and fate were inevitable, and therefore any reward or rank derived from these inequalities was acceptable. The present inequality of *condition*, however — the vastly widening gulf between wealth and destitution — was inexcusable, he argued; and inequality of *opportunity* — the lack of education or of a "fair chance in life" — was intolerable. As an editor and author, Loudon felt a grave responsibility to inform and instruct, as well as to entertain. "The present population can only be saved by the press," he wrote in the April 1831 issue of the *Gardener's Magazine*, "and the coming generation by the schoolmaster."[24]

The urgency of his message must have been clear to the readers of that issue. Just months earlier, an organized revolt of agricultural laborers had swept across the face of southern England, leaving a trail of broken threshing machines and creating reverberations of unrest in the towns. In December 1830 William Cobbett reported that even middle-class tradesmen in the metropolis sympathized with the machine breakers.[25] In May 1831 the National Union of the Working Classes was formed in order to further the political goals of William Lovett and the Association for the Promotion of Co-operative Knowledge.[26] Meanwhile, the not-so-radical Society for the Diffusion of Useful Knowledge had just launched its *Quarterly Journal of Education*. An article on New England free schools argued that education was a "great moral police" that had safeguarded life and property in some of the American states, particularly in Massachusetts, where universal education had been known for two centuries.[27] Concurrently, Lord Brougham, in his capacities as lord chancellor and as chairman of the Society for the Diffusion of Useful Knowledge, continued to advocate a national system of education in Britain. To a few keen observers, the choices were clear: education and political reform, or revolution.

Loudon, reassured by Brougham's efforts, continued to report on the progress of education and offered his own versions of the current pedagogical wisdom: knowledge was pleasure as well as power; education was self-realization as well as moral policing. Loudon was optimistic that, given educational tools, the rising generation of working people would be able to seek knowledge independently in whatever art or science they chose to pursue. And in recognizing a fundamental harmony of interests with the rest of society, they would learn how and when to cooperate.[28]

Robert Owen's cooperative experiments stimulated Loudon to design projects for semicooperative living, with some shared facilities for washing, cooking, and dining.[29] Even traveling might be enjoyed on the cooperative system, Loudon observed. He suggested that men of very humble means could pool their resources and, by turns, operate a locomotive steam carriage that would run on the public roads. "It is delightful," he wrote, "to think of a party of London or Birmingham journeymen, with their wives, making a tour in a hired or joint-stock mechanical carriage, to North or South Wales, or the lakes; and to think of the ease with which all the finest scenery in the island might be seen by everyone."[30]

On the wider implications of Owen's cooperative experiments, however, Loudon reserved judgment. Owen believed that external circumstances — birth and environment — condition man's character and beliefs to a far greater extent than Loudon was willing to admit. He had risen to a position of prominence in the horticultural world by virtue of self-cultivation and extraordinary inner drive. Of course, he had received the necessary encouragement along the way, but he was, by nature, too much an individualist to accept those of Owen's theories like the notion that "man does not create his own belief or character," that these are "uniformly created for him."[31]

In 1826 Loudon had noticed among the British agricultural laborers certain regional differences in living conditions that seemed to influence their character. In the course of economic research, he found that these laborers' material conditions were worse, on the whole, than they had been fifty years before. The morale of agricultural laborers was low; they were either despondent or militant. Now, in the late 1820s, Owen's theories demanded a response to an important question: Does character act on condition? Or condition on character? In Loudon's view, the action was mutual, so he tried to stimulate improvements in both areas. [32] Herein lies the basis for the warm, human sympathies that tempered the cool calculations of the unofficial Utilitarian and amateur political economist who taught the rudiments and refinements of gardening and home building: Loudon recognized that the elusive, precious attribute *character* needed refinement as much as the façade of a house, the heating of its interior, or the precise grouping of trees and shrubs on the lawn.

Material conditions, character, sensibility, and the quality of the environment — ultimately, all these concerns were related. Fascinated by the interrelations, Loudon was continually recommending some improvement in the public or private domain, some new opportunity for people to better their own condition or refine their tastes. He would urge that museums, painting and sculpture galleries, gardens and parks be opened to all the people, that they might have their sensibilities nourished, their minds expanded, and their scope of enjoyment enlarged. He sprinkled the pages of his magazines with thoughts from such luminaries as Sir John Herschel, the astronomer, who once reflected, "If I were to pray for a taste which should stand me in stead under every variety of circumstances, and be a source of happiness and cheerfulness to me through life, and a shield against its ills, however things might go amiss, and the world frown upon me, it would be a taste for reading."[33] From Goethe, Loudon quoted these thoughts:

Men are so inclined to content themselves with what is commonest, the spirit and the sense so easily grow dead to the impression of the beautiful and the perfect, that every one should study to nourish in his mind the faculty of feeling these things, by every method in his power: for no man can bear to be entirely deprived of such enjoyment; it is only because they are not used to taste of what is excellent, that the generality of people take delight in silly and insipid things, provided they be new. For this reason, one ought every day to hear a little song, read a good poem, see a fine picture, and, if possible, to speak a few reasonable words. [34]

To this list of excellencies Loudon would add fine landscapes, beautiful trees, and all the delightful creatures of the animal kingdom. Soon after the Zoological Society opened its gardens in Regent's Park, Loudon urged that the public should be generally admitted on Sunday afternoons, not just during the week. Otherwise, servants and the poorer tradesmen would never be able to visit them. "These also have a curiosity to be gratified," he noted, "affections to be cultivated, and minds expanded."[35]

In the process of being exposed to the wondrous creations of the "Author of nature" and to the finest works of man, somewhere along the path toward understanding, appreciation, and creative thoughts or deeds, people ought to find a species of happiness, Loudon reasoned. Surely happiness had something to do with the self-willed, vigorous exercise of all one's faculties; and yet, what pleasure there was in quiet contemplation. . . Loudon's thoughts on happiness were never collected in a treatise, but tossed out now and again. He once recalled a feeling of enchantment upon first hearing music among the trees in the park of Karlsruhe, "a sudden burst coming sometimes in one direction, and then in another."

He wondered if those occasional concerts in the duke of Baden's park, open to all, had had any influence in forming the peculiarly mild, gentle character of the people of the town.[36] On another occasion, having returned from a gardening tour in the north of England, Loudon quoted the words of one W. Pare, of the Birmingham Mechanics' Institution: that the end of all education was "the improvement of the moral character and the habits, and the diffusion of happiness." Loudon then added, "Nothing is more conducive to the happiness of the individual (the means of comfortable existence being first provided for) than the cultivation of the heart and of the affections. To teach man how to pursue this kind of cultivation is one of the most important, though almost wholly neglected, branches of education."[37]

Because the means of a comfortable existence were not yet generally available to the great mass of society, Loudon devoted much of his own writing to their material needs. At very least, he aimed to diffuse the kind of knowledge that would enable people to know what material comforts they could expect, or hope for, in a house and garden. In the public domain, Loudon recognized the need for some guidance and control on matters of taste, but in the home, he wanted individual tastes to be freely expressed. Though an outspoken critic, Loudon consciously aimed to instruct, and not to lead. Emphasizing general principles, he encouraged his readers to think for themselves, to make their own choices. In their small portion of the earth's surface, he noted, the master and mistress of the house could alter the ground as they pleased, at a trifling expense, often with their own hands. "It is this," Loudon observed, "that gives the charm of creation and makes a thing essentially one's own."[38]

One of the choices which Loudon saw possible for more people, with the arrival of steam carriages and railways, was the choice of living in town, in the country, or — what seemed increasingly appealing — on the fringes of the metropolis, in the suburbs. In one of his last works, the *Suburban Gardener and Villa Companion*, Loudon noted that in the suburbs, an individual could achieve health, enjoyment, and the respect of society. And no man, Loudon insisted, could ever attain more than these three things, whatever his status or genius. Health and enjoyment could be found in the cultivation of one's own garden. The respect of society could be attained through the solid relationship of the individual to some larger group. In the country, the lord of the manor superintended the general management of his estate and was responsible, to some extent, for the laborers living in cottages on his estate or in the nearby villages. In the suburbs, the master of a villa personally cultivated his garden and adopted the responsibilities of a citizen of the town or metropolis (fig. 113).

Loudon was himself the master of a small suburban villa, and he prized his role as a responsible citizen of the metropolis. Mindful of Loudon's personal journey from country seats to the metropolis, one might expect that in his maturity he would no longer dream of a Utopia in the British countryside, tilled by the grateful tenants of a benevolent, far-sighted landlord. Yet the vast potential for improvements in rural Britain still intrigued him. On one of his last garden tours of England, he indulged in a lengthy sketch of rural felicity as he himself would arrange matters, were he the proprietor of a great house with thousands of acres, responsible for the livelihood and happiness of many dependents.[39]

In the thirty-six years since Loudon had first let his imagination play on this Utopian theme at the end of *Country Residences*, the character of his ideal landlord had not greatly changed; but the tone and the light finishing touches of his portrait — an ideal *self*-portrait — were altered. There were no gloomy mountains or lengthening shadows in the background. Gone was the chorus of weeping cottagers and servants that had stood as witnesses while their father and friend, the old nobleman, was buried on an isle of pines and cypresses beneath the heaven-pointing spire in the churchyard. There is no mood of elegy now, no language of pastoral romance. The words are plain, and the images are seen in the clear light of day. Here is the actual context:

It is September 1842. The previous year's census had reported an increase of two million people in England and Wales since 1831. For several years harvests have been poor, and a severe trade depression still lingers. In the manufacturing districts to the north, men are demanding that the tax on a necessity of life — bread corn — be abolished. The Corn Laws have not yet been repealed, but Prime Minister Peel has revived the

income tax that had been in effect during the later years of the Napoleonic
Wars. After more than a year and a half of fighting, the Opium war has just
ended, and China has ceded Hong Kong to Britain. Another expensive,
diastrous war has erupted in Afghanistan, claiming the lives of thousands
of native and British troops. At home in Westminster, the quality of
civilians' lives is under discussion. Edwin Chadwick has presented the
House of Lords with his report on the sanitary conditions of the British
laboring people. Lord Ashley (later to become the earl of Shaftesbury) has
proposed a bill to prohibit the employment of women in mines and colli-
eries, the employment of children under the age of thirteen, and the forced
unpaid "apprenticeship" of pauper children. And, with amendments that
will delay and diminish Lord Ashley's reform measures, his bill has
passed.[40]

Meanwhile Loudon is traveling with his wife, Jane, and their nine-
year-old daughter, Agnes, along the country lanes of Devonshire, somewhere between Sidmouth and Barnstaple.[41] The family has just spent a
week at Nettlecombe Court in Somerset, seat of Sir John Trevelyan, where
Loudon has been enchanted by the romantic setting of steep hillsides
crowned by oak woods; green meadows grazed by sheep and cattle; the
rich, red soil of fertile fields; and the fine park and pleasure grounds near
the house. He has perused the Trevelyan family papers and marvelled at
their antiquity; it reveals the Trevelyans' long lineage, for which he has
great respect. The comfortable whitewashed cottages of the Trevelyan
estate were similar to the cottages he is now passing in Devonshire. Here
the hedges are choked with weeds, however. The "thrashing" machines
are badly constructed; the current harvesting reveals foul stubble and
shallow plowing; the narrow, unidentified roads banked by impenetrable
hedgerows confound the traveler. Loudon begins to speculate on what he
would do, were he in the position to improve the land, the roads, the
buildings, and the relations among laborers, tenants, stewards, and
landlord.

First, no matter what the current skills or abilities of the tenant
farmers and laborers on his estate, Loudon writes that he would drive no
one from the land; rather, he would hire a skilled agriculturist to teach the
most appropriate methods of culture and management. Second, he would
commission a survey of all cottages and gardens on his estate, before
building new villages with community laundries, bakehouses, playgrounds, and so forth. He would also erect a nondenominational school,
which all children up to the age of fifteen or eighteen not already enrolled
in a school would be obliged to attend. Special courses for illiterate adults
would also be offered. Third, wages for laborers would be paid both in
cash and in kind; they would be assured of vegetables, meat, and access to
the estate's mill and malthouse, and would be given lessons in cooking
and "housewifery." Fourth, laborers would receive plants, roots, seeds,
and saplings from Loudon's own garden and nursery, as well as instructions in cottage gardening. Loudon would also offer prizes for the best
produce and for order and neatness. Fifth, no aged poor would be sent to
the workhouse. Those not able or willing to live with relations would be
encouraged to join in group living arrangements, where their meals would
be prepared by a neighbor or a housekeeper.

Loudon devoted his sixth guideline to his tenants' amusement, specifying the construction of a large community center for lectures, concerts, dances, theatricals, and reading aloud. Seventh, Loudon would attend to the rural infrastructure, including roads, drainage, fences, woods, orchards, farmhouses, and the parish church and churchyard. A main drive from his own house would traverse the estate, passing under tunnels or along overpasses where necessary to avoid gates. Eighth, after providing for the comfort of everyone around him, including the parish clergyman, he would finally attend to his own home farm, park, woods, and gardens, attempting to make them models of their kind. He concluded:

> So much for our *beau idéal* of what we think we should do if we were an
> extensive landed proprietor in Devonshire; but, to realise our suggestions,
> would require a degree of moral courage and devotion to the subject that can
> hardly be expected to be met with. Such a course of reformation would, in
> many, perhaps in most, cases, be met by the opposition of all the stewards,
> agents, and upper servants, whose business it is to get through their duties
> with as much ease to themselves as possible; and it would even be resisted at
> first by the tenantry and by the labourers. A determined spirit, however, on
> the part of the proprietor, and perseverance, would overcome every difficulty;
> and the consciousness of effecting a great good directly to a number of
> individuals, and by example to the public, while we were at the same time
> greatly increasing the value of our own estate and benefiting our offspring,
> would be an ample reward.[42]

Thus in his sixtieth year, Loudon proposed improvements which, a century and a half later, still demand attention, but now on a much greater scale: housing for the elderly, education for adults as well as children, and measures for the survival of family farms. (See portrait of Loudon, fig. 121.) Some of his suggestions were taken up, perhaps independent of his influence, by builders of small industrial towns, such as George Cadbury, whose employees at Bourneville received instructions in gardening from a professional trained at Kew Gardens, and Lord Leverhulme, who offered prizes for the best flowers and vegetables raised by his employees in their back gardens at his company town, Port Sunlight.[43] Frederick Law Olmsted and Calvert Vaux created one of the best-known systems of carriage drives on under- and overpasses — in their case, designed not to avoid farmers' gates, but to avoid collisions with other vehicles and pedestrians in New York's Central Park.[44]

Loudon could not claim originality for every aspect of his Utopian yet pragmatic program of improvements; its importance lay in its publication as a model for improving one's immediate environment and furthering the happiness of one's fellow man. One individual was already doing just that, on his estate of "Heanton Satchville," near Torrington, Devonshire; and Loudon was delighted to publicize his efforts.[45] Lord Clinton had formed a local agricultural society, built a school, improved the farmhouses and laborers' cottages, and refused to drive any of his tenants from the land, preferring to offer them agricultural instruction instead. In 1842 Loudon was honored to stake out a new approach road for Lord Clinton, a man who was already doing so much for the happiness of other human beings.

# 15

## At Home in Bayswater

For twenty years, No. 3, Porchester Terrace was Loudon's home, framed by fruit trees, shrubs, and vines. Recollections of his wife, his daughter, and his friends give a picture of Loudon's house, garden, and private life.

Coming home from London on a summer evening when winds were blowing from the west, Loudon could breathe in the fragrance of his own honeysuckles — *Lonicera japonica* — from nearly a quarter of a mile away.[1] As he approached the house, he would pass Hopgood's nursery on the right side of Bayswater Road, then his own half-acre reserve ground, rented from Hopgood's. Beginning at Craven Lane, where his experimental gardens ended, Loudon had pits for cucumbers and melons, and beds for asparagus, sea kale, rhubarb, strawberries, and Lancashire gooseberries — a cheerful prospect. But on the left side of the road, barring the view into Kensington Gardens, was a mean brick wall some eighteen to twenty feet high. Loudon had circulated several petitions asking to have it replaced by an open iron-rail fence and shrubberies, but the Office of Woods and Forests moved slowly.

At Porchester Terrace, Loudon would turn right. About forty yards down this unpaved street, again on the right, was his own black iron gate, sheltered by a pedimented, flat-arched gateway (fig. 114). He could inspect his variegated hollies and thorns, planted just inside the dwarf wall and iron railing. His double-blossomed *Crataegus tanacetifolia* came into leaf a week before the other deciduous shrubs; in May it blossomed with profuse white flowers that gradually faded to pale pink. Behind these shrubs, along the southwest boundary wall, Loudon had originally planted dark green laurels, but a giant ivy and a Virginia creeper overtook the laurels and formed their own rich mantle, spilling out over the coping of the wall at about shoulder height.[2]

*In the autumn of 1844, when the American nurseryman Charles Mason Hovey called on Jane Loudon, he paused to admire some of the trees in the front garden — a cedar of Lebanon, a mountain ash, two cherries (Cerasus Padus and C. semperflorens), a plum (Prunus myrobalana), a shadbush (Amelanchier Botryapium), a Persian lilac, a rose acacia, and other trees.*

Fig. 114
E. B. Lamb, View of Loudon's house, Porchester Terrace, ca 1838.

Just inside the gate, Loudon would enter a cool, dark tunnel of space created by the mass of vegetation around him — a cedar of Lebanon, a walnut, a sweet chestnut, a purple beech, several pears, lilacs, a cherry, a scarlet thorn, *Clematis Vitalba*, common ivy, laburnum, magnolia, and other trees and shrubs. The effect was that of a leafy telescope, drawing his eye towards the steps of his own front door — which did not face west, toward the street, but south, in the direction of Kensington Gardens.

In the center of the street façade of Loudon's plain, symmetrical three-story brick house, instead of a ceremonial entrance there was a small glass-domed conservatory filled with camellias that were reflected and multiplied in the panes of looking-glass behind them. It was a striking picture: camellias looked like bright precious gems in a larger setting of honeysuckles and wisteria, climbing roses, pyracantha, quinces, and grape vines, all clinging to the piers of the glass-roofed veranda; while behind the piers, the foliage of figs and the vines of claret grape clustered round the dining room windows on the west façade. Loudon's house was actually a double house, a fact scarcely evident on the west side in the thin wire fence running down the center of the front garden. All was unified, however, by abundant, luxuriant plantings, slightly different on either side of the fence. The house was set back only thirty feet from the street on roughly a half acre, yet at least one visitor remarked that it appeared immersed in the country, far from the crowded city.[3]

If any man's house and gardens ever reflected his own decided tastes, Loudon's home in Bayswater did — with all of the clarity and ordered chaos that one might expect from a logical but expansive and overextended writer and journalist. His house and garden combined were a vivid metaphor of his own mind and sensibilities, always developing, expanding, open to change. The house was constructed so as to accommodate additions over time, and the gardens were always in the process of growth and change. Over two decades, the experimental gardens were maintained as a microcosm of the known vegetable kingdom — at least in its higher orders, including tropical plants and vines under glass. In the open air, collections of strawberries, bulbs, and alpine plants were eventually removed to create space for representative collections of all the herbaceous plants and hardy trees and shrubs known to survive in the climate of Britain.[4]

Today Loudon's experimental gardens are gone and Bayswater is subsumed in the densely built metropolis. The front garden shows only a pale shadow of the horticultural splendor it once offered to the street.[5] The gardens and the house are no longer an integrated whole; the house alone remains largely intact, lately restored to some of its former dignity (fig. 115). Although this house eventually owed much to Mrs. Loudon's skill and manual labor, it was originally constructed as a bachelor's home; Loudon designed it seven years before he met and married Jane Wells Webb.

By the autumn of 1823, the shell of the house and the boundary walls of the garden were completed. Loudon was, at that time, suffering from rheumatism, which contracted the thumb and two fingers of his left hand. His right arm, recently broken and improperly healed, was constrained in an iron case night and day. Nevertheless, Loudon rose at four each morning so as to be on hand when the workmen came to begin their daily tasks. He had already had the soil drained with four-foot trenches and treated with lime and stable dung. With the earth excavated from the basement, he had raised the level of the surrounding land about two feet; thus, the house would appear to rise from the same earthen platform that he would later prescribe for all dwellings, even the humblest cottage.

The main mass of the double house (like that of Tew Lodge) forms a cube — the most economical form by which to enclose a maximum of space for a minimum of materials and labor. The materials are the familiar natural stone, Coade stone, yellow brick, wood, and stucco of late Georgian and Regency houses. The plain detailing includes brickwork of Flemish bond, simple guaged flat arches over the square-headed windows, narrow window reveals without prominent frames, and quoins in high relief. Similar fenestration, proportions, and detailing could be found near his old neighborhood in Bloomsbury — in the plain houses of Gower Street and the slightly more ornamented houses of Russell Square, built in the 1790s and early 1800s.[6]

The most prominent feature of Loudon's house is the small glass- and iron-domed conservatory. A glass appendage of some sort would become a familiar feature in later Victorian houses, and all those containing curvilinear wrought-iron sashes would owe something to Loudon's invention of the solid wrought-iron sash bar. Less commonly seen was the sort of glass-roofed veranda that surrounded the house, supported by sturdy, square piers (fig. 116). Under this sheltered walkway, Loudon's frail mother took exercise while she lived in her son's house until her death in October 1831.[7]

The double house is not sited as Loudon had originally planned. He had hoped to let the sunlight strike all four sides of the house — on the northeast, southeast, southwest, and northwest. Since Porchester Terrace

*Loudon designed this "double-detached" house for his own residence in 1822. As so often happens, the house has been restored, but the grounds have been truncated and the landscape gardening has disappeared.*
Fig. 115
View of Nos. 3 and 5, Porchester Terrace, Bayswater.

*While trees other than Lou-
don's shade the veranda,
the handsome railing —
possibly of his own de-
sign — remains.*
Fig. 116 (see also p. 280)
No. 3, Porchester Terrace,
Bayswater, detail of veranda.

runs north-south, this would have entailed rotating the house forty-five degrees and facing a corner to the street. However, the surveyor from whom Loudon acquired a ninety-nine year lease refused to allow a diagonal orientation, claiming that it would disfigure the street. Loudon's double house therefore confronts the street squarely, facing west. His own front door faced south, and that of his future tenant, north.

In plan, the two houses are virtually identical (fig. 117). Each has a ground floor and two upper stories, three exposures, a glass-roofed veranda on three sides, a private main entrance, and a private service entrance. On the ground floor of each, in front is the dining room (*h*); the back room is a library (*i*). In the half-basement, apparently duplicated for each house, are the front and back kitchens; the cellars for wine, beer, and coals; the pantry, the closets, and two servants' bedrooms; a water cistern; a dust-hole; a fixed safe; a lumber-closet; and the servants' lavatories. At the eastern corners of the verandas were the families' lavatories. Loudon's own house had sole access to two central features — the office of the *Gardener's Magazine* (*n*) on the east, and the conservatory (*g*) on the west.

While this house was being built, Loudon was also at work on the *Green-House Companion,* which later went through at least three editions.[8] It was a popular manual, intended mainly for the edification of gentlemen and ladies. In clear, nontechnical language, the *Companion* briefly explained the basic construction of glasshouses, gave hints on how to harmonize plant houses with dwellings, and furnished practical instructions on the cultivation of greenhouse plants. One might suppose this work would give some insight into Loudon's ideas about architectural design and, in particular, his intentions for the design of his own house and attached conservatory. Because the book was published anonymously, however, one wonders how much editorial control he had over the result.

In the *Green-House Companion* there is nothing of the young inventor's sense of discovery after a patient search for the right form calculated to serve a particular function; no manifesto about the liberation of glasshouses from all dependence on historical styles. In 1822 Loudon had insisted that the greatest progress in the construction of plant houses had begun when they were finally freed from the domination of "mansion architects."[9] How odd then to find him, two years later, proposing the decoration of conservatories with Grecian columns or Gothic pinnacles!

This book for amateurs, more cautious and conciliatory in tone than Loudon's earlier works for specialists, shows his willingness to use classical or medieval ornaments on glasshouses, in keeping with the style of the main house — as long as the plants inside were given sufficient light, warmth, and ventilation. For glasshouses to be constructed further away from the house, he recommended more original structures: the semidome constructed by W. & D. Bailey, ironmongers, with Loudon's curvilinear sash bar; and another, cheaper semidome without curving lines — simply a polygon of flat planes (fig. 118). (Had the flat planes been triangles, not parallelograms, this structure would have resembled Buckminster Fuller's now-familiar geodesic domes.)[10] Compared with these glass structures, the ornamented ones are disappointing. Nonetheless, they demonstrate Loudon's general principle of harmony; as an appendage to a house, each conforms "with that whole of which it is a part."[11]

This principle accounts for the heavy piers and thick cornice of

Loudon's domed conservatory — the centerpiece of a veranda with similar piers and cornice. The principle of harmony also accounts for his manner of addressing controversial issues, from reform of government and national education to architectural taste and the wages of gardeners. He expressed his radical views most forcefully in letters and short works written for the activist or specialist. In works for a general audience, the radical edge of his message was gently relieved by some literary filing and

*From the east-facing projection* (n), *the office of the* Gardener's Magazine, *Loudon looked out over his experimental gardens toward London.*

Fig. 117 (*bottom left*)
J.C. Loudon, Plan of his own residence, Porchester Terrace.

*A less expensive alternative to Loudon's curvilinear glasshouses was this polygonal conservatory, designed to be placed against a garden wall. The recommended orientation was southeast; otherwise, south or east.*

Fig. 118 (*see also p. 290*)
J.C. Loudon, Polygonal conservatory, ca. 1823.

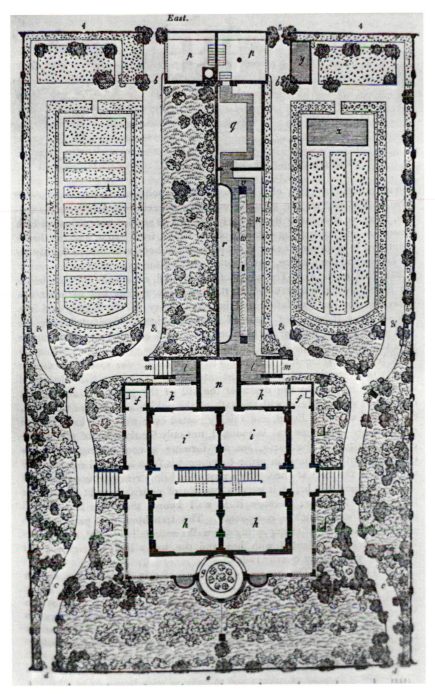

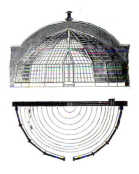

Fig. 119 (opposite)

*During his last twenty years, Loudon lived in the double house on the east side of Porchester Terrace, just off the Uxbridge (now Bayswater) Road, which ran along the northern boundary of Kensington Gardens.*

Fig. 119 (*opposite*)
John Britton, Map of St. Pancras and Marylebone, 1834, detail of Bayswater.

smoothing; alternatively, sharp, potentially abrasive remarks were "published in" a minute typeface. Just as he adjusted both message and medium to accommodate different audiences, Loudon adapted his conservatory, as viewed from the street, to the general tone of the neighborhood. Behind his house, in the experimental gardens, he erected more utilitarian glazed structures and laid out the regular beds of his horticultural collections. This space for his scientific pursuits was less picturesque — more private.

As forms of personal expression, Loudon's house and gardens in Bayswater should be "read" with the same degree of attention and sympathy that his writings deserve. The home can tell something about both Loudon's public face and his private sensibility, as one progresses from the western gate to the eastern end of the house — where, from the office of the *Gardener's Magazine,* Loudon could look out over his experimental gardens, toward Hopgood's nursery and, beyond, toward the London metropolis (fig. 119).

On the bright morning of September 14th, 1830, Loudon stood in the office of the *Gardener's Magazine,* and dictated one of the shortest, most spirited articles of his journalistic career.[12] As usual, he had more than one assistant in the room, and more than one subject on his mind. This morning, however, his remarks had to be brief, for he had "other important business to transact" before noon.

Consulting his notes from a recent tour of France, he suggested that the orange blossoms in the Tuileries should not be plucked off, as they currently were, for the profit to be made in selling them to perfume manufacturers. Rather, the delicious fragrance of these blossoms should be allowed to scent the air — of the Tuileries and perhaps half of Paris — as did the orange blossoms in Genoa and Naples. Loudon mused over the possibility of distributing of orange trees, or even mignonettes, so that "the air of any city might be rendered as odoriferous as that of a garden."

Then Loudon's mind soared away from his main subject for the second or third time that morning: "When the many have once conquered from the few what is necessary and convenient, they will then attempt what is agreeable and refined; and, with the knowledge of the wonderful resources of nature and art, requisite to give them the sovereignty of society, they will succeed." (p. 531) In the article he was composing, Loudon had already alluded to the glorious second French revolution of 1830, whereby a king who would not respect the charter of the people had just been replaced by a king who would. (This revolution had been brief and relatively peaceful, with none of the horrors that had sullied the first one.) Now he explained his digressions: "We feel that it would be a species of profanation, even in a Magazine of Gardening, to say much on any subject in which Paris is concerned, foreign from the glorious events which took place on the 27th, 28th and 29th of July last; events which, sanguine as we are as to the destiny of the human race, and great as have been our expectations from the French, have produced results of which 'we dare not have dreamed'" (p. 529). Some British political analysts had seen the fall of Charles X as the prelude to the fall of the conservative government in London. As Lord Brougham would exclaim in an exuberant article in the

*Edinburgh Review* (October 1830), "The battle of English liberty has really been fought and won at Paris."[13]

Loudon was among those who were delighted with the new shift toward the left in the French government, but his magazine article did not contain predictions for the immediate political future of London or Paris. Here, as usual when his main subject was not explicitly political, Loudon alluded to his own ideological views in passing. This time he cloaked them in the garb of the gardener:

When once society is freed from the trammels of antiquated institutions, the rapidity with which the natural rights of man will gain the ascendancy can only be compared to the rapid growth of a tree, which, after having been for many years clipped, is at last permitted to shoot forth in all the character and beauty of truth and nature; when its widely-spreading and vigorous branches soon burst through the limits to which the tree had been previously confined by the tonsor, and a formal and insipid piece of verdure becomes in time one of the noblest subjects of the forest. (529–30)

At the end of the article, Loudon returned to the orange trees of the Tuileries, commenting that they might look more attractive if their tubs were sunk into the borders of the paths, giving the illusion of trees growing in the ground.

The "other important business" Loudon had to transact that morning was not specified. However, a note appended to this article gave a clue to the reader. One J.L.Cobham explained that sprigs and wreaths of orange blossoms were customarily sold in the markets of Paris throughout the year, to be used in wedding ceremonies. The bride would be crowned with a wreath, and her attendants would carry bouquets. In the evening of the wedding day, all the young female friends of the bride would eagerly seek fragments of the bride's wreath, as in England they would seek pieces of the bride-cake. The custom was being adopted in England; sprigs from orange trees now were being worn at marriages. On that September morning in 1830, Loudon had been dictating to an amanuensis while he was being dressed by his manservant. Later in the morning he was due to appear in church, to wed Miss Jane Wells Webb, formerly of Birmingham and Bartley Green, Worcestershire, and lately of London (fig. 120).

At twenty-three years of age, Jane Webb was about to marry a forty-seven-year-old man of decided opinions on taste in gardening, the rights of man, free trade, religious tolerance, national education, the wages of gardeners, the siting of public buildings, the ennui of ladies, and much more. By her own admission, Jane Webb came to Loudon utterly ignorant of his fields of expertise; but she was willing and able to learn, having had, earlier in her life, the benefits of a private governess, a good home library, and a few years' residence on the Continent with her father, a Birmingham business man and a widower. (Her mother had died when Jane was twelve.)[14] Jane Webb would also have gathered odd details of manufacturing and engineering from the dinner table conversations of her father's business acquaintances and friends. These men may have provided some technical background for her science-fiction novel, *The Mummy* (1827) — the work that led to her introduction to Loudon in February 1830.[15]

Jane Webb had been writing stories and poems for publication since

1824, when her father died. She was then seventeen, a young woman left without parents or legacy to support her. Determined to earn her living by her pen, she had her first volume, *Prose and Verse*, privately printed in Birmingham in 1824.[16]

Before she became Mrs. Loudon, Jane Webb had suffered some trials that were later delicately explained by William Jerdan, the distinguished and kind-hearted editor of the *Literary Gazette*. "I saved her from sinking," he wrote, "when [she was] first exposed to the struggle which a female venturing upon the rugged path of literature is sure to experience." According to Jerdan, Jane "fought a stirring fight with literary exertion, as her 'Hungarian Tales,' 'Conversations on History and Chronology,' 'Stories of a Bride,' and other clever works amply testify."[17] When she became ill, Jerdan came to her rescue and also served as literary father-confessor. "I have naturally an independent spirit," Jane confided to him,

and wish to maintain myself; but I am not fitted to struggle with the world. I cannot put myself forward, and I cannot make bargains [with publishers]. I am

*After her marriage to John Claudius Loudon, Jane Loudon continued to write fiction and enlarged her sphere of interests to accommodate his. In one of her books,* The Lady's Country Companion *(1845), she advises a young city-bred friend, "Seek nature, then, my dear Annie; leave your trim flower garden, and your tame poultry, and wander in the woods, admiring the poetry of forest scenery, and watching the habits of the various creatures which people what seems to the careless observer only one vast solitude."*

Fig. 120
Jane W. Loudon (1807–1858). Portrait reproduced by kind courtesy of Bea Howe.

soon depressed, and when any one finds fault with any of my productions, instead of defending them, I throw them into the fire. I try to overcome this feeling, but I cannot. The phrenologists say that conscientiousness and love of approbation are my two strongest qualities, and that I have no self-esteem. I believe they are right. Forgive this loquacity.[18]

In Webb's best-known work, *The Mummy*, Jerdan found evidence of "great talent and imaginative power." He was flattered when Webb invited him and the poet Letitia E. Landon to be advisors for her forthcoming *Tabby's Magazine* — a joint project with another writer, Elizabeth Spence. The periodical never materialized, however.[19] Eventually, Jerdan explained, Jane Webb "wisely abandoned the unsuccessful struggle" and married one of his esteemed friends. Loudon had been a salaried contributor to the *Literary Gazette*. Of his protégée Jane Webb, Jerdan concluded, "Leaving the fields of romance, she happily became the helpmate of Mr. Loudon in the true spirit of his practical and solid productions."[20]

Among all of Jane Webb's writings, the work which first attracted Loudon's attention and admiration was a bold, light-hearted satire, published anonymously, which revealed nothing of its author's timidity. *The Mummy! A Tale of the Twenty-Second Century* is a three-volume frolic of science fiction, in which reformers, inventors, planners, and the working classes are all gently satirized. A celibate queen reigns over dim-witted ministers and pedantic servants. Civilization has progressed to such an extraordinary degree that mysticism and superstition have returned to haunt the most enlightened of kingdoms.

Loudon was intrigued. *The Mummy* was remarkably original, he thought, comparable only to Mary Shelley's *Frankenstein*.[21] He also enjoyed seeing inventions and improvements pushed to the level of absurdity. Along with descriptions of steam mowing-machines and inflatable aerial horses, *The Mummy* contained some curious and useful ideas about smokeless cities, chemically heated and ingeniously ventilated houses, and terraced public gardens along the Thames, to be filled with clean and handsome British sculpture. In the Egypt that she described, irrigation channels prevented the Nile from flooding. And in London, Jane Webb wrote, a law in operation for two centuries prohibited the burial of the dead within the city walls. Loudon gave an enthusiastic review to *The Mummy* in March 1828 and let it be known privately that he wished to meet the author.[22] Through a mutual friend, Loudon at last met the demure Jane Webb at a party in February, 1830.

Little is known of the Loudons' courtship. Reticent in print, Jane confessed only that, from their first meeting, she believed, "he formed an attachment for me."[23] Having recently toured Germany and France, Loudon found his mind was charged with new enthusiasm for national education, political reforms, planning and municipal government, and new scientific institutions; and these were the subjects he discussed in writing — not the wooing of Jane Webb. However, Loudon may have had something to do with the naming of a new plant after his fiancée. In the *Gardener's Magazine* of October 1830 this tribute appeared:

*Pelargònium Webbiànum* . . . This hybrid has been named in compliment to the accomplished Miss Webb, the elegant authoress of *The Mummy*, from which an extract may be seen in Vol. III, p. 478; who, to her numerous acquirements, is adding, with unparalleled ardour, an extensive knowledge of botany. A most desirable plant, raised from *P. Hùmei*, which had been fertilised with some unknown kind.

The Loudons' only child, born on October 28, 1832, was a girl, christened Agnes, for Loudon's mother. Bea Howe has written sympathetically of the girl's beauty and her somewhat melancholy charm; her popularity among the talented young men in London (Wilkie Collins, Charles Kean, Charles and Edwin Landseer, Augustus Egg, and John Everett Millais); her close friendship with Bella Martin, the painter's daughter; parties at the home of Charles Dickens in London and evenings with the Brownings and the Trollopes in Florence; unhappy romances with dashing and mysterious Italian and Greek gentlemen on the Continent; marriage to a solicitor from Yorkshire (who became Chief Agent of the Conservative Party under Disraeli); children; and an early death.[24] Unfortunately, Loudon never knew his daughter as a young woman; he died when she was eleven. The Agnes he knew was the impetuous child who appears as "Agnes Merton" in many of Jane Loudon's published tales.

In *Agnes; or, The Little Girl Who Could Keep Her Promise*, six-and-a-half-year-old Agnes Merton is allowed to accompany her parents on their excursions into the countryside. One day the family arrives at a village where Agnes's papa intends to see a blacksmith who has invented a curious sort of plow. Mr. Merton stops the carriage at the green and walks to the blacksmith's shop. Agnes slips out of the carriage and races across the green, while her mother follows at some distance. Sheep are grazing, and a donkey lingers under the branches of an old oak. Agnes stops running when she arrives at a brook where dragonflies dart close by the water's edge. When she leans over the bank, Agnes can see crystal-clear waters sparkling in the sunlight and pebbles lying in the sand on the bottom. She dangles her pretty little green silk glove over the water and, when her mother has caught up with her, asks, "Why can't the shops be in the country? And the factories? Why can't people *live* in the country?"[25] Mrs. Merton explains the requirements of concentration, capital, machinery, workers, and the pricing of goods. One wonders what the absent Mr. Merton — or Loudon, the planner of greenbelts for cities — would have replied.

Agnes appears again in Jane Loudon's *Glimpses of Nature . . . During a Visit to the Isle of Wight*. At home in the garden, ten-year-old Agnes sits on a swing, melancholy and lost in thought. Her father is ill, her mother is preoccupied, and Agnes feels neglected. The narrator explains that Mr. Merton is fond of his daughter when he is well, but sick people cannot bear the fatigue of children. Later, the family travels by carriage to Southampton, where it crosses to the Isle of Wight, for the sake of Mr. Merton's health. Along the way, the Mertons find occasions to pique the child's curiosity:

"Every seed," said Mr. Merton, "contains an embryo — that is, a miniature plant, which has one or two leaves, a root, and generally an ascending shoot, quite small, and curiously folded up, but still plainly to be distinguished, either by the naked eye, or with a microscope. Now a sporule has no embryo, and no traces of a plant can be discovered in it till it has begun to grow."

"I am afraid that I do not quite understand you, Papa," said Agnes.

"It can hardly be expected that you should," said Mrs. Merton; "but it will be sufficient for you to remember that cryptogamous plants have no flowers, and no regularly formed seeds."[26]

One can well imagine that these fictitious conversations were drawn from life, as the Loudons' carriage lumbered along a country road toward Southampton, or, as members of the family drew together for breakfast or dinner from different areas of the house and gardens. Many threads of their everyday existence are woven into both parents' works on horticulture, botany, agriculture, and other subjects. Now and again a detail appears more fictitious than real. Was there, in fact, a child's swing in Loudon's garden, where fruit trees were sometimes cut down, due to lack of space, just when they were producing bountiful crops of fruit? Certainly the back gardens were less a playground for a little girl than an outdoor classroom and laboratory. As Loudon explained in 1838, his interest in these gardens was scientific knowledge, not ordinary enjoyment.[27]

A flued brick wall, or hot wall, with a sloping, south-facing glass façade ran along the north side of Loudon's experimental gardens. It led to a hothouse, a greenhouse, and, at the east end, a shed. Within the shed, located on different levels, were a potting bench; a pump; a carpenter's bench; a wooden safe for preserving fruit; bulbous roots; specimens of plants; and a glass-enclosed bookcase containing a garden library; as well as shelves for seeds, roots, tallies, and so forth. The machinery for the clock in the shed's tower was located in the loft, along with bins for onions and other bulbs, and mats for protecting half-hardy shrubs against frost. In the basement of the shed was the fireplace (a source of heat for the hothouse, greenhouse, and hot wall), storage bins for fuel and lumber, and space for growing mushrooms and forcing rhubarb and chicory. Outside, Japanese quince and honeysuckle clung to the south wall of the shed; and, along the brick boundary wall, near the public footpath of Craven Lane, Loudon grew black Hamburg grapes, various roses, and a prize *Magnolia Soulangeana,* which Soulange-Bodin had sent as a gift in 1828.[28]

For many years at Porchester Terrace, Loudon was able to employ at least one gardener (for whose benefit he had installed the garden library). From the latter part of September 1830, Loudon also enjoyed the willing assistance of his wife. Judging from Jane Loudon's writings and her husband's enthusiastic reviews in the *Gardener's Magazine,* she must have been mistress of all the floricultural treasures of their house and grounds — mistress, but dirt-gardener as well! Reviewing Jane Loudon's *Instructions in Gardening for Ladies,* Loudon observed, "Labour is the root of all enjoyment." For a gentleman, a lady, or any practical gardener, the full enjoyment of flowers and other delightful productions involved sowing, watering, transplanting, and thinning, as well as hoeing, raking, digging, pruning, pushing a wheelbarrow, handling a syringe, and working a "garden engine" if necessary.[29]

Jane confessed to her readers that she had had to learn about these operations as an uninitiated adult — and this was her claim to legitimacy as a writer on gardening:

When I married Mr. Loudon, it is scarcely possible to imagine any person more completely ignorant than I was, of every thing relating to plants and gardening; and, as may be easily imagined, I found every one about me so well acquainted with the subject, that I was soon heartily ashamed of my ignorance. My husband, of course, was quite as anxious to teach me as I was to learn, and it is the result of his instructions that I now (after ten years' experience of their efficacy) wish to make public, for the benefit of others. I do this because I think books intended for professional gardeners are seldom suitable to the wants of amateurs. It is so very difficult for a person who has been acquainted with a subject all his life, to imagine the state of ignorance in which a person is who knows nothing of it, that adepts often find it impossible to communicate the knowledge they possess. Thus, though it may, at first sight, appear presumptuous in me to attempt to teach an art, of which, for three fourths of my life, I was perfectly ignorant, it is, in fact, that very circumstance which is one of my chief qualifications for the task.[30]

Jane Loudon was beginning to teach ladies the art and craft of gardening at a time when the very idea of a duchess — or even a lady of lesser rank — wheeling a barrow and nailing espaliered trees would have been dismissed by most people as absurd. Readers knew the stories of Marie Antoinette playing dairymaid in her picturesque hamlet at Versailles, of course. And, in his review of his wife's book, Loudon recalled the eminent Girardin, vicomte d'Ermenonville, whose wife and daughters had dressed as peasants in their picturesque country residence north of Paris, at about the time that Rousseau was enjoying a philosopher's retreat in one of their cabins. But Loudon went further, observing that "the grand and all-pervading evil among ladies of independent fortune is *ennui*."[31] He had already hinted at the consequences of boredom in 1806, when he had encouraged gentlemen and ladies to take an active interest in the management of their country residences.[32] In the 1840 essay, Loudon spoke more directly: "Ladies of rank are as much subject to *ennui*, as ladies without rank; and every lady, as well as every gentleman, has a portion of the day that she can call her own, when she may indulge in what she likes. If she has not, her life is not worth keeping."[33]

Jane Loudon may have agreed, but she would never have made such a strong statement in print — unless she did so indirectly, through satire. She may have won over more ladies to the horticultural cause with sweet good sense than her husband ever did with tart, bold phrases, for Jane, by Loudon's own admission, was the one who wrote with elegance and poetic feeling. She was a mistress of English grammar. He was a master of a kind of forthright statement of fact mingled with feeling and utterly sincere, indomitable belief for which there may be no precise word in the English language.

The gardening world was indeed fortunate that, as John Gloag has pointed out, J.C. Loudon found in Jane Webb a "perfect partner."[34] One wonders if the *Encyclopaedia of . . . Architecture*, the *Arboretum Britannicum, The Suburban Gardener*, and other late works would ever have appeared without Jane's constant, cheerful assistance. As Agnes recalled, her mother was always "so patient and forebearing, always thinking of saving others trouble, so gentle, so kind, so utterly unselfish."[35] Jane may have had some influence on Loudon's temperament, which became milder and more reflective over time. If he taught her all she knew about gardening, Jane communicated her new knowledge on her own terms, in her own distinctly feminine voice. Loudon remained more truly sanguine and idealistic than his sensible, practical wife. *He* was the one who wrote about reform, amelioration, and paradise on a global scale. And yet, on that bright morning of their wedding, and during the years that followed, Jane may have reinforced in Loudon that extraordinary sense of self-confidence and optimism for the fate of humanity that can only well up in a person who loves deeply and is truly loved in return.

We have seen Loudon, his house, his garden, and his family much as a reader or a passerby might have seen them. A few glimpses of the inside of the house may reveal something about the character of the man who built it.

The dining room was apparently the place where Loudon could be most at ease with his family and his guests. One close friend was the *Gentleman's Magazine* reviewer known as J.M., who accompanied Loudon on garden tours in the south of England.[36] Having enjoyed Loudon's hospitality in Bayswater, he later recalled that "whoever was a guest at [Loudon's] table, was sure to be gratified by the company of persons of superior intelligence and information; of naturalists, travellers, men conversant with literature, or art, or science, of various characters and pursuits, but almost all of attainments that inspired respect, and conversation that was listened to with enjoyment."[37] This company included men and women of different generations, some of whom would become famous only after Loudon's death. Among them were John Leech, Mark Lemon, and Douglas Jerrold, of *Punch;* Charles Dickens, and W.H.Wills, of *Household Words;* William and Mary Howitt, Mrs. Gaskell, and William Makepeace Thackeray; Noel Humphreys, the artist and naturalist; Robert Chambers, the Edinburgh journalist, and his wife Anne; Charles Waterton, the naturalist; Dr. Anthony Todd Thompson, the surgeon; and John Martin, the painter, and his family.

On Saturday evenings the Loudons enjoyed giving dinner parties for twelve or more — at least before the *Arboretum Britannicum* became an all-consuming occupation.[38] Friends were also welcome to share humbler fare. Thomas Sopwith, the mining engineer and inventor from Newcastle-upon-Tyne, used to make frequent visits to the metropolis, and he enjoyed Loudon's hospitality. He later recalled, "I had for many years the privilege of dining with him at his plain family dinner any time I chose to go, and I not unfrequently had this very great pleasure. No ceremony as to dress. Conversation in a free and unmeasured and most friendly manner was the true charm of the feast."[39]

William Jerdan, Loudon's editor and his friend for over twenty years, fondly remembered Loudon's occasional lapses of the pen: "Earnestness and simplicity were prominent traits in his character. His earnestness hurried him at times into strenuous pursuit of whatever was in hand, whether likely or not to lead to profitable result. His simplicity, delightful in the transparency of his personal and domestic life, betrayed him, as an author, into the use of language and illustrations not suited for the eye of the general reader. Expressions which would have excited public amazement escaped from his pen."[40] Jerdan then alluded to some casual remark of Loudon's concerning the growth of asparagus, that, had it not been excised, would have banned the *Literary Gazette* from all parlors and drawingroom tables.

Jerdan, a Scot, had left the border town of Kelso to settle in London, in a cottage in Old Brompton. Another of Loudon's friends, Robert Chambers, remained in Scotland and edited *Chambers's Edinburgh Journal,* in the pages of which he recommended Loudon's works on gardening and agriculture. Loudon did not possess the "higher gifts of genius," Chambers believed; but he appreciated Loudon's talents for eliciting, analyzing, and conveying information:

He possessed to an extraordinary degree the art of drawing forth the knowledge of others; and as soon as he had formed a plan of one of his works, he seemed endowed with an instinctive feeling which guided him at once to the persons who could give him the best information on the subjects he had in view — information which they were often not aware they possessed. Around him in his study, masses of knowledge, thus gleaned from practical men, were arranged in labelled compartments, ever ready when needed; and by the alchemy of his mind, and the incessant labours of his pen, he gave these thoughts to the public in an inviting and useful form.[41]

One of his draftsmen described the customary order and neatness of Loudon's workrooms in this way: "The books in the library and manuscripts in his study, were so arranged that he could at any time put his hand upon any book or paper that he might want, even in the dark. He instilled this system of order into the minds of his clerks, too; for, when any new one came, his inevitable instructions were — 'Put every thing away before you leave at night, as if you never intended to return.'"[42]

One vivid description of the office and ground floor of Loudon's house appears among the letters of John Ruskin, who used to visit in Bayswater when he wrote for Loudon's magazines of architecture and natural history.

Loudon had been the first editor to publish a prose piece of Ruskin's — a brief article in the *Magazine of Natural History,* in September 1834, in which Ruskin discussed the peculiarly clear green color of the Rhine as it emerged "purified" from the Lake of Constance.[43] Ruskin later recalled that the first sight of the article in print brought tears to the eyes of his father; his fifteen-year-old son was a published author![44] Within a few years, Ruskin began a series of essays for Loudon on "The Poetry of Architecture." Loudon wrote numerous letters of recommendation for the young Ruskin, and the elder Ruskin repeatedly advised his son to use them to make his way in the literary world.[45]

As a well-known author and editor, Loudon was certainly a "useful" person to know. He provided Ruskin, as an Oxford undergraduate, with contacts and an outlet for his first architectural writings. But Loudon was also a family friend whose home and office were always open to the younger man. Though their views on architecture would not always coincide, Loudon, the aging, ailing editor, enjoyed a genial relationship with the young prodigy — advising him on places to see and write about while in Scotland. In turn, he received at least one letter from Ruskin, a puckish description of the extravagance of Sir Walter Scott's "Gothic" residence, Abbotsford.[46]

Ruskin was equally irreverent about Loudon's house in Bayswater. One Saturday in January 1837, Ruskin paid a visit and found that Loudon was out, but he stayed for conversation with Loudon's friend and architectural colleague E. B. Lamb. The casual observer, Ruskin wrote to his father, might have considered Loudon's house on that occasion a "chaos of literary confusion"; but Loudon, its master or presiding genius, would have viewed it otherwise:

Dust covered fossils and lack lustre minerals, their crystals shattered, their polish destroyed, and enveloped in cobwebs of duration so antique and size so formidable as to render the specimens far more interesting to the entomologist than the mineralogist, occupy the landing places and passages, while the floors of the rooms themselves are paved with books and portfolios. On entering the company room of Mr Lamb, I found myself in the midst of an admired disorder of such architectural specimens as in their native land or spot would have been beautiful, while where they were, they were only so many causes of lamentation and instigators of indignation. Here, on a wooden bracket — over a narrow cupboard which suggested involuntary ideas of papers of tea and loaves of sugar — was a Corinthian capital from Tivoli! There, in a fantastic niche, his knightly heel kicking a rush bottomed chair, stood some ancient Saxon monarch, whose marble brows, which had long frowned down the shadowy and echo-voiced aisles of some ruined abbey — now held the same dignified expression, while gazing on the poker, tongs, shovel, and ashes, which were the accompaniments of the parlour grate — while a richly carved Gothic altar, which had long stood in the noble cathedral, ⟨ . . . ⟩ the burial place of Alfred, now occupied a corner in dangerous ⟨pro⟩ximity to the fire broom. I had however the pleasure of knowing that a good many of the relics which lay about the room like rocks to confound and swallow the navigation up of the unwary stranger were casts.[47]

This dusty chaos would seem incomprehensible in light of Loudon's legendary love of order. However, Ruskin's letter was written while the *Arboretum* was in its final, frenetic months of completion. By 1835 Loudon had had to give up his gardener to economize. As the strain of laboring on the *Arboretum* increased, under pressure of time and mounting debts, he may have been forced to relax his standards of order; hence the dusty fossils and cobwebs.

Grant Thorburn, the Scottish emigré who became a successful seedsman in New York City, revealed that to complete the *Arboretum* Loudon had knowingly risked bankruptcy; for it was he, not the publishers, who bore the financial responsibility. The publishing company, Longmans, had warned Loudon that the work would ruin him. But Loudon confessed to Thorburn that "he could not yield to their advice, as his whole mind was bent on it." Thorburn continued, "He told me himself it was well patronized by the nobility and the public, but the capital was very heavy and returned comparatively slow, — hence his trials; and withal he was so upright in the whole matter, as to make every order for his work to be paid over to his bookseller."[48] The project had doubled in size since it was first begun, and during the last six years of Loudon's life, many of his other works were also pledged to Longmans to pay the debts incurred on the *Arboretum*. Though he was seriously ill for nearly two years after the last installment of the *Arboretum* was sent to the printers, in 1839 Loudon once again advertized his services as a landscape gardener and consultant (fig. 121).[49] Meanwhile, he and Jane continued to produce useful works on gardening, horticulture, and the design and management of cemeteries.

An unabashed admirer of Loudon, the columnist known as J.M., once confessed, "We never close the gates of his delightful suburban home without a sigh, when we think of our solitary lares, and the phalanx of grim and grisly authors who stand in hope or fear, glaring round the Reviewer's Cave."[50] And so we may descend the south-facing steps, well aware that all was not paradise in that suburban home. In the late 1830s and early 1840s, it was troubled by infirmities, mounting debts, and, finally, fatal illness. Loudon's family would have been left with even greater burdens but for the gallant efforts of friends, including Joseph Paxton; Charles Waterton; Sir William Jardine; John Stevens Henslow; Joseph Strutt; George Charlwood, a seedsman in Covent Garden; Robert Marnock, curator of the Royal Botanic Garden in Regent's Park; Sir Walter and Lady Pauline Trevelyan of Wallington Hall, Northumberland; and other kind persons who rallied to help Jane Loudon and her daughter after Loudon's death on December 14th, 1843.[51]

Paxton, in particular, was a devoted friend and benefactor to Loudon's widow and child. He immediately issued a circular reminding the friends of horticulture of their responsibilities. He explained in another context, "To immediately release this distinguished man's family from embarrassments is a debt the horticultural world owes to his memory; his

*During her husband's last years, his body was succumbing to fatal illness, Jane Loudon knew; yet, she wrote, his mind remained clear to the very end — vigorous, and full of projects for the future.*

Fig. 121
John Linnell, Portrait of J.C. Loudon (1840–41).

name must ever be associated with the brightest era in Gardening, for to him we are principally indebted for having raised Horticulture from a state of ignorance and empiricism to the rank it now holds amongst other scientific professions."[52] On the initiative of Paxton and a few others, a public meeting was held on February 17th, 1844, in the rooms of the Horticultural Society in Regent Street. A committee was appointed to receive subscriptions for the purchase of Loudon's works and contributions from those who already possessed complete libraries of his works.[53]

A complete listing of those who gave contributions or made purchases would be impressive. The name of Prince Albert could head such a list, to be followed by the names of dukes, earls, noble ladies, eminent scientists, architects, literary men, nurserymen, statesmen, amateur gardeners, and others. Among them would be Charles Barry, Thomas Cubitt, Joseph Hume, the bishop of Winchester, the duke of Devonshire, the earl of Radnor, and Sir W.J.Hooker. The Royal Agricultural Society, the Royal Botanic Society, and the Hull Subscription Library also made purchases.[54]

Jane Loudon was grateful for these efforts, which had, in six weeks after her husband's death, reduced his debts by about a thousand pounds, but, as she revealed in the *Times* in March 1844, more than half the debt remained.[55] The *Westminster Review* considered Loudon's death a "public calamity."

Jane Loudon was never free of financial worries, but she continued to write books and bring out revised editions of her late husband's works. Even her daughter began to write. At the age of eleven, Agnes Loudon published her first story, "The Lost Gloves," in *Chamber's Edinburgh Journal*.[56] Prime Minister Peel had used his influence to grant Mrs. Loudon an annuity in recognition of her late husband's contributions to science.[57] Somehow mother and daughter managed.

Jane Loudon went on to win her own laurels. Her works on horticulture and botany were well received, and apparently well used, in Britain. A new edition of her *Gardening for Ladies* was edited in America by Andrew Jackson Downing.[58] In Paris, Jane Loudon's works (including some of the Agnes Merton stories) found their way into the Bibliothèque Nationale. And, on the strength of her own horticultural contributions, as well as in honor of her much-esteemed husband, Madame Loudon was elected a corresponding member of the Royal Horticultural Society of Paris in January 1844.[59]

Alexandre Poiteau, the botanist and editor of *Le Bon Jardinier*, was one of the men who had proposed Jane Loudon's election to the society. Poiteau admired the lucidity and perfect execution of her works. On behalf of the society, he also expressed deep regret for the loss of her husband. "Personally," he wrote, "I will retain the precious memory of the friendship with which he honored me as long as I live, and I will never cease to deplore his loss."[60] Grant Thorburn considered Loudon "the most extraordinary man in our age." He asserted that Loudon, in spite of his amputated right arm, was a more prolific writer than anyone since Shakespeare. Thorburn's parting comment on Loudon was terse: "He is a Scotchman, a man of strong *mother wit*, and a clear head."[61] Downing had not known Loudon personally, but he observed, "His herculean labors as an author have at last destroyed him; and in his death we lose one who has done more than any other person that ever lived, to popularize, and render universal, a taste for Gardening and domestic architecture."[62]

Loudon's colleagues in Britain found various ways to honor him. Robert Sweet named a dazzling, blood-red hybrid *Pelargonium Loudonianum*.[63] Noting that Loudon's works were "well known in every part of the civilized world," John Lindley named two plants in Loudon's honor: *Adesmia Loudonia,* an evergreen plant from Chile with an erect stem, grey-green leaves, and golden flowers that blossomed in May or June; and the genus *Loudonia* (pl. 9, fig. 122).[64] In 1872 William Robinson dedicated the first volume of his periodical *The Garden* to the memory of Loudon. The *Arboretum Britannicum,* among others of his works, Robinson wrote, had "tended to ennoble the art of gardening."[65] And there were other kind words and deeds — perhaps none more endearing than the following:

In 1829 Loudon learned about the fate of some seeds from the Scotch pine of Haguenau, which he had procured from Vilmorin in Paris and sent to two gentlemen in Perthshire. These men planted the seeds on some exposed hilly grounds and named their future pine groves "Loudon's Howe" and "Loudon's Brae." Loudon remarked:

Here are a valley and a hill dedicated to our memory, which will be recorded in the maps of the country, and exist, bearing our name in these maps and in

*Dr. John Lindley, appointed Professor of Botany at University College London in 1829, had assisted Loudon previously by writing a considerable portion of the* Encyclopaedia of Plants. *Lindley named the new genus* Loudonia *just after Loudon completed the* Arboretum Britannicum.

Fig. 122

*Loudonia aurea,* from John Lindley, "A Sketch of the Vegetation of the Swan River Colony," South Australia, ca. 1839.

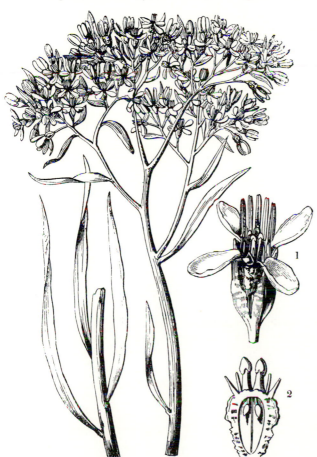

Fig. 1. represents a flower of *Loudonia aurea,* magnified, after three of the front stamens have been removed.

Fig. 2. is a section of the centre of the ovary, with two stigmas remaining, the two pendulous ovules, and the cord that separates them.

this Magazine, during the remainder of the interval between the past and the next geological change of our island's surface. We feel this to be an ample gratification for the act of procuring and bringing home the seeds — in itself a pleasure.[66]

In the end, it is almost impossible to feel sorry for this man, in spite of all his infirmities and struggles. Like J.M., one can only close the gate of Number 3, Porchester Terrace, and recognize that Loudon's lifework was in itself a pleasure.

# Appendix A
# Southampton and the Garden Cemetery

Loudon designed cemeteries with the mind of an engineer and the eye of a landscape gardener. Places of remembrance could also be scenes of mild exercise and the subdued enjoyment of trees, shrubs, and open space.

Loudon visited Stoke Park, Buckinghamshire, in the summer of 1833. In the churchyard he found Thomas Gray's tomb and, in the park, a massive pedestal and sarcophagus inscribed with excerpts from Gray's "Elegy." There he paused to reflect on that mid-eighteenth-century poem, a melancholy, wistful plea for rembrance:[1]

> Beneath those rugged elms, that yew-tree's shade,
> Where heaves the turf in many a mouldering heap,
> Each in his narrow cell forever laid,
> The rude forefathers of the hamlet sleep.
>
> (Lines 13–16)

> Yet even these bones from insult to protect,
> Some frail memorial still erected nigh,
> With uncouth rhymes and shapeless sculpture decked,
> Implores the passing tribute of a sigh.
>
> (Lines 77–80)

Whatever compassion Loudon may have felt for Gray's deceased neighbors, his purpose was to report on garden design and management, and his brief comments on Stoke Churchyard were unsentimental. Most of Gray's "rugged elms" were gone, although the yews were still standing. Unfortunately, most of the ruins of a fine old Elizabethan mansion near the churchyard had been removed.[2]

Over the years, particularly in the *Gardener's Magazine* articles which were collected in *On the Laying out, Planting, and Managing of Cemeteries* (1843), Loudon discussed the state of country churchyards, suburban cemeteries, suitable trees, proper drainage, costs and capacities, styles of chapel architecture, and cremation. He acknowledged the utility of some great funeral monuments, because they served as examples of good taste in architecture. The poor man, too, merited a dignified burial, if not an impressive tombstone. But, in the future, Loudon predicted, most of the dead would be cremated, not buried; and this change would come much sooner than even his most enlightened contemporaries might imagine. Disease, noxious vapors, and contaminated waters were the results of common burial practices such as interment in crowded urban churchyards and in above-ground catacombs or churches. In the future,

"Every large town will . . . have a funeral pile, constructed on scientific principles, instead of a cemetery; and the ashes may be preserved in urns, or applied to the roots of a favourite plant."[3]

The seriously ill Loudon may have had his own imminent death on his mind as he wrote. Compare the different sensibilities of Loudon and Gray, both nurtured in the eighteenth-century landscape:

> Even from the tomb the voice of Nature cries,
> Even in our ashes live their wonted fires.

> (Lines 91–92)

Gray suggests that human ashes retain something of Nature's vitality, in a metaphysical sense. Loudon emphasized only the physical reality of ashes, which could nourish a living plant.

Typically avoiding metaphysics, Loudon sought straightforward explanations for anything complex or mysterious. Because of his lack of subtlety and reverence, then, the *Quarterly Review*, generally appreciative of Loudon's literary works, was sternly critical of his book on cemeteries. "It was impossible for a mere utilitarian mind rightly to embrace a subject which hangs so closely on the confines of another world," wrote the *Quarterly* reviewer some months after Loudon's death. "His book, therefore, though useful in many of its suggestions, falls short as a guide to what a Christian cemetery ought to be."[4] These words point to a major opposition between Loudon and his early-Victorian, Christian contemporaries — in the abstract, an opposition between adherents of science and of religion.

Loudon did not dwell on the spiritual comforts of a Christian burial. He wrote about cemeteries as a public health official or a biologist might, and kept his religious views to himself. To him, a cemetery was, above all, the site of the decomposition of deceased bodies and, therefore, a potential threat to the health of the living. It was secondarily a place of remembrance of the dead, and could also provide an open space for exercise, liberal and moral education, and peace of mind for the living.[5]

In a cemetery, as elsewhere, Loudon insisted, the feelings of rich and poor were to be respected equally. He went so far as to censure the economical practice of grazing sheep in cemeteries, for the animals also ate the flowers on the burial mounds of the poor. (The wealthy deceased did not depend on flowers for remembrance; they had monuments of stone.) Loudon also observed that churchyard paths should be adequately wide and level to allow pallbearers a dignified passage without fear of stumbling. But the *Quarterly* reviewer was outraged by Loudon's businesslike, irreverent approach to cemetery management. Loudon suggested, for instance, that paupers be buried in a "temporary cemetery." This could be rented on a twenty-one-year lease, then cultivated as common land seven years after the last burial. "He himself proposes to convert paupers into manure!" the reviewer exclaimed.[6]

In many of his less radical views, Loudon was not alone. He shared the concerns of John Evelyn, Sir Edwin Chadwick, and George Alfred Walker, all of whom had sought to prohibit burials within the limits of large towns and cities.[7] Loudon believed that cemeteries should be sited just outside of towns, so that — properly laid out, "ornamented" with tombs, and planted with labeled trees, shrubs, and herbaceous plants —

the cemetery might become a "school of instruction in architecture, sculpture, landscape gardening, arboriculture, botany and the important points of general gardening: neatness, order, and high keeping."[8] As an example of a well-kept "garden cemetery," Loudon cited St. James's Walk, Liverpool — a few acres in the center of town that had been converted from an old quarry into a place of remembrances of the dead and breathing space for the living.[9]

In *Necropolis Glasguensis* (1831) John Strang observed, "A garden cemetery and monumental decoration are not only beneficial to public morals, to improvement of manners, but are likewise calculated to extend virtuous and generous feelings. . . . A garden cemetery gives a token of a nation's progress in civilisation and in arts, which are its result."[10] Loudon agreed wholeheartedly. He also commended George Frederick Carden who, in 1824, first suggested the creation of public cemeteries in England.[11] Loudon added that, eventually, both botanic gardens and cemeteries should be formed and maintained by municipal societies, not by churches or profit-making companies. But he felt that the time (1834) might not yet be ripe for such public expenditures.

Less than ten years after he made that remark, Loudon was commissioned to design a public cemetery to be maintained by the Corporation of Southampton. He had recently submitted a plan and report to the new Cambridge Cemetery Company, a private concern, and had published the report in the *Gardener's Magazine* for 1843.[12] Later, just months before his death, Loudon was to design a cemetery for the rector of Bath Abbey. These three cemeteries — one public, one private and speculative, one private and ecclesiastical — constitute Loudon's practice in cemetery design, excluding those London cemeteries on which he consulted or advised.[13] Each of the three merits a study in itself. Only the Cambridge Cemetery, however, has received more than passing attention in recent studies — from N. B. Penny.[14] Historians of nineteenth-century cemeteries — notably J. S. Curl, N. B. Penny, and John Morley — have tended to concentrate on the broader issues of cemetery design and management, rather than on individual examples.[15]

Among Loudon's commissions, only the Cambridge Cemetery continues to resemble his original design, with some replanting and demolition. The Bath Abbey Cemetery is by far the most beautiful, owing much to careful planting, benign neglect, and the idyllic views of Perrymead, Widcombe Hill, and Bath. But the Southampton Cemetery, truly a product of committee design, is hardly recognizable today as the subject of Loudon's original report.[16]

The history of the design and execution of the Southampton Cemetery reveals the distinctions between Loudon's approach and concerns for the subject and those of the contemporary articulate public. Loudon's cemetery designs were difficult for the cemetery committee to accept on two counts: they were not truly "picturesque" and they were not "Christian." His relative success in Southampton was to depend on the extent to which the committee would accept a gardenesque, utilitarian design.

The Corporation of Southampton submitted to Parliament a petition for a municipal cemetery. It passed the House of Lords and received royal assent on July 6, 1843.[17] One week later, a Mr. Doswell, surveyor to the borough council, was instructed to mark off fifteen acres in the southwest

*To give the cemetery a char-*
*acter distinct from that of a*
*pleasure ground, Loudon*
*insisted on the predomi-*
*nance of straight walks. Va-*
*riety would be achieved*
*mainly by the planting of*
*trees — some tall, solemn*
*evergreens, such as yews,*
*lining the straight walks,*
*and many common and or-*
*namental kinds in the*
*periphery.*

Fig. 123
Reconstruction of a plan for the
Southampton Cemetery, drawn
by the author, from Loudon's
written description, 1843.

corner of Southampton Common for the new cemetery. Ten acres were to be enclosed at once, and five marked off and reserved. As the cemetery was to be constructed on "the most ornamental and tasteful design," Loudon's consultation was sought. On July 24 Loudon appeared before the committee to offer his views on the subject; he was invited to submit a plan and report.

On August 31, 1843, Loudon's report was read before the cemetery committee and four sets of plans were submitted. As these plans have since disappeared, my reconstruction (fig. 123) is based on Loudon's verbal description in the report and on contemporary town maps. Certain specifications had previously been fixed by the committee: The site was one and one-half miles from town. It was rectangular, running north-

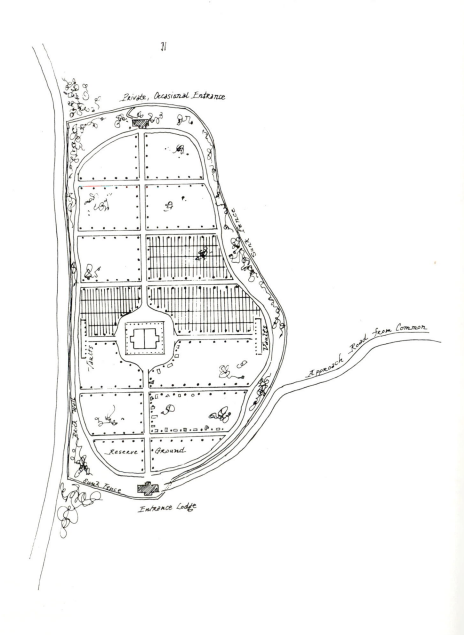

south, sloping gently to the south and to the center. Of the fifteen acres, ten were to be consecrated and five to be set apart for Dissenters. The boundary as planned comprised a seven-foot wall on the west and a sunken fence on the north, east, and south. Loudon was asked to site the lodge and chapels and to decide whether the entire fifteen acres, or only ten, should be appropriated at once. The roads, drainage, plantings, and capacity of the cemetery were also to be determined. The total expenditure was set at seven thousand pounds.

Drainage was Loudon's first concern. The natural slope of the land and the plan to build sunken fences would help to drain surface water from the periphery. To drain the interior, Loudon proposed installing an eighteen-inch barred drain 12 to 15 feet below the intended main road, running north/south. This was meant to dry the subsoil and to serve as an arterial drain for branch drains that might be constructed along the crosswalks. Branch drains from border vaults, catacombs, and the foundations of the chapels could also lead to the arterial drain. Two tile drains sunk two feet below the surface would border the central road to complete the surface drainage of the interior.

Loudon recommended that the entire fifteen acres be appropriated at once in order to avoid the expense of two consecrations. He added that to defer the execution of part of the plan would be false economy, liable to result in neglect or error. If funds were limited, Loudon advocated postponing the erection of the chapels, or reducing their cost, rather than executing only part of the plan for roads and boundaries.

The main road was to run north-south and separate the Dissenters' ground from consecrated ground. Loudon's original scheme appears to differ only slightly from his previous design for the smaller Cambridge cemetery. The central straight avenue would be intersected by several crosswalks — not just two, as in Cambridge. The main roads and walks, including borders, would be slightly raised, and the chapels would be sited relatively close to the main entrance lodge on the south. (The Cambridge chapel, now demolished, had occupied the center of the cemetery.)

With his familiar instinct for equality, Loudon had planned the two Southampton chapels (for the Church of England and for the Dissenters) back-to-back, facing east and west, with an open arcade around the entire block to shelter monumental tablets. Should vaults be needed someday, they could be erected along the eastern and western boundaries, facing their respective chapels. If any catacombs beneath the chapels were desired, Loudon wrote, they should be used only for temporary deposit of coffins, until suitable vaults or catacombs could be prepared in the borders of the cemetery. (He believed that catacombs constructed beneath buildings meant for human use were unsanitary, because of the noxious gases that sometimes escaped from coffins.)

The layout of individual graves for the Southampton cemetery was to be governed by an original principle of Loudon's: that the earth excavated for each coffin should be continuously spread over the adjacent land surface. [18] To understand the utility of this practice, one must be aware of the contemporary situation. In cemeteries which had religious affiliations, most of the land was consecrated. Each interment resulted in the displacement of some "superfluous" soil — the soil displaced by the coffin. This soil, being consecrated, could not be sold; yet it had to be disposed of. Loudon's solution to this problem was to lay out rows of graves in what he called "imaginary squares." Ideally, gravestones and monuments would be restricted to the borders of main walks and roads around the squares, while the interiors remained open space. At any given time, only alternate rows of graves were to be excavated; and the soil left over from interment was to be spread over the adjacent rows. When a row was completely filled, to a depth of four coffins per grave, the adjacent row could be excavated. In time, the interior of these imaginary squares, four rows wide, would have risen several feet above the main walks and roads. If, in fact, individual headstones were erected within these squares, they would have to be continually raised, too — "at a moderate expense."

Loudon assumed that only a few imaginary squares would be under excavation at one time; the rest of the cemetery would thus resemble a garden, though a somber and restrained one. The ground was to be sown with rye grass and white clover. The trees — hollies and thorns already existing in the cemetery grounds — would remain largely intact. The central road and main walks were to be lined with cypresses or Irish yews planted at regular intervals, thirteen or fourteen feet apart. This regularity was not sacred, however. As graves, gravestones, and tombs were needed, trees might be transplanted to accommodate them. Irish yews were preferable to cypresses for this purpose, since they could withstand transplantation at any size.

In his discussion of the number of graves that might be contained within the fifteen-acre cemetery, Loudon's words were brief, his manner businesslike:

In addition to the above calculation of graves if it were determined to close the Cemetery forever, all the four-feet paths might be buried in, and all the walks and roads, which would give at least 4000 additional interments. As it is, reckoning the interments at 600 a year, there is accommodation for about 80 years. But as it may be reasonably supposed that there will be an annual increase of interments proportionate to the rapidly increasing population of Southampton, if we say fifty years we shall probably be nearer the truth.

For his journey to Southampton, his report and plans, Loudon was paid £34.3.4 — perhaps posthumously, as the payment was recorded on January 31, 1844. In any event, Loudon did not live to see the faint shadow of his plans that was realized at the Southampton cemetery. Though the committee apparently had high regard for his opinions, they did not follow his advice entirely. In February 1844 they considered alternate plans for the cemetery by two Southampton nurserymen, W. Page and W. H. Rogers. On February 27th Rogers's plan was in part adopted. Both nurserymen were paid five pounds for their efforts. Today the cemetery is credited to Rogers, and rarely is Loudon's work acknowledged.

The cemetery records reveal a history of vacillation concerning various specifications given by Loudon and Rogers. Initially the committee approved of Loudon's simultaneous appropriation of the entire fifteen acres. Then, on October 30, 1843, the borough council insisted on appropriating only ten acres, with five to be held in reserve. By January 25, 1844, Doswell, the surveyor, had marked out the roads and drains "strictly" to Loudon's plans, given the ten-acre limitation. He also excavated the sunken fence and diverted all springs leading into the cemetery from the periphery, as Loudon had directed. In May, however, the committee disapproved the excavation for the fence and ordered it to be filled with soil displaced by new graves.

Other measures that frustrated Loudon's plan to drain the land included the leveling of his intended elevated site for the two chapels. These were not built as Loudon had proposed — back-to-back in the center of the main road — but free-standing, as the Bishop of Winchester insisted. Each chapel was sited along its own curving side road, screened by trees. The chapel of the Church of England was entirely surrounded by consecrated land, and that for the Dissenters, by unconsecrated land.

In December 1844 W. H. Rogers issued a formal complaint that his plans had not been fully realized. The committee had done away with the circular ring road he had proposed and also had rejected his proposal that Loudon's straight main road be made serpentine. The committee wanted a straight vista, unencumbered by Loudon's back-to-back chapels. This they achieved by compromising Rogers's plan with a curving east-west road that crossed the straight north-south road.

The Southampton Cemetery today displays a few traces of Loudon's original design. Not all the Irish yews bordering the walks and roads are overgrown. Pruned and clipped, they stand like sentinels in perfect equidistance. Some imaginary squares remain fairly open, without gravestones and trees in the interior (fig. 124). The old oaks in the southwest corner remain, along with hollies and thorns, as Loudon had desired. But the cemetery falls short of Loudon's ideal and belies the description given by the *Hampshire Advertiser* two days after it was consecrated:

No site ever selected for a Cemetery has been so favourably situated as this, being backed by a dense mass of wood, having in front some of the finest park scenery in England, and disclosing in all directions, save the Hill Lane side, a variety of View, yet quietness of tone, which harmonises most agreeably with the associations belonging to the place. . . . Mr. W. H. Rogers . . . has

*These large squares were meant to remain open, to accommodate the continual shifting of consecrated earth from successive excavations and burials. Tombs and trees were to appear mainly on the periphery.*

Fig. 124
Remnants of "imaginary squares" designed by J. C. Loudon for the Southampton Cemetery, 1843.

contrived to unite all the requirements of a Cemetery, as regards plotting out of the ground, giving easy access by paths to every part, and yet has deprived it of all formal character, and contrived to retain the fine trees which were already on the land.[19]

Loudon's design for the Southampton Cemetery was apparently too "formal" for the taste of his clients and competitors. His roads and walks did not meander. His drainage system demanded certain artificial elevations and excavations that did not conform to the committee's taste for picturesque landscape. Though removed from town, Loudon's municipal cemetery was urban in character. It demonstrated the order and efficient land use of densely settled towns. The imaginary squares suggest blocks of terrace houses or avenues of monumental buildings with trees lining the streets and gardens or large courtyards on the interior. The cypresses and yews, of course, were to give the specific somber character of a necropolis — a "city of the dead."

Loudon's cemetery plan considered both the dead and the living. The large open squares were meant to allow currents of air to dry the ground and aid in decomposition. The bordering narrow cypresses and yews would not obstruct air currents to any great extent. The trees on the periphery would have been appropriate for an arboretum.

The Southampton Cemetery Committee seems to have shared Loudon's interest in trees, for in 1846 the *Hampshire Advertiser* reported the following collection:

Here are to be seen, for instance, the largest oak, thorn, and holly, on the Common. The shrubs are so disposed as to form vistas, and each plot or division is an arboretum in itself, consisting of hundred varieties [*sic*], among which are to be found some of the handsomest of the Coniferae tribe, as Pinus Cambra [*sic*], Excelsa Douglasii, Cephalonia, Morinda, Cedar of Lebanon, and Laricis [*sic*]. Here are all the weeping trees of the lime, willow, birch, Chinese ash, elm, poplar, and oak, also the Irish junipers, arbor vitae, new hollies, the elegant juniperus repandus, ditto chinense, cyprus [*sic*], laburnums (six varieties), flowering acacias, almonds, thorns, many sorts of arbutus, scarlet and yellow chestnuts, hemlock spruce [Abies Canadensis Michx.], hybrid rhododendrons and magnolias and others. These are all planted twenty feet apart along the borders of the walks, and when they have grown to a proper size will have a most beautiful effect.[20]

Loudon would have objected to the weeping willows. As he had explained to John Ruskin, who enjoyed seeing weeping willows in old churchyards — these trees had associations with water and dampness inappropriate for the image of a properly drained cemetery.[21] But on the whole Loudon would have been pleased to see this cemetery-arboretum at Southampton, maintained by the municipal corporation "at the expense of all, for the benefit of all."

The problems inherent in design by committee Loudon never resolved. In 1831 several directors had ruined his plan for the Birmingham Botanical Garden by eliminating his major focus, the circular greenhouses. Frustrated by the partial realization of that plan, Loudon would have been irked as well by the actions of the committee in Southampton. True, in speaking as a compiler of design possibilities in the *Encyclopaedia of Architecture*, Loudon had announced his intention "to instruct and not to lead." But when he worked as a professional landscape gardener, he expected his instructions to be followed. The Southampton Cemetery Committee was willing to listen, but, in the end, they would not follow. They had tastes of their own — and the interests of the Church of England — to gratify.

What traveller or tourist is there that does not make the churchyard of the village one of the first scenes which he visits; and does not receive from it his first impressions of the clergyman, the people, and consequently the general character of the inhabitants?[22]

Tomb of J.C.Loundon (Fig. 4)

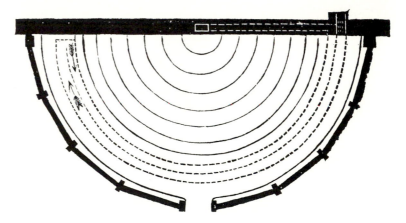

# Appendix B
# Works by J.C.Loudon

The following list includes all works by Loudon cited in the text and notes, as well as certain other works, with brief notes on later editions, impressions, revisions, and additional supplements. For more complete bibliographic information, the reader is advised to consult the catalogues of the British Library (London), the National Library of Scotland (Edinburgh), and the Bibliothèque Nationale (Paris); the National Union Catalogue of the Library of Congress (Washington, D.C.); and the Union Catalogue of Harvard University (Cambridge, Massachusetts). Other sources for bibliographic information include Ben Weinreb's list of Loudon's works in volume 1 of the five-volume collection of the *Architectural Magazine* (London: Cornmarket Reprints Limited, 1972) and the list found in *John Claudius Loudon and the Early Nineteenth Century in Great Britain*, edited by Elisabeth B.MacDougall (Washington, D.C.: Dumbarton Oaks, 1980), pages 127–33.

## Published Works:
## Books and Articles

### 1803
"Hints respecting the manner of laying out the grounds of the Public Squares in London, to the utmost picturesque advantage." *Literary Journal* 2, no. 12 (December 31, 1803): cols. 739–42 (London).

### 1804
"Hints on Hedges and Hedge-Row Timber." *Gentleman's Magazine* 74, pt. 1 (January 1804): 20–21.

*Observations on the Formation and Management of Useful and Ornamental Plantations; on the Theory and Practice of Landscape Gardening; and on Gaining and Embanking Land from Rivers or the Sea.* Edinburgh: A.Constable.

### 1805
*A Short Treatise on several improvements recently made in Hot-houses; by which from four-fifths to nine-tenths of the fuel commonly used will be saved; time, labour, and risk, greatly lessened; and several other advantages produced. And which are applicable to hot-houses already erected, or to the construction of new hot-houses.* Edinburgh: Printed for the Author.

### 1806
*A Treatise on Forming, Improving, and Managing Country Residences; and on the Choice of Situations Appropriate to Every Class of Purchasers. In All Which the Object in View is to Unite in a better manner than has hitherto been done, a Taste Founded in Nature with Economy and Utility, in constructing or improving Mansions, and other Rural Buildings, so as to combine Architectural Fitness with Picturesque Effect.* 2 vols. London: Longman. Reprinted, in facsimile. Westmead, Farnborough, Hampshire: Gregg International Publishers Ltd., 1971.

### 1807
*Engravings, with Descriptions, illustrative of the difference between the modern style of rural architecture and the improvement of scenery, and that displayed in a treatise on country residences, and practiced by Mr. Loudon.* London.

### 1808
*An Immediate and Effectual Mode of Raising the Rental of the Landed Property of England; and Rendering Great Britain Independent of Other Nations for a Supply of Bread Corn. With an Appendix containing Hints to Commercial Capitalists, and to the Tenantry of Scotland.* By a Scotch Farmer, now Farming in Middlesex. London: Longman.

"On Rural Embellishments." *Farmer's Magazine* (Edinburgh) 9 (June 1808): 158–61.

### 1809
*The Utility of Agricultural Knowledge to the Sons of the Landed Proprietors of England — And to Young Men intended for Estate Agents: Illustrated by what has taken place in Scotland. With an Account of an Institution formed for Agricultural Pupils in Oxfordshire.* By a Scotch Farmer and Land Agent, resident in that County. London.

### 1811
*An Account of the Paper Roofs used at Tew Lodge, Oxon. So decidedly preferable for Churches, Warehouses and Agricultural Buildings, in point of Economy, Durability and Elegance.* London: J. Harding.

*Designs for Laying out Farms and Farm-Buildings, in the Scotch Style; adapted to England: Including an account of Tew Lodge Farm, Oxfordshire, with an Opinion on the subject of Breaking up Grass Lands.* London: Harding. Reprinted, 1812. An edition that appeared in 1812 was titled *Observations on Laying out Farms.*

### 1812
*Hints on the Formation of Gardens and Pleasure Grounds. With Designs, in Various Styles of Rural Embellishment: Comprising plans for laying out flower, fruit and kitchen gardens, To which is added, a priced catalogue of fruit and forest trees, shrubs and plants, adapted to villa grounds.* London: Harding and Wright for J.Harding. Another edition appeared in 1813.

*A Treatise on the Culture of Wheat, Recommending a System of Management founded upon the successful experience of the Author.* By a Practical Farmer. London.

### 1817
*Remarks on the Construction of Hot-houses, pointing out the most advantageous forms, materials and contriv-*

*ances to be used in their construction; also, a review of the various methods of building them in foreign countries as well as in England.* London: J. Taylor.

### 1818

*A comparative View of the common and curvilinear Mode of roofing Hot-houses.* Folio. London.

"Design for a Bridge across the Mersey at Runcorn. *Annals of Philosophy; or, Magazine of Chemistry, Mineralogy, Mechanics, Natural History, Agriculture, and the Arts* 11 (January 1818): 14–27.

*Sketches of Curvilinear Hot-houses; With a Description of the Various Purposes in Horticultural and General Architecture, to which a solid Iron Sash Bar (lately invented) is applicable.* London.

### 1820

"On the Origin of English Gardening." *New Monthly Magazine* 13 (February 1820): 191–92.

### 1821

*Esquisse pour une Histoire Générale du Jardinage, etc./Outline for a General History of Gardening, and an Account of its Present State Throughout the World.* London: Printed for the Author.

### 1822

*The Different Modes of Cultivating the Pine Apple, from its first Introduction in Europe to the Improvements of T.A.Knight, Esq.* By a member of the Horticultural Society. London: Longman.

*An Encyclopaedia of Gardening; Comprising the Theory and Practice of Horticulture, Floriculture, Arboriculture, and Landscape Gardening. Including all the Latest Improvements; A General History of Gardening in all Countries; and a Statistical View of its Present State, with Suggestions for its Future Progress in the British Isles,* ed. J.C.Loudon. London: Longman. Several later editions and revisions were brought out between 1824 and 1878. The work was translated into German as *Encyclopädie des Gartenwesens.* Two 8vo. vols. of text and one 4to vol. of plates. Weimar, 1823–26.

### 1824

*The Green-House Companion, Comprising a General Course of Green-House and Conservatory Practice throughout the Year; A Natural Arrangement of all the Green-House Plants in Cultivation with a Descriptive Catalogue of the most desirable to form a collection, their proper soils, modes of propagation, management, and references to botanical works in which they are figured. Also, the proper treatment of Flowers in Rooms, and Bulbs in Water Glasses.* London: Harding, Triphook, and Lepard, and J.Harding. Two later printings appeared, in 1825 and 1832.

### 1825

*An Encyclopaedia of Agriculture: Comprising the Theory and Practice of the Valuation, Transfer, Laying out, Improvement, and Management of Landed Property, and of the Cultivation and Economy of the Animal and Vegetable Productions of Agriculture, Including all the latest Improvements; A General History of Agriculture in all Countries; A Statistical View of its Present State, with suggestions for its Future Progress, in the British Isles.* Ed. J.C.Loudon. London: A. and R.Spottiswoode for Longman. This work ran through several editions from 1826 through 1833. A four-volume translation into French by Oscar Le Clerc was completed about 1834.

### 1826

*Encyclopädie des Landwirthschaft.* Weimar. Published in parts, beginning in March.

### 1827

*Remarks on the Benefits which would Result to Gardening and Gardeners, from the Establishment of Garden Libraries, and to Labourers and others of the Rural Population from the Establishment of Village Libraries and Labourers' Institutions.* London.

### 1829

*An Encyclopaedia of Plants. Comprising the description, specific character, culture, history, application in the arts, and every desirable particular respecting all the plants indigenous, cultivated in, or introduced to Britain, combining all the advantages of a Linnaean and Jussieuean* species plantarum, *an historia plantarum, a grammar of botany, and a dictionary of botany and vegetable culture.* . . . Ed. J.C.Loudon . . . , the specific characters by an eminent botanist [John Lindley], the drawings by J.D.C.Sowerby, F.L.S.; and the engravings by R.Branston. London: Longman. This work was reprinted, with supplements, several times between 1836 and 1880, and was translated into German as *Encyclopädie Der Pflanzen* (Jena, 1836–41; 1836–47). The London edition of 1855 was reprinted in India (Jaipur: Prakash Publishers, 1973).

*Des Etablissements pour l'éducation publique en Bavière, dans le Würtemberg, et dans le pays de Bade, et remarques sur les améliorations à introduire dans ces établissements pour les faire adopter en France, en Angleterre et autres pays.* Paris.

*Parochial Institutions; or, Outline of a plan for a National Education Establishment suitable to the children of all ranks, from infancy to the age of puberty; as a substitute for the National Churches of England, Scotland and Ireland.* London: Privately printed. An abridged version — with all references to the disestablishment of the national churches omitted — appeared in Loudon's *Gard. Mag.* 5 (December 1829): 692–704.

### 1830

*Elementary Details of Pictorial Map drawing in 154 lessons, explained in English, French and German.* London.

*The Great Objects to be Attained by Reform; In a Letter to the Editor of the Morning Advertiser.* London.

*Loudon's Hortus Britannicus. A Catalogue of all the Plants indigenous, cultivated in, or introduced to Britain.* London: Longman. This work was published in new editions, with supplements, from 1832 through 1850.

*A Manual of Cottage Gardening, Husbandry, and Architecture: Including plans, elevations, and sections of three designs for model cottages; descriptions of a mode by which every cottager may grow his own fuel; a* new mode of heating cottages; a scheme for labourers and others to build their own cottages, on the cooperative system; calendarial tables of the culture and produce of cottage gardens throughout the year; directions for brewing, baking, etc. and the process for making sugar from mangold wurzel. Assisted by Mr. Ellis, Mr. Gorrie, Mr. Taylor, etc. London: A. and R. Spottiswoode for the Author. This work was extracted from Loudon's article "On Cottage Husbandry and Architecture, Chiefly with reference to certain Prize Essays received on Cottage Gardening, and to projected Encyclopaedias on these Subjects," *Gard. Mag.* 6 (April 1830): 139–67. It reappeared as *The Cottager's Manual of Husbandry, Architecture, Domestic Economy, and Gardening* in 1834 (London), and was republished in 1840 in *British Husbandry*, edited by J.F.Burke, which was issued as volume 3 of the *Library of Useful Knowledge*.

*Traité de la composition et de l'exécution des jardins d'ornement . . . Extrait, sur un nouveau plan, de "l'Encyclopédie du Jardinage" de M.J.C.Loudon, et traduit de l'anglais par J.-M.Chopin; revu et annoté par M. le Chevalier Soulange Bodin.* In *Encyclopédie Portative, ou Résumé universel des Sciences, des Lettres et des Arts.* Under the direction of C.F.Bailly de Merlieux. Paris, 1825–30. This French translation and abridgment was further abridged, also in 1830, as *Précis de l'art de la composition et de l'exécution des jardins d'ornement.* Paris: au bureau de l'Encyclopédie Portative, etc.

### 1830–33

*Illustrations of Landscape Gardening and Garden Architecture; or, A Collection of Designs, Original and Executed for Laying out Country Residences, of every degree of extent, from the cottage and farm to the national palace and public park or garden; kitchen gardens, Flower Gardens, Cemeteries, &c., In different styles, by different artists of different periods and countries. Accompanied by Letter press descriptions in English, French and German.* Ed. J.C.Loudon. London, Paris, Strasburg.

### 1832

"Colleges for Working Men." *Mechanics' Magazine* 16, no. 443 (February 4, 1832): 322–24. The article is based on a project Loudon developed in 1818.

### 1832–33

*An Encyclopaedia of Cottage, Farm, and Villa Architecture and Furniture; Containing Numerous Designs for Dwellings, from the Villa to the Cottage and the Farm, Including Farm Houses, Farmeries, and other Agricultural Buildings; Country Inns, Public Houses, and Parochial Schools: With the Requisite Fittings-up, Fixtures, and Furniture; and Appropriate Offices, Gardens, and Garden Scenery; Each Design Accompanied by Analytical and Critical Remarks.* London: Longman. This work went through several editions, with supplements, from 1835 through 1869. An American edition (New York) appeared in 1883.

### 1836–38

*The Suburban Gardener and Villa Companion: Comprising the choice of a suburban villa residence, or of a situation on which to form one; the arrangement and furnishing of the house; and the laying out, planting and general management of the garden and grounds.* London: H.Bohn. This work, first brought out in monthly installments, was revised and edited by Jane Webb Loudon, and reappeared as *The Villa Gardener* in 1850.

### 1838

*Arboretum et Fruticetum Britannicum; or, The Trees and Shrubs of Britain, native and foreign; Pictorially and Botanically delineated, and Scientifically and Popularly described; with their propagation, culture, management, and uses in the arts, in useful and ornamental plantations and in landscape gardening, preceded by a historical and geographical outline of the trees and shrubs in temperate climates throughout the world.* 8 vols. London: A. Spottiswoode for the Author. This work went through several impressions and at least two editions from 1838 through 1854.

*Hortus Lignosus Londinensis; or, A Catalogue of all Ligneous Plants, indigenous and foreign, hardy and half-hardy, cultivated in the gardens and grounds in the neighbourhood of London.* London: Printed for the Author. Another edition appeared in 1842.

### 1839

*Coniferae Britannicae, Pictorially and Botanically Delineated and Scientifically and Popularly Described, with their Propagation, Culture and Management.* London. Extracted from the *Arboretum et Fruticetum Britannicum.*

### 1840

*The Derby Arboretum: Containing a catalogue of the trees and shrubs included in it; a description of the grounds and directions for their management; a copy of the address delivered when it was presented to the Town Council of Derby; by its founder, Joseph Strutt, Esq. And an account of the ceremonies which took place when it was opened to the public, on September 16, 1840.* London: Longman.

*The Landscape Gardening and Landscape Architecture of the late Humphry Repton, Esq., Being His Entire Works on these Subjects. A new edition, with an Historical and Scientific Introduction, a Systematic Analysis, a Biographical Notice, Notes and a Copious Alphabetical Index.* Ed. J.C.Loudon. London: Whitehead for the Editor. Reprinted in facsimile. Edinburgh: Longman, 1969.

### 1842

*An Encyclopaedia of Trees and Shrubs; Being the Arboretum et Fruticetum Britannicum, Abridged: Containing the Hardy Trees and Shrubs of Britain, Native and Foreign, Scientifically and Popularly Described; With their Propagation, Culture, and Uses in the Arts; and with Engravings of nearly all the Species. Abridged from the Large Edition in Eight Volumes, and Adapted for the use of Nurserymen, Gardeners and Foresters.* London: Printed for the Author and Longman. This work was published in several editions in London through 1883; an American edition (New York) appeared in 1875.

*The Suburban Horticulturist; or, An Attempt to teach the Science and Practice of the Culture and Management of the Kitchen, Fruit, and Forc-*

ing Garden to those who have had no previous Knowledge or Practice in these Departments of Gardening. London: Bradbury and Evans for the Author. This work was reprinted in 1845, and a revised version appeared in 1849 and 1860 as *The Horticulturist*. It was edited and revised by William Robinson in 1871 and reprinted in 1875 in London.

[Contrib.], *A Dictionary of Science, Literature and Art . . . With the derivation and definition of all the terms in general use*. Ed. William Thomas Brande, assisted by Joseph Cauvin . . . [and others, including J.C.Loudon]. London. The New York edition appeared in 1847.

### 1843

*On the Laying out, Planting, and Managing of Cemeteries and on the Improvement of Churchyards*. London: A.Spottiswoode for the Author. Reprinted in facsimile. Redhill, Surrey: Ivelet Books Ltd, 1981.

### 1845

*Self-Instruction for Young Gardeners, Foresters, Bailiffs, Land-Stewards and Farmers; in Arithmetic and Bookkeeping, Geometry, Mensuration, and Practical Trigonometry, Mechanics, Hydrostatics, and Hydraulics, Land-Surveying, Levelling, Planning and Mapping, Architectural Drawing, and Isometrical Projection and Perspective; With examples showing their application to Horticultural and Agricultural Purposes*. By the late J.C.Loudon . . . With a Memoir of the Author. London: A.Spottiswoode for Longman. The memoir was written by Jane Loudon. The work was completed by one Dr. Jamieson with contributions from John Robertson, one of Loudon's former draftsmen; a Mr. Osborn of Fulham Nursery; a Mr. Wooster, Loudon's last amanuensis; Samuel Taylor; Richard Varden; a Professor Donaldson; and James Munro. The work was reprinted in 1847 and 1848.

## Periodicals Edited by Loudon

### 1826–44

*The Gardener's Magazine, and Register of Rural and Domestic Improvement*. 19 vols. London: Longman.

First series, 1826–34. Second series (or "decade"), 1835–44. Completed, January 1844. (This magazine first appeared quarterly, beginning in January 1826. By January 1827 it was published every two months, and by April 1834, it was published monthly.)

### 1828–36

*The Magazine of Natural History, and Journal of Zoology, Botany, Mineralogy, Geology, and Meteorology*. Ed. J.C.Loudon, with assistance from John Denson. London: Longman. From 1837 to 1840 the magazine was edited by Edward Charlesworth. It then merged into the *Annals of Natural History*, which continued as *The Annals and Magazine of Natural History, including Zoology, Botany, and Geology*. Ed. Sir William Jardine, P.J.Selby, et al.

### 1834–39

*The Architectural Magazine, and Journal of Improvement in Architecture, Building, and Furnishing, and in the Various Arts and Trades Connected therewith*. 5 vols. London: Longman. Completed, January 1839. Reprinted in facsimile. London: Cornmarket Reprints Ltd., 1972.

### 1840–41

*The Gardener's Gazette* (begun January 7, 1837, London). Loudon conducted the horticultural department of the *Gazette* from November 14, 1840, through November 6, 1841.

## A Selection of Loudon's Published Letters

This list includes both personal correspondence and untitled articles appearing in British periodical literature.

### 1805

June 5. *Farmer's Magazine* (Edinburgh), 6 (August 1805): 356–62. On principles of landscape gardening, and replying to criticism of his *Obs. on Gard*.

### 1818

May 12. *Gentleman's Magazine* 88, pt. 1 (June 1818): 494–96. On extending the Regent's Canal, London, and on improving Kensington Gardens and Hyde Park, London.

### 1824

February 20. To J.D.C.Sowerby, Esq. Published in John Gloag, *Mr. Loudon's England* (Newcastle-upon-Tyne: Oriel Press, 1970), 54. Gives instructions for Sowerby's illustrations for the *Encyc. Gard*.

### 1829

March 17. To William Jerdan. Published in Jerdan, "Characteristic Letters," *Leisure Hour* (February 1, 1869): 140. On cuckoos, chrysanthemums, and the small size of Loudon's garden in Bayswater.

September 13. To T.A.Knight, Esq. Published in *Gard. Mag*. 5 (December 1829): 719. On Knight's controversial paper "On the Culture of the Potatoe" in *Trans. Hort. Soc*. 7, pt. 3: 405, which had been abridged in *Gard. Mag*. 5 (June 1829): 294–96.

### 1830

November 22. *The Morning Advertiser* (London), November 24, 1830. On the need for parliamentary reform. Later printed as a pamphlet, *The Great Objects to be Attained by Reform* (London, 1830).

### 1832

N.d. *Times* (London), April 12, 1832. On a proposal for hastening passage of the Reform Bill in Parliament by collective action on the part of consumers.

### 1833

March 9. To William Jerdan. Published in Jerdan, "Characteristic Letters," *Leisure Hour* (February 1, 1869): 141. On William Wilkins's National Gallery, London, and on Nicholas Carlisle's *Hints on Rural Residences*.

### 1834

May 23. *Blackwood's Edinburgh Magazine* 36 (September 1834): 96. Replies to Blackwood's review of Loudon's *Encyc. Gard*.

### 1837

September 2. To William Jerdan. Published in Jerdan, "Characteristic Letters," *Leisure Hour* (February 1, 1869): 141. On Jerdan's review of Loudon's *Encyc. Arch*., and on the Loudons' preoccupation with work.

### 1838

November 30. To John James Ruskin. Extract published in *The Works of John Ruskin*, ed. E.T.Cook and

Alexander Wedderburn, 39 vols. (London: George Allen & Unwin Ltd., 1903–12), 1: xxxvii. On John Ruskin, aged nineteen, the "greatest natural genius" Loudon says he has ever known.

### 1839
April 5. *Times* (London), April 11, 1839. On the current improvements in Hyde Park.

April 22. *Times* (London), May 9, 1839. On the beneficial effects of a uniform, cheap rate of postage on periodical literature.

May 9. *Times* (London), May 10, 1839. On the design for the Royal Botanic Society's garden in Regent's Park.

### 1840
October 30. *Morning Chronicle*, November 3, 1840. On the rumored plans to convert part of the kitchen gardens of Kensington Palace for building, and on Loudon's preference for retaining the land as public parkland.

October 30. *Times* (London), October 31, 1840. Urges that the kitchen gardens of Kensington Palace be conserved for public parkland.

November 2. *Times* (London), November 4, 1840. Continues to press for conservation of the Kensington Palace land.

November 3. *Morning Chronicle*, November 4, 1840. Continues the struggle for conservation of the former kitchen gardens.

November 7. *Morning Chronicle*, November 11, 1840. Recommends the formation of a public sunken north-south road across Kensington Gardens, discusses the benefits of carrying one road or path over another in both public and private grounds, and warns against lining such a public road with private houses.

### 1843
October 3. *Gardener's Chronicle*, October 7, 1843: 694. Refutes the rumor that he is "lying dangerously ill at Southampton," explains recent visit to Isle of Wight and Southampton "for change of air," and cites his more recent professional

visits to Bath and Oxfordshire as proof of his physical recovery.

## Unpublished Works: Manuscripts, Reports, Letters, and Miscellany

### 1803
"A Treatise on the Improvements proposed for Scone, an estate pertaining to the Right Honorable, the Earl of Mansfield, in Perthshire; Illustrated with Sketches and detached plans of the estate." By J. Loudon, Landscape Gardener and Improver. Edinburgh. 10th October. In the Muniments of the Earl of Mansfield, Scone Palace, Perth, vol. 117, which can be examined in the National Register of Archives, West Register House, Edinburgh.

### 1806
"Sketches of the Alterations and Additions proposed to be made on Barnbarrow House . . . " This folio is accompanied by a letter of explanation. Barnbarrow House was the residence of Robert Vans Agnew in Wigtonshire (or Kirkcudbrightshire; references differ). In the Paul Mellon Collection/Abbey Scenery, Upperville, Virginia.

### 1807
"Report on the intended Embankments and Shorelands of Tremadoc, the Property of W.A. Madocks, Esq., M.P., etc., etc., in Carnarvonshire," December 23, 1807; with a footnote dated 24 December 1807, Tremadoc. In manuscript copy at the National Library of Wales, Aberystwyth.

### 1811
"Hints for a National Garden," An Address delivered to the Linnaean Society (London), December 17, 1811. The original manuscript is preserved in the Library of the Linnaean Society, London. A photocopy of the manuscript is kept in the library of Kew Gardens.

### 1818
"Report on Certain Plans of Improvement, Proposed for the Park, and Demesne Lands, of Bullmarsh Court, the Property and Residence of James Wheble, Esq., in Berkshire." Report is accompanied by a large atlas, "Maps and Panoramic

Views Relative to Bullmarsh Park," dated December 1818. In the Abbey Collection of the Yale Center for British Art, New Haven, Connecticut.

### 1820
"Remarks on certain improvements proposed for the park and grounds at Dovecot House [South Lancashire], the property of Adam Dugdale Esqre, referring to a folio volume of delineations by J.C. Loudon." London. Signed, "J.C. Loudon, Bayswater House, 5th April 1820." In the Abbey Collection of the Yale Center for British Art, New Haven, Connecticut.

### 1835
Letters to Sir Walter Calverly Trevelyan, of Wallington Hall, Northumberland, dated 29 January and 10 August, 1835, from Bayswater. (On various topics, including information on trees for the *Arboretum et Fruticetum Britannicum*). In the Walter Calverly Trevelyan Papers, Box 175, in the Library of the University of Newcastle-upon-Tyne. This box also includes letters from Jane and Agnes Loudon to Sir Walter and Lady Pauline Trevelyan.

"Remarks Relating to the Plan for Improving the Approach Road to Gunnersbury Park, the Residence of N.M. Rothschild, Esq." Dated 1 December 1835. A typescript of the original report is kept in the Gunnersbury Park Museum, Old Brentford, West London. The essence of these remarks was published in *Gard. Mag.* 12 (February 1836): 53–59, with a plan; the proprietor and residence were not, however, identified.

### 1836
Letter to Joseph Hume, M.P., on a proposed new site for the houses of Parliament. Mention of an attachment refers to twenty-five copies of Loudon's article "A New Site for the Houses of Parliament," reprinted from *Arch. Mag.* 3 (March 1836): 100–03. In the Library of University College, London, under the listing "Hume Tracts."

### 1838
The last will and testament of John Claudius Loudon, of No. 3, Porchester Terrace, London. Dated 30

November 1838. In Public Records
Office, London, PROB–11–1998, p.
379.

    1843

"Report on Certain Improvements
proposed to be made at Coleshill
House, the seat of the Earl of Radnor." Signed, "J.C.Loudon, Bayswater, May 2nd 1843." In the
Berkshire County Record Office.

"Report on the Design for a Cemetery Proposed to be formed at Southampton by authority of an Act of
Parliament and under the Direction
of the Mayor and the Town Council." Signed, "J.C.Loudon, Bayswater, August 31st/43." In the
Southampton Civic Record Office.

Letter to Professor John Stevens
Henslow. Dated December 1, 1843,
Bayswater. (Explains Loudon's financial embarrassment and physical
infirmities; requests that Professor
Henslow order a copy of *Arboretum
et Fruticetum Britannicum*.) Facsimile copy, (AAF, E76/35) with
manuscript note, preserved in the
University Library, Edinburgh.

# Appendix C
# Chronology

The following is an outline of Loudon's activities as a professional landscape gardener, as well as of some of the main events in his personal life. No attempt has been made to list all of his projects in their various stages of completion. Where doubts about the precise date of an event or project have been raised, the earliest reasonable date is generally given. Loudon's own recollections of dates and events have been corroborated, when possible, by the recollections of others and by various sources cited in the notes to each chapter.

The main sources for this chronology are Loudon's own works and Jane Loudon's "Life of Loudon," which first appeared in Loudon's posthumous *Self-Instruction for Young Gardeners*. Further information on Loudon's early practice in Scotland is found in A. A. Tait, *The Landscape Garden in Scotland, 1735–1835* (Edinburgh: Edinburgh University Press, 1980).

## 1783
Born April 8 in Cambuslang, Lanarkshire, at the home of his mother's only sister. Was the eldest of several children of William Loudon, farmer, of Kerse Hall, near Gogar and Edinburgh; and of Agnes Loudon, daughter of Claudius Somers, an elder of the Church of Scotland in Cambuslang.

## 1794
Begins part-time work in Dalry, near Edinburgh, as draftsman and general assistant to John Mawer, nurseryman, landscape gardener, and hothouse designer. Studies in an Edinburgh school and boards with an uncle.

## 1798
Death of Mawer. Becomes part-time apprentice to the nurserymen and landscape gardeners Messrs. Dicksons and Shade, at Leith Walk, Edinburgh.

## 1798–1802
Attends Andrew Coventry's lectures on agriculture and rural economy at the University of Edinburgh. Also attends an unnamed architectural school. During vacations, works on father's farm.

## 1802
First appearance in print (before eighteenth birthday): translation of the life of Abelard for the periodical *Shrarton's Encyclopaedia*.

## 1803
First visit to London. With Coventry's letters of introduction, meets James Sowerby, Sir Joseph Banks, and Jeremy Bentham. Is commissioned to propose improvements for the grounds of Scone Palace, Perthshire, seat of the third earl of Mansfield.

## 1804
To date, has been employed by the duchess of Brunswick at Brunswick House, Blackheath; by Colonel Duncan at Glenfuir, Stirlingshire; by Richard Howat, Esq., at Maybo (or "Mabie"), Kirkcudbrightshire (or Dumfriesshire; references differ); and by Gideon Bikerdyke (or "Bickerdike"), Esq., at Kingswood Lodge, Surrey. Has made estimates for embankment projects of Lord Keith and the earl of Selkirk. Exhibits three landscapes at the Royal Academy: a scene at Scone; a view of the Crammond River, near Edinburgh; and a house at Balliad, Perthshire, for P. Campbell, Esq.

## 1805
By February has been employed by Sir Hew Hamilton Dalrymple, Bart., at Leuchie (or "Leughie") House, North Berwick, Haddingtonshire (East Lothian); and by the end of 1805, by T. Botfield, Esq., at Hopton Court, Shropshire; by the earl of Wemyss at Gosford, Haddingtonshire; by Walter Fawkes, Esq., at Farnley Hall, Yorkshire; and by Thomas Johnes, Esq., at Havod (or "Hafod"), Cardiganshire. Is elected to the Society of Arts, Commerce, etc., London, March 13.

## 1806
Publishes *Country Res.*, October. Gives address as 90, Newman Street, London. By 1806 has been employed by Robert Vans Agnew, Esq., at Barnbarrow, Wigtonshire (or Kirkcudbrightshire; references differ); by General Drummond, at Machany Castle, Perthshire; by Thomas Allan, Esq., at Linkhouse, Haddingtonshire; by John Hawthorn, Esq., at Castlewigg, Wigtonshire; by Lord Gwydir (?) at Drummond Castle, Perthshire; by James Gillespie, Esq., at Mountwhannie (or "Mountquhanie"), Fifeshire; by the earl of Mansfield at Schaw Park, Clackmannanshire; by J. B. Howell, Esq., at Priknash, Gloucestershire; by William Everett, Esq., at Palatine House, Middlesex; by Walden Orme, Esq., at Trigger Hall, Middlesex; and by the earl of Harewood at Harewood, Yorkshire. Is elected a fellow of the Linnaean Society, London, February 4. Visits Tremadoc, North Wales, to consult on William Madocks's embankment projects. Knee becomes ankylosed and right arm permanently contracted as result of contracting rheumatic fever.

## 1807
Retires to a farmhouse in Pinner, Middlesex. William Loudon joins son as a tenant farmer of Wood Hall Farm, Pinner, and takes lease on Kenton Farm, Middlesex.

## 1808
In April, publishes *Landed Prop.* (dedicated to George Harley Drummond, Esq., of Dumtochty Castle, Kincardine, and Stanmore, Middlesex). Summoned by G. F. Stratton, Great Tew, Oxfordshire, to revalue

lands. Becomes tenant of Tew Lodge Farm.

### 1809

Establishes small agricultural college at Tew. In February, publishes *Utility of Agricultural Knowledge* (dedicated to Stratton). Employed by Richard Mytton, Esq., at Garth, Montgomeryshire, to improve mansion and stables. Purchases Mimbury Fort, in Ramsbury, Wiltshire, intending to improve farm and erect a Lancasterian School. William Loudon dies, December 29.

### 1811

Leaves Tew, February. Address is now 42, Pall Mall, London. On May 30 publishes *Designs for Farms* (dedicated to the Prince Regent). By 1811 has been employed by Edward Moulton-Barrett at Hope End, near Ledbury, Herefordshire.

### 1812

Publishes *Treatise on Wheat* (dedicated to Stratton). Exhibits a landscape at the Royal Academy. Has accumulated £15,000 through labors as landscape gardener, farmer, and land agent.

### 1812–13

Travels through the south of England.

### 1813–14

First Continental journey, sailing from Harwich, March 16. Visits Gothenburg, Memel, Königsberg, Elbing, Marienburg, and Danzig. Stays two weeks in Berlin, then continues to Frankfort, Posen, Warsaw, Tycocyn, Grodno, Wilna, Kosnow, and Mitton. Arrives Riga, September 30. Spends three or four months in St. Petersburg. Arrives Moscow, March 4; departs June 2. Arrives Kiev, June 15. Visits Cracow, Vienna, Prague, Dresden, Leipzig, Magdeburg, Hamburg. Arrives Yarmouth, September 27. En route, has been elected to the Imperial Society of Moscow, Natural History Society of Berlin, Royal Economical Society of Potsdam, and various other societies.

### 1814

In London, finds that banker has mishandled finances and depleted his fortune. Health suffers. Designs a ducted hot-air heating system for the earl of Radnor at Coleshill, Berkshire (now Oxfordshire).

### 1815

First trip to Paris. Attempts to recover part of financial losses. Visits Girardin's seat, Ermenonville, and Boursault's nursery garden, rue Blanche, Paris.

### 1816–17

Moves from 82, Newman Street to "The Hermitage," or "Bayswaterhouse." Mother and sisters join him. Health still impaired. Experiments with construction of hothouses.

### 1817

In April publishes *Remarks on Hothouses* (dedicated to Sir Joseph Banks). Exhibits painting of the Church of St. Anne, Wilna, Poland at Royal Academy.

### 1818

In *Sketches of Hot-houses*, published in March, describes his recently invented sash bar. Designs eight-story apartment block for working men and families in May. Consults with Banks about feasibility of erecting such a structure. Becomes ill; housing project is not undertaken. In December, completes elaborate manuscript, plans, and views of proposed improvements at Bullmarsh Court, Berkshire, residence of James Wheble, Esq.

### 1819

Second Continental journey, to gather material for *Encyc. Gard.* Reaches Paris May 30 with letters of introduction from Banks. Visits Lyons, Avignon, Marseilles, Nice. Sails from Genoa to Leghorn, arriving July 8. Visits Pisa, Florence, Rome, Naples, Pompeii, Herculaneum. Returns August 21 to Florence. Visits Bologna, Ferrara, Venice, Padua, Vicenza, Milan, Borromean Isles, Isola Bella. Visits Geneva, Basel, and Strasbourg. Proceeds to Brussels, Ghent, Bruges, Ostend. Arrives back in Bayswater, October 9.

### 1820

Proposes landscape improvements for Dovecot House, South Lancashire, residence of Adam Dugdale, Esq., in March or April. Manuscript report completed by an amanuensis as Loudon suffers from chronic rheumatism in right arm. Visits Brighton to try Mahomed's vapor baths. Submits to pain of "shampooing" and stretching the arm. The operation fractures his arm, close to the shoulder; it never heals properly.

### 1822

In March, publishes *Encyc. Gard.*, which establishes his horticultural reputation in Britain and abroad.

### 1823–24

Designs and supervises the construction of his own house, No. 3, Porchester Terrace, Bayswater. Suffers acute pain, as rheumatism contracts thumb and two fingers of the left hand.

### 1826

Begins *Gard. Mag.*, January, as quarterly supplement to *Encyc. Gard.* The German translation of *Encyc. Gard.* is published serially in Weimar through May. In October tours gardens in Rutlandshire, Nottinghamshire, Lincolnshire, Yorkshire, Derbyshire, Staffordshire, and Worcestershire. Spends ten days at unnamed country residence near Gainsborough, Lincolnshire, staking out improvements.

### 1827

In *Gard. Mag.* (January) announces competition for forming libraries for benefit of working gardeners. Earliest libraries formed at his suggestion include Northwick Park Garden Library (near Moreton in the Marsh, Gloucestershire, seat of Lord Northwick, established January 6); Mackay's Clapton Nursery Library (near London, est. January 8); and Thompson's Welbeck Garden Library (Nottinghamshire, seat of duke of Portland, est. January 13).

### 1828

Is elected to Paris Horticultural Society (founded 1827) in February. Reviews anonymous novel *The Mummy* in March. In April calls upon John James Audubon in London and persuades him to write an article for *Mag. Nat. Hist.* Departs London on August 29 for third Continental tour. Via Brighton, Dieppe, and Rouen, arrives Paris, September 6. Remains until October 10. Meets Etienne Soulange-Bodin and

P.P.A.deVilmorin. Visits Nancy, Roville, Epinal, Lunéville, Strasbourg, Donaueschingen, Ulm, and Augsburg, arriving Munich before November 1. Praises English Garden in Munich and F.L. von Sckell's work at Nymphenburg gardens, near Munich. Meets Charles Sckell, nephew of F.L. von Sckell. Visits Ratisbon, Nuremburg, Stuttgart, Heilbron, Schweizingen, Karlsruhe, Baden, Haguenau (Haut-Rhin, France), Saverne, and Château Saline, arriving Metz by December 9. Arrives Paris, December 10.

### 1829

Leaves Paris, mid-January, for London having been elected to Paris Society for Elementary Education and Agricultural Society of Rouen. By this time, is also a member of the literary societies of Warsaw and Cracow, and an honorary member of Horticultural Society of New York. Publishes multiple greenbelt plan for London (December).

### 1830

Meets Jane Webb in February and marries her in September. Elected to Massachusetts Horticultural Society (est. 1829). Abridgment of *Encyc. Gard.* entitled *Traité . . . des jardins d'ornement*, edited by Soulange-Bodin, appears in Paris.

### 1831

Leaves Bayswater, April 24, for garden tour in London, Manchester, Lake District, and Scotland. Prepares plans and stakes out walks for Birmingham Botanical Garden. Visits Moor Park, Stowe, Warwick Castle, Alton Towers, Haddon Hall, Chatsworth, Heaton Park, and other places. Departs Manchester, July 1. Visits Tatton Park, Eaton Hall, Levens Hall, and homes of the poets Southey (near Keswick) and Wordsworth (Rhydal Mount, near Grasmere). Public dinners held in his honor at Ayr and Kilmarnock. Visits Jardine Hall, Culzean Castle, and Loudon Castle. Learns of mother's illness and returns immediately to Bayswater. Mother dies October 14.

### 1832

Publishes "Colleges for Working Men" (project for multifamily hous-

ing, based on scheme of 1818) in *Mechanics' Magazine*. Begins publication of *Encyc. Arch.* (completed June 1833). Only child, Agnes, born October 28.

### 1833

Tours gardens in south of England, leaving Bayswater, July 27. Via Acton, Brentford, Twickenham, Slough, arrives Reading by August 7. Visits Swainson's Botanic Garden; Twickenham; Stoke Park; Dropmore; Windsor Castle; Frogmore; White Knights; Nuneham Courtenay; and Blenheim. Arriving Oxford August 13, visits Oxford Botanic Garden; Highclere; The Grange, and other places. Visits Page's Botanic Garden and Nursery, Southampton, August 23. Visits Stourhead, Fonthill Abbey, Wardour Castle, Stonehenge, and Wilton House. Returns to Bayswater, September 16.

### 1834

Begins *Arch. Mag.* in March as monthly supplement to *Encyc. Arch.* By this time, has been elected honorary member of horticultural societies of Lisle, Baltimore, Philadelphia, and Toronto.

### 1835

First number of *Arb. Brit.* appears (January). Tours gardens in Surrey, Berkshire, Hampshire, and Sussex, August 12–22. Visits Syon, White Knights, Farnham Castle, Deepdene, and several nurseries expressly to examine trees for *Arb. Brit.* Designs small public garden for unnamed English corporate town; plan published in *Gard. Mag.* January 1836. Completes design for new approach road to Gunnersbury Park, seat of N.M.Rothschild, Esq., Old Brentford, near London, December 1.

### 1836

Letter to Joseph Hume, M.P., urging reconsideration of the site for new Houses of Parliament. Begins to publish *Sub. Gard.* in monthly numbers, along with four other monthly serials: *Gard. Mag.*; *Arch. Mag.*; *Mag. Nat. Hist.*; and *Arb. Brit.* Relinquishes editorship of *Mag. Nat. Hist.* to Edward Charlesworth at end of year.

### 1838

In May completes *Arb. Brit.* (dedicated to the Duke of Northumberland). In July completes *Sub. Gard.*

### 1839

Completes *Arch. Mag.*, 5 vols., January. Lays out Derby Arboretum in May. Spends three weeks visiting gardens in Derbyshire and Yorkshire, including Chatsworth, Kedleston Hall, Elvaston Castle, Bretby Hall; the botanic garden and cemetery in Sheffield; and factories and schools in Milford and Belper. Tours gardens from London to Cheshunt, passing through Muswell Hill, Hornsey, and Southgate, July 24 to August 10.

### 1840

Publishes his edition of Repton's *Landscape Gardening and Landscape Architecture* (Repton's complete works). In May visits gardens in Lincolnshire, Staffordshire, and Middlesex, including Harlaxton Manor and village, near Grantham; Belton House; Chatsworth; Alton Towers; and Trentham. Last trip to Paris. Leaves Bayswater June 28. In Paris meets with César Daly, Alexandre Poiteau, and P.P.A. deVilmorin. Visits public gardens in Paris, Fontainebleau, Versailles, Meudon, St. Cloud, Sceaux, and Verrières (the residence of Vilmorin), among others. Begins campaign to preserve the former kitchen gardens of Kensington Palace for public parkland in October. Begins to edit the horticultural department of *Gardener's Gazette*. As editor, praises highly Prince Pückler-Muskau's writings on landscape gardening, which are being serialized in *Gardener's Gazette*.

### 1841

Tours gardens in North of England and Scotland, June 22 through September 30, and publishes accounts in *Gardener's Gazette* and *Gard. Mag.* Commissioned to design a plan for reforming grounds of Castle Kennedy, near Stranraer, seat of earl of Stair. From September 1, revisits scenes of his youth in Edinburgh with wife and daughter. Tours necropolis and botanic garden in

Glasgow, Dryburgh Abbey, Blair-Adam, Valleyfield, Blair-Drummond, and Stirling Castle. Ceases to edit horticultural department of *Gardener's Gazette* with number for November 6.

1842

Attack of inflammation of lungs in early March; to Brighton for health in early autumn. Tours gardens in Somersetshire, Devonshire, and Cornwall, arriving Nettlecombe Court, near Bridgewater, August 29. Visits Old Cleeve Abbey, Dunster Castle, Powderham Castle, Luscombe Castle, Torquay and environs, Tor Abbey, Mount Edgecumbe, Endsleigh, Bicton, Killerton Park, and others. Tours gardens in Sussex, leaving London October 14. Visits Wadhurst Castle, Battle Abbey, and Tunbridge Wells. Inspects grounds for Cambridge Cemetery,

November 8, and publishes plans and direction for management in *Gard. Mag.* (1843).

1843

Completes plans for improving grounds of Coleshill House, Berkshire, for Lord Radnor on May 2. On June 12 serves as witness before parliamentary commission of inquiry into the "State of Large Towns," giving testimony on housing, building codes, water closets, and other matters. Examines arrangements for Kensal Green Cemetery in early July. Visits Isle of Wight for health. Examines ground for laying out Southampton General Cemetery and completes report, August 31. Inspects grounds for laying out Bath Abbey Cemetery; Kiddington, Oxfordshire, seat of Mortimer Ricardo; and seat of a Mr. Pinder, near Bath. Advised of fatal

lung disease. Completes plans for laying out grounds of Baron Rothschild, Mr. Ricardo, Mr. Pinder, and for laying out Bath Cemetery. While standing and dictating text of *Self-Instruction for Young Gardeners*, dies in wife's arms at about noon, December 14. Burial in Kensal Green Cemetery, London, December 21.

1858

Death of Jane Loudon, July 13. Burial in Kensal Green Cemetery, July 17. Marriage of Agnes Loudon to Markham Spofforth, December 21.

1863

After birth of her third child, death of Agnes Loudon Spofforth, June 13. Burial in Kensal Green Cemetery, beside parents.

# Notes

Full bibliographic data not present in these notes can be found in Appendix B: Works by J.C. Loudon.

## Preface

**1**

T.H.D. Turner has recently suggested that the first publicly owned park in England was the three-acre Terrace Garden in Gravesend, Kent, designed by Loudon in 1835 and sold for building development in 1875. Loudon's unidentified plan for this garden was published in *Gard. Mag.* 12 (January 1836): 14–15. See Turner, "John Claudius Loudon and the Inception of the Public Park," *Landscape Design, Journal of the Landscape Institute*, no. 140 (November 1982): 33–35.

**2**

Henry Noel Humphreys, "Recollections," *Garden* 2 (December 7, 1872): 488.

**3**

Loudon, *Gard. Mag.* 6 (August 1830): 483.

## Introduction

**1**

Loudon, quoted in Henry Noel Humphreys, "Recollections," *Garden* 3 (January 18, 1873): 48. The main sources for biographical information on J.C. Loudon are Jane Loudon's "Life of Loudon" and Loudon's published works. His papers are believed to have been destroyed by bombings during the Second World War.

**2**

The itinerary of Loudon's first northern European journey closely resembles the first Continental trip of Sir John Sinclair, president of the Board of Agriculture and member of Parliament for Caithness, Scotland. (The itinerary for Sinclair's journey, along with his impressions, was printed for private circulation. See Rosalind

Mitchison, *Agricultural Sir John* (London: Geoffrey Bles, 1962), 53–57.

**3**

Loudon, *Landed Prop.*, 41; and *Gard. Mag.* 5 (December 1829): 672.

**4**

Loudon, *Parochial Institutions . . .* (1829), 2.

**5**

Loudon, *Treat. Hothouses*, 157–58.

**6**

Ibid.

**7**

Chambers, "Biographic Sketches: John Claudius Loudon," *Chambers's Edinburgh Journal* (May 4, 1844): 284.

**8**

Quotations are taken from Coventry, *Discourses Explanatory of the Object and Plan of the Course of Lectures on Agriculture and Rural Economy* (Edinburgh: A. Constable, and London: John Murray, 1808), 52.

**9**

Loudon, "Treatise on Scone." For Birmingham design, see *Gard. Mag.* 8 (August 1832): 407–28.

**10**

Price, *Essays on the Picturesque* (London: Mawman, 1810), 3: 168–69.

**11**

Price influenced Loudon not only through his writings, but through personal contact. In 1842 Loudon praised Price, whom he had known personally, "as an author and as a man." *Gard. Mag.* 18 (1842): 377–78.

**12**

Loudon, *Gard. Mag.* 10 (February 1834): 60.

**13**

Compare Bentham's panopticon, described in his *Panopticon; or, The Inspection House* (London, 1791), with Loudon's glasshouses for the Birmingham Botanical Garden, de-

scribed in *Gard. Mag.* 8 (August 1832): 407–28.

**14**

Loudon, quoted in Humphreys, "Recollections," *Garden* 2 (July 20, 1872): 47.

**15**

Alexandre Poiteau, *Annales Soc. Hort.* 34 (February 1844): 87.

**16**

Jane Loudon, "Life of Loudon," 194.

**17**

*Remarks on Hot-houses, Sketches of Hot-houses*, and *Encyc. Gard.* (1830 ed.), 314–18.

**18**

For a reproduction of Loudon's "cathedral conservatory," see Nikolaus Pevsner, "Early Iron," *Architectural Review* 106 (September 1949): 189.

**19**

Loudon, *Sketches of Hot-houses*.

**20**

Loudon, *Encyc. Gard.*, 1150ff. Thouin's plans remained in this section of the *Encyc. Gard.* until the 1835 ed., when some illustrations in this section were omitted. For Loudon's estimation of Thouin's and Blaikie's talents, see *Encyc. Gard.* (1830 ed.), pt. 1, bk. 1, chap. 3, subsection 3.5, p. 42.

**21**

Loudon, *Gard. Mag.* 7 (June 1831): 262–64.

**22**

See *Parochial Institutions . . .* (1829) and *Gard. Mag.* 9 (June 1833): 257ff.

**23**

See A Country Gentleman, *The Consequences of a Scientific Education to the Working Classes of the Country pointed out, and the Theories of Mr. Brougham on that subject confuted, in a letter to the Marquess of Lansdowne* (London, 1826).

**24**

Loudon's *Des Etablissements . . .* (1829) received a favorable review in the *Athenaeum* (April 22, 1829), which noted that "the brochure now before us is the only detailed account we have met with of the state of those schools since [John Quincy] Adams published his Letters [from Silesia] more than twenty years earlier."

**25**

Loudon, "Parochial Institutions,"

*Gard. Mag.* 5 (December 1829): 692–704.

26

Loudon, Letter to the *Times* (London), 12 April 1832.

27

Loudon, *Gard. Mag.* 5 (February 1829): 3.

28

See Loudon's letters to the *Morning Chronicle*, November 3, 4, and 7, 1840; the letter published November 7 was reprinted in the *Gardener's Gazette*, November 21, 1840, p. 741. See also *Gard. Mag.* 3 (March 1828): 470.

29

*Gard. Mag.* 5 (December 1829): 686ff.

30

Quatremère de Quincy, *Essai sur la nature, le but, et les moyens de l'imitation dans les Beaux-Arts* (Paris: Treuttel et Wurtz, 1823).

31

Loudon, *Mag. Nat. Hist.* 8 (1835), preface.

32

*Mag. Nat. Hist.* 1 (May 1828): 6ff.

33

See Humphreys's articles in *Arch. Mag.*, vols. 4 and 5 (1837, 1838). Grant Thorburn (1773–1863), a native of Dalkeith, Scotland, and a correspondent to *Gard. Mag.*, emigrated to New York, where he became a seedsman and horticultural writer.

34

Benjamin Ward Richardson, *Thomas Sopwith, with Excerpts from his Diary of Fifty-seven Years* (London, 1891), 196.

35

J.M., *Gentleman's Magazine* 21 (February 1844): 209.

36

*Times* (London), February 7, 1839.

37

Loudon, Letter to Professor John Stevens Henslow, Manuscript Collection, University Library of Edinburgh; and *Quarterly Review* 62 (October 1838): 332–60.

38

Loudon, *Gard. Mag.* 10 (1834): iii, iv, 558ff.

39

Sylvanus Urban, *Gentleman's Magazine* n. s., 8 (July 1837): 59.

## Chapter 1:
## Farming in Time of War

1

See Arthur Young, "On the Price of Corn, of Land, and of Labour," *Annals of Agriculture* 43 (1805): 36.

2

Alexander Allardyce, ed., *Scotland and Scotsmen in the Eighteenth Century, from the MSS. of John Ramsay, Esq. of Ochtertyre*, 2 vols. (Edinburgh: Blackwood, 1888), 2: 283. See also John, Lord Sheffield, *Remarks on the Deficiency of Grain* (London: Debrett, 1800).

3

Lord Sheffield, speech in the House of Lords, February 22, 1803, quoted in *Annals of Agriculture* 40 (1803): 166ff.

4

Arthur Young, *Annals of Agriculture* 40 (1803): 79ff.

5

Loudon, *A Treatise on the Culture of Wheat* . . . (London, 1812), 4–5 (hereafter, *Treatise on Wheat*).

6

Ibid., 25.

7

Ibid., xi.

8

For more details of Loudon's practice in Scotland, see A.A.Tait, *The Landscape Garden in Scotland, 1735–1835* (Edinburgh: Edinburgh University Press, 1980).

9

Loudon, *The Utility of Agricultural Knowledge to the Sons of the Landed Proprietors of England* . . . (London, 1809), 23 (hereafter cited as *Agricultural Knowledge*). For a discussion of the "primacy of agriculture," see G.E.Mingay, ed., *Arthur Young and His Times* (London: Macmillan, 1975); and F.M.L.Thompson, *English Landed Society in the Nineteenth Century* (London: Routledge & Kegan Paul, 1971).

10

*Gentleman's Magazine* (February 1810): 89. For William and J.C.Loudon's work at Wood Hall Farm, see *Designs for Farms*; and John Gloag, *Mr Loudon's England* (Newcastle-upon-Tyne: Oriel Press, 1970). See also chapter 5 in this book.

11

Sir Joseph Banks to Sir John Sinclair letter, ca. 1809, quoted in *Designs for Farms*, introduction.

12

Loudon, *Landed Prop.*, and *Encyc. Ag.* (1844 ed.), 1138. Loudon credits the introduction of Scotch farming into England to the Scottish *Farmer's Magazine*; a Scottish farmer named Gourlay, of Wiltshire; and his own *Landed Prop.* Sir Joseph Banks, however, wrote to Sinclair on October 13, 1819; "I rejoice to hear that your Scottish Agriculture has met with so extensive a sale . . . To have been the cause of imparting to Englishmen, the skill of Scots farmers, is indeed a proud recollection." See Sir John Sinclair's *Correspondence* (London: Colburn & Bentley, 1831), 1: 405.

13

Loudon, *Landed Prop.*, 74ff., 151.

14

See also Loudon, *Country Res.*, vol. 1 (1806); *Agricultural Knowledge* (1809); *Designs for Farms* (1811); and *Treatise on Wheat* (1812).

15

Loudon, *Landed Prop.*, 148.

16

Coventry, *Discourses Explanatory of the Object and Plan of the Course of Lectures on Agriculture and Rural Economy* (Edinburgh: A.Constable, and London: John Murray, 1808).

17

Loudon, *Landed Prop.*, 134. See James Mill, *Commerce Defended, An Answer to the Arguments by which Mr. Spence, Mr. Cobbett, and others, have attempted to prove that Commerce is not a Source of National Wealth* (London: Baldwin, 1808).

18

Loudon, *Landed Prop.*, 135.

19

[Thomas Stone], *A Letter to the Rt. Hon. Lord Somerville* . . . *to shew the inutility of the plans and researches of* [*the Board of Agriculture*]. By a Society of Practical Farmers (London: Cawthorn et al., 1800).

20

Banks, in Sinclair, *Correspondence*, 1: 404.

21

Loudon, *Landed Prop.*, 142ff., 86.

22

Loudon, *Gard. Mag.* 2 (January 1827): 108–20.

23

Marshall, *An Elementary and Practical Treatise on . . . the Landed Property of England* (London, 1804), 444.

24

John G. Gazley, *The Life of Arthur Young, 1741–1820* (Philadelphia: American Philosophical Society, 1973), 20ff.

25

Ibid., 360ff.

26

Young, *Annals of Agriculture* 40 (1803): 80.

27

Accounts of the annual Woburn and Holkham sheep shearings, indicating a remarkable diversity among participants, appeared regularly in the *Annals of Agriculture*. In June 1803 the duke of Bedford hosted a dinner at Woburn for 126 "friends of agriculture," including the duke of Manchester; Lord Somerville; Prince Esterhazy (of Hungary); Mr. Gore (the American ambassador); Sir John Sinclair; Arthur Young; Mr. Coke of Holkham; W. Beaver, a butcher, of Finsbury Square; and W. Chapman, also a butcher, Fleet-Market. See *Annals of Agriculture* 40 (1803): 481ff.

28

For Loudon's praise of the *Farmer's Magazine*, see his *Encyc. Ag.* (1844 ed.), 131.

29

See W. G. Hoskins, *The Making of the English Landscape* (London: Penguin, 1973); and David Spring, *The English Landed Estate in the Nineteenth Century: Its Administration* (Baltimore: Johns Hopkins University Press, 1963).

30

Thompson, *English Landed Society*, 213.

31

Loudon, *Landed Prop.*, 137ff.

32

See William Marshall, *On the Management of Landed Estates* (London, 1806); and W. G. Hoskins and L. Dudley Stamp, *The Common Lands of England and Wales* (London, 1963).

33

Cobbett, editorials in the *Political Register;* excerpts are found in *Selections from Cobbett's Political Works*, ed. J.M. and J.P. Cobbett, 6 vols. (London, 1835). [Hereafter, *Political Works*]

34

Cobbett, *Political Works*, vol. 2 (August 27, 1807). Cobbett was born in 1763; he died in 1835. See also his *Cottage Economy* (1821; reprint ed. [from 1850 ed.], with introduction by G. K. Chesterton, London, 1916).

35

Loudon, *Designs for Farms*, 96–97. Loudon intended to improve Mimbury Fort with a new approach road, a house with gardens and pleasure grounds, new cottages, a chapel, and a Lancasterian school. (Lancaster's system was controversial because it purported to be nondenominational. Some members of the Church of England insisted that such godless education would be harmful.) All the buildings would be centrally located, and the hedges between fields would radiate, without strict regularity, from the center. Loudon also planned to redesign the house in the "castle style," in keeping with the romantic landscape and the name of the farm. It is not clear to what extent these plans were carried out.

36

According to the mid-seventeenth-century Act of Settlement, an unemployed laborer could not leave his parish to seek work in another parish — unless he went to a northern industrial town, where there was a demand for labor. See Brian Inglis, *Poverty and the Industrial Revolution* (London: Panther, 1972); and J.L. and Barbara Hammond, *The Village Laborer* (London: Longmans, 1966).

37

Loudon, *Landed Prop.*, 51.

38

William Mason, *Works*, 4 vols. (London: Cadell and Davies, 1811), 1: 211ff, "The English Garden, A Poem in Four Books." Book 1 was begun in 1767 and first published in 1772; book 4 was published in 1781. For biographical information on Mason, see John Ingamells, "A Candidate for Praise," *Apollo* (June 1973): 605.

39

George Crabbe's poems "The Village" (1783) and "The Parish Register" (1807) were greatly admired by critics who disapproved of Wordsworth's innovations. See *Annual Review* 6, pt. 2 (1807): 521ff; and *Edinburgh Review* 12 (April 1808): 131–51.

40

Mason, "The English Garden," bk. 2, ll. 224–26, in *Works*.

41

Loudon's picturesque imagery was not entirely Utopian; in his *Encyc. Gard.* (1830 ed., p. 1089), he describes the unusually well mannered, dignified working people of Paisley, Renfrewshire, Scotland, whose amusements included writing verses, and keeping bees and a variety of fine pigeons.

42

See Robert Forsyth, *The Beauties of Scotland*, 5 vols. (Edinburgh: Bonar & Brown, 1805), vol. 1: *Midlothian*.

43

Ibid., 48. For further information on education in Edinburgh, see also John Robertson, *A View of the System of Education pursued in the Public Schools and University of Edinburgh* (London: Warren, 1818).

44

Fergusson, *Lowland Lairds* (London: Faber and Faber, 1949), 15.

45

Forsyth, *Beauties of Scotland*, 1: 387.

46

Kames, *The Gentleman Farmer: Being an attempt to improve Agriculture, by subjecting it to the Test of Rational Principles* (Edinburgh, 1776).

47

Kames (or "Kaimes"), cited in Loudon, *Encyc. Ag.* (1844 ed.), 127–28.

48

For a vivid account of the clearances, see John Prebble, *The Highland Clearances* (London: Penguin, 1975). See also Fergusson, *Lowland Lairds*.

49

See Allardyce, *Scotland and Scotsmen*, 2:212ff.

50

James Thomson, *The Seasons*,

(1726–46), quoted in Loudon, *Agricultural Knowledge*, 20–21.

51

See Fergusson, *Lowland Lairds*.

## Chapter 2: Gardeners and Poets, Landlords and Laborers

1

Loudon, *Country Res.* 2: 684ff.

2

Ibid., 655ff.

3

Ibid., 673–74.

4

William Cowper, quoted in Loudon, *Country Res.* 2:674. See Cowper, "The Task," bk. 5, ll. 738–47, in vol. 2, William Cowper, *Poems*, (London: J.Johnson, 1811). Loudon altered the poetic spelling of "composed," "heaven," etc. He again cited "The Task" in *Country Res.*, 2: 723, in the course of lamenting some of the practices of landscape improvers since Brown's time (Cowper criticized Brown's destruction of "venerable piles," in bk. 3). Cowper's *Letters on Taste* are also cited in *Country Res.*, 2: 668, where Loudon satirizes Repton's placing a proprietor's family arms on "milestones," in order to indicate the proprietor's ownership over the adjacent land.

5

When Loudon began his practice, Repton's most recently published works were *Sketches and Hints on Landscape Gardening* (1795) and *Observations on the Theory and Practice of Landscape Gardening* (1803).

6

Loudon exhibited five paintings at the Royal Academy in London between 1804 and 1817: (1804) *Scene on Lord Mansfield's estate, Perthshire, View of the Crammond River, nr. Edinburgh,* and *Elevation of a house at Balliad, Perthshire, for P. Campbell,* (1812) *A landscape,* and (1817) *Church of St. Anne at Wilna, Poland, built, so they say, by Freemasons invited to Poland by King Ladislaus in 1434.* See Algernon Graves, *The Royal Academy of Arts, A Complete Dictionary of Contributors and their Work . . . ,*

*1769–1904* (London: Henry Graves; and London: George Bell, 1906).

7

Loudon, *Country Res.* 1: 66.

8

Ibid., 124–25.

9

Loudon, *Country Res.* 1: 125.

10

Ibid., 140–41.

11

Ibid., 2: 642ff.

12

Ibid., 1:144ff.

13

Ibid., 146–47.

14

See Loudon's accounts of his travels in northern Europe in 1828–29 in *Gard. Mag.*, vols. 5–9 (1829–33).

15

Barrell, *The Dark Side of the Landscape: The Rural Poor in English Painting, 1730–1840* (Cambridge: Cambridge University Press, 1980).

16

Loudon, *Country Res.* 2:678.

17

Compare Loudon's passage with "Summer," ll. 1730ff.

18

Thomson, "Winter," lines 378–83, 1068–69.

19

Alexander Pope, *Epistle to Burlington* (1731), lines 65, 57, 50. Loudon quoted from Pope's *Epistle to Lord Bathurst* (1733) in *Landed Prop.*; and as late as 1820, he quoted from the "*Epistle to Burlington*" in his "Remarks on . . . Dovecot House . . . ," a manuscript in the Abbey Collection of the Yale Center for British Art, New Haven, Connecticut.

20

*The Seasons* was translated into French by J. Poulin (Paris, 1803). In reviewing this translation (*Edinburgh Review* 7 [January 1806]: 328ff), William Herbert noted that Thomson's poetry was still generally popular. For a study of Thomson and other eighteenth-century poets, painters and gardeners, see John Dixon Hunt, *The Figure in the Landscape* (Baltimore, Md.: Johns Hopkins University Press, 1976).

21

Price, *Essay on the Picturesque* (1794); Knight, *The Landscape*

(1794; see below); and Knight, *An Analytical Inquiry into the Principles of Taste* (1805).

22

See Peter Willis, *Charles Bridgeman* (London: Zwemmer, 1978); Michael Wilson, *William Kent: Architect, Designer, Painter, Gardener, 1685–1748* (London: Routledge & Kegan Paul, 1984); Kenneth Woodbridge, "William Kent as Landscape Gardener, A Reappraisal," *Apollo* 100 (August 1974): 126–37; and Dorothy Stroud, *Capability Brown* (London: Country Life, 1957).

23

George, the first Baron Lyttleton, was Thomson's patron and the proprietor of Hagley Park, Worcestershire. Henry Hoare II, the banker, directed the creation of Stourhead, Wiltshire. Charles Hamilton was the "creative genius" of Painshill, Surrey. William Shenstone, the poet and author of "Unconnected Thoughts on Gardening" (1764), laid out a small park farm at The Leasowes, Shropshire.

Loudon considered English versus Continental claims for the invention of the landscape garden in *Encyc. Gard.* (1835 ed.), 317–20.

24

For Loudon's announcement that he was following Price's and Knight's lead, see Loudon, *Obs. on Gard.*, 215ff.

25

Ibid., 194; 210ff.

26

Knight, *The Landscape: A Didactic Poem* (1794); 2nd ed. (London: Nicol, 1795; reprint ed., Westmead, Farnborough: Gregg, 1972), bk. 1, lines 279–86.

27

For Loudon's Utopian visions, see below, and chapters 13 and 14.

28

Knight, *The Landscape*, bk. 3, ll. 377–400.

29

Knight, *The Landscape*; Humphry Repton, "Letter," in *Sketches and Hints on Landscape Gardening* (London, 1795); and Sir Uvedale Price, *A Letter to H. Repton, Esq.* (London, 1798). For the picturesque aesthetic and controversy, see Christopher Hussey, *The Picturesque* (London, 1927); and Patrick Goode, "The

Picturesque Controversy," in George Carter et al., eds., *Humphry Repton, Landscape Gardener, 1752–1818* (Norwich: Sainsbury Center for Visual Arts, 1982), 34–41.

30

Repton, *An Enquiry into the Changes of Taste in Landscape Gardening* (London, 1806), 137.

31

Loudon, *Country Res.* 2: 432–33.

32

Girardin, *De la composition des paysages* (Geneva and Paris, 1777). Girardin's principles of design may be translated as "Unity; and Connection among the (related) parts."

33

Loudon's agreement with Girardin on these points can be found in his *Country Res.* 2:358; and his *Obs. on Gard.*, 205ff. For biographical information on Girardin, see André Martin-Decaen, *Le Marquis René de Girardin, 1735–1808* (Paris: Perrin, 1912), 10ff. Girardin would have seen Blenheim, Stowe, and The Leasowes, between 1763 and 1766.

34

Price, *Essay on the Picturesque*, 381. That Loudon had grasped the analogy between landscape and language is evident in a note in *Country Res.*, 2:714: "[The ferry-boat which Repton proposed for Holkham] is of a piece with the rest of Mr. Repton's improvements, they tend to prettyness, which, like *puns* in conversation, may produce momentary amusement."

35

Price, *Essay on the Picturesque* (1796), 383.

36

*Monthly Review* 64 (February 1811): 189.

37

See *Annual Review* 5, pt. 2 (1806): 722, which generally concurred with the *Monthly*'s assessment of Loudon's works.

38

William Robinson, who first successfully popularized the "wild garden" in England, published a book of that title in 1870. See Mea Allan, *William Robinson, 1838–1935, Father of the English Flower Garden* (London: Faber and Faber, 1982).

39

*Monthly Review* 54 (November 1807): 276.

40

*Edinburgh Review* 11 (October 1807): 214; 231.

41

Wordsworth to Lady Beaumont, May 21, 1807, letter, collected in *Memorials of Coleorton*, ed. William Knight (Boston: Houghton Mifflin, 1887), 2: 9.

42

Wordsworth, preface to the *Lyrical Ballads*, 4th ed. (1805; a new edition, London: Methuen, 1961), 8–9. For a study of the development of Wordsworth's voice and vision, see Geoffrey Hartman, *Wordsworth's Poetry, 1787–1814* (New Haven: Yale University Press, 1964); and Kenneth R. Johnston, "The Idiom of Vision," in *New Perspectives on Coleridge and Wordsworth*, ed. Geoffrey Hartman (New York: Columbia University Press, 1972).

43

See David Perkins, *Wordsworth and the Poetry of Sincerity* (Cambridge: Harvard University Press, 1964), 176ff.

44

For Loudon's hothouses, see chapter 7. His writings on hothouses were reviewed in *Anti-Jacobin Review* 23 (1806): 332; *Universal Magazine* 4 (1805): 240–42; *Monthly Review* 54 (November 1807): 320–21; and *Gentleman's Magazine* 88, pt. 1 (March 1818): 255.

45

Loudon, *Country Res.* 2: 360–61. The italics are mine.

46

Charles Bridgeman (d. 1738) and Sir John Vanbrugh (1664–1726) worked at Stowe from about 1719; William Kent (ca. 1685–1748), in the 1730s; and Lancelot "Capability" Brown (1716–1783), in the 1740s. See George Clarke, "William Kent: Heresy in Stowe's Elysium," in *Furor Hortensis*, ed. Peter Willis (Edinburgh: Elysium Press, 1974).

47

Whately, *Observations on Modern Gardening* (London: Payne, 1771), 213ff.

48

Loudon, Letter to the Conductor,

*Farmer's Magazine* 6 (August 1805): 358.

49

Hartley, *Observations on Man*, 3 vols., 4th ed. (London: Johnson, 1801), chap. 1, sec. 2. *Observations* was originally published in 1749. Loudon, in *Country Res.*, noted that Hartley has "beautifully explained" the association of ideas. For Wordsworth's early interest in Hartley and associationism, see Christopher Salvesen, *The Landscape of Memory: A Study of Wordsworth's Poetry* (London: Edward Arnold, 1965).

50

Wordsworth to Lady Beaumont, May 21, 1807, letter, collected in Knight, ed., *Memorials of Coleorton*, 2:13–14.

51

See Wordsworth's "To the Spade of a Friend . . ." (1806) and "The Leech-Gatherer" (1802). Loudon's discussion of a church spire that conferred a "degree of dignity on everything around" (*Country Res.* 1: 122) recalls Wordsworth's depiction of the church in book 4 of *The Prelude* (written 1805; published, with revisions, 1850).

52

Wordsworth to Lady Beaumont (undated letter; prob. December 1806) collected in Knight, ed., *Memorials of Coleorton* 1:191–209. The following details of the winter garden are taken from this letter. See also Russell Noyes, *Wordsworth and the Art of Landscape* (Bloomington: Indiana University Press, 1968); and Margaret Greaves, *Regency Patron: Sir George Beaumont* (London: Methuen, 1966).

53

In his letter to Lady Beaumont (cited in note 55), Wordsworth mentioned Thomson's "Ode on Solitude." Actually, he was referring to the final stanza of Thomson's "Hymn on Solitude" (1729).

54

I am indebted to James H. Broderick for calling my attention to Wordsworth's annotated copy of Knight's *Principles of Taste* (1805), as well as to Dorothy Wordsworth's reading of Knight's *The Landscape* (1794) in 1800. Broderick's observations appear in his paper, "Making all kindness Registered and Known:

Wordsworth as a Landscape Gardener" (May 1984), written for my Radcliffe seminar.

55

*Spectator*, no. 477 (September 6, 1712), cited in Wordsworth to Lady Beaumont (undated letter; prob. December 1806), collected in Knight, ed., *Memorials of Coleorton* 1:192–93.

56

Wordsworth to Sir George Beaumont, October 17, 1805, letter, collected in Knight, ed., *Memorials of Coleorton* 1: 104–118. This letter is a concise statement of Wordsworth's ideas on laying out grounds and on rural land management.

57

Repton, *Observations on . . . Landscape Gardening* (1803), in *The Landscape Gardening and Landscape Architecture of the Late Humphry Repton, Esq.*, ed. J.C. Loudon (London: Longmans, 1840), 207.

58

Loudon, *Gard. Mag.* 7 (October 1831): 551–52.

59

Loudon, *Treat. Hot-houses*, postscript.

60

Loudon, *Landed Prop.*, 154–55.

61

Loudon, *Obs. on Gard.*, 226. For a discussion of analogies between landscapes and women, see Carole Fabricant, "Binding and Dressing Nature's Loose Tresses: The Ideology of Augustan Landscape Design," in *Studies in 18th-Century Culture* 8 (1979): 109–35.

62

Loudon, *Landed Prop.*, 154–55. Here Loudon quotes Cicero, inserting love (*amor*) for friendship: "Non aqua, non igni, pluribus locis utimur, quam *amore*."*** "Solem enim e mundo tollere videntur, qui *amorem* e vita tollunt; qua a diis immortalibus nihil melius habemus, nihil jucundius!"

63

For an analysis of Wordsworth's complex feelings regarding the French Revolution, see F.M. Todd, *Politics and the Poet: A Study of Wordsworth* (London: Methuen, 1957).

64

See Price's recollections of his own benevolent uncle in *Essay on the Picturesque*, 379.

65

See Repton's discussions of Bulstrode and Sherringham Hall in his *Fragments on the Theory and Practice of Landscape Gardening* (London: Taylor, 1816), 234, 206.

66

The marquis of Huntley, son of the duke of Gordon, of Gordon Castle, Banff, volunteered to command a Highland regiment during the Napoleonic wars. Wounded, he returned to Scotland, where people of all ranks "celebrated his arrival with every expression of transport; and their fond attachment to his name and family was redoubled by his personal bravery and sufferings." His father, the duke, was known for liberality to his tenantry, and they held him in high regard: "I beheld him enter a miserable hut, among these moors, and inquire with familiar kindness into the family affairs" (John Stoddart, *Remarks on the Local Scenery and Manners in Scotland during the years 1799 and 1800*, 2 vols. [London: Miller, 1801] 141ff.). Rousseau died in 1778 at Ermenonville, Girardin's country residence near Paris. He was buried there, one midnight, on the Isle of Poplars. While a small black boat carried his coffin to the Isle, the local villagers stood by the water's edge, bearing torches. See Martin-Decaen, *René de Girardin*; and Jean Guéhenno, *Jean-Jacques, Histoire d'une Conscience*, 2 vols. (Paris: Gallimard, 1962).

67

Loudon, *Country Res.* 2: 694–97.

## Chapter 3:
## Scone Palace,
## Picturesque and Romantic

1

Sir Iain Moncreiffe, *Scone Palace, The Home of the Earls of Mansfield* (Perth, Scotland, ca. 1970), 2–6, 25–32; and Loudon, "Treatise on Scone."

2

Loudon, *Landed Prop.*, 39–40. William Atkinson (1773–1839), a pupil of James Wyatt, won the Gold Medal of the Royal Academy in 1797.

3

Robert Thomas in Sir John Sinclair, *The Statistical Account of Scotland*, vol. 18 (Edinburgh: Creech, 1796), 67ff.

4

Ibid. See also *The Gazeteer of Scotland* (Dundee: Chalmers, 1803); and *The Traveller's Guide through Scotland and its Islands* (Edinburgh: J. Thomson, 1808), 354. The first earl of Mansfield twice served simultaneously as lord chief justice and chancellor of the exchequer. His eloquence as a member of Parliament commanded a silent attention, unusual in the House of Commons. When he freed a slave named Somersett, he struck "the first real blow" against the slave trade (see Moncreiffe, *Scone Palace*; and Thomas, in Sinclair, *Account of Scotland*). The second earl was a distinguished statesman and diplomat. On his death in 1796, his son, Loudon's employer, succeeded to the earldom. The third earl erected a school for children on his lands at Stormontfield. Both the third and fourth earls were commended for charitable gifts and for creating jobs for laborers unable to work outdoors (see Sinclair, *Account of Scotland*, vol. 10, *Perth* [Edinburgh: Blackwood, 1845], 1060ff; 1075).

5

Thomas, in Sinclair, *Account of Scotland*, 86.

6

*Sketch of a Tour in the Highlands through Perthshire, Argyleshire and Inverness-shire, in September and October, 1818* (London: Baldwin, Craddock and Joy, 1819), 5ff; *The Scottish Tourist and Itinerary* (Edinburgh: Stirling, Kenney & Co., 1838), 113ff; and *Black's Picturesque Tourist: Scotland* (Edinburgh: A. and C. Black, 1844), 307ff.

7

Thomas, in Sinclair, *Account of Scotland*, 87.

8

Loudon, "Treatise on Scone," preface, 25.

9

In *Country Residences*, Loudon mentions the fine undergrowths of rhododendrons and arbutus at Kenwood. Partly for its naturally picturesque setting, partly for its rich variety of plants, Loudon (*Gard. Mag.* 4 [August 1828]: 303) considered Painshill "the most delightful and instructive place described by Thomas Whately" (Whateley, *Observations on Modern Gardening* [London, 1770]). While he was living in London earlier in 1803, Loudon may have visited Painshill (See *Obs. on Gard.*, 214).

10

Like Repton, Loudon focused on the natural character of a place to be improved and emphasized the importance of the approaches to a residence.

11

Loudon, "Treatise on Scone," 130ff. See also A.A.Tait, "The Scottish Garden: A Picturesque Quarrel," *The Scottish Review* 2, no. 5 (Winter 1976), 31–36, for a discussion of Loudon and the Thomas Whites, father and son, at Scone.

12

Loudon, "Treatise on Scone," 44.

13

These plans were folded and inserted at the back of Loudon's "Treatise on Scone."

14

Girardin, *De la composition des paysages* (Paris, 1777), quoted in Loudon, *Obs. on Gard.*, 239–48. Loudon was probably quoting from the English translation of 1783, attributed to Daniel Malthus. As late as 1820, Loudon was still quoting Girardin as an authority on landscape gardening. (See Loudon, "Remarks on . . . Dovecot House".)

15

Loudon, *Country Res.* 2: 520.

16

Thomas Whateley, *Observations on Modern Gardening* (1771 ed.), 243–44.

17

Jean-Jacques Rousseau, *Julie; ou, La nouvelle Héloïse* (Paris, 1761; a new ed., Paris: Garnier Frères, 1960), pt. 4, letter 11, 453–57. In *Country Res.*, Loudon twice referred to Rousseau and Julie. Her aviary was mentioned, and Loudon quoted Rousseau's observation from pt. 4, letter 4: "An air of greatness has always something melancholy in it" (*Country Res.* 2: 611). For details of Lord Harcourt's garden and an illustration by Paul Sandby, see John

Dixon Hunt and Peter Willis, eds., *The Genius of the Place* (New York: Harper & Row, 1975), 308. For a discussion of Julie's garden and Rousseau's comments on Stowe (which he had never seen), see Peter Willis, "Rousseau, Stowe and Le Jardin Anglais: Speculations on Visual Sources for La Nouvelle Héloïse," *Studies on Voltaire and the Eighteenth Century* 90 (1972): 1791–98.

18

De Lille, *Les Jardins; ou, L'Art d'embellir les jardins* (Paris, 1782), 66–67. In his first book (*Obs. on Gard.*) Loudon referred to the "excellent observations" in De Lille's poem. Later he stated that he had availed himself "principally of the ideas of Price, Knight, Gilpin and De Lille, so far as they were in unison with my own preconceived notions" (see Loudon, *Farmer's Magazine* 6 [August 1805]: 358).

19

For a concise introduction to Jussieu's natural system, see M.A.Brogniart, "Historical Notice of Antoine-Laurent de Jussieu," trans. from the *Annales des Sciences Naturelles* (January 1837) in *Mag. Nat. Hist.* n.s. 1, no. 12 (December 1837): 609–25.

20

In 1803 Loudon may have been aware of the garden which Erasmus Darwin had laid out, beginning in 1777 in Staffordshire, according to the system of Linnaeus. The novelty of Loudon's approach, however, was the use of a system of classification (and of arrangement) that was more suitable than that of Linnaeus for achieving visual harmony among the plants. See Erasmus Darwin, *The Botanic Garden, A Poem in Two Parts* (London: Jones, 1825).

21

Two framed plans in the estate office of Scone show details of these gardens: (1) "Plan of Part of the Estate showing the proposed improvements delineated by J.Loudon, 1803," and (2) "Plan showing the improvements to be made on Scone supposing the Bridge of Isla Road not to be removed and only the Kirk Manse and a few houses in the Village, removed to the Coupar Angus Road at Burnside," J.Loudon, 1803.

22

Young, *Annals of Agriculture* 37 (1801), 465ff. The following account of Croome is taken from this source. See also Dorothy Stroud, *Capability Brown* (London: Country Life, 1950), 48ff.

23

Loudon, *Country Res.* 2: 376–77.

24

Loudon, *Country Res.* 2: 548.

25

"Minutes of Planting," muniments of Lord Mansfield, vols. 113–15, preserved in the National Register of Archives, Edinburgh.

26

Loudon, "Treatise on Scone," pl. 12 (which consists of the plan of the village of Scone).

27

*Gard. Mag.* 13 (1837), 123–24.

28

*Scone Palace, The Home of the Earls of Mansfield* (Scone, 1980). Among the Mansfield Papers, I have examined those materials which relate to Scone Palace at the time of Loudon's commission. I have not seen any private correspondence between Loudon and the third earl. Evidence that some of Loudon's ideas were implemented is derived from the above-mentioned published works, unpublished manuscripts, and my visits to Scone.

29

Loudon, *Designs for Farms*, 102ff, pl. 36.

30

Loudon, "Treatise on Scone," 150–51.

# Chapter 4:
# Tremadoc and the Sublime

1

James Macpherson, trans., *The Poems of Ossian* (Boston: Phillips, Sampson, 1851; reprint ed., St. Clair Shores, Michigan: Scholarly Press, 1970), 213–14. The first edition of the Ossianic poems, purporting to be Macpherson's translations from ancient texts, appeared as *Fragments of Ancient Poetry Collected in the Highlands of Scotland* (Edinburgh: 1760).

2

William Gilpin, *Observations on sev-*

24

*Prospectus of the Royal Institution of Great Britain* (London: W.Bulmer, 1800), 18–19. Rumford's authorship is confirmed by Sanford C. Brown, in Brown, ed., *Collected Works of Count Rumford* (Cambridge: Harvard University Press, 1969).

25

Loudon kept one model of a sheep house in his office at Tew Lodge. He twice referred to the "National Institution" as a repository of his agricultural and landscape models. This must have been the "Royal Institution of Great Britain," founded by Benjamin Thompson, Count Rumford, in 1799 and housed in Albemarle Street, Piccadilly, London (see *Farmer's Magazine* 6 [February 1805]: 126–27). Loudon presented Sir Hew with the model for his estate at North Berwick, along with an "elegant" manuscript volume illustrated by Loudon's own drawings and sketches.

26

Humphreys, "Recollections," *Garden* 2 (December 21, 1872), 532–34; and *Garden* 3 (January 18, 1873): 47–49.

27

Humphreys, "Recollections," *Garden* 2 (December 21, 1872): 533.

28

Loudon, *Designs for Farms*, 19ff.

29

Stratton, "Scotch System of Husbandry," 19.

30

Ibid., 29–30.

31

Loudon, *Encyc. Ag.*, 1095. After the Bullion Committee's *Report* was published in 1807, there was a general fall of prices for land and produce. As Loudon explained, "Anxiety to increase the rent-roll" induced Stratton to let the nearly four-thousand-acre estate of Great Tew to two Scottish tenants (Loudon and Stenhouse Wood) who offered much higher rents than those paid by the incumbent English tenant farmers— nearly twenty in all. Eight months later Stratton nearly sold Great Tew for four times the figure he had asked a year earlier, but the purchase was not completed. Stratton had difficulties paying for the new buildings, roads, and drainage, and

he had to buy back the leases of some English tenants. Loudon wrote, "He soon found that though one person had been willing to buy the estate held on twenty-one year leases, yet that it would sell much better if held by tenants at will; and was thence induced to buy up from the Scotch tenants the leases granted to them two years before." Still, he could not sell the estate. At last Stratton had most of his lands in hand. One farm was put under the management of an Irishman who, Loudon wrote, "rendered himself notorious by some parts of his conduct, and finally left the country clandestinely; and whose actions have unfortunately often been confounded with those of the Scotch farmers, after all the latter had completely left that part of the country." In 1814, when peace was concluded, land prices fell still lower. In 1815 Great Tew was sold to Matthew Robinson Boulton for less than half the selling price of 1809, but about double the asking price in 1807. (See Loudon, *Encyc. Ag.* [1844 ed.], 1137–38.)

32

For an account of Great Tew and the old site of Tew Lodge Farm today, see Frank Emery, *The Oxfordshire Landscape* (London, 1974), 140ff.

33

Michael Hanson, "Great Tew's Expectations," *Country Life* (October 16, 1980): 1419. See also Mavis Batey, "Pioneer in Preservation," *Country Life* (March 8, 1979): 656–60. Mrs. Batey kindly read an earlier version (1976) of the present chapter and consulted with me before writing her article. A comparison of Loudon's "before and after" plans of Great Tew reveals that he planned to add only a few new cottages to the village, which was built between August 1808 and September, 1810, and the layout of the village is not noticeably altered in his design.

34

*Book of British Villages*, ed., Reader's Digest Association Ltd., for Drive Publications Ltd. (Basingstoke, Hampshire: The Automobile Association, 1981), 209.

## Chapter 6:
## Architecture and
## the Beautiful Economy
## of Nature

1

Price, *Essay on the Picturesque* (London: J.Robson, 1798).

2

Ibid., 389ff; 428ff.

3

Loudon, *Obs. on Gard.*, 276.

4

George Robertson, *A General View of the Agriculture of the County of Midlothian* (Edinburgh: G.Nicol, 1795), 136.

5

Ibid., 135.

6

Loudon, *Treat. Hot-houses*, 15.

7

Rumford, *Essays, Political, Economical and Philosophical* (London: Cadell & Davies, 1802); and Nicol, *The Scotch Forcing Gardener* (1797; a new ed., Edinburgh, 1802).

8

Loudon, *Treat. Hot-houses*, 162.

9

Ibid., 113.

10

Ibid., 165ff.

11

Ibid., 247ff.; and *Gard. Mag.* 11 (December 1835): 619. For a Mr. Smith of Leith Walk, Edinburgh, Loudon erected a vinery and installed his improved furnace. For Colonel Duncan, at Glenfuir, near Falkirk, he erected a cucumber pit; there, and at Underley Park, near Kendal, he heated the soil of pineries by steam. He also erected a pinery for the Dicksons in Edinburgh.

12

Loudon, *Treat. Hot-houses*, 200.

13

Loudon, *Country Res.* 1: 346ff.

14

Ibid., 347n.

15

Ibid., 138.

16

Rumford, "Chimney Fireplaces" (1796) in *Collected Works of Count Rumford*, ed. Sanborn C. Brown (Cambridge: Harvard University Press, 1969), 2: 221–95.

**17**

Rumford, "Observations Relative to the Means of Increasing the Quantities of Heat obtained in the Combustion of Fuel," in *Collected Works of Rumford* 2:160.

**18**

Rumford, "Chimney Fireplaces," 265.

**19**

Loudon, *Country Res.* 1: 135.

**20**

Gandy, *Designs for Cottages* (London, 1805); idem, *The Rural Architect* (London, 1805).

**21**

*Annual Review* 4 (1805): 890. In *Heavenly Mansions* (London: Cresset, 1949), "The Vision of J.M.Gandy," Sir John Summerson described Gandy as a "frustrated Wordsworth of architecture," who reflected in his own medium Wordsworth's interest in a plain, emphatic language. Summerson had no evidence of communications between Wordsworth and Gandy; but at least one contemporary critic noted similarities between them. See *Annual Review* 4 (1805): 890, on Gandy: "In a wild pursuit of novelty, he has adopted a style of frigid extravagance, disregarding the requisites of climate, manners, and convenience, and with a singular dereliction, or rather, inversion, of usual proportions." Compare *Annual Review* 6 (1807): 524, on Wordsworth's *Poems in Two Volumes* (1807): "It is this, this spirit of paraphrase and periphrasis, this idle parade of fine words, that is the bane of modern verse writing. . . . Thus much for the system of Mr. Wordsworth, which appears to us a frigid and at the same time an extravagant one."

**22**

In 1831 Loudon referred to Gandy as a "first-rate architect." See *Gard. Mag.* 7 (August 1831): 407.

**23**

Robert Adam, *Works*, 3 vols., folio (1778; reprint ed., facsimile, Paris: Thezard, 1900), vol. 1, preface.

**24**

Culzean Castle, seat of the earl of Casillis (or Cassilis), was considered the finest country seat in Ayrshire. See Robert Forsyth, *The Beauties of Scotland* (Edinburgh, 1805), vol. 2; and Robert Chambers, *The Picture of Scotland* (Edinburgh, 1828), vol. 1.

**25**

Loudon, *Country Res.* 1: 113. This purist streak is a departure from Payne Knight's tolerance of mixing Grecian and Gothic in a single building. See George Hersey's discussion of Knight, Alison, and Loudon, in his *High Victorian Gothic: A Study in Associationism* (Baltimore: Johns Hopkins University Press, 1972), 10–22.

**26**

Loudon, *Country Res.* 1: 69ff. In 1801 Loudon attended an architectural school in Edinburgh and studied "all the details of classical architecture" (*Arch. Mag.* 1 [May 1834]: 113). This school may not have been part of the University of Edinburgh; it is not mentioned in contemporary accounts of the university. The five orders alluded to are, of course, the Tuscan, Doric, Ionic, Corinthian, and Composite.

**27**

Loudon, *Country Res.* 1: 185.

**28**

Price, *Essays on the Picturesque* (1798), 2: 212.

**29**

Loudon, *Country Res.* 1: 185–86.

**30**

Ibid., 83ff.

**31**

Ibid., 101–02.

**32**

Price, *Essays on the Picturesque* (1798), 2: 337.

**33**

Loudon, *Country Res.* 1: 88, 185–86.

**34**

Ibid., 2: 712, for example. See Reynolds's *Discourses on Art*, no. 13 (1786), for observations on the sound rules of Grecian architecture and the compositional skills of Vanbrugh.

**35**

See Loudon's *Encyc. Arch.* (1834 ed.), 1123, for discussion of Laugier.

**36**

For Loudon's discussions of Thomas Hope, see *Gard. Mag.* 5 (October 1829): 589–93; 7 (June 1831): 384; 11 (October 1835): 508; and *Arch. Mag.* 2 (November 1835): 504. For Loudon's discussions of Durand, see *Arch. Mag.* 3 (March 1836): 108; 2 (February 1835): 88; and 4 (July 1837): 351.

**37**

See David Watkin, *The Triumph of the Classical: Cambridge Architecture, 1804–1834* (Cambridge: Cambridge University Press for the Fitzwilliam Museum, 1977), 4ff.

**38**

Hope, quoted in Watkin, *Thomas Hope (1769–1831) and the Neo-Classical Idea* (London: John Murray, 1968), 62.

**39**

Watkin, *Triumph of the Classical*, 4.

**40**

Loudon, *Gard. Mag.* 5 (October 1829): 589–93.

**41**

Loudon, *Encyc. Arch.* (1834 ed.), 1122.

**42**

Compare J.N.L.Durand, *Précis des leçons d'architecture* (Paris: Bernard), vol. 1 (1802) and vol. 2 (1805); with Loudon, *Country Res.* 1: 67ff.

**43**

Archibald Alison, *Essays on the Nature and Principles of Taste*, 2 vols. (1790; another edition, Edinburgh: Constable, 1815), 2: 138ff.

**44**

Durand, *Précis des leçons*, vol. 1, introduction, p. 13. For further discussion, see Emil Kaufmann, *Architecture in the Age of Reason* (Cambridge: Harvard University Press, 1955). For a detailed discussion of Vitruvius's seminal speculations on the origins of architecture, during the first century B.C., see Joseph Rykwert, *On Adam's House in Paradise: The Idea of the Primitive Hut in Architectural History* (Cambridge: MIT Press, 1981).

**45**

Durand, *Précis des leçons* 2: 6.

**46**

In the following reviews of *Country Residences*, one finds extracts from that work in which buildings are discussed; but the reviewers dwell on principles of landscape design, rather than on principles of architecture per se: *Monthly Review* 54 (November 1807): 269–81, and *Annual Review* 5, pt. 2 (1806): 722–24.

47

Loudon, *Country Res.* 1:61ff.

48

Loudon, "Hints for a National Garden," dated December 10, 1811, an address delivered to the Linnean Society on December 17, 1811. The original manuscript is preserved in the library of the Linnean Society, London, and a photocopy is kept in the library of Kew Gardens, London.

49

Ibid.

50

Loudon, *Hints on Gard.*, 43ff; pl. 20. Many of the plans for gardens in this work were reproduced in the *Encyc. Gard.*

51

Loudon, *Hints on Gard.*, x.

## Chapter 7: Engineering for Splendor and for Health

1

The main sources of information on Loudon's journeys in northern Europe and Russia in 1813–14 are the following: Jane Loudon's "Life of Loudon" and, by J.C. Loudon, *Remarks on Hot-houses, Sketches of Hot-houses, Encyc. Gard., Encyc. Arch.*, and "General Survey of the present State of Domestic Architecture in the Different Countries on the Continent of Europe: chiefly from personal Recollection," *Arch. Mag.* 2 (March 1835): 111–23.

2

For a study of the major building and planning projects in St. Petersburg during the eighteenth and early nineteenth centuries, see Iurii Alekseevich Egorov, *The Architectural Planning of St. Petersburg*, trans. E. Dluhosch (Athens, Ohio: Ohio University Press, 1969). See also a work from which Loudon quotes extensively in his *Encyc. Gard.*: A.B. Granville, *St. Petersburgh: A Journal of Travels to and from that Capital*, 2 vols., 2nd ed. (London: Colburn, 1829).

3

Thomas de Thomon (b. 1756, Paris; d. 1814, St. Petersburg) built the Great Theatre (1803) and the mausoleum of Peter I (1810) as well as the Maritime Exchange Building, all in St. Petersburg. See Egorov,

*Planning of St. Petersburg*, 71ff; 218n. For a reproduction of a view of the Exchange ca. 1810, see Anthony Cross, *Russia Under Western Eyes, 1517–1825* (London: Elek, 1971); and the catalogue of the exhibition, *Landscape Masterpieces from the Soviet Museums*, Royal Academy (London: 18 October–30 November 1975), pl. 4.

4

Loudon, "Design for a Bridge across the Mersey, at Runcorn," in *Annals of Philosophy* 11 (January 1818): 14–27. Loudon showed his completed design to his friend, the engineer Thomas Telford, who had also designed a bridge for the same site along similar lines. For an engraving of Telford's bridge, see John Rickman, ed., *Thomas Telford, Civil Engineer, written by Himself* (London, 1838).

5

Loudon, *Arch. Mag.* 1 (July 1834): 208–09. See also Jeremy Bentham, *Panopticon; or, The Inspection House* (London, 1791). In 1834 Loudon admired the same kind of central planning and arrangements for classification, separation, inspection, and security in London's new Tothill Fields Prison in Pimlico, designed by Robert Abraham.

6

Jane Loudon, "Life of Loudon," 197.

7

Chrétien Müller, *Tableau de Petersbourg; ou, Lettres sur la Russie écrites en 1810, 1811, et 1812*, trans. C. Léger (Paris: Treuttel & Würtz, 1814), 99ff.

8

Adams, *Memoirs*, vol. 2 (Philadelphia: Lippincott, 1874), 65. When Loudon arrived in St. Petersburg in the autumn of 1813, Adams was there, and the city was then being considered for the mediation between Britain and the United States concerning the War of 1812.

9

Loudon, *Arch. Mag.* 2 (March 1835): 123.

10

Loudon, *Encyc. Gard.*, 50–59.

11

Loudon, *Arch. Mag.* 2 (March 1835): 111ff.

12

Madame de Staël, *Oeuvres complètes*

(Brussels: Hauman, 1830), vol. 15, *Dix années d'exil*, 194–201.

13

Loudon, *Arch. Mag.* 2 (March 1835): 114ff. For further details of the typical Russian stove and its superiority to German stoves, see Müller, *Tableau de Petersbourg*, 87ff. The German stove produced heat mainly from the flame and the coals. In the earthenware tubes of the Russian stove, the hot air of fumes lasted longer and could be employed for heat. Russian stoves also conserved fuel, consuming only about one-fifth to one-sixth of the wood burned in a German stove.

14

Loudon, *Arch. Mag.* 2 (March 1835): 119–20.

15

Loudon, *Arch. Mag.* 2 (March 1835): 122.

16

Ker Porter, *Travelling Sketches in Russia and Sweden, During the Years 1805, 1806, 1807, and 1808* (Philadelphia: Hopkins and Earle, 1809), 48–49. Porter notes that the pleasure grounds of the Taurida palace were laid out by (William) Gould (of Lancashire) — "the Repton of Russia." See also "History of the First Introduction of the Modern Style of Laying out Grounds into Russia . . . ," by One of the Imperial Gardeners, in *Gard. Mag.* 2 (July 1827): 385–90.

17

Loudon, *Encyc. Gard.*, 52.

18

Loudon, *Remarks on Hot-houses*, 49. See also his *Encyc. Gard.* (1835 ed.), 250, where he notes that the residence at "Gorenki" [sic] was built by an English artisan. The glasshouses may owe something to a study Loudon cites in *Remarks on Hot-houses*, "A Didactic Epistle to General Showalow on the Utility of Glass," by the Russian poet and philosopher, Mikhaïl Lomonosow (1711–1765).

19

Loudon, *Remarks on Hot-houses*, 89n.

20

Loudon, *Remarks on Hot-houses*, 89.

21

Thomas Andrew Knight, "A Description of a Forcing House for

Grapes; with Observations on the best Method of constructing Houses for other Fruits" (Read on May 3, 1808), in *Trans. Hort. Soc.* 1 (1812): 99–102.

22

Loudon, *Remarks on Hot-houses*, 9ff.

23

Mackenzie, "On the Form which the Glass of a Forcing-house ought to have, in order to receive the greatest possible quantity of Rays from the Sun" (Read on August 1, 1815), in *Trans. Hort. Soc.* 2 (1817): 171–77.

24

Thomas Andrew Knight, "Suggestions for the Improvement of Sir George Stuart Mackenzie's Plan for Forcing-houses" (Read on April 1, 1817), in *Trans. Hort. Soc.* 2 (1817): 350–53. For a wider discussion of glasshouses over the centuries, see John Hix, *The Glass House* (Cambridge: MIT Press, 1974). See also a comprehensive work in which Loudon is featured: Georg Kohlmaier and Barna von Sartory, *Houses of Glass: A Nineteenth-Century Building Type*, trans. John C. Harvey (Cambridge: MIT Press, 1986).

25

Loudon, *Remarks on Hot-houses*, 21.

26

Loudon, *Sketches of Hot-houses*, unpaged. See the favorable review of this work in *Gentleman's Magazine* 88, pt. 1 (March 1818): 255.

27

Loudon, *Treat. Hot-houses*.

28

Banham, *The Architecture of the Well-tempered Environment* (London: Architectural Press, 1969), 21ff. Banham identifies the "massive" tradition with the "conservative" mode of environmental management (having chosen the term in honor of the Conservatory Wall at Chatsworth, in Derbyshire, devised by Sir Joseph Paxton in 1846). Banham also recognizes two other modes, the "selective" mode of admitting certain desirable environmental elements from the outdoors — such as light and air — without introducing for instance, rain or snow, and the "regenerative" mode of applying energy, such as heat or electricity, to operate devices for environmental management.

29

Loudon, *Remarks on Hot-houses*, 39.

30

Alison, *Essays on the Nature and Principles of Taste* (1790); and Loudon, *Sketches of Hot-houses*. For a discussion of Loudon's debts to Alison, see George L. Hersey, *High Victorian Gothic: A Study in Associationism* (Baltimore: Johns Hopkins University Press, 1972).

31

Loudon, *Encyc. Gard.*, 358ff.

32

Ibid., 337–39.

33

Ibid. (1824 ed.), 310–11.

34

Loudon gives an engraving and description of this hothouse in *Gard. Mag.* 5 (December 1829): 681. The engraving is also reproduced in Hix, *Glass House*, 26.

35

The Crystal Palace had ridge-and-furrow roofing, but the sashes were of wood. See unsigned article in *Household Words* 2 (1850–51): 390: "The apex of each 'ridge' is a wooden sash bar, with notches on either side for holding the sloping laths in which are fitted the edges of the glass. The bottom or 'furrow' bar — otherwise a rafter — is hollowed in the middle, to form a gutter, into which every drop of rain glides down from the glass and passes through the transverse gutters into hollow columns."

36

Loudon, *Encyc. Gard.*, 353.

37

Le Corbusier, *Vers une architecture* (Paris, 1923).

38

For a view in St. Giles's Parish, ca. 1840, see chapter 12, and *Camden History Review* (London) 1 (1973):19.

39

For an overview of housing conditions, see J.N. Tarn, *Working-Class Housing in Nineteenth-Century Britain* (London: Lund-Humphreys for the Architectural Association, 1971), and Enid Gauldie, *Cruel Habitations, A History of Working-Class Housing*, 1780–1918 (London: George Allen & Unwin, 1974).

40

See John Nash, "Report . . . to the Commissioners of His Majesty's Woods, Forests and Land Revenues" (ca. 1811) in *Some Account of the Proposed Improvements of the Western Part of London* (London: W. & P. Reynolds, 1814), xxv ff.

41

Loudon, "Colleges for Working Men," *Mechanics' Magazine* 16, no. 443 (February 4, 1832): 321–24 (hereafter, *Mech. Mag.*).

42

Bentham, *Panopticon*.

43

See William Bridges Adams (1797–1872) in *DNB* and *Wellesley Index*, vol. 3. Adams used the pseudonym "Junius Redivivus" for his political pamphlets, especially at the time of agitation for the Reform Bill, ca. 1832.

44

Junius Redivivus, "Plan for the Better Housing of the Working Classes," *Mech. Mag.* 16 (December 3, 1831): 170.

45

Ibid., 169.

46

See Loudon, *Arch. Mag.* 3 (January 1836): 40–41; *Arch. Mag.* 3 (March 1836): 138. The viaduct was built in 1863–69 by William Heywood, Surveyor of the City. See Nikolaus Pevsner, *The Buildings of England: London 1* (London: Penguin, 1973), 250.

47

See "University Place Development," in *HGSD News* 10, no. 2 (Cambridge: Harvard Graduate School of Design, Winter, 1982): 9.

48

M. Dorothy George, *London Life in the Eighteenth Century* (London: Penguin, 1965), 86. The window tax, first imposed in 1696, was not repealed until 1851. As George points out, this tax induced people to block up windows permanently and reduce the admission of light to a minimum. See also John Burnett, *A Social History of Housing, 1815–1970* (London: Methuen, 1978), 27ff.

49

For a description of Frost's floors and Witty's furnace, see note 41. The earl of Shrewsbury was pleased with the furnace that Witty had installed at the earl's residence, Alton Towers, Staffordshire. See *Gard. Mag.* 7 (August 1831): 482ff for a section and description of the furnace.

50
Junius Redivivus, *Mech. Mag.* 16 (February 25, 1832): 372.

51
Junius Redivivus, "Plan for Better Housing," 170.

52
Loudon, *Encyc. Arch.* (1834 ed.), 244ff.

53
A nineteenth-century view of Akroydon, along with an enlightening discussion of Akroyd's intentions, is found in Walter Creese, *The Search for Environment. The Garden City: Before and After* (New Haven: Yale University Press, 1966), 40–46. Creese points out that Akroyd's homeowners had access to allotment gardens and to the central public garden, but not to private attached gardens. Instead of Loudon's centralized public facilities, the square park featured Colonel Akroyd's monument to Queen Victoria in the center of two intersecting paths.

54
Loudon, *Encyc. Arch.* (1834 ed.), 251. This was probably Francesco Camporesi, one of the architects who designed the palace of Ostankino in Moscow.

55
Junius Redivivus, "Plan for Better Housing," 170.

56
Loudon, *Encyc. Arch.* (1834 ed.), 251.

57
Loudon, *Gard. Mag.* 8 (February 1832): 60.

58
Ibid. 3 (September 1827): 101–02.

59
Tredgold, *Gard. Mag.* 1 (January 1826): 37–42. Atkinson is discussed in *Gard. Mag.* 2 (March 1827): 200–03.

60
Loudon, *Gard. Mag.* 3 (January 1828): 366–67.

61
Ibid., 368.

62
Junius Redivivus, *Mech. Mag.* 16 (February 25, 1832): 371.

# Chapter 8:
# Progressive Architecture

1
For readers' comments on the influence of the *Encyc. Arch.* during its early years, see *Arch. Mag.* 1 (April 1834): 94; ibid. (May 1834): 141; ibid. (July 1834): 212; ibid. (August 1834): 246–47; and *Gard. Mag.* 10 (February 1834): 56.

2
Loudon, *Arch. Mag.* 1 (1834), preface and introduction.

3
Two British architectural journals that appeared after the *Arch. Mag.* were the *Civil Engineer and Architect's Journal*, begun in October 1837, and *The Builder*, begun in December 1842.

4
See Sebastiano Serlio (1475–1552), *On Domestic Architecture: Different Dwellings from the meanest hovel to the most ornate palace*, bk. 6, ed. Myra N. Rosenfeld (New York: Architectural History Foundation, 1978); and Andrea Palladio (1508–80), *Quattro libri d'Architettura* (Venice, 1570), trans. as *The Architecture of A. Palladio; in Four Books*, with notes and remarks of Inigo Jones (London: Ward, 1742).

5
Loudon, *Arch. Mag.* 3 (April 1836): 179. Although the numbers of gardeners had increased in Loudon's lifetime, the nursery business was suffering from a recession. See chapter 9.

6
*Times* (London, February 2, 1839). See also *Westminster Review* 41 (March 1844): 225ff; *Athenaeum* (March 7, 1835); Ibid. (October 8, 1842); *Penny Magazine* 2 (August 31, 1833): 339–40; *New Monthly Magazine* 36 (July 1, 1832): 300; Ibid. (October 1, 1832): 443; *Annales Soc. Hort.* 28 (1841): 145–47.

7
Poiteau, *Annales Soc. Hort.* 28 (1841): 145–47; ibid. 34 (February 1844): 94–95.

8
*Gentleman's Magazine* 102, pt. 2 (September 1832): 244–45.

9
Addison, "On the Pleasures of the Imagination," *The Spectator*, no.

411 (June 21, 1712); idem, no. 412 (June 23, 1712).

10
Loudon, *Encyc. Gard.* (1830 ed.), 74.

11
Loudon, *Treat. Hot-houses*, preface.

12
Jane Loudon, "Life of Loudon," 209.

13
See Loudon, *Encyc. Arch.* (1834 ed.), 841, 965, 816–20 (Barry), 846 (Fowler). Robertson's and Lamb's designs are found throughout the *Encyc. Arch.*

14
Loudon, *Encyc. Arch.* (1834 ed.), 790–821 ("Selim" and Barry), 790 (Loudon). For illustrations of Harlaxton Manor, see Mark Girouard, *The Victorian Country House* (New Haven: Yale University Press, 1979), 90ff.

15
Loudon, *Encyc. Arch.* (1834 ed.), 1018–27 (the Mallets), 711–15 (Rumford), 686–90 (Laxton), 251–57 (Manning), and 637, 650–51, 675 (Robison). For a discussion of William (or John) Manning's cottages, see Gilbert Herbert, *Pioneers of Fabrication: The British Contribution in the Nineteenth Century* (Baltimore, Md.: Johns Hopkins University Press, 1978), 9ff; idem, "The Portable Colonial Cottage," *Journal of the Society of Architectural Historians* 31 (December 1972): 261, where the confusion over Manning's first name is discussed.

16
Loudon, *Encyc. Arch.* (1834 ed.), 257ff.

17
Loudon, *Gard. Mag.* 6 (April 1830): 139–67, and *Encyc. Arch.* (1834 ed.), 8–20.

18
For Loudon's views on heating the floors of buildings (and notes on the baths of Pompeii and houses in China), see *Arch. Mag.* 1 (April 1834): 79.

19
Loudon, *Encyc. Arch.* (1836 ed.), 15. Loudon again warned about dampness in *Gard. Mag.* 16 (1840): 337–38, where he discussed cottages in Harlaxton, Lincolnshire.

His remarks were quoted by Edwin Chadwick in his *Report on . . . the Sanitary Condition of the Labouring Population of Great Britain*, Parliamentary Papers (1842), vol. 26, p. 266.

20

Loudon referred to *Country Res.* as a "juvenile work of ours published at a time when we had hardly attained the years of manhood" in *Gard. Mag.* 8 (December 1832): 700–01.

21

George L. Hersey, *High Victorian Gothic: A Study in Associationism* (Baltimore, Md.: Johns Hopkins University Press, 1972), 10ff.

22

Loudon, *Encyc. Arch.* (1834 ed.), 1114ff.

23

Loudon, *Encyc. Arch.* (1834 ed.), 1119–20.

24

A.-C. Quatremère de Quincy, *Essai sur la nature, le but, et les moyens de l'imitation dans les Beaux-Arts* (Paris: Treuttel & Würtz, 1823), and Charles Percier and P. F. L. Fontaine, *Recueil de décorations intérieures* (Paris, 1801).

25

See the general index to the *Arch. Mag.* in vol. 5 (1838), and the section titled "Original Communications" in each volume.

26

See *Arch. Mag.*, vols. 2 (1835), 3 (1836), and 4 (1837) for Thomas Hope; *Arch. Mag.* 2 (1835) for Quatremère de Quincy; and *Arch. Mag.* 4 (1837), and 5 (1838) for Ruskin ("Kata Phusin").

27

Ruskin, *Arch. Mag.* 4 (November 1837): 505–08.

28

*Arch. Mag.* 5 (March 1838): 99.

29

Ibid., 102.

30

Loudon, *Gard. Mag.* 7 (April 1831): 177ff.

31

Carlyle, *Past and Present and Chartism* (New York: Putnam, 1848), 66.

32

Ibid., 277.

33

Loudon, *Country Res.* 2:693–97.

34

Pugin, *Contrasts* (London, 1836), reviewed by Loudon in *Arch. Mag.* 4 (March 1837), 132.

35

Loudon, *Arch. Mag.* 4 (March 1837): 142.

36

Ibid., 143.

37

Loudon, *Gard. Mag.* 17 (August 1841): 399–404. Pierre Philippe-André L'Evêque de Vilmorin (1776–1862) was one of a long line of scientific and commercial seedsmen. At Verrières-le-Buisson, his residence just south of Paris, he laid out a landscape garden with rare trees and shrubs (some of which still exist). Loudon spoke of Vilmorin's residence as "a beautiful rural retreat, kept at all times in the highest order"; and he considered Vilmorin & Cie. "the first seedsmen in the world." Alexandre Poiteau (1766–1850), a botanist with field experience in the Dordogne, Haiti, and Guyana, became head of the nurseries at Versailles in 1815; head gardener at Fontainebleau, ca. 1821; and, later, head of the botanic garden of the School of Medicine, Paris. He taught at the Institut de Fromont and, from 1825–44, was editor-in-chief of the *Almanach du Bon Jardinier*, which Loudon considered "one of the best standard works on gardening and agriculture published in Europe." (*Gard. Mag.* 16 [1840]: 296).

38

Poiteau, *Annales Soc. Hort.* 28 (1841): 41.

39

Loudon, *Arch. Mag.* 3 (April 1836): 185ff.

40

Loudon to William Jerdan, March 9, 1833, in Jerdan, "Characteristic Letters," *Leisure Hour* (February 1, 1869): 141.

41

Loudon, *Encyc. Arch.* (1834 ed.), 963.

42

Loudon, *Arch. Mag.* 1 (July 1834): 186–88.

43

See chapter 15, and Loudon, *The Green-House Companion* (1824);

idem, *Sub. Gard.* (1838) and *Suburban Horticulturist* (1842).

44

Loudon, *Sketches of Hot-houses*.

45

E. E. Viollet-le-Duc, *Discourses on Architecture*, trans. Benjamin Bucknell (Boston: Ticknor, 1872), "Discourse 10," 446ff. Originally published as *Entretiens sur l'architecture*, 2 vols. (1863).

46

Loudon, *Arch. Mag.* 2 (January 1835): 1–2.

47

Ibid., 40–41, 44.

48

Ruskin, *Seven Lamps of Architecture* (London, 1849). For Pugin's views, see note 34; for Viollet-le-Duc's views, see Neil Levine, "The Romantic Idea of Architectural Legibility: Henri Labrouste and the Neo Grec," in *The Architecture of the Ecole des Beaux-Arts*, ed. Arthur Drexler (New York: Museum of Modern Art; distrib. MIT Press, 1977), 325ff.

49

Loudon, *Arch. Mag.* 2 (January 1835): 2–3. The Pantheon Bazaar was designed by James Wyatt and built by Samuel Wyatt, 1769–72. In 1790–91, it was converted to a theater. See J. M. Robinson, *The Wyatts: An Architectural Dynasty* (Oxford: Oxford University Press, 1979), 243. The Pantheon was rebuilt in the early 1830s. See *Arch. Mag.* 1 (April 1834): 91.

50

Kahn, interviewed in John Cook and Heinrich Klotz, *Conversations with Architects* (New York: Praeger, 1973), 183.

51

See *Arch. Mag.* 2 through 5 (1835–1838). For Hosking, see *Encyc. Arch.* (1834 ed.), 1123.

52

See chapter 10.

53

Loudon, *Gard. Mag.* 16 (January 1840): 35.

54

Levine, "Romantic Idea of Architectural Legibility."

55

In the summer of 1840, Loudon met with Daly in Paris, and the two discussed street widenings and building set-backs. See Loudon, *Gard. Mag.* 17 (April 1841): 195–96.

56

Daly, *Revue Générale* 1 (June 1840), cols. 327–33.

57

Pugin, *Contrasts*, 5. See also Loudon, *Arch. Mag.* 4 (March 1837): 142–43.

58

Loudon, *Gard. Mag.* 17 (1841): 292.

59

Ruskin, *Seven Lamps of Architecture* (New York: Noonday, 1969), 44.

60

Ibid., 194.

61

Loudon to John James Ruskin, November 30, 1838, in *Works of John Ruskin*, ed. E.T.Cook and Alexander Wedderburn, 39 vols. (London: George Allen & Unwin, 1903–12), vol. 1, p. xxxvii.

62

See Nikolaus Pevsner, *Some Architectural Writers of the Nineteenth Century* (Oxford: Clarendon, 1972), 139–56.

63

For evidence that Loudon's influence on architecture was spread round the world, see note 1.

64

Blau, *Ruskinian Gothic: The Architecture of Deane and Woodward, 1845–1861* (Princeton: Princeton University Press, 1982).

65

Downing, *The Architecture of Country Houses* (1850; reprint ed., New York: Dover, 1969), 461–84. Loudon favorably reviewed Downing's *Cottage Residences* (1842) in *Gard. Mag.* 18 (1842): 570; and Downing's *Treatise on Landscape Gardening* (1841) in *Gard. Mag.* 17 (1841): 421, 472.

66

Scully, *The Shingle Style and the Stick Style* (1955; revised ed., New Haven: Yale University Press, 1971), xliii.

67

Downing, *Architecture of Country Houses*, 8–9.

68

The style of rendering in *Cottage Residences* is closer to that of the engravings in Loudon's *Country Res*.

than to that of the woodcuts in *Encyc. Arch*.

69

Loudon, *Gard. Mag.* 7 (June 1831): 275–77.

70

Ibid., 272.

71

Loudon, *Arch. Mag.* 5 (January 1839): 673–77. The article on Covent Garden, from which the quotations that follow were taken, originally appeared in *Gard. Mag.* 7 (June 1831): 265–77.

## Chapter 9: Progressive Gardening

1

Loudon, *Encyc. Gard.*, 2.

2

Ibid., 1. Other treatises that offer the gardener a cosmic perspective on his art include Jacques Boyceau, *Traité du jardinage* (Paris, 1638), and Claude Mollet, *Théâtre des plans et jardinage* (Paris, 1652).

3

*Gentleman's Magazine* n.s., 1, (May 1834): 497–501. The author was "J.M.."

4

*Literary Gazette* (26 October 1822): 672–74.

5

Loudon, *Esquisse pour une histoire générale du jardinage/Outline for a General History of Gardening and an Account of its present state throughout the World.* (London: Printed for the Author, 1821). A copy of this pamphlet, containing about ninety closely printed pages, is preserved in the Bibliothèque Nationale, Paris.

6

*Quarterly Review* 24 (January 1821): 400–19.

7

Ibid., 415.

8

Ibid., 418–19. In *Remarks on Hot-houses*, Loudon had written, "The horticultural societies of London and Edinburgh, composed of men of rank and influence, scientific amateurs and practical gardeners, give a degree of *éclat* and salutary consequence to the study; and from this circumstance, as well as the known skill and activity of many members,

the public may expect to reap considerable advantage" (p. 1).

9

See Knight's original paper (read on March 7, 1820) in *Trans. Hort. Soc.* 4:77. For Loudon's response, see *Gard. Mag.* 5 (June 1829): 367.

10

Loudon, *Gard. Mag.* 5 (February 1829): 87.

11

Loudon, *Gard. Mag.* 10 (February 1834): 73. For more details of the controversy, see *Gard. Mag.* 5 (June 1829): 364–68; (October 1829): 534–39; (December 1829): 718–22.

12

Christopher North [John Wilson], *Blackwood's Edinburgh Magazine* 35 (May 1834): 691ff. Loudon's reply appears in vol. 36 (September 1834): 96.

13

Poiteau, *Annales Soc. Hort.* 27 (December 1840): 347.

14

Loudon, *Gard. Mag.* 3 (September 1827): 108. This paragraph originally appeared in my review of Phillada Ballard's *An Oasis of Delight: The History of the Birmingham Botanical Gardens* (London: Duckworth, 1983) in *Journal of Garden History* 5, no. 4 (October–December 1985): 386.

15

Loudon, *Gard. Mag.* 3 (September 1827): 109.

16

Loudon, *Gard. Mag.* 3 (March 1828): 443–44. See also *Annales Soc. Hort.* 1, no. 2 (1827): 81–87. Before the revolution of 1789, Malmaison was one of the finest landscape gardens in France.

17

A picturesque view of Fromont, looking towards the Seine, is found in M.Audot, *Traité de la composition et de l'ornement des jardins*, 2 vols., 6th ed. (Paris, 1859), pl. 22.

18

Loudon, *Gard. Mag.* 7 (February 1831): 16. In vol. 9 (April 1833): 141–42, when Loudon praised Etienne Soulange-Bodin as a gentleman, a man of science, and a tradesman, he added, "There is nothing of the kind that we know of in England; nor can there be in the present state of things. It is, perhaps, one of the finest moral features in France, that most gentlemen are either manufacturers, tradesmen, or farmers; and that nearly all of the persons practicing these professions are, in education and manners, gentlemen."

19

Soulange-Bodin, "Sur les jardins de l'ornement," *Annales de l'Institut Royal Horticole de Fromont* 3 (June 1831), hereafter cited as *Annales de Fromont*.

20

Loudon, *Gard. Mag.* 1 (January 1826), preface.

21

J.M., in *Gard. Mag.* 7 (February 1831): 117 (not to be confused with J.M. of the *Gentleman's Magazine*, whose home was apparently in Suffolk).

22

A Lady Florist, *Gard. Mag.* 7 (April 1831): 245.

23

Loudon, ibid.

24

S.T., ibid., 244.

25

A would-be suburban gardener, ibid. (December 1831): 720–21.

26

See Robert Abraham's house for a gardener in *Gard. Mag.* 6 (February 1830): 34–35; and the series of designs which begins with vol. 8 (October 1832): 551ff.

27

Sensitivus, *Gard. Mag.* 2 (January 1827): 36–38.

28

Archibald M'Naughton (of Hackney, East London), *Gard. Mag.* 1 (January 1826): 24–26.

29

Burnard, I.P., of Eden Grove, Holloway, ibid. (April 1826): 141.

30

G.R.C., ibid. (October 1826): 411.

31

A.B.C., *Gard. Mag.* 5 (February 1829):100; *Gard. Mag.* 6 (December 1830): 721.

32

Loudon, *Gard. Mag.* 8 (December 1832): 645.

33

Loudon, *Gard. Mag.* 5 (February 1829): 112.

34

Rollins, ibid., 101–02.

35

Loudon, ibid., 102–03.

36

Loudon, *Gard. Mag.* 7 (August 1831): 414; ibid. (October 1831): 557.

37

Loudon, *Encyc. Gard.* (1830 ed.), 1135.

38

Q., Doncaster, Yorkshire, *Gard. Mag.* 7 (April 1831): 139–40.

39

The following articles were originally contributed to the *Gard. Mag.*: grafting [3 (November 1827): 149ff]; gardener's house [10 (February 1834): 24ff]; on *Ericae* [1 (April 1826): 131ff]; heat and moisture [1 (January 1826): 37ff]; on hothouse in Vienna [8 (October 1832): 535ff]; landscape gardening [10 (May 1834): 197ff]; Whateley's "Observations" [7 (April 1831): 144ff].

40

Q., *Gard. Mag.* 7 (April 1831): 139–40.

41

See J.L. and Barbara Hammond, *The Town Labourer, 1760–1832* (London: Longmans, 1966), 295; and J.T. Ward, *Chartism* (London: Batsford, 1973), 63.

42

Loudon, *Gard. Mag.* 7 (August 1831): 419.

43

Loudon, ibid., 420. See Friedrich Engels, *The Condition of the Working Class in England,* trans. and ed., W.O. Henderson and W.H. Chaloner (Stanford, Ca.: Stanford University Press, 1958), 31ff.

44

See Asa Briggs, *Victorian People* (London, 1954); and E.P. Thompson, *The Making of the English Working Class* (London: Penguin, 1970).

45

Loudon, *Gard. Mag.* 7 (August 1831): 420.

46

Jane Loudon, "Life of Loudon," 206.

47

Loudon, *Gard. Mag.* 7 (October 1831): 609.

48

See George F. Chadwick, *The Works of Sir Joseph Paxton* (London: Architectural Press, 1961).

49

See Loudon's review in *Gard. Mag.* 10 (May 1834): 230–32.

50

Loudon, *Gard. Mag.* 8 (April 1832): 130.

51

E., *Gard. Mag.* 10 (October 1834): 521. E. suggests that the real cause of the depressed state of the nursery business was the London Horticultural Society's overextending themselves in creating the large garden in Chiswick and in distributing plants to its members. In effect, he charges that the society had become a competitor of the nurserymen.

52

Desmond, "Loudon and Nineteenth-Century Horticultural Journalism," in *John Claudius Loudon and the Early Nineteenth Century in Great Britain,* ed. E. MacDougall (Washington, D.C.: Dumbarton Oaks, 1980), 85.

53

Loudon, *Gard. Mag.* 8 (April 1832): 130–31.

54

Loudon, *Gard. Mag.* 9 (April 1833): 145–50; *Encyc. Gard.* (1830 ed.), 38. Boursault's garden was near the Barrière de Montmartre, in the northern periphery of Paris.

55

Loudon, *Gard. Mag.* 8 (April 1832): 256; and ibid. (October 1832): 593.

56

Soulange-Bodin, *Annales de Fromont* 4 (1832): 214–16.

57

Loudon, *Gard. Mag.* 8 (October 1832): 593. See chapter 14.

58

Ibid.

59

Loudon, *Gard. Mag.* 11 (December 1835): 654.

# Chapter 10:
# Art and Science
# in the Landscape

1

*Arb. Brit.* 3:1766ff.

2

Ibid., 2:511–12. Loudon quotes four stanzas in all, from the Harleian Manuscript No. 5396.

3

Ibid., 1:193ff, and preface.

4

Loudon, *Gard. Mag.* 2 (May 1827):
301, and Julius von Sachs, *History
of Botany, 1530–1860*, trans.
H.E.F.Garnsey (Oxford: Clarendon
Press, 1906), 82–107, 116–22.

5

John Lindley, quoted in *Gard. Mag.*
7 (February 1831): 76ff. See also
William T. Stearn, "Linnaean Classification, Nomenclature, and Method," in Wilfred Blunt, *The Compleat
Naturalist, A Life of Linnaeus* (New
York: Viking, 1971), 242–45.

6

Antoine-Laurent de Jussieu, *Genera
Plantarum, secundum Ordines Natu-
rales disposita* (Paris: Herissant,
1789). The rudiments of this long
work were developed in Jussieu's
paper "Exposition d'un nouvel ordre
de plantes adoptés dans les démon-
strations du jardin royal," in
*Mémoires de l'Académie Royale des
Sciences. Histoire de l'Académie*
(Paris, 1774), 175–97. Frans A.
Stafleu, in a new edition of Jussieu's
*Genera Plantarum* (New York:
Stechert-Hafner Services Agency,
ca. 1970), observes that this work
was difficult to obtain outside France
during the Revolution, but by September 16, 1789, Sir Joseph Banks
owned a copy. Loudon, who occasionally had the use of Banks's library, may have read Banks's copy
sometime in 1803, the year Loudon
first met Banks.

7

Loudon, *Arb. Brit.* 1:200ff.

8

See Erasmus Darwin, *Loves of the
Plants* (London, 1789); idem, *The
Botanic Garden* (London, 1791).

9

*Quarterly Review* 62 (October 1838):
334.

10

Loudon, *Arb. Brit.* 1:viiiff.

11

See the album containing more than
seventy letters addressed to J.C.
Loudon (and later presented to Miss
Jane Jukes [1791–1873], a geol-
ogist, of Birmingham), now in the
Yale Center for British Art, New
Haven, Connecticut. Extracts of
these letters were quoted by W.
Roberts (a previous owner of the
album), in "The Centenary of Loudon's 'Arboretum'," *Journal of the*

*Royal Horticultural Society* 61
(1936): 277–84.

12

Roberts, "Centenary of Loudon's
'Arboretum'," 281.

13

Ibid., 282.

14

Loudon, *Arb. Brit.* 1:190–91.

15

For examples, see W.E.Hickson,
*Westminster Review* 35 (April 1841):
418–56; and A.J.Downing, *Magazine of Horticulture* (Boston, Mass.)
4 (1838): 201ff. (Hickson, the radical reformer, became co-owner of
the *Westminster Review* in 1840; see
*Wellesley Index* 3:540. Downing is
discussed in chapter 11 of this
book.) For a sampling of reviews
written by such authorities as Sir
W.J.Hooker, Sir William Jardine,
and Alphonse de Candolle, see *Gardener's Chronicle* (October 30,
1841): 714, where excerpts are
given from the *Quarterly Review*, the
*Edinburgh Review*, the *Annales Soc.
Hort.*, the *Berlin Garten Zeitung*, the
*Bib. Universelle de Genève*, and other
works. Etienne Soulange-Bodin offered an objective explanation of
Loudon's views on the gardenesque
(without critical discussion) in *Annales de l'Institut (Royale) Horticole
de Fromont* 6 (1834): 343–51 (hereafter cited as *Annales de Fromont*).

16

Loudon, *Country Res.* 1:65–66,
2:712. See Reynolds, *Discourses on
Art* (London: Collier-Macmillan,
1969), discourse 6, 93ff.

17

Loudon, *Arb. Brit.* 1:200.

18

Loudon, *Gard. Mag.* 7 (April 1831):
155.

19

Loudon, *Gard. Mag.* 2 (May 1827):
301.

20

Loudon, ed., *The Landscape Gardening and Landscape Architecture
of the late Humphry Repton, Esq.*
(London, 1840), introduction. Recently it has been suggested that
Loudon was not really interested in
combining the charms of Repton's
school with the sciences of gardening and botany. See T.H.D.Turner,
"Loudon's Stylistic Development,"
*Journal of Garden History* 2, no. 2

(April–June 1982). Turner argues
that Loudon grew to "favour the
regular style of garden layout based
on abstract geometrical forms" (p.
185). That I disagree will become
apparent in this chapter.

21

Loudon, *Gard. Mag.* 11 (December
1835): 612. Loudon had tried to
plant lawns with masses, or drifts, of
wildflowers as early as 1803, at
Scone Palace.

22

Loudon, *Gard. Mag.* 7 (April 1831):
151.

23

Loudon, *Sub. Gard.*, 136.

24

Walpole, quoted in Loudon, *Encyc.
Gard.*, 1154.

25

Loudon, *Gard. Mag.* 8 (December
1832): 701.

26

Viart, *Le jardiniste moderne* (Paris,
1827), 5. In the first edition (1819),
Viart states that it is necessary to
have genius, reason, and taste to
succeed in the art of gardening, or
"le jardinisme." In 1827, in place of
*le jardinisme*, Viart substitutes the
word *jardinique*. Two important features of Viart's art of gardening are
the isolated tree—which can be
grouped in "masses of isolated
trees"; and the "chain," or sequence, of landscape scenes. Alexandre Poiteau, in *Annales Soc. Hort.*
13 (1833), describes Viart's park,
Brunehaut, near Etampes, as "the
most beautiful park that now exists
on French soil" (p. 124).

27

See Loudon, *Encyc. Gard.*, 1305,
and idem, *Gard. Mag.* 4 (August
1828): 261.

28

Soulange-Bodin, *Annales de Fromont*
6 (1834): 343–51.

29

Quatremère de Quincy, *Essai sur la
nature, le but, et les moyens de
l'imitation dans les Beaux-Arts*
(Paris: Treuttel & Würtz, 1823), 1–
28 (hereafter, *Essai sur l'imitation*).

30

Ibid., 5–6, 149–50.

31

Loudon, *Arch. Mag.* 4 (January
1837): 43–44, idem, *Gard. Mag.* 10

(November 1834): 559, and *Gard. Mag.* 13 (1837): 597ff.

**32**

Loudon, *Gard. Mag.* 14 (1838): 434.

**33**

*Gard. Mag.* 10 (November 1834): 559. See Quatremère de Quincy, *Essai sur l'imitation*, 95–102, 149–50. Loudon's mature interest in a free, rather than literal, imitation of nature is parallel to his mature views on the "fictive truth of construction" in architecture (see chapter 8). Though Loudon never discussed in print his sources for these architectural ideas, he was probably intrigued by Quatremère de Quincy's statement that there is an element of fiction in *all* works of art; and he may have gone on from there to consider the fictive truth of construction.

**34**

Loudon, *Gard. Mag.* 13 (1837): 600.

**35**

Reynolds, *Discourses on Art*, discourse 13, 210–11.

**36**

Scott, *Quarterly Review* 37 (March 1828): 310–11.

**37**

Loudon, *Gard. Mag.* 13 (1837): 600.

**38**

*Gard. Mag.* 15 (December 1839): 715.

**39**

*Gard. Mag.* 16 (December 1840): 621.

**40**

Ibid., 622.

**41**

*Gard. Mag.* 11 (December 1835): 648.

**42**

Ibid., 649.

**43**

Ibid., 650–51.

**44**

Ibid., 652.

**45**

For Loudon's views on Versailles, see *Gard. Mag.* 17 (August 1841): 383; and *Gard. Mag.* 7 (February 1831): 7. For his view of Le Nôtre's work at Fontainebleau, see *Gard. Mag.* 17 (August 1841): 402.

**46**

Compare the plan of Sceaux (en-graved from a plan originally made by a Parisian land surveyor), which was published in *Gard. Mag.* 7 (February 1831): 3–4, with an earlier plan of Sceaux (dated 1785): "Nouveau plan des jardins de Sceaux," seat of the duc de Penthièvre, in Georges Poisson, *Sceaux, Domaine Princier*, in the series *Les Monuments historiques de la France, edition de la Caisse Nationale des Monuments Historiques* (Paris, ca. 1975).

**47**

Loudon, *Gard. Mag.* 7 (February 1831): 3–4.

**48**

*Gard. Mag.* 6 (October 1830): 529.

**49**

*Gard. Mag.* 17 (August 1841): 383.

**50**

Loudon laid out St. Peter's Square, Hammersmith, London, in the late 1820s. See Thomas Faulkner, *The History and Antiquities of the Parish of Hammersmith* (London, 1839). I am indebted to John Gloag for the suggestion that Loudon may have had something to do with the layout of St. Peter's Square. Loudon also laid out the grounds of the duchess of Brunswick's residence at Blackheath (*Obs. on Gard.*, dedication). Later in life, he designed a small garden "within 2 miles of St. Paul's" (*The Villa Gardener*, ed. Mrs. Loudon [London, 1850], 95).

**51**

Loudon, *Gard. Mag.* 8 (August 1832): 407–28. See also Phillada Ballard, *An Oasis of Delight, The History of the Birmingham Botanical Gardens* (London: Duckworth, 1983).

**52**

Nash, "Plan of . . . Marylebone Park Farm" (later called Regent's Park), 1811–12, in *Parliamentary Papers, First Report of the Commissioners of . . . Woods, Forests and Land Revenues*, June 4, 1812.

**53**

For a study of English traits in the arts, see Nikolaus Pevsner, *The Englishness of English Art* (New York: Penguin, 1978), 95ff. According to Pevsner's theory, Nash's plan could be compared with the ground plans of the English Perpendicular-style cathedrals, because of their "additive" quality, as opposed to the organic quality of the plans of twelfth- and thirteenth-century French cathedrals.

**54**

Few of the garden designs in *Gard. Mag.* are actually by Loudon, and none are taken from his own finished drawings. His right arm was amputated in 1825; thereafter his crude left-handed sketches were redrawn by draftsmen.

**55**

Thouin, *Plans raisonnés de toutes les espèces de jardins*, 2nd ed. (Paris, 1820), pl. 19.

**56**

Viart, *Jardiniste moderne* (1819), 30ff.

**57**

Loudon, *Gard. Mag.* 9 (August 1833): 387; *Gard. Mag.* 4 (December 1828): 494. Loudon published some of von Sckell's writings in *Gard. Mag.* 17 (1841) and 18 (1842).

**58**

Loudon, *Gard. Mag.* 16 (December 1840): 620.

**59**

See Vincent Scully, Jr., *Frank Lloyd Wright* (New York: Braziller, 1969), 30ff.

**60**

Loudon, *Gard. Mag.* 4 (December 1828): 496. In *Gard. Mag.* 5 (December 1829): 676, Loudon gives a rare account of his trials as a mature landscape gardener. In 1826, at forty-three, an established authority on landscape gardening, he found it difficult to persuade a client to accept his recommendations, and added, "When an artist is not great enough to be an autocrat in matters of his profession, and at the same time is not little enough to chime in with whatever is proposed to him; when he has to address himself to a mind that is without faith in his taste, that cannot reason on what is proposed, and that has a morbid feeling of opposition to all ideas that are not already familiar; every change which it is proposed to introduce produces a battle. At least fifty of these stormy but perfectly good-natured discussions, took place during the ten days which we remained at _____" (an unnamed residence near Gainsborough, Lincolnshire).

61
Loudon, *Gard. Mag.* 8 (August 1832): 423.

62
See chapter 11, and *Gard. Mag.* 12 (January 1836): 13ff.

63
As a result of recent redistricting, Coleshill village is now officially in Oxfordshire. For attributions to Inigo Jones, see *Antiquities in Bedfordshire, Berkshire, etc.* in *Bibliotheca Topographica Britannica*, vol. 4 (London: Nicols, 1790).

64
Summerson, *Architecture in Britain, 1530–1830* (Baltimore, Md.: Penguin, 1970), 152.

65
John Britton and E. W. Brayley, *Beauties of England and Wales* (London: Longmans et al., 1801), 1:133ff.

66
Cobbett, *Rural Rides*, ed. G. Woodcock (London: Penguin, 1967), 355–58.

67
Ronald E. Huch, *The Radical Lord Radnor: The Public Life of Viscount Folkestone, Third Earl of Radnor, 1779–1869* (Minneapolis: University of Minnesota Press, 1977), 4.

68
Mark Girouard, *The Victorian Country House* (New Haven: Yale University Press, 1979), 23. Loudon's plan for the heating system at Coleshill was discussed in C. J. Richardson, *Popular Treatise on the Warming and Ventilation of Buildings* (London: Weale, 1837). Richardson includes a cross-section of the heating system and notes that it was found defective because soot in the flues frequently caught fire; later these iron flues were removed.

69
Loudon's "Report on . . . Coleshill House," May 2, 1843, is preserved in the Berkshire County Record Office, Reading. All improvements were "projected" at the time.

70
Huch, *Radical Lord Radnor*, 157–58.

71
The house was destroyed in 1952 (Summerson, *Architecture in Britain*, 152) or in 1953 (Olive Hill and John Cornforth, *English Country Houses:*

*Caroline* [London: Country Life, 1966], 91).

## Chapter 11:
## The Derby Arboretum

1
Loudon's view reported by Robert Chambers in *Chambers's Edinburgh Journal* (May 4, 1844): 285. The following account is based mainly on Loudon's catalogue *The Derby Arboretum* (London: Longman, 1840), which describes the history, formation, opening day ceremonies, and proposed management scheme of the arboretum, and gives a complete list of plants. The catalogue was abridged in *Gard. Mag.* 16 (1840): 521ff. See also Stephen Glover, *The History of the Borough of Derby* (Derby, 1843).

2
Granville, *The Spas of England*, 2 vols. (1841; reprint ed., Bath: Adams & Dart, 1971). See vol. 2, 60ff, 121ff.

3
Loudon, *Gard. Mag.* 16 (1840): 535.

4
Gilpin, *Observations on the Mountains and Lakes of Cumberland and Westmoreland* (London, 1792).

5
*Second Report of the Commissioners of Inquiry into the State of Large Towns and Populous Districts*, Parliamentary Papers, vol. 18 (1845), pt. 2, appendix, 275 (hereafter cited as *State of Large Towns*).

6
Ibid., 271.

7
Loudon, *Gard. Mag.* 2 (May 1827): 371–72 (on Buckingham Palace).

8
*State of Large Towns*, 275.

9
Jane Loudon, *Lady's Magazine of Gardening* 1 (1842): 231ff, and J. W. Allen, "Bygone Derby," in *Derby Evening Telegraph* (October 2, 1950).

10
*State of Large Towns*, 67ff.

11
Ibid., 68.

12
Chadwick, *Report on the Sanitary Condition of the Labouring Popula-*

*tion of Great Britain*. Parliamentary Papers, vol. 26 (1842): 276ff (hereafter cited as *Sanitary Condition*), *Westminister Review* 35 (1841): 418ff. Chadwick was secretary to the Poor Law Commission from 1834 to 1837. See also Loudon's review of Chadwick's *Sanitary Condition* in *Gard. Mag.* 18 (1842): 472.

13
Loudon, *Gard. Mag.* 16 (1840): 534.

14
Rauch was probably identical with (or related to) Charles Rauch, the court gardener in Laxenburg, Germany, whose article "On the Construction of a double-roofed Hothouse at Vienna" appeared in *Gard. Mag.* 8 (October 1832): 535ff. In *Gard. Mag.* 8 (August 1832): 400, Loudon noted that "C. Rauch," formerly of Vienna, was currently employed in the Chiswick Garden of the Horticultural Society, in London.

15
Loudon, *The Derby Arboretum*, 8ff.

16
Loudon, "Hints for a National Garden," an address delivered to the Linnaean Society, December 17, 1811. The original manuscript is preserved in the Library of the Linnaean Society, London.

17
Loudon, *Gard. Mag.* 16 (1840): 542ff.

18
Ibid., 544.

19
Strutt, "Presentation of the Derby Arboretum," address before the mayor, aldermen and councillors assembled in the Guild Hall, Derby, September 16, 1840. A copy of the address is preserved in the Derbyshire County Library, Derby Local Studies Department.

20
Ibid.

21
Loudon, *Derby Arboretum*, 93.

22
Strutt, "Presentation of Derby Arboretum."

23
Loudon, quoted in *Westminster Review* 35 (1841): 427.

24
Ibid., 429.

25
Granville, *Spas of England* 2:123–24.

26
Hickson, *Westminster Review* 35 (1841): 418–57.

27
Hickson, *Westminster Review* 35 (1841): 438.

28
Jerdan, "Characteristic Letters," *The Leisure Hour* (February 1, 1869): 140.

29
Mott, in Chadwick, *Sanitary Condition*, 240ff.

30
Martin, *State of Large Towns*, pt. 2, appendix, 275.

31
Jane Loudon, *Lady's Magazine of Gardening* 1 (1842): 231ff. A version of this paragraph appeared in my review essay on *John Claudius Loudon and the Early Nineteenth Century in Great Britain*, ed. Elisabeth B. MacDougall (Washington, D.C.: Dumbarton Oaks, 1980), in *Journal of Garden History* 3, no. 1 (January–March, 1983): 59–64.

32
Martin, *State of Large Towns*, 272.

33
William Baker, M.D., "Description of a Court in Bridge Street, Derby, called Robinson's Yard, and of the Fever which prevailed there in the months of August, September, October, and November, 1843," in *State of Large Towns*, pt. 2, appendix, 279ff.

34
Hovey, *Magazine of Horticulture* 11 (1845): 122–28.

35
Downing, *Horticulturist* 5 (1850): 266–68. As if to make amends for criticizing the design of the arboretum, Downing reprinted Loudon's essay on taste from the *Arch. Mag.* 1 (May 1834): 97–103.

36
Downing, *Horticulturist* 5 (1850): 268–71.

37
Loudon, *Gard. Mag.* 9 (August 1833): 468.

38
Allen, "Bygone Derby."

39
Since the early 1970s, the Derby Department of Town Planning and local citizens have tried to maintain the arboretum and some housing in adjacent Arboretum Street and Arboretum Square as a conservation area. Restoration of the arboretum is planned for 1987, and some of the houses in Arboretum Square have already been restored. In 1981 alone, the Derby City Council voted to spend three-quarters of a million pounds on the arboretum. See *Derby Evening Telegraph* (April 14, 1981; December 17, 1979; January 26, 1977), and other materials in the Derbyshire County Library, Derby Local Studies Department. See also John E. Heath, "The First Public Park in England," *Derbyshire Life and Countryside* (October 1975): 66–68; and Roy Christian, "Forgotten Oasis in an Urban Desert," *Country Life* (November 25, 1976): 1582–83. I am indebted to Mr. Kay of the Derby Department of Town Planning for making available a draft of the plan entitled "Borough of Derby Arboretum Conservation Area," ca. 1975. A comparison of this draft with Loudon's original plan reveals very little change in the basic layout of the arboretum; however, as of 1977, only about a dozen trees could be identified with Loudon's original planting plan. See *Derby Evening Telegraph*, January 26, 1977.

## Chapter 12:
## Metropolitan Improvements

1
Loudon's changes of address in London can be traced in his published works. In 1803–05, he had lodgings in 4, Chapel St., Bedford Row. Later addresses were (1806) 90, Newman St.; (1808) 82, Newman St.; (1811) 42, Pall Mall; (1814–16) Newman St.; (1817) Bayswater House (or The Hermitage), Bayswater; (1823–43) 3, Porchester Terrace, Bayswater.

2
Peter Quennell, ed., *Mayhew's London* (London: Spring Books, Hamlyn, 1969), 18.

3
Cobbett, *Rural Rides* (1830; a new edition, London: Penguin, 1967), 81.

4
Grant, *The Great Metropolis* (New York and London: Saunders and Otley, 1837), 1–22.

5
Quennell, ed., *Mayhew's London*, 17.

6
Evelyn, *London Revived: Considerations for its Rebuilding in 1666*, ed. E.S. de Beer (Oxford: Clarendon, 1938).

7
Marcus Whiffen, "Academic Elysium: The Landscaping of the Cambridge Backs," *Architectural Review* 101, no. 1 (January 1947): 13–17.

8
Summerson, *John Nash, Architect to King George IV*, 2nd ed. (London: Allen & Unwin, 1949), 170ff. Nash's commission for Price was the design of Castle House, in Aberystwyth, North Wales. For this project and for Nash's collaborations with Repton — including Corsham Court, Wiltshire — see Summerson, *The Life and Work of John Nash, Architect* (Cambridge: MIT Press, 1980), 33ff. For Nash's work in London, see Hermione Hobhouse, *A History of Regent Street* (London: Macdonald and Jane's, and Queen Anne Press, 1975).

9
Summerson, *John Nash* (1949), 180.

10
John Gloag first suggested to me that Loudon may have designed St. Peter's Square in Hammersmith, London. Evidence is scanty; see Thomas Faulkner, *The History and Antiquities of the Parish of Hammersmith* (London, 1839). Faulkner states that Loudon "planned" the square, and other statements of his suggest a date of ca. 1827 for Loudon's participation in this project. See also Melanie Louise Simo, "Loudon and the Landscape: A Study of Rural and Metropolitan Improvements, 1803–1843" (Ph.D. diss., Yale, 1976), for more information on St. Peter's Square. In 1835 Loudon also laid out an approach road to Gunnersbury Park, West London (near Acton Station), the residence of N.M. Rothschild. See *Gard. Mag.* 12 (February 1836): 54.

11
Summerson, *John Nash* (1949), 180–81.

12

Loudon, *Gard. Mag.* 5 (December 1829): 672.

13

Loudon, letter to the editor, dated December 22, 1803, in *Literary Journal* 2, no. 12 (December 31, 1803), cols. 739–42. See Laurence Fricker, "John Claudius Loudon, The Plane Truth?" in *Furor Hortensis*, ed. Peter Willis (Edinburgh: Elysium Press, 1974), 76–85. After locating this article (not an easy task), Fricker exposed a myth perpetuated unwittingly by Jane Loudon in her "Life of Loudon," that is, that her husband had recommended Oriental and Occidental plane trees for London squares in 1803; he had not.

14

Loudon, "Hints for a National Garden," 1811.

15

See the plan of the Loddiges' arboretum in *Encyc. Gard.* (1830 ed.), 1035. Loudon considered Conrad Loddiges and his sons "eminent" botanical nurserymen. See *Encyc. Gard.* (1830 ed.), 1108.

16

Loudon, letter to the editor, *Gentleman's Magazine* 88, pt. 1 (June 1818): 494–96.

17

Peter Smith, *Waterways Heritage* (Luton, Bedfordshire: Luton Museum and Art Gallery, 1975), 6.

18

*Gentleman's Magazine* 89, pt. 2 (August 1819): 105. See also Summerson, *John Nash* (1949), 171ff.

19

John Nash made a similar observation on canal boats in a park in the *First Report of the Commissioners of His Majesty's Woods, Forests, and Land Revenues* (June 4, 1812), appendix 12B. For a detailed discussion of Nash's intentions for Regent's Park, see Summerson, *Life and Work of Nash*, 58ff.

20

Loudon, *Gard. Mag.* 1 (January 1826): 89–90. See also the *Fifth Report of the Commissioners of His Majesty's Woods, Forests, and Land Revenues*, Parliamentary Papers (May 12, 1826).

21

John Martin, *Plan for Supplying with Pure Water the Cities of London and Westminster* (London, 1828).

22

Loudon, *Gard. Mag.* 6 (August 1830): 490. In 1829 Loudon circulated a petition, signed by the "principal inhabitants of Bayswater," in favor of pulling down the north wall of Kensington Gardens and replacing it with an open iron-rail fence and mounds on the interior planted with evergreens (all of which suggestions have since been followed). At the time, the wall was a "hideous, old, crooked, lofty wall, disfigured by handbills and chalk-writing," and by buttresses that collected "all kinds of impurities." As late as October 1837, however, the wall remained. See *Gard. Mag.* 13 (1837): 469ff.

23

James Henry Leigh Hunt, *The Old Court Suburbs; or, Memorials of Kensington, Regal, Critical and Anecdotal* (London: Hurst & Blackett, 1855), 277ff.

24

Loudon, *Gard. Mag.* 1 (July 1826): 284.

25

Loudon, *Encyc. Gard.*, 1187–88.

26

See Violet Markham, *Paxton and the Bachelor Duke* (London: Hodder & Stoughton, 1935), 277–80; and George F. Chadwick, *The Works of Sir Joseph Paxton, 1803–1865* (London: Architectural Press, 1961), 201–12.

27

See An Architect [A.W.Hakewill], *An Apology for the Architectural Monstrosities of London* (London, 1835), Sir Edward Cust, *Letter to Sir Robert Peel, Bart., M.P., on the Expediency of a Better System of Control over Buildings Erected at Public Expense* (London, 1835), and others, including *Gentleman's Magazine, Literary Gazette, Mechanics' Magazine*, and *Gardener's Magazine*.

28

Pugin, *True Principles of Pointed or Christian Architecture* (London, 1842); idem, *Contrasts* (London, 1836).

29

Charles Fowler, *Arch. Mag.* 2 (September 1835): 381–84; Hakewill, *Architectural Monstrosities; idem, Thoughts on the Style of Architecture to be adopted in the Rebuilding of the Houses of Parliament* (London, 1835).

30

Hazlitt, "The Periodical Press," *Edinburgh Review* 38 (May 1823): 351.

31

An Admirer of Good Taste, *Letter to . . . Sir Charles Long on the Improvements Proposed and Now Carrying on in the Western Part of London* (London, 1825).

32

*Mechanics' Magazine* 8 (July 28, 1827): 18.

33

Loudon, *Gard. Mag.* 2 (May 1827): 371–72.

34

Loudon, *Arch. Mag.* 3 (March 1836): 100–03.

35

A Member of Parliament, *Considerations upon the Expediency of Building a Metropolitan Palace Dedicated to King George IV* (London, 1825).

36

Ibid.

37

Loudon, *Gard. Mag.* 19 (1843): 596. Loudon was in Southampton to advise on the laying out of the new cemetery. See Appendix A.

38

Loudon, *Gard. Mag.* 7 (August 1831): 407.

39

Loudon, *Arch. Mag.* 1 (June 1834): 179–80.

40

Loudon, *Gard. Mag.* 6 (August 1830): 514.

41

Ibid. See also J.C.Platt, "Smithfield," in Charles Knight, ed., *London*, vol. 2 (London: Knight, 1842), 318–28.

42

Loudon, *Gard. Mag.* 5 (February 1829): 3.

43

Loudon's notes on travels in 1828–29 were published in *Gard. Mag.*, vols. 5 through 9 (1829–1833).

44

*Gard. Mag.* 5 (February 1829): 8.

45

*Gard. Mag.* 6 (February 1830): 11.

46
*Gard. Mag.* 5 (February 1829): 8–9.
*Gard. Mag.* 9 (August 1833): 385.
47
*Gard. Mag.* 5 (April 1829): 115–16.
*Gard. Mag.* 9 (August 1833): 413.
48
*Gard. Mag.* 7 (October 1831): 522.
49
*Gard. Mag.* 5 (April 1829): 113–25.
50
Ibid., 114.
51
Smirke, *Suggestions for the Architectural Improvement of the Western Part of London* (London: Priestley & Weale, 1834), 23–29.
52
Ibid., 60ff.
53
Loudon, *Arch. Mag.* 1 (June 1834): 177–80; ibid. (December 1834): 382.
54
Loudon gave testimony before the Commission of Inquiry into the State of Large Towns and Populous Districts on June 12, 1843. See *First Report . . .* (on) *the State of Large Towns,* Parliamentary Papers (1844), 55–60.
55
Ibid., 55–56, 59–60. For other co-operative housing schemes in Britain (though most of the book concerns America), see Dolores Hayden, *The Grand Domestic Revolution: A History of Feminist Designs for American Homes, Neighborhoods and Cities* (Cambridge: MIT Press, 1981).
56
Loudon, *Gard. Mag.* 7 (April 1831): 224.
57
*Gard. Mag.* 5 (June 1829): 329.
58
*Gard. Mag.* 12 (October 1836): 550.
59
See note 54.
60
Loudon, *Gard. Mag.* 18 (1842): 139, 566. One of Loudon's letters to the *Morning Chronicle* (November 11, 1840) was reprinted in the *Westminster Review* 35 (1841): 440–41, and in the *Gardener's Gazette* (November 21, 1840): 741. Another of Loudon's letters on this subject appeared in the *Morning Chronicle,* November 3, 1840.
61
Loudon, *Mag. Nat. Hist.* 3 (September 1830): 434.

## Chapter 13:
## Planning for London and the Ideal Capital

Another version of this chapter, with more emphasis on Hampstead Heath, past and present, was published as "John Claudius Loudon: On Planning and Design for the Garden Metropolis" in *Garden History* 9, no. 2 (Autumn 1981): 184–201. Reproduction of parts of this article is by kind permission of the Honorary Editor, *Garden History.*

1
Loudon, *Gard. Mag.* 5 (December 1829): 686–90.
2
Ibid., 669.
3
Ibid., 653–56.
4
*Mechanics' Magazine* (October 31, 1829): 167.
5
*Scotsman* (October 21, 1829), quoted in Loudon, *Gard. Mag.* 5 (December 1829): 686.
6
Loudon, *Gard. Mag.* 5 (December 1829): 692–704.
7
Ibid., 701–02.
8
Ibid., 659, 662, 695, 658–59.
9
F.M.L.Thompson, *Hampstead: Building of a Borough, 1650–1964* (London, 1974); C.W.Ikin, *Hampstead Heath* (London: Printed for the Greater London Council, 1972); idem, "The Battle for the Heath," *Camden History Review* (London) 4 (Autumn 1976): 13–16.
10
For imagery of the city as a prison, see Wordsworth's *The Prelude* (1805) and Dickens's *Little Dorrit* (1857).
11
Summerson, *John Nash, Architect to King George IV* (London: George Allen & Unwin, 1949), 175.
12
*Times* (London), editorial, June 17, 1829.
13
W.H., letter to the editor, *Times,* May 30, 1829, p. 6.
14
T., letter to the editor, *Times,* June 17, 1829, p. 3.
15
See W.E.Hickson, *Westminster Review* 25, no. 1 (1836): 71–103. See also David Owen, *The Government of Victorian London, 1855–1889* (Cambridge: Harvard University Press, 1982).
16
See chapter 14, note 19.
17
Loudon, *Arch. Mag.* 1 (June 1834):179.
18
Loudon, "Design for a Bridge across the Mersey at Runcorn," *Annals of Philosophy,* ed. Thompson, 11 (January 1818): 14–27. Loudon's bridge was never built.
19
Loudon, *Landed Prop.,* 50. This vision is quite removed from that of the elegant women in George Stubbs's late eighteenth-century paintings entitled *The Reapers.* Loudon imagined female laborers who would enjoy far greater mental activity than is apparent in the distracted gazes of Stubbs's figures. See his two versions of reapers, one at the Yale Center for British Art, New Haven, Connecticut; the other, the property of the National Trust, in the Bearsted Collection, Upton, England.
20
In *Gard. Mag.* 5 (December 1829), Loudon's article on "Breathing Places for the Metropolis" immediately preceded his "Hints for a Plan for saving the Manure lost in the Common Sewers of London, and for rendering the Thames Water fit for Domestic Purposes."
21
Loudon, *Gard. Mag.* 11 (December 1835): 650–51.
22
Loudon, *Gard. Mag.* 5 (December 1829): 689.
23
*Gard. Mag.* 6 (December 1830): 644.
24
See W.Eric Jackson, *Achievement: A Short History of the London County*

*Council* (London: Longmans, 1965); and S.K.Ruck and Gerald Rhodes, *The Government of Central London* (London: George Allen and Unwin, 1970).

**25**

See Loudon's review of the *Report of . . . Mr. Martin's Plan for Rescuing the Thames River from Every Species of Pollution* (London, 1836), in *Arch. Mag.* 3 (August 1836): 360–81.

**26**

For Loudon's views on public parks, cottages and cemeteries, see the following Parliamentary Papers: Edwin Chadwick, *Report on . . . the Sanitary Condition of the Labouring Population of Great Britain* (1842), vol. 26, appendix, 395–99; and *Supplementary Report* (to the above) *on the Practice of Interment in Towns* (1843), vol. 12, pp. 132, 145. For multifamily housing, see chapter 12, note 54.

**27**

The *First Annual Report of the Metropolitan Improvement Society* (July 30, 1842) listed sixty members of the committee, including Ch. Barry, Esq.; John Bowring, LL.D., M.P.; Sir Edwin L. Bulwer, Bart.; E. Chadwick, Esq.; Ch. Fowler, Esq.; W.E.Hickson, Esq.; Joseph Hume, M.P.; The Earl of Lovelace; J.C.Loudon, F.L.S., H.S.; J. Martin, K.L.; Sydney Smirke, Esq.; Southwood Smith, M.D.; and Maj. Gen'l Sir F.Trench, M.P. The *Fourth Annual Report* (July 31, 1845) lists three additional members: Dr. N.Arnott, F.S.A.; Charles Dickens, Esq.; and G.A.Walker, Esq.

**28**

W.E.Hickson, review of Loudon's *Arb. Brit.*, *Westminster Review* 35 (April 1841): 419.

**29**

Percy J. Edwards, *History of London Street Improvements, 1855–1897* (London: Printed for the London County Council, 1898), 9–11; and Jackson, *History of the London County Council*, 3–7, 15.

**30**

Abercrombie, *Greater London Plan* (London: Macmillan, 1944), 4.

**31**

Abercrombie, *County of London Plan* (London: Macmillan, 1943), 36–47. Abercrombie may never have known of Loudon's plan for

London; it is not mentioned in standard works on the history of town planning.

**32**

Frank Smallwood, *Greater London: The Politics of Metropolitan Reform* (New York: Bobbs-Merrill, 1965), 48.

**33**

Peter Hall, "The Future London," in *Planning for London*, ed. Judy Hillman (London: Penguin, 1971), 139.

**34**

Hall, *London 2000* (London: Faber and Faber, 1971), 20.

**35**

Evelyn, *London Revived: Considerations for Its Rebuilding in 1666*, ed. E.S.de Beer (Oxford: Clarendon, 1938).

**36**

Gwynn, *London and Westminster Improved* (London, 1766), 16.

**37**

[James Stuart], *Critical Observations on the Buildings and Improvements of London* (London, 1771), 49.

**38**

Bentham, "Manual of Political Economy," first assembled by John Bowring, in *Works of Jeremy Bentham* (London, 1838–43), 3:74.

**39**

Bentham, *Panopticon; or, The Inspection House* (London, 1791).

**40**

See Loudon, *Gard. Mag.* 9 (June 1833): 259–60, and *Encyc. Gard.* (1830 ed.), 1028, for a plan of Karlsruhe.

**41**

Ledoux, *L'Architecture considerée sous le rapport de l'art, des moeurs, et de la législation*, 2 vols. (Paris, 1804). Partially realized, Chaux exists today, in its half-elliptical plan, in Franche-Comté, thirty-five kilometers southwest of Besançon.

**42**

Thouin, *Plans raisonnés de toutes les espèces de jardins* (Paris, 1819), fig. 51: "Projet d'une ferme expérimentale de la zone torride." Thouin received the program for this project from his brother André, a member of the Royal Academy of Sciences and professor of agriculture at the Natural History Museum in the Jardin des Plantes, Paris.

**43**

Thouin, *Plans raisonnés*, fig. 51. The three buildings which Thouin

specifically located on the central island were the central church and two buildings on its longitudinal axis: *b*, the house of the director, and *c*, the hospital.

**44**

Soane, *Designs for Public and Private Buildings* (London, 1828), pl. 34: "Design for a Royal Palace [in Hyde Park], Made in Rome, 1779." Loudon may have seen this, and similar designs of Soane for palaces in the royal parks, exhibited in the 1820s.

**45**

Jane Loudon, *The Ladies' Companion at Home and Abroad* (London: May 18, 1850): 331–33, and Noel Humphreys, "Recollections," *Garden* 1 (June 29, 1872): 698. A case in point was Loudon's suggestion, expressed in *Arch. Mag.* 3 (August 1836): 379ff., that sewage in London could be disposed by constructing a system of intercepting sewers, which would accommodate any potential overflow caused by flooding and prevent sewage from escaping into the Thames. In 1843 Loudon recommended such a system for the town of Southampton (*Gard. Mag.* 19 [1843]: 593–94). Intercepting sewers were later to become the key factor in the ultimate solution of London's drainage problems determined by Sir Joseph Bazalgette, an engineer for the Metropolitan Board of Works in the 1850s. As Bazalgette modestly explained, the ideas for his plans were derived from various sources, "so often repeated in some shape or other, that it would be difficult to determine who were the first authors" (Bazalgette, *Report on Drainage*, April 3, 1856, quoted in Owen, *Government of Victorian London*, 49).

**46**

Humphreys, "Recollections," *Garden* 1 (June 29, 1872): 698.

**47**

Howard, *To-Morrow: A Peaceful Path to Real Reform* (1898; revised ed., *Garden Cities of To-Morrow*, London, 1902).

**48**

George L. Hersey first suggested the phrase "garden metropolis" to me in conversation.

**49**

Through his contacts with Andrew Jackson Downing, Olmsted knew of

Loudon's writings, and he recommended several of them, including the *Encyc. Gard.* and the *Arb. Brit.*, as references on landscape architecture (F.L. Olmsted to William Hammond Hall [designer and superintendent of Golden Gate Park, San Francisco], October 5, 1871; this reference was pointed out to me by Charles E. Beveridge). Still, Olmsted appears to have been more directly influenced by Joseph Paxton's landscape design at Birkenhead Park, near Liverpool, and by the writings of Repton and Ruskin than by anything Loudon wrote or designed. See Frederick Law Olmsted, *Walks and Talks of an American Farmer in England* (New York, 1852), and Charles C. McLaughlin, Charles E. Beveridge, et al., eds., *The Papers of Frederick Law Olmsted*, vols. 1–4 (Baltimore, Md.: Johns Hopkins University Press, 1977–1986).

50
Olmsted, "Public Parks and the Enlargement of Towns," in *Civilizing American Cities: A Selection of Frederick Law Olmsted's Writings on City Landscapes*, ed. S.B. Sutton (Cambridge: MIT Press, 1971), 74.

51
Loudon, *Gard. Mag.* 7 (February 1831): 2–4.

52
*Gard. Mag.* 9 (August 1833): 468.

## Chapter 14: The Greatest Happiness

1
Loudon, *Gard. Mag.* 10 (February 1834): 60.

2
Loudon, *Gard. Mag.* 6 (June 1830): 344. See also M.P. Mack, *Jeremy Bentham* (London: Heinemann, 1962), 2ff., and *Edinburgh Review* 78 (October 1843): 460ff., on Bentham (1748–1832).

3
See note 1.

4
Humphreys, "Recollections," *Garden* 1 (June 29, 1872): 698.

5
Loudon's unnamed draftsman, quoted in Jane Loudon, "Life of Loudon," 219. The line of poetry is from James Thomson, *The Seasons* (1726–46), "Summer," line 1143.

6
Extract from Carlyle's journal, quoted in J.A. Froude, Thomas Carlyle, *A History of the First Forty Years of his Life* (1795–1835), vol. 2 (London, 1882), 72–73.

7
Mill, *Autobiography* (1873; a new edition, New York: Signet, 1964), 93ff.

8
Loudon, *Treatise on Wheat* (1812) and *Landed Prop.* (1808).

9
J. Saunders, "The Thames Tunnel," in *London,* ed. Charles Knight, 6 vols. (London: Knight, 1842), 3:49–64.

10
Loudon, *Gard. Mag.* 3 (March 1828): 467–68.

11
Ibid., 468.

12
*Gard. Mag.* 4 (April 1828): 54.

13
*Gard. Mag.* 6 (February 1830): 105. A few years later, the *Westminster Review* would agree: "Despotic governments build pyramids; a reformed Parliament would do itself no wrong by attaching its memory to the more useful glories of a tunnel" (vol. 19 [1833]: 10–22).

14
Michael Harrison, *London Beneath the Pavement* (London: Davies, 1971), 131ff., 148–49.

15
Loudon, *Gard. Mag.* 18 (1842): 476, 667, 643.

16
*Gard. Mag.* 7 (October 1831): 523.

17
Ibid., 522.

18
Carlyle, "Signs of the Times," *Edinburgh Review* 49 (June 1829): 439–59. In *Chartism* (1839), Carlyle was still critical of the "panacea" of suffrage.

19
Primogeniture was the system by which the first-born male would customarily inherit an entire estate, thereby perpetuating the consolidation of wealth in relatively few families. Entail legally prevented the disposal or division of landed property handed down from one generation to another.

20
Loudon, *The Great Objects to be Attained by Reform* (London, 1830), a pamphlet reproducing Loudon's letter of November 22, 1830, published in the *Morning Advertiser*, November 24, 1830.

21
Froude, *Carlyle, First Forty Years* 1:1–7.

22
See Loudon's articles and editorial comments in *Gard. Mag.* 5 (1829).

23
Loudon, *Gard. Mag.* 7 (April 1831): 224.

24
Ibid.

25
Cobbett, *Political Register,* December 4, 1830, quoted in E.P. Thompson, *The Making of the English Working Class* (London: Penguin, 1970), 253.

26
Francis Sheppard, *London, 1808–1870: The Infernal Wen* (London: Secker & Warburg, 1971), 314. In 1838 the People's Charter was drawn up by William Lovett, the founder of the London Working Men's Association, and Francis Place. Loudon did not publicly espouse Chartism, per se, but in his pamphlet *The Great Objects to be Attained by Reform* (1830), he anticipates two main points of the Charter — suffrage and the secret ballot.

27
*Quarterly Journal of Education* 2 (October 1831): 251–59. The Society for the Diffusion of Useful Knowledge also sponsored the *Penny Magazine*, edited by Charles Knight, which first appeared on March 31, 1832, a few weeks after *Chambers's Edinburgh Journal*. See Knight, *Passages of a Working Life* (London: Bradbury & Evans, 1864), 2:180ff.

28
Loudon, *Gard. Mag.* 7 (August 1831): 499.

29
These designs first appeared in the *Mechanics' Magazine* (1832) and in Loudon's *Encyc. Arch.* (1832–33).

30
Loudon, *Gard. Mag.* 7 (October 1831): 522–23.

31
Owen, *Two Discourses on a New*

*System of Society* (London, 1825), 19ff. See also Owen, *A New View of Society* (1813/14); a new edition, ed. V.A.C.Gatrell (London: Penguin, 1969), 28ff. For a discussion of Owen's well-meant paternalism, which conflicted with the goals of self-determination held by Radicals (and by Loudon), see E.P. Thompson, *English Working Class*, 857ff.

32

Loudon, *Gard. Mag.* 2 (March 1827): 178ff. See also *Gard. Mag.* 1 (April 1826): 175ff., *Gard. Mag.* 2 (January 1827): 51ff., and *Gard. Mag.* 2 (May 1827): 321ff. These articles make up Loudon's four-part review of Robert A. Slaney's *Essay on the Beneficial Direction of Rural Expenditure* (London, 1826).

33

Sir John Herschel, quoted from the *Penny Magazine*, in Loudon, *Gard. Mag.* 10 (February 1834): 54.

34

Goethe, quoted in Loudon, *Arch. Mag.* 1 (November 1834): 351.

35

Loudon, *Mag. Nat. Hist.* 2 (September 1829): 371.

36

Loudon, *Gard. Mag.* 17 (1841): 282–83.

37

Loudon, *Gard. Mag.* 7 (October 1831): 530.

38

Loudon, *Sub. Gard.*, introduction.

39

Loudon, *Gard. Mag.* 18 (October 1842): 481–89.

40

W.N.Molesworth, *The History of England from the Year 1830*, 3 vols. (London: Chapman & Hall, 1872), 2:80–130; Sidney Low and Lloyd C. Sanders, *The History of England During the Reign of Victoria, 1837–1901*, vol. 12 of *The Political History of England*, ed. William Hunt and Reginald L. Poole, 12 vols. (London: Longmans, 1907), 27–47; and Edwin Chadwick, *Report on the Sanitary Condition of the Labouring Population of Great Britain* (London: HMSO, 1842), reprint ed., edited and with introduction by M.W.Flinn (Edinburgh: Edinburgh University Press, 1965).

41

Loudon, *Gard. Mag.* 18 (October 1842): 481–89, *Gard. Mag.* 19 (1843): 238–50.

42

Loudon, *Gard. Mag.* 19 (1843): 250.

43

Wilhelm Miller, "What England Can Teach us about Garden Cities," *Country Life in America* (March 1910): 531–34, and Walter L. Creese, *The Search for Environment. The Garden City: Before and After* (New Haven: Yale University Press, 1966), 108–43. Bourneville, located near Birmingham, was the site of Cadbury's chocolate manufacturing company. Begun in 1895, it was largely a company town. Port Sunlight, wholly a company town, was built in 1888 for the employees of Lord Leverhulme's soap factory near Liverpool.

44

Charles E. Beveridge and David Schuyler, *The Papers of Frederick Law Olmsted*, vol. 3, *Central Park* (Baltimore, Md.: Johns Hopkins University Press, 1983), 121ff. Olmsted and Vaux won the competition for the design of Central Park in 1858.

45

Loudon, *Gard. Mag.* 19 (1843): 243.

# Chapter 15:
# At Home in Bayswater

1

Many details of Loudon's house and garden are given in his *Sub. Gard.*, 325–50, and the revised edition entitled *Villa Gardener* (1850), ed. Mrs. Loudon, 134–45. Other sources are the *Gard. Mag.* and letters and reminiscences of Loudon's friends and colleagues. See also Miles Hadfield, "A House in Porchester Terrace," *Country Life* 146 (October 23, 1969): 1054–55.

2

Loudon, *Villa Gardener*, 142.

3

Hovey, *Magazine of Horticulture* (Boston, Mass.) 12 (1846): 86. In the autumn of 1844, when Hovey visited the Derby Arboretum (see chapter 12), he also called on Mrs. Loudon in Bayswater, but she happened to be out. Regretting that he could not return, he glanced at the library, which was "filled to over-flowing with most of the works on horticulture, botany, etc., of the present century." In the front garden, Hovey particularly admired one "highly picturesque" group of trees then bearing fruit—a bird-cherry (*Cerasus Padus*) with dark purple berries, a *Sorbus hybrida* with red berries, and a snowberry (*Symphoria racemosa*) with white berries.

4

Loudon, *Sub. Gard.*, 337ff.

5

In 1850 Jane Loudon updated her husband's description of the garden: "In 1849, twenty-six years after these gardens were laid out and planted, that on the south side [Loudon's side] still preserved much of its original character; though nearly a third of the trees and shrubs originally planted had died, or had been cut down for want of space. In the north garden, only a few trees were left, and the greater part of the ground was covered with grass" (*Villa Gardener*, 145).

6

See Nikolaus Pevsner, *The Buildings of England: London*, vol. 2 (London: Penguin, 1974), 216–17.

7

Bea Howe, *Lady with Green Fingers: The Life of Jane Loudon* (London: Country Life, 1961), 53.

8

Three editions appeared in London—in 1824, 1825, and 1832.

9

Loudon, *Encyc. Gard.*, 353.

10

Loudon, *The Green-House Companion* (London: Harding, Triphook & Lepard, and J.Harding, 1825), 6–22. See also R.Buckminster Fuller's dome (384 ft. in diameter) for the Union Tank Car Company, Baton Rouge, Louisiana (1958). For a photograph of Fuller's U.S. pavilion dome at Expo 1967, in Montreal, see Reyner Banham, *Megastructure: Urban Futures of the Recent Past* (London: Thames & Hudson, 1976).

11

Loudon, *Green-House Companion*, 13.

12

Loudon, *Gard. Mag.* 6 (October 1830): 529–31.

13

Henry Brougham, *Edinburgh Review* 52 (October 1830): 1.

14

Howe, *Lady with Green Fingers*, 26ff.

15

*The Mummy! A Tale of the Twenty-Second Century*, 3 vols., published anonymously (London: Henry Colburn, 1827). A second edition appeared in 1828.

16

Howe, *Lady with Green Fingers*, 26–37. This work is based on Jane Loudon's unpublished diaries, fiction, and books on gardening.

17

Jerdan, *Autobiography*, 4 vols. (London: Hall, Virtue, 1852), 4:321–22.

18

Jane Loudon, quoted in Jerdan, *Autobiography* 4:322–23.

19

Jerdan, *Autobiography* 4:322. Jerdan was also the devoted supporter of Landon (known as L.E.L.).

20

Jerdan, "Characteristic Letters," *Leisure Hour* (February 1, 1869), 140. Other contributors to the *Literary Gazette* included Faraday, Lockhart, Bowring, Sandby, Haydon, Ker Porter, Miss Mitford, J.S.Buckingham, and Mill. See Jerdan, *Autobiography* 2:282.

21

Leopold Martin, son of John Martin, the painter, later recalled hearing Loudon make this remark. See Mary L. Pendered, *John Martin, Painter, His Life and Times* (London: Hurst & Blackett, 1923), 115.

22

Loudon, *Gard. Mag.* 3 (March 1828): 478–79.

23

Jane Loudon, "Life of Loudon," 205.

24

See note 7.

25

Jane Loudon, *Agnes; or, The Little Girl Who Could Keep Her Promise* (London: Harvey & Darton, 1839), 3ff.

26

Jane Loudon, *Glimpses of Nature* (London: Grant & Griffith, 1844), 89.

27

Loudon, *Sub. Gard.*, 349.

28

Loudon, *Gard. Mag.* 4 (June 1828): 148, and *Villa Gardener*, 143.

29

Loudon, *Gard. Mag.* 16 (1840): 350–52.

30

Ibid., 350.

31

Ibid., 351.

32

Loudon, *Country Res.* 2:685–86.

33

Loudon, *Gard. Mag.* 16 (1840): 352, 351.

34

Gloag, *Mr Loudon's England* (Newcastle-upon-Tyne: Oriel Press, 1970), 61ff.

35

Agnes Loudon to Lady Pauline Trevelyan, July 15, 1858 (two days after Jane Loudon's death). Sir Walter C. Trevelyan Papers, Box 175, in Special Collections, the Library of the University of Newcastle-upon-Tyne. Quotation of this letter is by kind permission of the Trevelyan family.

36

J.M., *Gentleman's Magazine* 21 (February 1844): 208.

37

Ibid., 209. At the end of one of J.M.'s articles in *Gent. Mag.*, his residence was identified as B——n——ll, near the eastern coast of Suffolk.

38

Howe, *Lady with Green Fingers*, 97–98.

39

Sopwith, quoted in B.W.Richardson, *Thomas Sopwith (1803–1879), with Excerpts from his Diary of Fifty-Seven Years* (London, 1891), 196. One evening at Loudon's home, Sopwith reported, a Miss Loudon (one of Loudon's sisters, Jane or Mary) instructed Sopwith in the rudiments of wood cutting. (Many of the woodcuts in Loudon's works were made by Loudon's sisters.

40

Jerdan, "Characteristic Letters," *Leisure Hour* (February 1, 1869): 140.

41

Chambers, *Chambers's Edinburgh Journal* (May 4, 1844): 286.

42

A draftsman described as having worked for Loudon for more than nine years (probably John Robertson), quoted by Jane Loudon

in her "Life of Loudon," 218. This passage first appeared in the *Derby Reporter* soon after Loudon's death.

43

Ruskin, "Enquiries on the Causes of the Colour of the Water of the Rhine," *Mag. Nat. Hist.* 7 (September 1834): 438–39.

44

Ruskin, *Deucalion: Collected Studies on the Lapse of Waves and Life of Stones*, 2 vols. (Boston: Dana Estes, ca. 1931), vol. 1, chapter 14.

45

John J. Ruskin to his wife Margaret, December 20, 1836, and December 26, 1836, in *The Ruskin Family Letters*, ed. Van Akin Burd, 2 vols. (Ithaca: Cornell University Press, 1973), 1:379, 391.

46

Ruskin to Loudon (September, 1838), in *Works of John Ruskin*, ed. E.T.Cook and Alexander Wedderburn, 39 vols. (London: George Allen & Unwin, 1903–12), 36:15–17. It appears that Loudon advised Ruskin to write an article on Scott's home, Abbotsford, for the *Arch. Mag.* Ruskin replied that he intended to write such an article, which would have been the first in a series of "Homes of the Mighty" — but Abbotsford disappointed him. Rather than "cast a stain on Scott's reputation" (for not appreciating the "real beauty and application of Gothic architecture"), Ruskin simply gave Loudon a few details of the place.

47

Ruskin to his father (January 10, 1837), in *Ruskin Family Letters*, ed. Burd, 1:415–16.

48

Thorburn, in *Magazine of Horticulture* (Boston, Mass.) 10 (1844): 77.

49

Loudon's charges for landscape design, consultation, travel, and so forth are given in *Gard. Mag.* 15 (1839): 716.

50

J.M., *Gentleman's Magazine* n. s. 8 (July 1837): 59.

51

These friends helped in various ways, including their purchases of Loudon's works. Sir Walter and Lady Pauline Trevelyan continued to offer moral and financial support to

Jane and Agnes throughout their lifetimes. See note 35. Howe (*Lady with Green Fingers*, 169) notes that, on December 21, 1858, when Agnes was married to Markham Spofforth, Sir Walter Trevelyan gave away the bride. In 1844 Charles Waterton assisted Jane, noting that her husband had published at his own expense Waterton's *Essays on Natural History, Chiefly Ornithology* in 1837. In turn, Waterton made his second series of *Essays* (published by Longmans) "an unsolicited donation to the widow of my poor departed friend, Mr. Loudon, whose vast labours in the cause of Science have insured him an imperishable reputation" (preface).

52
Paxton, *Gardener's Chronicle* (February 10, 1844): 86.

53
Paxton, *Magazine of Botany* 11 (1844): 48, and *Gardener's Chronicle* (February 24, 1844). Dr. John Lindley, the first professor of botany at the University of London, chaired the public meeting. He had provided most of the descriptions in *Loudon's Encyclopaedia of Plants* (London: Longman, 1829).

54
See note 53, *Gardener's Chronicle* (March 30, 1844): 207, and succeeding numbers of the *Gardener's Chronicle*, through July 1844.

55
Jane Loudon to the (London) *Times*, March 23, 1844.

56
Howe, *Lady with Green Fingers*, 89.

57
*Westminster Review* 41 (March 1844): 225–26, and W.Roberts, "The Centenary of Loudon's 'Arboretum'," *Journal of the Royal Horticultural Society* 61 (1936): 279. Roberts states that Mrs. Loudon was granted an annuity of £100 in March, 1846.

58
Jane Loudon, *Gardening for Ladies*, ed. A.J.Downing, from the 3rd London edition (New York: Putnam, 1843).

59
Alexandre Poiteau and M.Tripet-Leblanc, *Annales Soc. Hort.* 34 (January 1844): 38–40.

60
Poiteau, *Annales Soc. Hort.* 34 (February 1844): 97. This sentiment ends Poiteau's twelve-page obituary of Loudon.

61
Thorburn, *Men and Manners in Britain* (New York: Wiley & Long, 1834), 67.

62
Downing, *Theory and Practice of Landscape Gardening*, 2nd ed. (New York: A.O.Moore, 1859), 21.

63
Sweet, *Geraniaceae, The Natural Order of Gerania* (London: James Ridgway, 1828–30), vol. 5, *Supplement*, pl. 17.

64
Lindley, in *Edwards' Botanical Register* 20 (London: J.Ridgway, 1835), 1720, on *Adesmia Loudonia*; idem, "A Sketch of the Vegetation of the Swan River Colony," *Edwards' Botanical Register, Appendix to the First 23 volumes* (London: J.Ridgway, 1839), xlii, on *Loudonia aurea*.

65
Robinson, *Garden* 1 (1872), dedication.

66
Loudon, *Gard. Mag.* 5 (December 1829): 663. See also *Gard. Mag.* 7 (February 1831): 17. The *pin de Haguenau* was a variety of Scotch pine growing in the Haguenau Forest (Haut-Rhin, France). Loudon procured the seeds from Vilmorin & Co., Paris, in September 1828. His *Encyclopaedia of Trees and Shrubs* (London: A.Spottiswoode for the Author, 1842), 953, gives the following description, from P. Lawson & Son's *Agriculturist's Manual* (Edinburgh, 1836): *Pinus sylvestris haguenensis* (*Pin de Haguenau*, Fr.): "The old trees are remarkably tall, straight, free from branches, except near the summit, with remarkably smooth reddish-coloured bark. The leaves of the young plants are longer than those of any of the preceding varieties; they are much waved or twisted, of a light green slightly glaucous colour, and minutely serrulated; the young terminal buds are of a peculiar reddish colour, and generally more or less covered with whitish resin. The young plants are, besides their difference in shade of colour,

readily distinguished by their stronger and more rapid growth."

## Appendix A: Southampton and the Garden Cemetery

This discussion is largely drawn from Melanie Louise Simo, "Loudon and the Landscape: A Study of Rural and Metropolitan Improvements, 1803–1843" (Ph.D. diss., Yale University, 1976). As it represents earlier research than does the main body of the text, it is presented separately here.

1
Loudon, *Gard. Mag.* 9 (October 1833): 528.

2
Ibid.

3
*Gard. Mag.* 19 (1843): 591.

4
*Quarterly Review* (March 1844): 451.

5
See J.S.Curl's discussion of this subject in *The Victorian Celebration of Death* (Newton Abbot, Devon: David and Charles, 1972), 81–82. The author is indebted to Mr. Curl for helpful comments in conversation.

6
See note 5.

7
See John Evelyn, *London Revisited: Considerations for its Rebuilding in 1666*, ed. E.S.de Beer (Oxford: Clarendon, 1938); Edwin Chadwick *Supplementary Report into the Practice of Interment in Towns*, Parliamentary Papers, (1843) vol. 32; and George Alfred Walker, *Gatherings from Graveyards* (London, 1839). See also N.B.Penny, "The Commercial Garden Necropolis of the Early Nineteenth Century and its Critics," *Garden History* 2, no. 3 (Summer 1974): 61–76; and J.S.Curl, "The Architecture and Planning of the Nineteenth-Century Cemetery," *Garden History* 3, no. 3 (Summer 1975): 13–41.

8
Loudon, *Gard. Mag.* 19 (1843): 104–05.

9
Loudon, *Gardener's Gazette* (August 7, 1841): 500.

10

Strang, *Necropolis Glasguensis* (Glasgow, 1831), quoted in Loudon, *Gard. Mag.* 19 (1843): 93ff.

11

Loudon, *Gard. Mag.* 10 (April 1834): 160.

12

*Gard. Mag.* 19 (1843): 354–67. The report and plan date from November 1842.

13

Loudon was paid ten guineas to advise on the Brompton Cemetery. See Curl, *Victorian Celebration of Death*, 116. See also "Minutes of the West London and Westminster Cemetery Company," in Public Record Office, London. Loudon also offered gratuitous advice on the London suburban cemeteries of Abney Park, Kensal Green, and Norwood. See *Gard. Mag.* 19 (1843) and *Gardener's Gazette* (July 24, 1841): 468. Further, Loudon made several proposals for a London metropolitan cemetery and for a cemetery on Arthur's Seat, Edinburgh. See *Gard. Mag.* 4 (June 1828): 163, for example.

14

N.B.Penny, "Commercial Garden Necropolis"; see also John Morley, *Death, Heaven and the Victorians* (London: Studio Vista, 1972).

15

My review of works in this field was made in 1976.

16

Loudon, "Report on the Design for a Cemetery Proposed to be formed at Southampton by authority of an Act of Parliament and under the Direction of the Mayor and the Town Council," August 31, 1843. In Southampton Civic Records Office.

17

Charles E. Deacon, Secretary of the Cemetery Committee, "The Southampton Cemetery, under the Management of the Corporation Established by Act of Parliament 6th and 7th Victoria, 1843." In Southampton Civic Records Office. The following account of the Southampton Cemetery is taken from this document, except where noted. Loudon's report of August 31, 1843 is contained in the Deacon document, but the plans and elevations he cites are missing.

18

For a detailed explanation of this principle, see Loudon, *Gard. Mag.* 19 (1843): 589ff.

19

Extract from the *Hampshire Advertiser*, May 9, 1846, in a typed transcription preserved in the Southampton Civic Record Office.

20

Ibid. The misspelled specimens were probably *Pinus cembra*, *Laricinus*, and cypress.

21

Loudon, Reply to *Kata Phusin* [John Ruskin], *Arch. Mag.* 5 (December 1838): 624. Ruskin was responding to Loudon's article, "On the Choice of a Situation for a Church; and on the Laying out and planting of the Churchyard," *Arch. Mag.* 5 (August 1838): 345–60.

22

Loudon, *On the Laying out, Planting, and Managing of Cemeteries* (London: A.Spottiswoode for the Author, 1843), 74.

# Index

French Revolution: of *1789*, 46; of *1830*, 266, 268
Fromont, horticultural fête at, 152
Frost (inventor), 121, 123

Gainsborough, Thomas, 4, 93, 133
Gandy, Joseph Michael, 131, 219; cottage designs of, 98, 99, 311*n*21; *The Rural Architect*, 84–85
Garden cities, 241–42
Gardeners: education of, 151, 158, 159; training of, 148–49; working conditions of, 155–57
*Gardener's Dictionary* (Miller), 149
*Gardener's Magazine* (Loudon), 10, 15, 118, 163, 168, 171, 227–28, 229; *Annals of Agriculture* (Young) compared to, 22; contributors to, 158; readership of, 152, 153–55, 156, 157–58; reception in Scotland, 159–60
Gardenesque, the, 13, 87–88, 180; role in Derby Arboretum, 198; the picturesque versus, 169, 170, 171
Gardening: progressive, 149, 164. *See also* Landscape gardening
*Gardening for Ladies* (Jane Loudon), 272–73, 278
Gardens: flower gardens, 56, 175; French, 177; geometrical, 176–77; public, 169; at Tew Lodge Farm, 86–87; winter gardens, 43–44, 136. *See also* Birmingham Botanical Garden
Gauen, Robert, 123, 124
*Gentleman Farmer, The* (Kames), 25
*Gentleman's Magazine*, 126, 148
Geometrical gardens, 176–77
Germany: education in, 11; training of gardeners in, 148–49; metropolitan planning in, 220–21
Gilpin, William, 4, 65, 169, 192; *Tours*, 34
Girardin, Louis-René de, 1, 171; *De la composition des paysages*, 53; *Essay on Landscape*, 37–38
Glaslyn River, proposed diversion of, 73
Glasshouses: curvilinear design proposed by Loudon, 8, 112, 114, 116; in Russia, 110–11. *See also* Hothouses
Glass ranges, 116
*Glimpses of Nature* (Jane Loudon), 271–72
Godwin, George, 132
Goethe, Johann Wolfgang von, 256
Goldsmith, Oliver, "The Deserted Village," 25
Gorinka, hothouses at, 111

Gothic architecture, 101, 104, 136, 139; Russian Gothic, 110
Government: local government, 233–34; reform of, 67, 252–53
Grant, James, 207
Granville, A.B., 192, 200
Gray, Thomas, 40; "Elegy in a Country Churchyard," 29, 281, 282
Grecian architecture. *See* Classical architecture
Greenbelts, 227, 231–33, 237, 244
*Green-House Companion* (Loudon), 264
Grenville, Lady, 168
Guggenheim Museum, 185
Gwynn, John, 237

Hakewill, A.W., 216
Hall, Peter, 237
Hamilton, Charles, 34, 52
*Hampshire Advertiser*, 287–88
Hampstead Heath, 230, 231
Happiness, Loudon's views on, 256–57
Harewood, earl of, 18
Harlaxton Manor, 128
Harmony, Loudon's views on principle of, 264–65
Harrington, Lord, 168
Harrison, Joseph, 160
Harrison, Renny, 71
Hartley, David, *Observations on Man*, 42
Hatfield House, 128
Hazlitt, William, 217
*Headlong Hall* (Peacock), 68, 75–76
Henslow, John Stevens, 14
Herschel, Sir John, 256
Hersey, George, 131
Hickson, W.E., 194, 201
"Hints for Breathing Places" (Loudon), 227
*Hints on the Formation of Gardens and Pleasure Grounds* (Loudon), 9, 106
Historical styles, of architecture, 135–36
Hoare, Henry, 34
Home, Henry. *See* Kames, Lord
Hope, Thomas, 102, 103, 104, 173; *Historical Essay on Architecture*, 132
Horticultural collections, loss of, 162–63
Horticultural fêtes, 151–52
Horticultural journalism, economic pressures on, 161
*Horticultural Register and Magazine of Botany*, 15, 160–61

Horticultural societies, 150; of London, 111, 112, 150–52, 317*n*51; of Paris, 126
Horticulture, British, economic recession affecting, 148, 149
Hosack, David, 165
Hosking, William, *Treatise on Architecture and Building*, 138
Hothouses: for Birmingham Botanical Garden, 182–83, 185; engineering design of, 94–97; Mackenzie on design of, 112; in Russia, 111
Housing: multifamily, 118, 120–22; for working classes, 104–05. *See also* Cottages
Hovey, Charles Mason, 202–03, 204, 326*n*3
Howard, Ebenezer, 241–43
Howe, Bea, 271
Huch, Ronald, 186
Hume, Joseph, 194, 236, 253
Humphreys, Noel, 4, 14, 65, 89, 132, 241, 248
Hunt, James Henry Leigh, 46, 214–15
Hunt, Thornton Leigh, 169
Huntley, marquis of, 306*n*66
Husbandry, Scottish methods of, 80
Hyde Park, 213–15, 223
"Hymn on Solitude" (Thomson), 44

Imitation, arts of. *See* Fine arts, theories of
Institute of British Architects, 138
Italianate architecture, 136

"Jardin fantastique anglais" (Thouin), 180–81
*Jardinique*, 171–72
*Jardiniste moderne, Le* (Viart), 172, 180, 318*n*26
*Jardins, Les* (De Lille), 56
Jefferson, Thomas, 12, 221
Jeffrey, Francis, 39–40, 69
Jerdan, William, 201, 274; relationship to Jane Loudon, 269–70
*Julie; ou La nouvelle Héloïse* (Rousseau), 56, 58
Junius Redivivus, 118, 120, 121, 122, 124
Jussieu, Antoine Laurent de, 56, 147, 318*n*6
Jussieu, Bernard de, 56
Jussieuean classification system, 57, 87, 166–67, 170–71, 196

Kahn, Louis, 138
Kames, Lord, *The Gentleman Farmer*, 25
Karlsruhe, town planning for, 238